Aging and Gender
in Literature

STUDIES IN CREATIVITY

Feminist Issues: Practice, Politics, Theory

ALISON BOOTH AND ANN LANE, EDITORS

Aging and Gender in Literature

STUDIES IN CREATIVITY

Edited by
Anne M. Wyatt-Brown
and
Janice Rossen

University Press of Virginia

Charlottesville and London

The University Press of Virginia
Copyright © 1993
by the Rector and Visitors
of the University of Virginia

First published 1993

Library of Congress Cataloging-in-Publication Data
Aging and gender in literature : studies in creativity / edited by
  Anne M. Wyatt-Brown and Janice Rossen.
    p.   cm. — (Feminist issues)
  Includes bibliographical references and index.
  ISBN 0-8139-1431-0. — ISBN 0-8139-1434-5 (paper)
    1. Authorship.   2. Creation (Literary, artistic, etc.)   3. Aging—
Psychological aspects.   4. Women and literature.   5. Literature—
Women authors—History and criticism.   I. Wyatt-Brown, Anne M.,
1939–   II. Rossen, Janice, 1955–   .   III. Series: Feminist issues
(Charlottesville, Va.)
PN151.A36   1993
801'.92—dc20   92-35305
                                                                     CIP

Printed in the United States of America

To Our Parents

Natalie J. Marbury and the late William L. Marbury

Mildred and Thomas Taecker

Contents

Contents

Contents

PART IV
The Phenomenology of Aging

Acknowledgments

Aging and Gender in Literature: Studies in Creativity has been in many ways a collaboration. Janice Rossen initiated the idea of producing such a study. Then both of us solicited submissions from people in literary gerontology and from others whose work indicated a potential interest in aging. The contributors from first to last have been extremely patient and cooperative. Many of them read the introduction at various stages and offered helpful suggestions. They have endured what must have seemed like entirely too many editorial comments from us with professional aplomb. When asked, they transferred their papers to disk so that Anne Wyatt-Brown could compile a common bibliography. Moreover, we owe a great deal to the moral support of Bill Rossen and to the assistance of Bertram Wyatt-Brown, who in many ways has been our unacknowledged coeditor. Bert has read many of the essays, offered astute comments, and helped assemble the bibliography.

To Nancy Essig of the University Press of Virginia, we owe a great debt of gratitude for championing the project from its early stages. Without her support and encouragement this book would have taken far longer to produce. The Press readers were helpful as well. Besides their suggestions for change, we were encouraged by the thought that readers in such diverse fields as medical sociology and literary theory were genuinely interested in our findings.

The authors and the editors express their thanks to those who have granted permission to print the following material: to Professor Ruth Limmer, for permission to reprint sections from Louise Bogan's poems "The Catalpa Tree," published in *Voices* (September–December 1941), and "Statue and Birds," published in *The Blue Estuaries: Poems, 1923–1968;* to Ms. Louise Gluck, for permission to reprint sections from "To Autumn," published in *The House on Marshland;* to Ms. Elizabeth Susan Howell, Literary Executrix of the Estate of D. M. Richardson, and to the Beinecke Rare Book and Manuscript Library at Yale University, for permission to quote from unpublished Richardson material; to Ms. Karla M. Hammond, for permission to quote from her interview with Josephine Miles; to the University of Illinois Press, for permission to quote from the poetry of Josephine Miles; and to Harcourt, Brace, Jovanovich, for permission to quote from Virginia Woolf's letters.

Aging and Gender in Literature

STUDIES IN CREATIVITY

ANNE M. WYATT-BROWN

Introduction:
Aging, Gender, and Creativity

AGING IS A missing category in current literary theory. Kathleen Woodward has observed that with the attention given to race, gender, and class, "only *age* has remained invisible, not subject to analysis"; this fact represents a special irony because women "are necessarily subject to—at the minimum—a double marginality." In June 1990 an advertisement for a "major new women's history text" boasted of its innovative use of "the issues of race, ethnicity, region, class, and sexuality" without mentioning age. This exclusion reveals our cultural blindness. As Ernest Becker argues in *The Denial of Death,* we suffer from a pervasive but almost completely repressed fear of death.[1] Given our ability to avoid reminders of unpleasant truths, it is not surprising that old age became a cultural taboo. Yet until the dimension of age is included in such a study, any investigation of women's lives and of human life in general inevitably will be incomplete. Moreover, to add age to the study of women and not of men furthers the myth that men are exempt from the influence of aging.

It is equally absurd to omit from an analysis of literature a close consideration of the alleged impact of old age and the concepts of aging. For example, as literary critic Mikhail M. Bakhtin points out, the novel is notable for two elements: its "indeterminacy, a certain semantic openendedness, a living contact with unfinished, still living contemporary reality," and its ready absorption of multiple languages and voices (what he calls its "polyglossia").[2] Aging is an important one of those "voices" in which writers and characters speak, and critics and readers must learn to hear its messages. To ignore that aspect of a writer's or character's life experience is to ignore a fundamental part of human nature.

Moreover, exploring the experience of growing old adds insight to our understanding of literature and life. Within the past twenty years, Constance Rooke suggests, the novel of "completion or winding up," what she calls the *Vollendungsroman,* has conveyed a remarkable sense of flux. It has avoided an overly determined sense of closure, even though paradoxically the plot may end with the character's death. Barbara Frey Waxman's term for late-life fiction, *Reifungsroman* or the "novel of ripening," adds another important dimension, by reminding us of the possibility of adventure and change in later life. Margaret Gullette adds the insight that powerful social and literary pressures have constructed our images of aging in literature. In *Safe at Last in the Middle Years,* she argues convincingly that a "decline narrative" of aging has dominated our literature, even though it does not accurately reflect real human experience. One of the culprits, she suggests, is "realism's typical plot of 'systematic disillusionment,'" which has so influenced our thinking that we have come to accept this plot as truthful, despite our skeptical reading of most other literary conventions. As a result, we have enshrined the notion that old age means decay and are likely to reject any other sort of interpretation as romantic nonsense.[3] Yet, as Rooke has suggested, some literary works demonstrate that even the act of dying may enhance the character's memory of the multiple voices of his or her past, a point beautifully illustrated by Penelope Lively's novel *Moon Tiger* (1987). By emphasizing the contributions of aging writers and the voices of aging characters, we hope in the following chapters to expand and sharpen the reader's awareness of literature and of human life.

Like Gullette's *Safe at Last in the Middle Years* and Kathleen Woodward's *Aging and Its Discontents,* this volume seeks to show how growing older affects literary creativity and psychological development and to examine how individual writing careers begin to change in middle age. Most important, these essays do not treat the dynamics of aging as an isolated single theme. Instead, in combination with other factors—among them the writer's psychology, gender, sexual orientation, and class—our analyses of the dynamics of aging generate literary insights and theory. In this we build on the pathbreaking and important work already done by Stuart F. Spicker, Woodward, and David D. Van Tassel in *Aging and the Elderly,* Van Tassel in *Aging, Death, and the Completion of Being,* Laurel Porter and Laurence D. Porter in *Aging in Literature,* and Thomas R. Cole and Sally A. Gadow in *What Does It Mean to Grow Old?* All of these excellent interdisciplinary studies have brought issues of aging to the attention of humanists. Our work in this volume also extends and complements recent collections, like Prisca von Dorotka Bagnell and Patricia Spencer Soper's *Perceptions of Aging in Literature,* which combines short introductory essays with selected readings about old age drawn from multiple cultures, and Cole, Van Tassel, and Robert Kastenbaum's *Handbook of the Humanities and Aging,* a basic reference work which seeks to guide future research in the field. In our view a study of aging should include not just the last years of life but the changes that emerge at midlife as well. As a result, our contributors treat aging as a multifaceted subject, one with roots deep in childhood experiences. In many ways our essays are an extension of the sophisticated literary and psychoanalytic approaches employed in Woodward and Murray M. Schwartz's *Memory and Desire.* [4]

Despite the contributions that these works have made, literary gerontology, like gerontology in general, is not rich in theory. Thus, in 1977 Daniel J. Levinson et al. felt justified in complaining that "gerontology has thus far provided considerable information, though little understanding, about" old age.[5] This volume seeks to stimulate the development of useful theories. By providing data at this level of detail about development across time, we seek to dispel glib generalizations about later-life writing or being. By emphasizing the cultural pressures on the later years, including the intersection of gender with age, we wish to preclude any superficial pronouncements about later life.

Literary gerontologists seek to challenge the preconceptions about aging that influence our thinking about later life. Our work reinforces the findings of humanistically inclined gerontologists, most of whom work in a variety of academic fields. If for example, as gerontologist Gary Kenyon claims, "aging can be defined as a series of problems, or as a developmentally interesting phenomenon," the contributors to this volume clearly espouse the latter position. Like many other gerontologists, we celebrate human diversity and the various ways individuals react to growing old. We also share Kenyon's conviction that the artists we write about have a "self-creative aspect." Like all human beings they are neither entirely "individual entities nor socially constructed" ones. Creativity provides an important source of self-discovery and self-creation. As anthropologist Mary Catherine Bateson attests, "Writing has been the constancy through which I have reinvented myself after every uprooting." These convictions affect our methodology. Although we sometimes borrow useful gerontological theories—such as Erik Erikson's well-known analysis of the sequential stages of life and their psychological tasks—we express reservations about strong theories that attempt to explain too much. Instead we endorse H. Thomae's warning against "the danger of assuming that there is a *modal adjustment pattern* that one must live up to in order to be considered competent." We, like all constructors of theories, should also keep in mind psychiatrist George Vaillant's modest remark that one of his chapters in *Adaptation to*

Life is "the very antithesis of the last word" and, like him, show respect for the artist's "special sense of creative potentiality."[6]

These essays also challenge some of the assumptions of social psychologists who specialize in the phenomenon of creativity, while reinforcing the findings of others. Rather than attempting to propose an overarching theory of creativity, the contributors to this volume have provided case studies of individual writers, whose lives demonstrate how complex the creative experience can be. Most of the essayists would disagree with Dean Simonton's assertion that "creativity is a form of leadership in that it entails personal influence over others." According to his model, those with true creative genius are accepted into the canon. Not surprisingly no women appear in his list of preferred geniuses, at least in the essays cited. Furthermore, Simonton de-emphasizes the collaborative aspects of artistic endeavor and disregards the influence of cultural forces. For example, he has repeatedly asserted that the creativity of lyric poets begins to peak in the early thirties and then drops off precipitously, a pattern which no doubt has been all too common in the past.[7]

Moreover, Simonton's quantitative methodology causes him to overlook the effect of cultural messages on aspiring writers. If, as some of our essayists demonstrate, for generations most authors assumed that sexual love and romance were the primary topics of poetry or of life itself, no wonder few poets were able to write once they entered middle age and no longer found romantic topics as compelling as they once did. Levinson et al. commented as late as 1978 that "humanity has as yet little wisdom for constructing the 'portrait of the hero as a middle-aged man.' That archetype is still poorly evolved." Carolyn Heilbrun has demonstrated that women artists had even less help in charting alternative courses until the generation of women poets born between 1923 and 1932 in middle age "transformed the autobiographies of women's lives."[8]

Instead, most of the contributors would endorse the view of David Harrington, a social psychologist, who urges his fellow psychologists to study creative individuals in relation to their environment. Harrington, drawing on Virginia Woolf's *A Room of One's Own* (1929), Tillie Olsen's *Silences* (1978), and Ralph Ellison's *Invisible Man* (1952), demonstrates the effect of alienating forces upon the productivity of an artist. He asserts that no matter how creative an individual may be, she still depends on "writers, agents, editors, and audiences able to see value in or create value from her work," as well as "the existence of economically viable or critically accepted genres" that are congruous with the artist's talents. As a result, some creative individuals lack the opportunity to develop their skills and achieve recognition, while others fail to hold their audience when they grow old.[9]

Serious examination of late-life creativity did not begin to enter the realm of scholarship until a few years after 1975, the date when, according to Gullette, "the culture was giving its writers permission to overthrow the traditional decline view" of middle age.[10] Before that date, most literary critics ignored the later lives of the poets, dramatists, and novelists they studied. Likewise, most biographers and theoreticians of biography and autobiography, who might reasonably have been expected to have a special interest in the life course of their subjects, have also overlooked the importance of development in later life. With the growth of interest in psychoanalytic theory, some scholars turned their attention to the creative products of later life, such as the psychoanalytically informed literary critics in Woodward and Schwartz's *Memory and Desire* (1986). Yet few of the writers in that volume were much interested in biographical questions, except as a peripheral issue, and this is a void which several of the following essays begin to fill.

In the theory of biography and autobiography, psychoanalytic ideas about aging emerged slowly. Indeed, the first attempts to generate a theory of biography were largely unpsychological, as well as woefully ignorant of "age studies," Gullette's term for our enterprise. This situation reflected the fact that the authors and subjects of life writing tended to be public figures, whose productive careers generated vast amounts of data. As a result, more attention was given to their activities than to their midlife concerns about growing old. Inevitably concentration on the public side of these subjects' lives tended to obscure study of their later years, however revelatory such an inquiry might have been. Still, in retrospect, it is apparent that the process of deconstructing one's own life in autobiography, so carefully described by Wallace Fowlie, could have been successfully illuminated by a deeper understanding of gerontological theory. Nonetheless, James Olney, the American dean of autobiographical studies, and the authors who appear in his influential edited volumes largely ignore the issues of old age and aging. Eventually, however, feminist researchers turned their attention to lesser-known subjects whose lives were more private. Aside from Kathleen Woodward's essay on Simone de Beauvoir that appears in *The Private Self,* most of the other feminist biographers in that volume ignore the effect of aging upon their subjects.[11] Ironically, not only would the later lives of these obscure women have been clarified by a knowledge of such theory, but the details of their later lives could have enhanced and expanded our understanding of the phenomenology of aging.

In time, however, the shift in focus from studying private rather than purely public lives led biographers to examine the psychological experiences of their subjects, partly to compensate for the absence of traditional data. At first scholars began to explore the subject of childhood, a preoccupation which reflected the psychoanalytic concepts of the time. Ira Nadel marks 1969 as the point at which psychobiography entered the canon of academic biography, but Steven Weiland argues that Erik Erikson's 1958 biography, *Young Man Luther,* had already "prompted methodological debates over the uses of psychology in history and life history." Of course, Freud's child-centered ideas have been influential as well. Yet, as Kathleen Woodward has convincingly demonstrated, his fears about growing older kept him from developing theories about old age, even though he was extraordinarily productive himself in his later years. As a result, for many years no one advanced new insights about late-life change, ideas that might have challenged the last remnants of rigid Aristotelian views about human development, discussed by Bakhtin in his study of time in the novel.[12] That venerable schema made a belief in the "becoming," or the evolution of an individual, almost impossible until the Darwinian era.

For all these reasons, psychoanalytic theory altered the methods by which biographers analyzed the early life of their subjects. Yet these same theories reinforced stereotypical attitudes about the nature of old age. Neglecting the potentiality of late life seems especially regrettable when one considers Park Honan's acute observation that in most lives much of the biographical material comes from the "years of the famous older person"— usually beginning at some point in middle age—rather than from "the youth or childhood of the same person." Indeed, many elders, especially gifted ones like those chosen as subjects for biography, tend to review their past lives and early experiences from the vantage point of old age, but these commentaries have not been scrutinized. Life review, as Robert Butler calls it, can be a complex phenomenon in which older people feel forced to confront the ghosts of their past in order to make peace with themselves.[13] In the process some individuals come to reevaluate the significance of their prior careers. If biographers hope to understand the importance of these life reviews, they must become conversant with research on aging.

Luckily for theorists of age studies, as Erik Erikson himself grew older he discovered that later life was more challenging and variable than he had once imagined. (His interest in the topic originally had been whetted by David Van Tassel, who invited Erikson to present a paper in 1975 at the Conference on Human Values and Aging, at Case Western Reserve University.) According to Steven Weiland, the experience of old age has become Erikson's primary topic in recent years. The analyst's own productivity has caused him gradually to refine his theories of the last years of life—a stage which he had largely undervalued in the work of his midlife. For example, in *The Life Cycle Completed,* he for the first time placed old age at the beginning rather than at the end of his famous chart of the life cycle, thereby achieving new insights into the pattern of human life. Six years later, he suggested that the psychic lessons of early life are reinterpreted and reintegrated in old age. In a 1988 interview he used terms such as "humility," "agape," and "caritas" to describe the culminating values of old age.[14]

Following Erikson's lead and reflecting the demographic fact that more people today are living into a fruitful old age, some biographers, according to Steven Weiland, have begun to turn their attention to the last phase of human development. Weiland cites examples of biographers during the 1970s and 1980s who explore with varying degrees of understanding the later lives of their subjects. In his judgment, however, only Justin Kaplan's *Walt Whitman* (1980) captures intuitively the complexities of his protagonist's last days. Perhaps as the productive longevity of elders becomes a norm, researchers will feel obliged to scrutinize more thoroughly the phenomenology of old age, but few do at the present moment. For example, Neal Tolchin's valuable account of the effect of blocked mourning on Herman Melville's writing pays almost no attention to life-course issues, even though Melville published his first novel when he was twenty-seven and began his last, *Billy Budd,* when he was sixty-seven.[15]

Despite the dominance of the Freudian and neo-Freudian focus on childhood and adolescence, other voices reflecting a more Jungian psychoanalytic viewpoint are beginning to affect gerontological theory. For example, in 1965 Elliott Jaques wrote an important essay on the connection between midlife crisis and a change in the pattern of creativity in the lives of male artists. He argues that male artists usually face the reality of death for the first time in their late thirties. The shock of that discovery can either stifle the creative impulse completely or alter its character, sometimes causing dramatic changes in their styles. They tend to paint or write thereafter in a more careful, sculpted style.[16]

Recently, Jaques's findings that some artists develop a late style have been confirmed to a degree by scholars, such as Kathleen Woodward, Amir Cohen-Shalev, Carolyn H. Smith, Mary Winkler, Mariolina Salvatori, and Anne M. Wyatt-Brown. In most cases, late-life depression, bereavement, or worries about aging and death prompt the change, indicating that artists are more able than most of us to voice their deepest fears. No matter how dramatic the change may be, however, important continuities also remain. Moreover, Wyatt-Brown's *Barbara Pym* demonstrates that in some cases writers revert at least temporarily to a earlier style once the depression has lifted. Thus, research supports Robert Kastenbaum's conviction that the issue of late style is much more complicated than Jaques had realized. Kastenbaum also argues convincingly that in some situations artists have changed their styles radically in response to "a sense of time urgency," a feeling which may not necessarily be related to growing older.[17]

Some clinicians, who find evidence of new developments in the later lives of their patients or subjects, challenge Jaques's idea that fear of death causes the changes. Psychiatrist George Vaillant believes that middle-aged individuals are troubled by worries about "decay" and "deterioration" rather than death. "Suicide," he argues, "reflects a fear of living, not of dying." Vaillant regards Jaques's "fear of death" as a metaphor for anxieties about our changing bodies and remarks that midlife, our "second coming of age," can be very stressful. David Gutmann also objects to the "catastrophic view of aging" implied by the Jaques model and prefers to stress the "particular resilience that the aged can show in the face of death" and the "special serenity" some exhibit even in the face of imminent extinction.[18] Of course, in fairness to Jaques, artists, unlike the rest of us, are more apt to express their anguish, because they may experience catharsis by so doing.

Finally, we must remember that Jaques's study was based on a small sample of Western white men, whose outstanding accomplishments made them obvious but unrepresentative choices for case studies. Most of the artists Jaques studied achieved recognition in youth, a circumstance which is not necessarily the case for women or for members of different cultural groups. For example, the lives of women, as Carolyn Heilbrun has remarked, follow a different trajectory. Since many have to postpone their period of creativity, their midlife often marks a flowering rather than a change in direction or a decline. As a result, Heilbrun argues, "life crises that have been identified as patterns in male lives often occur at a later age in women." The noted anthropologist Margaret Mead theorized that most women experience renewed energy in their later years, what she called "postmenopausal zest." Yet despite the urgent necessity to modify and modernize Jaques's theory, we must acknowledge his contributions. He pioneered the inquiry into male midlife creativity. The moment has arrived to broaden his inquiry by examining the creativity of older women and less privileged men.[19]

Because so few have recognized that conventional attitudes toward middle and old age are socially constructed, much remains to be done. This volume extends the inquiry about creative development over the life span, focusing most intensely on late-life creativity. We raise a series of questions about how artists work. What role do depression and loss play in the creative process? For example, does losing one's parents at an early age inhibit or spur creativity? Are the experiences of women artists fundamentally different from those of men? Do the changes that Jaques describes happen later for women than for men, if they occur at all? Can facing the threat of death at an early age quicken the alterations in style that we have learned to associate with later life? How do individual artists develop and change over the life course? What are the classic precipitating events? Are the artists affected by the cultural matrix in which they age, particularly its ideas about the value and creative power of later stages of life? Might the idea of "creativity" itself be culture-bound?

Happily, the writing of old age suggests that our society is hardier than we thought. The creative patterns of writers differ dramatically depending upon their life situations. Understandably, the stereotype of a young male artist who finds his subject by reacting against his family's desiccated values has generated much powerful and important fiction and poetry. This view, however, overlooks the possibility that every stage of the life course has its own topics, crises, and turning points, processes or moments, any one of which can also cause a flowering of creativity, a revitalization, or a new beginning.

Our essayists take literary texts as their starting points. They include some that were undervalued or misunderstood in their time, such as Elizabeth Bowen's *The Little Girls* and *Eva Trout* or D. H. Lawrence's *The Virgin and the Gipsy*. These are interpreted in the light of more recent critical and scholarly techniques, including post-Freudian psychoanalysis, literary gerontology, and biographical theory, as well as the insights of genetics and biology. Our collective understanding is that Anglo-American literary criticism, like the society from which it springs, until recently has been uncritically ageist. For many years most novelists, poets, and playwrights have hesitated to make older characters the central protagonists for fear that such works would not attract many readers. When an occasional artist like Henrik Ibsen, who prided himself on fighting the dominant culture of his time, created older heroes, they often exemplify what Levinson et al. identify as a pattern of "mid-life defeat." More commonly, however, fear of losing one's audience has inhibited artistic creativity. For example, three years after publishing his most successful novel, *A Passage to India* (1924), E. M. Forster abandoned a promising idea for a new work. He recorded in his commonplace book that the idea of "a *middle-aged* novel, i.e. by myself as an M. A., does attract. Would anyone want to read it though?" To him the dilemma was to "get nearer myself. . . . how get out my wit and wisdom without this pretence that it is through the young and on behalf of the young. Puberty-sauce—hiding the true flavour of M. A. dishes." [20]

Fortunately, as the population has aged, fewer novelists and poets have felt obliged to pretend that their writing is "puberty-sauce." Instead, beginning in the 1960s and 1970s, many have begun the task of exploring the experience of growing old. Besides the midlife progress novels that Gullette discusses, Carolyn Smith and Constance Rooke argue that more contemporary middle-aged and aging writers have placed midlife and elderly protagonists at the center of their fiction and poetry than have their predecessors. At the same time, some scholars have begun to incorporate gerontological theory into their analyses of literary texts. Several essays analyzing the effect of aging on the creative process have appeared in gerontological journals.[21] By taking up the individual cases of various authors, we plan to extend these insights, both to reveal more about individual texts and to learn how growing old affects creativity.

Our essays reflect the complexity of later life, observing moments of both despair and unexpected joy. In the first section of our book, the authors develop theories about late life and fiction. First, Margaret Gullette analyzes the multiple voices of aging subjects that she finds in medical, journalistic, and literary sources from 1910 to 1935. She argues that societal attitudes toward late life are constructed historically and vary from era to era. We are still, she thinks, influenced in part by the negative attitudes toward old age that were given credence in that period and by the assertion that decline begins in the middle years. Since so many of our writers reached maturity then, we can assume that they were exposed to some of these negative attitudes or to others specific to their families and/or social class. Refusing to oversimplify her interpretation, she offers the paradoxical insight that although decline overrode the positive features during that period, we now find the optimistic response more convincing than it once seemed.

Following Gullette's historical overview, Anne M. Wyatt-Brown identifies three models of late-life writing: one of continuity, another of late-life revival, and the third, an unexpected politics of old age. Using the novels of May Sarton, she shows that their composition has offered Sarton the chance to construct and then affirm a life for herself. The literary enterprise substitutes friends for lost and missing family members. Next, Thomas C. Caramagno asserts that biology and genetics present a theoretical challenge to the excesses of psychobiography in general, and to our understanding of suicide in later life in particular. His examination of Virginia Woolf's life challenges the views of those scholars who blame Woolf or her husband Leonard for her suicide. Caramagno reviews the recent findings in biology that have revolutionized our thinking about affective disorder and aging, all of which studies make Woolf's decision to commit suicide much more understandable. Finally, Kathleen Woodward theorizes that Freud's distinction between mourning and melancholia overlooks the interim position that Roland Barthes, among others, almost defiantly created, between finite mourning and infinite depression. Barthes, she argues, did not suffer from an uncontrollable melancholia; instead, he chose to sustain his sense of loss, in order to memorialize his mother. Indeed, he rejoiced in the discovery that his grief stimulated his imagination.

In the second section a terminal illness haunts the late career of D. H. Lawrence and a private vision and depression the career of Louise Bogan. The two followed radically different trajectories. When Lawrence received word in his fortieth year that he had only a year or two to live, he set about writing a puzzling novella. It was a chronicle of unsolved conflicts and wounding intimacies. In his youth he had created psychologically delicate and brilliant fictional portraits of children—which, according to M. M. Lally, he then abruptly and silently abandoned. In his own life children had become the most painful of subjects because his wife Frieda had given up her three young children to be with him. Now the threat of death urged him one last time, in *The Virgin and the Gipsy,* to deal with that prospect. This fictional life review has a shrill, unsettling quality, and not surprisingly it is an unfinished story. Bogan, on the other hand, had been sentenced to live; but she, who had always equated poetry with sexuality, could not make poems out of the emptiness she experienced in old age. Thus, Marcia Aldrich writes, Bogan's poetic career attenuated toward its own premature and self-imposed end. In retrospect, Bogan's definition of poetry was too narrow to sustain her creativity in late life. Fortunately, in more recent times women poets have broken out of the narrow mold that constrained Bogan; in many cases their later lives have been marked by artistic fertility.[22]

In the third section the writers had longer lives and sustained careers. Yet bouts of depression and despair plagued most of them and hindered their productivity, at least for a time. According to Brian Connery and Anne Wyatt-Brown, writing provided a lifeline for Jonathan Swift and Elizabeth Bowen when fears of mental illness and the anguish of bereavement threatened to overwhelm them. In part, the innovations of their late style can be traced to new insights gained from this intense struggle. Both regretted the absence of heirs and family, but neither was inclined to indulge their sense of despair. Instead, Swift created a memorial to himself in his poetry, while Bowen concocted a fictional memorial for her entire family by charting the decline and fall of the Trout dynasty in her final novel.

In contrast to the efforts of Swift and Bowen to maintain sanity in the face of threatened dissolution, the artistic careers of John Cheever and Henry de Montherlant, a twentieth-century French novelist, essayist, playwright, and pederast, were complicated by the necessity of hiding their homosexuality. Constance Rooke and Josephine V. Arnold argue that the burden of secrecy Cheever and Montherlant carried became too heavy for them in their old age. In their final works each invents characters with whom he feels a bond as a way to "calibrate" or work through his sexual experiences while still maintaining the aesthetic distance that narrative provides. Despite the woes of these writers, they had moments of inspiration that redeemed the pain and suffering of their daily existences. Their art is enriched by their battle against despair. Their final works provide examples of what Kathleen Woodward calls "a love story, a death story, a writing story" and Roger Salomon calls "desperate storytelling." Although Salomon is discussing the fate of the heroic tradition that has passed its prime, rather than that of aging individuals, his phrase can be applied to these swan songs as well.[23]

In their prime the writers in the final section had exhibited considerable resilience and serenity. Later life brought its burdens, but as long as they continued to write, they found it possible temporarily to transcend physical exile, physical infirmity, and the fear of death. Judith de Luce argues that Ovid's final poems should be read as an extended life review, created partly to express his displeasure at being exiled where he could not even speak the language. His final poems provide a remarkable combination of celebration and complaint. He rejoices in the power of creativity even as he reflects upon the difficulties facing aging writers. The same creativity sustained Colette in her last days. According to Bethany Ladimer, Colette was capable of redefining herself and her eroticism in old age. Unlike Louise Bogan, whose poetic inspiration withered in later life, Colette became the sort of masculinized but powerful woman David Gutmann finds typical among the older women he has studied.[24] In midlife she mourned the loss of her sexual attractiveness, but in old age she substituted an erotics of visual sensuousness for the intense gender analysis of her earlier fiction. Her newly developed capacity to respond viscerally to nature compensated her for severe physical disabilities.

In a similar fashion, Gloria Fromm argues, Dorothy Richardson as she aged discovered a new dimension and power to her consciousness, experiencing enhancement and "wealth" rather than restriction and poverty. Old age brought with it—to her surprise—a flexibility and mobility of the mind that resulted in "renewed and recharged creativity." Colette and Richardson are both examples of individuals who learn to accept their limitations in certain aspects of their lives, as long as they can find new gratifications. Margaret Gullette would argue that they learn to compartmentalize. Instead of despairing "about the other spheres and about the 'incoherence' of the whole self as well," they celebrated the victories that remain.[25] According to Carolyn Smith, the American poet Josephine Miles had an extraordinarily active life despite being afflicted with arthritis at an early age. Not only did she write poetry, but she was also a successful professor at Berkeley. Despite Miles's accomplishments, however, her early poetry is remarkably self-effacing. Not until old age did she feel free to explore her own feelings as a teacher, a lifelong sufferer from a debilitating disease, and an old woman facing death.

The two writers who are still alive, Peter Taylor and Maxine Kumin, have been greatly affected by the travails of others, as well as by their own. Bertram Wyatt-Brown argues that Taylor shows a rare sensitivity to the psychological and social experiences of his aged characters, men and women alike. Taylor is especially compassionate about the problems of elders who must adjust to a world that no longer shares the social values of their youth. Maxine Kumin describes herself as a survivor. Like the bereaved Allen Dow in John Updike's "His Mother Inside Him," Kumin sometimes feels like the last remaining speaker of a dying language.[26] Over the years since the suicide of her friend and fellow poet Anne Sexton, Kumin has created poems that Diana Hume George believes combine elegy with an epitaphic poetics. Thus, in all of the creative works in this final section, the authors have examined their own experiences of aging, as well as those of their friends and relatives. Knowing themselves to be living in an uncertain world, many have created a new kind of life review in their elegies as a way of coming to terms with exile, bodily infirmity, loss, and suffering.

In sum, despite our shared cultural anxiety about anomie, death, and decay, most of these novelists and poets confront the prospect of their decline with a mixture of grim humor and courage. Their late-life writing— in some cases their actual swan songs—suggest that even the threat of imminent death can inspire writers to new creativity.[27] Time may be short, but for many their later writing marks a new beginning, a bold attempt to re-create their identities for the remainder of their lives.

Notes

I am grateful to Margaret Gullette and M. M. Lally, who made a number of substantive suggestions for improving the introduction and to Janice Rossen, Gloria Fromm, Carolyn Smith, and Bertram Wyatt-Brown for expert editorial guidance.

1. Kathleen Woodward, "Simone de Beauvoir," 90; advertisement, *New York Review of Books*, June 28, 1990, 40; Ernest Becker, *The Denial of Death*, 11–24.

2. M. M. Bakhtin, "Epic and Novel," 7, 12.

3. Constance Rooke, "Hagar's Old Age," 31, 40, "Old Age in Contemporary Fiction," 245, and *"Oh What a Paradise It Seems"* in this volume; Barbara Frey Waxman, *From the Hearth to the Open Road,* 2, 16; Margaret Morganroth Gullette, *Safe at Last in the Middle Years,* xviii-xix. See also Gullette's forthcoming "The Deaths of Children and the Fear of Aging in Contemporary American Fiction." Lilian R. Furst, "Realism and Its 'Code of Accreditation,' " 102, says that since the mid-1970s contemporary theorists have begun to challenge the status of realism as representing some sort of inviolable truth, but remnants of that belief still exist.

4. Gullette, *Safe;* Kathleen Woodward, *Aging and Its Discontents;* Stuart F. Spicker, Kathleen M. Woodward, and David D. Van Tassel, eds., *Aging and the Elderly;* David D. Van Tassel, ed., *Aging, Death, and the Completion of Being;* Laurel Porter and Laurence M. Porter, eds., *Aging in Literature;* Thomas R. Cole and Sally A. Gadow, eds., *What Does It Mean to Grow Old?;* Prisca von Dorotka Bagnell and Patricia Spencer Soper, eds., *Perceptions of Aging in Literature;* Thomas R. Cole, David D. Van Tassel, and Robert Kastenbaum, eds., *Handbook of the Humanities and Aging;* Kathleen Woodward and Murray M. Schwartz, eds., *Memory and Desire.*

5. Daniel J. Levinson et al., *The Seasons of a Man's Life,* 18. James E. Birren and Vern L. Bengtson, eds., Preface to *Emergent Theories of Aging,* ix, state that their 1988 volume attempts to "address the data-rich but theory-poor state of current research on aging."

6. Gary M. Kenyon, "Basic Assumptions in Theories of Human Aging," 5, 7 (Kenyon, 12, paraphrases H. Thomae's remarks from "Personality and Adjustment to Old Age," in *Handbook of Mental Health and Aging,* ed. J. Birren and R. Sloane, 1980); Mary Catherine Bateson, *Composing a Life,* 223; Erik H. Erikson, *Childhood and Society* and *The Life Cycle Completed;* George E. Vaillant, *Adaptation to Life,* 236, 359. When a participant in the Grant Study of Adult Development complained about one of his conclusions, Vaillant listened to his arguments, leaving the interview "stunned but thinking," 355. As a result of such sensitivity to alternate viewpoints, Vaillant's study provides a remarkable example of effective "grounded theory," to borrow Barney G. Glaser and Anselm L. Strauss's useful term from their classic work, *The Discovery of Grounded Theory.* Besides Erikson and Vaillant, another influential practitioner of sequential stage theory is Levinson et al., *Seasons.*

7. Dean Keith Simonton, "Creativity, Leadership, and Chance," 386, "History, Chemistry, Psychology, and Genius," 98–99, and "Does Creativity Decline in the Later Years?" 86, 89.

8. Levinson, et al. *Seasons,* 215; Carolyn G. Heilbrun, *Writing a Woman's Life,* 61.

9. David M. Harrington, "The Ecology of Human Creativity," 149–50. Robert Kastenbaum, "The Creative Process," 304, agrees that creativity in old age is affected "by cultural expectations, by economic opportunity," and by many other less obvious variables.

10. Gullette, *Safe,* xii-xiii. Cf. Harry R. Moody, *Abundance of Life,* 14, who emphasizes the pessimism Americans felt in the 1970s partly because the population was aging; he calls that chapter "The Specter of Decline."

11. Margaret Morganroth Gullette, "Creativity, Aging, Gender," this volume; Wallace Fowlie, "On Writing Autobiography," 165; James Olney, *Metaphors of Self;* James Olney, ed., *Autobiography;* James Olney, ed., *Studies in Autobiography;* Woodward, "Beauvoir." With the exception of the work mentioned in this essay and cited in the remainder of the volume, few feminist critics are aware of the research on aging.

12. Ira Bruce Nadel, *Biography,* 113; Steven Weiland, "Aging according to Biography," 192; M. M. Bakhtin, "Forms of Time and of the Chronotope in the Novel," 140. See Woodward, *Aging,* for a powerful and convincing analysis of Freud's attitudes toward aging.

13. Park Honan, "The Theory of Biography," 112; Robert N. Butler, "The Life Review," 66. Cf. Gullette, *Safe,* 158, who argues that life review occurs periodically throughout life; "after a point that I would put in adolescence, we do it all the time."

14. Erik H. Erikson, "Reflections on Dr. Borg's Life Cycle"; Weiland, "Aging," 191; Erik H. Erikson, *The Life Cycle Completed;* Daniel Goleman, "Erikson, in His Own Old Age, Expands His View of Life," 16.

15. Weiland, "Aging," 192–94; Neal L. Tolchin, *Mourning, Gender, and Creativity in the Art of Herman Melville.*

16. Elliott Jaques, "Death and the Mid-Life Crisis," 502–3.

17. Kathleen Woodward, *At Last, the Real Distinguished Thing,* "May Sarton and Fictions of Old Age," "Beauvoir," and "Late Theory, Late Style" in this volume; Amir Cohen-Shalev, "Old Age Style"; Carolyn H. Smith, "Images of Aging in American Poetry, 1925–1985"; Mary G. Winkler, "Walking to the Stars"; Mariolina Salvatori, "Thomas Hardy and Eugenio Montale"; Anne M. Wyatt-Brown, "Late Style in the Novels of Barbara Pym and Penelope Mortimer," "Creativity in Midlife," and *Barbara Pym,* 142; Kastenbaum, "Creative Process," 301.

18. Vaillant, *Adaptation,* 234, 220–21, 224; David L. Gutmann, "Psychoanalysis and Aging," 490, 509.

19. Heilbrun, *Writing,* 39, 49, 59; Bateson, *Composing,* 28. Anne M. Wyatt-Brown, "Late Style" and "Creativity," finds that creative women who began their careers early sometimes experience dramatic shifts in their artistic vision at midlife, often at a slightly later age than thirty-seven. Sally H. Rankin, "The Emergence of Creativity in Later Life," 177, has found that creativity has three ways of developing in women's lives. Sometimes it emerges as a reaction to "loss and loneliness." Other times it is a lifelong occupation. Occasionally it represents a new beginning in later life.

20. Levinson et al., *Seasons,* 216; E. M. Forster, *Commonplace Book,* 29. Levinson's one-sided argument that "mid-life defeat" is the dominant message of literature can be countered by Gullette's findings in her essay in this volume, "Creativity." See Anne M. Wyatt-Brown, "A Buried Life," for a discussion of Forster's struggle to remain creative in later life.

21. Smith, "Images of Aging," and Rooke, "Old Age in Fiction." See Anne M. Wyatt-Brown, "The Coming of Age of Literary Gerontology" and "Literary Gerontology Comes of Age," for reviews of research in the field.

22. Heilbrun, *Writing,* 62–63.

23. The term "calibrate" is borrowed from Gregory Bateson, whom Constance Rooke quotes in "*Paradise,*" this volume. Woodward, "Late Theory," this volume. Roger B. Salomon, *Desperate Storytelling,* 9, borrows James Joyce's phrase to describe writers who respond to loss by creating "an 'enabling' context that makes possible the transformation of nostalgia and despair into renewed engagement with the heroic values of the past."

24. David Gutmann, *Reclaimed Powers,* 157.

25. Gullette, *Safe,* xxiii.

26. John Updike, "His Mother Inside Him," 35–36.

27. Gullette, *Safe,* xxvi, believes that for some artists "writing life-course fiction might particularly assist personal transformation."

I

Theories of Creativity, Aging, and Gender

I

MARGARET MORGANROTH GULLETTE

Creativity, Aging, Gender: A Study of Their Intersections, 1910–1935

Learning to Deconstruct at the Intersections

A FOG OF bitterness and failure always envelops those divergently valued abstract nouns "creativity" and "aging" when they are put together in our culture. Creativity is one of our highest attributes; aging, one of our saddest. The *decline* of creativity because of age—that's what the combination forebodes. Although Sophocles and Goethe, Beckett and I. B. Singer can be flung into the discourse as counterexamples of prestigious late-life production, does any collection of empirical examples prove that people can be become *more* creative by aging? Does any myth support the idea? Similarly for "gender": if "high" creativity is male—if, *they say,* women "can't write, can't paint," if "there can never be a woman of genius"[1]—can older women conceivably do better? Whenever these three abstractions are put together, they produce the effect of a construct composed of inert, ahistorical, unalterable materials.

No one writing for this book believes that this is true. On the contrary, we probably all believe something like this: that the culture surrounding us manufactures stories blaming aging for (among other things) causing the decline of creativity, and holding femaleness responsible for (among other things) producing works of feeble quality. Thus, as feminists and life-course theorists interested in age as a socially constructed category, we have an obligation, voluntarily assumed, to demolish such stories. So we chop away at the hydra, only to find—with the unsurprise of the historian confronting idiot ideology—that this hydra too has innumerable duplicable heads. Moreover, whenever we put these abstractions together (as in the title of this chapter), we too, entirely against our intention, put another head on the hydra—we reproduce the same essentialist illusion. No wonder the task seems complicated, fatiguing, and endless. For the sake of resistance, then, we stop for a moment to ask "Who created this monster? And when?"

These being historicizing questions, we need to locate a period, the more recent and influential the better, when creative decline first began to be solidly glued to aging, and, more particularly, a period when the creativity of women could first be asserted and then (of course), in expectable back-lash, be denied. I felt I had located age-correlated creative decline when I came upon indisputable signs of the monster's existence in the mind and, in-deed, on the bodies of well-known writers themselves. For Anglo-American culture, these signs become decisively and unmistakably visible between 1910 and 1935. But it was still startling to find that a debate about late-life female creativity was joined in exactly the same period. What follows is a study in some of the ways in which one culture, at one time, correlated age, gender, and creativity. Different voices—female and male, feminist and antifeminist, of various ages, speaking out of medical and sexual, eco-nomic and sociological context, publishing in diverse media—were at work making meanings out of *age, gender,* and *creativity,* at the multiple places where they were said to intersect. Much of what they produced, we still endure.

Aging Glands

In 1934 William Butler Yeats (one familiar story goes) underwent a "monkey-gland" operation to restore his sexual potency. This story, when-ever I've heard it, is told with a smirk by men many years younger than Yeats was then, as if to mock the "old man" (he was sixty-nine) for inappro-priate yearnings and at the same time fend off their own embarrassment at hinting at their own future desires. For the record, Yeats's operation most likely involved not transplantation but a partial vasectomy, an operation (associated with the name of Eugen Steinach) that supposedly stimulated the gonads to produce more internal secretion of testosterone. The opera-tion did not specifically promise to produce increased sexual performance. Its promise was to rejuvenate the whole body, restore health, and—cru-cial point for our purposes—revive flagging mental energies. Yeats was not in particularly good health at the time, and there was nothing organically wrong with him (these are not good indicators for elective surgery). But he was willing to undergo this particular surgery at his age because he had read one hard-sell book, Norman Haire's 1924 *Rejuvenation,* linking "vitality"

with hormones, and the failure of vitality with age-related hormonal decline, and hormone reproduction with this operation. He felt his poetic
energies flagging; he, who had ten years earlier implied that old men were
at least "monuments of unaging intellect," now attributed this decline to
aging. Popular science and medical and health guides had made all these
associations widely available; Norman Haire packaged them enthusiastically: Yeats simply made a leap of faith in the ageist sexual "science" of
his time that was required to put himself in some bodily and psychic risk.
Although he reported no major health gain—he thought his blood pressure
was lowered afterward—he believed it had restored his sexual "desire." The
myth (abetted by one of his biographers, Richard Ellmann, but reported
rather more neutrally by another, Norman Jeffares) goes that the operation produced rather than preceded another burst of poetic creativity.[2] The
operation had, we would now say, a placebo effect.

Gender symmetry was at work in the hormone-recharge field. About
ten years earlier the American novelist Gertrude Atherton at age sixty-six
had undergone a nonsurgical procedure for the same "creative" reasons.
We would now consider this one even riskier, as it involved a series of
X-ray treatments directed at the ovaries. The medical theory behind X-rays
was similar to that behind partial vasectomy: the ovaries were supposed to
be stimulated to produce more internal secretion. The operation for men
had been invented first (which is one reason why Yeats's vasectomy comes
first in my account). Doubts remained about whether an equivalent procedure could be invented that would "benefit" women. During that lapse in
time, a certain amount of commiseration could be heard over the fact that
"rejuvenation" was possible for men but not for women.

Atherton too felt that her creative powers had flagged, and the fault
was "age." Some years before, a German physiotherapist had assured her
that if she kept herself healthy, "my creative faculty would remain active
as long as I lived. There were scientists in Germany working as brilliantly
in extreme old age as in their middle years, and had not Sophocles written
Oedipus at Colonus when he was past eighty? But . . ." Empiricism is weak
in the face of ideology backed by medicine backed by press hype. There
was enormous coverage of rejuvenation operations. She read a newspaper
article about a man who chose between the "slight operation . . . or increasing senescence with all its attendant ills." After the operation Dr. Lorenz
"sometimes worked fourteen hours a day, and hardly knew what it was to
feel fatigue." She read another interview about women getting treatments
to "restore their exhausted energies and enable them to make a living"
and rushed off that morning to make an appointment with the doctor.[3]

Widowed young and never remarried and opposed to marriage for herself ("There are enough martyrs in the world," she wrote in her autobiography), she seems not to have cared about sexual rejuvenation. Indeed, she was at some pains afterwards to let the world know that vitality and creativity, not sexuality, were her issues. Like Yeats, she believed that the operation was responsible for her next creative effort. In fact, it *was,* because it gave her the subject matter for her next novel: about a fifty-eight-year-old woman who has the ovary treatment and appears in New York society looking thirty in the brightest light and ready for all that life can bring to a beautiful, rich, cultivated, Europeanized thirty-year-old woman. Large-scale wish fulfillment in a climate of anxiety about aging made *Black Oxen* the best-seller of 1923, a cause célèbre banned in some towns, Atherton's most famous novel. The book, the movie made from it, and her autobiography cultivated the image that she was a magically beautiful older woman. She was overrewarded for believing in the operation.

What these two accounts tell us—and I could add others, although the procedures were by no means all considered "successful"—is that in this period writers of both genders in both Great Britain and America could believe that a lull in writing was caused by a "decline" in creative "energy," that "aging" was responsible, and that "science" could "reverse" the trend. They believed these correlations in no casual way, since they were willing to put their bodies on the line for their sake. In order to believe this, they had to ignore other possible causes for having an unproductive period. Atherton, for example, had to ignore a fact of her experience, that she had such a hiatus after finishing other works. "It was true that I had had—like all writers, I fancy—these sterile periods before. . . . Each time I was sure that my fiction tract had dried up and that I'd never write another novel. Experience should have taught me better but never did" (*AN,* 553). Many writers of the early twentieth century interpreted their fallow times, however painful, as contingent and passing moments in a professional career: Virginia Woolf, for example, and Joseph Conrad. In other words, lulls in production occurred, and could recur, at every stage in life. For older writers worrying about the silent spells, a range of ad hoc, personal, and idiosyncratic explanations was available: exhaustion consequent on concentration, a crisis in the lives of one's adult children, ill health unrelated to age, temperament, poor reviews, fear of poor reviews, lack of ideas, creative rest. A range of extrinsic historical or economic explanations was also possible: the state of "letters," the exigencies of publishing, the inadequacies of the audience. Aging need not figure as paramount in these lists. It need not figure at all. Indeed, how could age come to count in later life as the overriding explanation for creative rest, when a writer's whole-life experience of writing and resting and writing again denied it?

Part of the answer lies in the way age-related depression was culturally constructed in the period. After the discovery of the hormones in the 1890s, many authorities believed that sex-hormone levels declined precipitously in the climacteric years of men and women. "Premature age, then, is in the nature of a deficiency disease," concluded Leonard Williams, writing one of the novelty books on the new stage of life, *Middle Age and Old Age* (1925). Deficiency and disease were becoming the standard metaphors for normal aging. Specifically, many writers vaguely but regularly linked the decline in hormone levels with decreases in general mental functioning. The highly respected author of *Senescence* (1922), G. Stanley Hall, wrapped in prestige from having invented adolescence and having brought sexuality to America in the person of Sigmund Freud, wrote: "Most important of all, and the chief source of human energy in man, are the sex glands, which distribute energy to all the sixty trillion cells of the body, making each carry out the function assigned it. . . . Sex glands stimulate not merely amorousness but all kinds of cerebral and muscular energy, pouring into the blood a species of vital fluid, and give a sense of vigor and well-being and plenitude of life, which later vanish when their source begins to run dry in age."[4]

A male climacteric, involving loss of sexual power for some men at some indeterminate age, had previously held a certain imprecise folkloric and medical status. But the discovery of the endocrine glands was treated as if it made the climacteric an absolutely universal discovery and inescapable experience, and the new discourse lowered the age at which it occurred, from way after sixty to any time from about forty-five on.[5] Most important for mental workers, especially artists, the losses attributable to aging had become systemic—tied not merely to the sexual system but to cerebration as well.

Even the weak denial "Genius is exempt" was not heard much. Indeed, once a decline in cerebral "energy" became a "known" correlate of aging, the original biological argument didn't need to appear; it was effaced. Men like Mencken who mocked "gland novels" like *Black Oxen* could write quite innocently of "authors in general" that "only too often the first half of their work is better than the second half."[6] It's a curious cultural case, in which intellectual men and women of mature age thoroughly invest themselves in an ideology that dooms them to increasing mental extinction.

The effort to make aging an unavoidable danger for mental workers was not aimed especially at women, for the obvious reason that considering women as skilled mental workers was not yet a necessary assumption for many men or perhaps for most women. "Woman" was a sort of after-thought to this universalizing decline discourse but was easily folded into it. Havelock Ellis, dean of sexologists, matched woman to man. The ovaries "not only form the ova, but they elaborate for internal use a secretion which develops and maintains the special physical and mental qualities of woman-hood, as the testicular secretion those of manhood." Blair Bell, in a 1916 book that became a classic text describing woman, echoed the party line. "The mental condition of a woman is dependent on her metabolism; and the metabolism itself is under the influence of the internal secretions." Leonard Williams particularized in more sinister ways. "But to whatever physical diseases or ailments the climacteric may be said to dispose the patient, it is upon her brain that the weight of the disturbances generally falls. . . . Then comes the hypertrophy of the Ego, written with a large capital, groundless fears, obstinate introspection, violent jealousies, sexual perversions, leading often enough to talk about suicide and profound melancholia."[7] Williams was only repeating one nineteenth-century discourse about the effect of menopause on women's psyche, a line that in its earlier form had fallen into some disrepute in the twenties. But in the new context of hormonal de-terminism and Freudian "perversions," that rather discredited menopause discourse carried with it new conviction and threat.

A brand-new and most disabling truism held that not merely the pres-ence of hormones was requisite for the production of art but sexual *activity*. The new sex enthusiasts narrowly linked (hetero)sexuality to creativity. Ilia Ilich Metchnikoff, who translated his Nobel Prize into book fame as a specialist in the prolongation of life (the title of his 1908 book), wrote, "The truth is that artistic genius and perhaps all kinds of genius are closely associated with sexual activity." Ellis applied this to women: "Ferrero has sought the explanation of the small part played by women in art, and their defective sense for purely esthetic beauty, in their less keen sexual emotions. This is doubtless an important factor." But in the early twentieth century it was becoming dogma that women were scarcely less keen about sexual activity than men. So Grete Meisel-Hess, a socialist-feminist whose 1917 book *The Sexual Crisis* was read by advanced people on both sides of the Atlantic, decided there were two different kinds of women. "It is the ardent women who can and must express themselves in the fields of art and re-search. Their antitypes, frigid women, lacking alike the fire of love and the divine flame of inspiration, are inapt also for social and artistic work. All that they do, all that they produce, is colorless, desexualized, and conse-quently valueless." Even Winifred Holtby, expressing the "common sense" of advanced women of her time, believed that women might regain what the culture was then blindly calling "second youth" (rather than, say, "a healthy midlife"), but, she went on, "it would be stupid to deny that under present conditions the majority of women do, from the ages of about forty-five to fifty, suffer from headaches, indigestion, low blood-pressure or some other form of disabling if not crippling disability. . . . To most young people in their twenties, middle-aged women all too often appear as physical crocks. And that discourages them." [8] Feminism, which was explaining male bias in so many realms of gendered difference, was rendered helpless whenever age overrode gender, medical authority about "menopause" overrode personal experience, and sexual "liberation" overrode all other considerations.

What was a celibate woman, or a woman no longer young, to do? Among older women writers, many were single, uninterested in marriage, lesbian, left behind in the rush for younger and more complaisant women, or postmenopausal. Many no doubt felt they suffered some combination of disqualifying factors. As we saw, Atherton's metaphors for her creative situation, "sterility," "dryness," and "fictional tracts," are derived from sexual science. An older woman writer would have had to stay ignorant of menopause "theory" (ignorance is still an excellent tactic); what were the grounds for denying it?

Not every authority accepted the link between age, sexual decline, and mental weakness. William Josephus Robinson, who produced easy-reading sex guides with titles like *Sexual Impotence* (1913) and *Sexual Problems of Today* (1921), contested the "false belief, shared by the common and the ignorant, that with the decay of the sexual powers there goes inevitably the decay of all mental power." [9] But since so many of the wise and respected upheld the false belief, it took on a life of its own, so that even as, very slowly through the century, sexologists have raised the upper age limit of the alleged decay of the sexual powers and gerontologists have tried to snap the bond between sex hormones and mental activity, some myths of age-related mental decline remain.

(Writers were also led to believe that their *material*—insofar as it depended on their sexual experience—was likely to wane as they aged. In a Storm Jameson novella about two women writers in their forties, one maliciously prognosticates about the other, who "dishes up her experience of life almost raw," that "when her experiences fall off—as they will with age, since they all come to her by her senses—her novels will become thinner and less lively. . . . She will re-hash old stuff." [10] One way or another, you could count on it: aging would bring a fall, and one's fiction would suffer.)

Culturally, the alleged correlations between mental decay and age can be blamed on the cult of youth, the youth rebellion that resulted in the creation of the generation gap, and the expansion and elevation of sexuality to formerly unimagined prominence in terms of the whole life. Stephen Heath has called D. H. Lawrence's novels "a decisive moment in the shift . . . to the more general representation of sex as the basic fact of experience and identity—and to which an intense value is now assigned." By another conflation, young people who were believed to possess the cultural goods that supposedly made sex so natural for them—"vigor," "health"—were also assumed to own the associated mental qualities: "young" ideas, "vision," "imagination." Randolph S. Bourne's 1913 *Youth and Life* implied on every page that the two abstractions in his title were identical. With the downright boys'-book brusqueness so fashionable then that it now seems the stylistic uniform of the second-rate, the twenty-five-year-old Bourne flaunted his era's pet biases and antagonisms. "Now the fact is, of course, that it is the young people who have all the really valuable experience. . . . It is only the interpretation of the ideas of this first collision with life that is worth anything. . . . If we get few ideas after we are twenty-five, we get few ideals after we are twenty." He associated "progress" with youth, "ashes" with middle age, and said of the old that they "sit in the saddle and ride mankind." [11]

Once "talent" was linked to youth, looking for talent in young people and of course finding it was a way to ally oneself with "youth," to share in it by sympathetic magic. The Bloomsbury set, the Harlem Renaissance, and the various groups calling themselves modernists felt they were a "young" generation overthrowing the outworn styles or ways of thinking of the old. When Amy Lowell wrote to Harriet Monroe to congratulate her on the success of *Poetry,* she put it this way: "I was immensely struck by the fact that there is not a single poet of distinction among the younger generation whom you have not printed." [12] Lowell was in her forties when she wrote those words, and Monroe, who repeated them proudly in her seventies, was then in her mid-fifties and knew very well that as a young poet she had had no success. And the culture at large reproduced these dramatic new reifications of the "stages" and abilities of life, even through the utterances of older creative people for whom it was masochism to agree.

Fictions of Creative Degeneration: Constructing Midlife Decline

As the new hormone and sex-based theories of mental decline throw a dark shadow over twentieth-century writers barely into their middle years, women as well as men, other more literary factors deepen the shade. The fact is that writers and educated people read, and in certain eras, for certain purposes, this can be a regrettable habit. One of the most striking phenomena of the new century is that literature (finally) began with some frequency to age its main characters into the middle years and beyond. Yet the advent of midlife fiction was badly timed. Suddenly a host of characters in their forties or fifties or in some vague middle age began to appear and simultaneously decay. Many of the most striking and ultimately canonical of these were about men. If I had to list ten reasons why a cultivated person today finds it hard to shed the idea of midlife decline, the list would include Oscar Wilde's *Portrait of Dorian Gray* (1891), Henry James's *The Ambassadors* (1904), Thomas Mann's *Death in Venice* (translated 1911), Dreiser's *Sister Carrie* (1900 and 1907 in America, 1901 in London) for the portrait of Hurstwood, T. S. Eliot's "Love Song of J. Alfred Prufrock" (1915), Proust's *Remembrance of Things Past* (trans. 1924), Willa Cather's *The Professor's House* (1925), F. Scott Fitzgerald's *Tender Is the Night* (1934) and "The Crack Up" (1936), and Evelyn Waugh's *Brideshead Revisited* (1944). The list does not include much-read novels of the time that have since been forgotten, that supported the tendency to think of aging-into-the-midlife as a traverse to loss, disaster, or possibly death, like Joseph Hergesheimer's *Cytherea*, the best-seller of 1922. Nor does it include decline novels by midlife women about midlife women: Rebecca West's *The Judge* (1922), Cather's *A Lost Lady* (1923), or Wharton's *The Mother's Recompense* (1925), and again, a host of popular novels.

And we can compare what we know of aging in works about the male midlife with equally well-known novels of male youth from the same period: Kipling's *Kim,* J. M. Barrie's *Peter Pan,* Booth Tarkington's *Penrod,* Fitzgerald's *This Side of Paradise*. Literary culture, not merely work by work, but in a kind of unconscious collaborative effort, was constructing an imagined life course for men. The trend it represented can be described only as a decline (beginning as young as four or five in Freud and Barrie), taking its final toll somewhere in the middle years. When Fitzgerald declared, "There are no second acts in American lives," he was not simply expressing his own personal sense of decline. He was grimly summing up (whether he knew it or not) a new Anglo-American—a western European—literary tradition and cultural interpretation of the life course.

Some of the protagonists of the midlife works mentioned above are presented initially as active writers or intellectuals: Mann's Gustav Aschenbach, Cather's Professor Godfrey St. Peter, Fitzgerald's Dr. Dick Diver. All these men lose their mental power and noticeably stop being productive through some complicated interactions with aging. These are subtle novels, full of substantial detail, psychological plausibility within the understandings of the time, layerings of loss, and aesthetic reinforcements and indirections. At bottom, each poignantly makes space for what was gradually coming to be considered universal aging-in-itself: physiological dwindling in the middle years. Aschenbach is in his fifties, St. Peter is fifty-two, Diver even younger. The writers were practicing: inventing the tones of voice of age-related fatigue, the tropes of lost strength and energy, the scenes expressive of diminished beauty, grace, self-control, physical confidence, bodily narcissism, or whatever else they prized that was vulnerable. Who could give subjective content to the otherwise empty rhetoric of the aging manuals so well as these great writers?

They constructed fear of aging far more devastatingly. In Cather's *The Professor's House*, St. Peter explains to his wife: "And now I seem to be tremendously tired. One pays, coming or going. A man has got only just so much in him; when it's gone he slumps." In *Tender Is the Night* we see Diver in the Mediterranean trying again and again to do a stunt on a surfboard that involves lifting another man, and however much a reader may share the belief of Dick's wife that this is a foolish test of power, we can't help feeling that his wanting to do it at all costs is a sign of genuine loss. Diver humiliates himself publicly, as an aging male body. As the narrator of Cather's *A Lost Lady* reports, about an aging woman, "He felt frightened for her. When women began to talk about feeling young, didn't it mean that something had been broken?" [13] When Aschenbach in *Death in Venice* watches a beauty doctor dye his hair and paint his cheeks, a new era in the representation of aging had begun. In the nineteenth century a midlife body could have been vaguely shown to be tired or less beautiful than when younger, but some kind of accommodation would have been found with these facts. Now they are made to loom in ruthless detail as a large part of identity, or rather, as an overwhelming of prior, true identity. On the spectrum of possible emotional response, they slide a man toward the surprise or even the degradation of physical aging—to newly coded signs of resignation or despair. One of these is the desperate, unavailing, and therefore humiliating effort to appear young.

But the losses are more than physical; they are systemic. By the time the pages to be read are few, Godfrey St. Peter has lost interest in every aspect of life and, having escaped dying by an effort of mere instinct, looks forward to nothing better than existence without joy. Dick Diver, the master of civilized discourse, has become rude to people; he who had yielded to their European dislocations only for his wife's sake winds up making motiveless moves to obscure provincial American towns. Aschenbach, at first merely following the boy he loves with his eyes, by the end kisses his door, keeps secret his knowledge of the plague, suffers ferocious erotic dreaming, and suddenly dies.

Plausible as the novels are at substantiating male bodily loss, all are finally weak—curiously weak—at explaining why the protagonists fall so far so fast. They leave vast gaps of explanation. St. Peter's wife says to him: "You are not old enough for the pose you take. That's what puzzles me. For so many years you never seemed to grow at all older, though I did. Two years ago you were an impetuous young man" (*PH,* 162). What is being constructed in all such novels is something unexpected, and at the end of the plot unexpectedly rapid, and absolutely irreversible—what would come to be called, many years later, a "midlife crisis," but without a resolution to follow. Some part of the protagonist's drastic decline remains under-explained because overdetermined, as if only heaping up a vast number of motives or agencies could yield the amount of loss the author's sense of aging requires. And no wonder. Now, with hindsight, using the tools of age analysis, we can begin to say why. Although their autobiographical circumstances were different, and the political circumstances as well (one novel is prewar, another postwar, and the third written during the depression), the constant that these writers shared was aging—in this particular place and time. The amount of desperation about aging that was circulating in the culture went far beyond what any writer could personally have experienced of loss through the processes of age alone. Or, to put it another way, this desperation colored each writer's interpretation of temporal experience, producing similar tropes, plots, and age-graded relationships between characters.

All three plots try to thicken the explanation by at least doubling the loss. The men lose not only their own younger self but a person they love who stands in for beautiful "Youth." In Aschenbach's case the plot involves the desperate lust of the climacteric (Havelock Ellis reported that Mann had meant it to be a story of the "pathological climacteric"). The young Polish boy who represents love to the long-ascetic Aschenbach also allegorically represents lost youth. He who could never regain his own boyhood could try to find it again—inappropriately, insanely—in some other boy.[14] Mann is the only one who unambiguously associates decline and "immorality"; in the other, later novels the attempt to possess the young person is not evil or crazy but simply impossible. Willa Cather's Professor too loses a young man, Tom Outland, an intellectual disciple and spiritual guide who had been a more valued intimate than his wife or daughters or sons-in-law. Dick Diver, with more varied gifts than either of the others, loses them all when he cannot find a way either to renounce or keep a "girl," eighteen-year-old Rosemary. The causality is vague (is it adultery or renouncing adultery that undoes him?). But the consequences of losing "Youth" are clear. In a continuous, remorseless sequence, Diver loses his ability to charm and entertain and control and cast a glow of glamour over life, his youthful energy and strength, and his interest in his clinical practice and psychological writing. The figure of Youth—Tadzio, Outland, Rosemary (they are all literally beautiful)—withdraws in all these plots. And whether the figure is male or female, objectively precious or precious mainly because of the protagonist's obsession, whether the withdrawal occurs through death or indifference, may be a matter of convincing detail but cannot obscure the structure of the allegory. The withdrawal of the embodied youth mimics or multiplies the losses that otherwise come "naturally" through the aging of the protagonist.

It seems to me that this set of early-century midlife decline novels constitutes a cultural meditation on "aging" in that time and place. (They do not concern "old age": the characters are not remotely old in years, and none is touched by actual ill health.) "Aging" means aging into the middle years. And none of these characters can bear the process. It is as if all the events that fill novels—their middles, their complications, what critics used to call "experience" or "life"—far from being a source of delight, or even a mixed bag, instead become a set of steps toward some level of misery. Not even creativity, in these rare cases where a character has a creative side, can bend the conclusion in another direction. By contrast, a youth-*Künstlerroman* like Joyce's *Portrait of the Artist as a Young Man* (1916) created expectation, as well as some skepticism, about the future of young Stephen Dedalus. These novels about midlife are counter-*Künstlerromane* in which neither the protagonist nor his work develops. If anything, the protagonist's mental work is present to show that mental work cannot save a man; that the richest natures walk downhill like the rest.

Oddly enough, only slightly earlier (indeed with some overlap in time) we can find true midlife *Künstlerromane*—about women who live to be almost the same ages, and who do develop as people and artists. These novels too seem to be talking to each other, in another quite separate and completely unconventional and feminist-inspired meditation about aging and (female) creativity. These early midlife progress novels include *A Woman of Genius* by Mary Austin (1912) and a novel by Willa Cather written ten years earlier than *The Professor's House. The Song of the Lark* (1915), written when Cather was forty-two and rejoicing that after years of journalism and editing, she had found her true voice as a novelist, is full of joy at Thea Kronberg's expanding art and self, her finding of her true "voice."

Thea is an opera singer who becomes famous at thirty and (in an Epilogue) at about forty "has given much noble pleasure to a world that needs all it can get," earns a thousand dollars a night, gives her one living relative "a draft for a good round sum" at Christmas, has "sung for the King at Buckingham Palace . . . but goodness, she was always doing something like that!"[15] In three sentences, we learn that she is also married, to a man who deserves her because he supported her career.

Aging a career woman to forty, even in an Epilogue, was notable. It proclaimed (insofar as fiction giving a single instance can proclaim) the possibility of effective artistic achievement and happiness for a woman who is not young. This was a combination that some women wanted to believe possible in 1915. Cather told her publishers to advertise the book in women's colleges "because, as she said, girls all wanted that combative, defiant sort of career."[16] Either she didn't have in mind, or didn't care to mention, the older professional women readers who would have wanted to see how skills and a career could be made not to end. At thirty Thea says, "I'm just beginning to see what is worth doing, and how I want to do it!" and her husband-to-be responds, "It's how long you're able to keep it up that tells the story" (*SL*, 399).

But Thea's final age may be less important than the developmental schema that Cather embeds her in at all ages. Behind Thea's high-level craft lies a set of stages of growth that Cather has set out one after another. We're told of her "greater positiveness, her whole augmented self" (*SL*, 329) after one change; then that "she's [changed] more than most of us" (*SL*, 348); then, "This woman he had never known; she had somehow devoured his little friend, as the wolf ate up Red Ridinghood" (*SL*, 359). The man who knows opera best details what she has learned technically and what her gifts are with a connoisseur's ravishment, and once she herself boasts about a triumph with charming "schoolboy" childishness. Unlike St. Peter, Aschenbach, Diver, or any other midlife decline figure, what she has done with sorrowful experience is to make art out of it. Her suffering over her mother's last illness has enriched one of her operas: "It's full of the thing every plain creature finds out for himself, but that never gets written down" (*SL*, 387). A reader of today might wonder, closing the Epilogue, whether there is any learning left to be thrilled about (is that why the novel has to stop, because there isn't?), but that thought might be precluded by the sense Cather has given that Thea's art is a permanent possession. Nothing in the ending implies that this achievement might fade. If "marriage" ended youth novels "happily ever after," creative power could serve the same proleptic purpose in the most ambitious midlife *Künstlerromane*. And in 1915 that genre could feature a Woman of Forty.

Yet in 1932, when Cather wrote a foreword to a new edition of *Song of the Lark,* she retracted the midlife progress features of the novel; she even denied they were there. Whatever decline story produced *The Professor's House* had supervened. Now she wrote: "The chief fault of the book is that it describes a descending curve; success is never so interesting as struggle. . . . I should have stopped where my first conception stopped . . . [with] the girl's escape . . . her vitality and honesty" (*SL*, xxxi, xxxii). *Song of the Lark* is now published with this interpretive preamble, so self-deprecating, so conscientiously repeating the culture's lesson that the best gifts of life—even those of art—somehow belong only to the young. If those who are gendered female get them, it can only be as "girls." An author can write a progress novel, but only for a young person. Cather herself had aged into success in that culture; she had reason to ponder not only age's losses but its gains. She said in the same place that art grows at the expense of life, but when we try to understand what she felt about that trade-off (which needn't, after all, be wholly despairing), concealing/revealing allusions to Oscar Wilde's *Portrait of Dorian Gray* interfere. But her anguish about the personal circumstances of her aging (no doubt partly connected with the marriage of her beloved friend, Isabelle McClung, to whom *Song of the Lark* was dedicated) is not merely personal.[17] It joins with the anguish of Mann, Fitzgerald, and all the other decline novelists mentioned earlier, to produce a joint, public, textual, and broadly applicable conclusion: that midlife progress novels and a fortiori *Künstlerromane* were (for the time being at least) a proscribed—a culturally impossible—form.

Success!

In 1905 when Ella Wheeler Wilcox, the author of much-quoted verse, published *The Story of a Literary Career,* she was fifty-five years old. Mary Augusta Arnold Ward, a novelist who had produced one of the nineteenth-century's best-sellers, reported *A Writer's Recollections* in 1918; she was sixty-seven. In 1923 Kate Douglas Wiggin, also sixty-seven, the author of *Rebecca of Sunnybrook Farm* (1903), brought out *My Garden of Memory.* Cora Harris offered her public *My Book and Heart* in 1924 and *The Happy Pilgrimage* in 1927. Kathleen Norris at forty-five published *Noon: An Autobiographical Sketch.* Jane Harrison responded to Virginia Woolf's request to write her memoirs and at age seventy-four saw the Hogarth Press produce *Reminiscences of a Student's Life.* Beatrice Webb published *My Apprenticeship* in 1926 at age sixty-eight. In the thirties autobiographies of women writers who had reached later life began to appear even more thickly: Mary Austin's *Earth Horizon* and Gertrude Atherton's *Ad-*

ventures of a Novelist in 1932, Gertrude Stein's *Autobiography of Alice B. Toklas* in 1933, Edith Wharton's *A Backward Glance* in 1934; in 1935 *The Living of Charlotte Perkins Gilman;* in 1936 Elizabeth Robins's *Both Sides of the Curtain* and Elinor Glyn's *Romantic Adventure (An Autobiography).* The following few years saw the publication of autobiographies by Harriet Monroe, Edna Ferber, and Mary Roberts Rinehart (as if with more self-consciousness about the tradition, *Writing Is Work*).[18]

What these older women writers (and many others) had in common was that they had all entered the star system. They had made themselves famous enough as writers at the time that an autobiography with their name on it could be expected to sell (even during the Depression). In writing autobiography on the basis of their fame as writers they were appropriating a form that had been largely a male prerogative before "first-wave" feminism in England and America.[19] They wrote as autonomous creators, confident of public support. Whatever their individual diffidence, the heft of some of these books suggests the amplitude both of their experiences as writers and the popularity and indulgence they currently enjoyed. Their reader is imagined as involved enough in the writer's life to be curious about details even of her childhood and her not-famous friends. All the works by professional writers validate their authors' authority as women of letters, sometimes explicitly in the titles that enshrine their profession. "Creativity" in these books has its romantic elements (if any) modified by their place in a career, which involves knowing publishers, having a quiet place to write, having one's books reviewed. To me this matter-of-factness about the business—the work—of writing confirms what the mere published presence of so many autobiographies suggests: the establishment of the older woman as literary success—some might say, her apotheosis. This was a cumulative, continuous process in the first third of the century. Insofar as the fame and wealth and publicity of individuals can elevate a "class," older women writers were elevated—into the empyrean indeed. It was the era of the mass-circulation magazine, the best-seller, the movie, and then the talkie. Success came to women in all the available public forms.

The public turned to some of them avid for personal contact. Kathleen Norris, now forgotten, tells how after her first book appeared, "the kindly letters began to come in, hundreds and thousands of letters. One was from Theodore Roosevelt. . . . Other big friends gathered about the little story, and all the critics were kind. I had letters from all the English-speaking countries."[20] Dorothy Canfield's mailman used to bring her letters in a special basket he had for the purpose.

The few earlier novelists who had imagined women artists as earning high salaries and living comfortably or luxuriously and being generous with their money could not have represented in fiction the actual wealth that some women writers achieved in their later years in the first third of the twentieth century, especially in America. *Rebecca of Sunnybrook Farm* made best-sellerdom for Wiggin when she was forty-seven. It then became a play and a film. Her *Mother Carey's Chickens* (1911) was also dramatized. In 1907 Elinor Glyn's sensational *Three Weeks* appeared: "Million of copies were sold, with translations in nearly every European language." She was forty-three. Eleanor Hodgman Porter published *Pollyanna* when she was forty-five; in 1913 "it was eighth on the best-seller list; in 1914 it was second, and in 1915 the newly published sequel, *Pollyanna Grows Up*, was in fourth place. For four more years Mrs. Porter's books were to be found among the annual ten best-selling works of fiction." Gene Stratton Porter published *Freckles* (1904) and *Girl of the Limberlost* (1909) when she was in her forties: "During her lifetime, Mrs. Porter's books enjoyed a phenomenal popularity, second only to the novels of Scott and Dickens in their day. . . . At the time of her death [1924], between eight and nine million copies of her nineteen works had been sold, for which she is reported to have received some $2,000,000." Mary Roberts Rinehart "was said to have been on the best-seller lists longer and more often than any other American author." Zona Gale, at forty-six, became famous in 1920 for *Miss Lulu Bett*. Olive Higgins Prouty's *Stella Dallas* sold 100,000 copies in 1922 and was dramatized and made into a movie. Mary Webb's *Precious Bane* (1924) "went through five editions in six months and continued for a decade to be a best-selling novel."²¹

Edna Ferber's first best-seller was *So Big,* published in 1924, when she was thirty-nine. "It sold 300,000 copies," Carolyn Heilbrun tells us, "in a time before the invention of the book clubs. . . . Ferber believed herself to be one of only 250 people in the United States who earned a living entirely from writing." Ferber said she was writing *A Peculiar Treasure* "at a typewriter in a penthouse apartment on top of a roof on Park Avenue, New York . . . middle-aged now and the curls are iron-gray. . . . I should say today that I have had an enchanting time of it; a rich, gay, exciting and dramatic life." Temple Bailey was called "the highest paid writer in the world. In 1933 *McCall's* Magazine paid her $60,000 for a serial, and *Cosmopolitan* Magazine commissioned three serials and from five to ten short stories, paying $325,000 for the lot." She sold at least three million books.²²

With the coming of the movies, which had vastly larger audiences than books, women and/or their works moved to Hollywood. (We usually hear about the men who were lured there.) Gertrude Atherton's best-seller *Black*

Oxen was filmed. Two motion pictures, a silent and a talkie, were made of Ferber's *So Big.* Dorothy Canfield's *The Home Maker,* a best-seller of 1924, was made into a film. Elinor Glyn also had a second, bigger helping of fame, this time at sixty-three, when her script for *It* (1927) added another word to the language and made Clara Bow a sex celebrity. Eleanor Hodgman Porter organized her own film company and made movies based on her own stories.

Older women could be found at the top of many trees. Selma Lagerlöf won the Nobel Prize for literature in 1909 and joined the Swedish Academy in 1914. In 1926 Grazia Deledda won at age fifty-five, and in 1928, Sigrid Undset—"still in her prime, an homage rendered to poetic genius," the citation thought it worth observing. She was forty-six. Pearl Buck won in 1938, after five of her eleven books had become international best-sellers. In 1937 Anne O'Hare McCormick was the first woman to receive a Pulitzer Prize in journalism. Constance Holme won the Femina–Vie Heureuse Prize in 1919 for *The Splendid Faring,* and Virginia Woolf won it a lustrum later for *To the Lighthouse.* Of the 950 women listed in *Who's Who in America, 1920–21,* 714 were writers, and women took 45.3 percent of all the slots for writers. *The Women of 1924 International* commented: "A few conclusions appear warranted. One is that women receive recognition for writing more readily than in most activities."[23]

The gatekeepers of culture gave some of these writers publicity and praise (the highest praise) and introduction into the canon and the clubs. The wall of prestige had many gates. And women themselves were becoming gatekeepers, networking and publicizing one another. The modernist women, writers and editors, "paid close attention to one another's work . . . took one another seriously as writers trying to support themselves by writing. . . . H.D. reviewed Marianne Moore in *The Egoist;* Marianne Moore reviewed H.D. in *The Dial;* May Sinclair reviewed Dorothy Richardson in both *The Little Review* and *The Egoist;* the list is almost endless."[24] When Jessie Fauset took over as literary editor of *Crisis* in her forties, she opened it to the female authors of the Harlem Renaissance. Women could also be reviewed in the mainstream newspapers and in the magazines that counted for sales, such as the *Bookman, Saturday Review of Literature, Review of Reviews, Smart Set,* and *London Times.* (Dorothy Sayers's photo, in costume, appeared on the front cover of the *Saturday Review* in 1936. Dorothy Canfield, with her editor-husband behind her, was drawn in kindly, aging, all-American profile by Norman Rockwell.)

A woman could write a book, and a man could call it a masterpiece. William Lyon Phelps, a noted critic, didn't hesitate to call a novel of

Canfield's "a masterpiece" and predict a Pulitzer Prize for it. Richard Littell in the *New Republic* asserted that "women novelists, Virginia Woolf, Katherine Mansfield, Rose Macaulay, Dorothy Richardson and Rebecca West, were showing the way to the men." William Stanley Braithwaite said that Jessie Fauset "stands in the front rank of American women novelists in general."[25] There could be testimonials of respect for an oeuvre of all the known kinds. Mary Webb's *Collected Works* came out in 1928–29. *A Vernon Lee Anthology* appeared in 1929. Perhaps most rarefied of all (since the model was Henry James's prefaces for his New York edition), Ellen Glasgow wrote a series of prefaces for the Old Dominion collection of her novels (1929–33). Grant Overton, capitalizing on the fascination with women writers, wrote *The Women Who Make Our Novels* in 1918 and then revised and expanded it in 1928, when it included sixty-five writers. "Genius," "perfection," "purely esthetic enjoyment" were words the enthusiastic Overton used with some freedom (Mencken mocked him for his effusiveness); he treated all with dignity. Carl Van Doren wrote on Glasgow and Gale and Wharton in *Contemporary American Novelists, 1900–1920*. Women's work appeared in anthologies of highly regarded prose. Colleges and collectors were asking them for their manuscripts and memorabilia. "Authors'" clubs that had been all-male began to invite women to speak and join. People (often men) started producing their biographies, sometimes while they were still alive. Percy Lubbock wrote on Mary Cholmondely in 1928, Violet Meynell on Alice Meynell in 1929, S. Foster Damon on Amy Lowell in 1935, and John Cowper Powys on Dorothy Richardson in 1931; Mary Webb had two biographies published (1931 and 1932). At the same time writers with reputations of their own were solidifying the reputations of earlier women writers: Vita Sackville-West wrote on Aphra Behn (1928), Romer Wilson on Emily Brontë (same year), May Sinclair on *The Three Brontës,* Virginia Woolf on many earlier figures. The history of women's writing was thickening, getting texture, power, reputation.

At the beginning of the era—March 1914, to be exact—*Vanity Fair* wrote with the effrontery of hypocrisy, "We dare to believe that [women] are, in their best moments, creatures of some cerebral activity; we even make bold to believe that it is they who are contributing what is most original, stimulating and highly magnetized to the literature of our day, and we hereby announce ourselves as determined and bigoted feminists." Their daring did not extend to finding very many women to publish. English playwright Cicely Hamilton disguised her gender behind a pseudonym before World War I but later wrote, "The woman playwright of the present year of grace [1935] would not dream of concealing her identity for fear of an unfavorable verdict." Anna Garlin Spencer, in *Women's Share in Social Culture,* pointed to "that cumulative guarantee of success which is the only way of impressing the mass intelligence"; in 1925 she thought women had proved to the mass audience that they could compete "on a high level" with men. Another feminist observer, Alice Beal Parsons, thought "the general public had already given up drawing the sex line where artists are concerned." In 1925 Mary Austin, who had identified herself in the public mind with/as *A Woman of Genius,* used that authority to produce an entire book on the "genius process," *Everyman's Genius.* Benjamin G. Brawley, defining and exemplifying *The Negro Genius* (1937), included a handful of women born between 1875 and 1891: Alice Dunbar-Nelson, Georgia Johnson, Jessie Fauset, and Zora Neale Hurston. By 1931 a male critic measured the change even more dramatically than Parsons had. "But woman has gradually emerged culturally self-confident. The history of the rise of American art is the history of woman's advance toward her present dominance in society and intellectual matters. In the arts, in literature, in music, America is the woman's own land." [26] In England as well as in America, many women (and men as well), impressed by literary phenomena like those collected here—the prizes, the prestige, the glory, the succès d'estime, the cash, the idealizations, the autobiographical self-exaltation, the public respect for and touching faith in the wisdom of women writers—might have concluded that literature was if not women's own land, then certainly a land whose pleasant (male) perquisites were now shared with women.

I am not implying that women no longer faced gender bias in entering upon a writing career and maintaining it over a lifetime; they faced that as well as race, class, and ethnic bias. But the backlash's "fact," "Women can't write," had been jeopardized by the immense quantity and popularity of women's writing of all kinds. Then came the second line of defense, "There can never be a woman of genius." In the "high/low" distinction and war, women figured richly on the low popular side, but they were found in the high aesthetic heavens as well. On the whole, though, they did not need to be "geniuses" to be professional writers. At all levels, they could feel themselves to be "breaking into the human race." [27]

How much, we may wonder, did these vast audiences notice that the prizes came with age? Rare indeed was the woman who could be spoiled, like F. Scott Fitzgerald, by early praise—although Edna St. Vincent Millay was twenty when *Renascence* became the poetic sensation of its year. Rarer yet was the woman who could "take up" writing after the children had left home, rather the way her mother had been told to take up tatting. This postmaternal woman, whom glorious expanded opportunities await, was a favorite new fictional character, created by Havelock Ellis and G. Stanley Hall and some of the rejuvenation boosters; everyone knew one such woman. Some of the autobiographies hint at these mingled truths: that women work long years and *wait* for success, and that if it ever comes, success then enriches their middle and later years. Harriet Monroe said that at forty "the professional outlook was rather discouraging." Poetry and *Poetry* came later. Edith Wharton talked about "a development naturally slow . . . retarded by indifference" but found "the drawbacks were outweighed by the advantages." Many women grew in confidence by producing book after book; only slowly did they convince themselves of their proficiency or talent. Surviving years of disappointment or neglect, they received the greatest gift of all from age, the sense of increasing powers. "Granted a mind which is no longer a shame or a battle to develop, women can look upon the passing of the years with as great an equanimity as does man," wrote Sylvia Kopald, an American labor specialist, in 1930.[28] Well, we know the equanimity of men about aging was not as great as all that. In any case, the optimistic assessment could have been true only for creative women whose fears and battles were behind them. Those who lost their battle, or lost their public, didn't write their autobiographies.

Ellen Glasgow, like Edna Ferber, shared with readers her sense of making progress through the life course. Indeed, even Gertrude Atherton, who gave details about her age-related creative problems, left the impression in her autobiography that age had granted her the friends and fame and travel she reveled in; on balance, time had not been her enemy. Glasgow said that around 1930 "my imagination was more vital and urgent than it had ever been . . . ; it is true to say I felt younger at sixty than I had felt at twenty. . . . Between fifty and sixty I lived perhaps my fullest and richest years."[29]

The Economics and Demographics of Creativity

Great writers, Virginia Woolf argued, require for their emergence a context of many minor writers, working and publishing. "For masterpieces are not single and solitary births: they are the outcome of many years of thinking in common, of thinking by the body of the people, so that the experience of the mass is behind the single voice." It is the women writers' forerunners who "earned them the right to speak their minds."[30] "Masterpieces" cannot be guaranteed, but success (measured in its different ways) has preconditions one can identify more exactly. For "older" writers to reach the top of the tree, they have to start, usually young, at the bottom. The basement of the creative pyramid was (and is) provided by education, and the ground floor by professional positions or institutions that pay for writing. (Finally, there must be readers buying the books, educated, in this case, to expect pleasure from the works of women and to find their pleasure increase as the writers continue to write.)

Success of any kind—even if defined merely by getting paid for writing—was thus mainly limited to women whose families were willing and able to give them an education, or who could earn it for themselves. In general, that pool grew extraordinarily in the years we are looking at for white, middle-class (and, in America, nonimmigrant) women. Then differential access to the mainstream white media provided a further narrowing. Poor women, women whose families arrived in America more recently, and African-American women are almost excluded from the statistics that follow. And we can assume that many women with some education internalized gender, class, racial, and/or ethnic stereotypes and never initiated a writing career. Yet some individuals with only marginally more privilege overcame the odds, had distinguished careers writing for smaller markets, and provided role models for younger women.[31]

Between 1890 and 1920, in Alice Echols's words, "the expansion of the economy's tertiary section created a great demand for a literate labor force that would work for relatively low wages." Year by year these better-educated women became as a group increasingly older and in higher percentages married. The statistics that follow are American, but the trends were visible in England as well. In 1924 the New York Bureau of Vocational Information observed that "specialized publications, trade papers, technical magazines, pamphlets, and books are, however, rapidly multiplying in answer to eager demand." The training guide mentioned some "prejudice" and women's "lack of business and technical experience" but said, "The number of women in newspaper work as reporters, special writers, editors and owners has been steadily increasing; more and more they are assuming all types of journalistic work rather than devoting themselves to subjects of particular interest to women."[32]

Between 1910 and 1920 the number of women authors, editors, and reporters went up 40 percent, to 8,736. The U.S. Census in 1920 listed 3,662 male writers and 3,006 women writers, relatively equal numbers. (Under "editors and reporters" it listed 28,467 men and 5,730 women.) If we expand beyond the career in letters, "a significant *proportion* of all women workers were professional. . . . During the 1920's women constituted nearly 45% of the professional workforce." According to Elaine Showalter, "This group of working professionals, however varied and low-paying its work, was an elite—14% of a female labor force which included less than a quarter of all women between the ages of 20 and 64." [33]

"The growth of women's higher education facilitated women's movement into professional work since it created a group of women who were well-educated and often career-minded," Echols continues. Eighty-eight percent of all the women in *Who's Who in America, 1920–21* reported receiving postsecondary training. Women writers of the era who had not been blessed with higher education (Edith Wharton and Virginia Woolf at one end of the class spectrum and Emma Goldman at the other) had found access to books or literary talk. A number who did go to college remember being helped by their mothers, who overcame enormous obstacles to get them there. Kate Gregg, who got a Ph.D. in English in 1916, wrote, "My mother's dominant passion for me, through these years, and for the five other daughters who came in the course of time, was a desire for our education, that we might fit ourselves for work and for salaries that would make us independent of marriage, or if we did elect it, able to leave it if it were unsatisfactory." [34] Many mothers of this generation had experienced having their own aspirations thwarted; some raised daughters to fulfill their dreams. Perhaps progressive midlife women, mothers of daughters, ought to be considered the subbasement of creativity. The bedrock.

In 1926 interviews were conducted with 100 professional women who were also married. Half of them were in "creative" work. A contemporary commentator, a woman at Columbia University, called these "experimental lives." "The New Woman of today is *consciously* experimenting with her own life to find out how women can best live." When investigator Virginia Collier asked why they worked, the women provided the same motives (over and above economic necessity) that were offered to postmaternal women: "creative urge" or vocational call, relief from depression, enhanced energy, avoidance of housework and escape from boredom, urge to activity, fear of the empty nest, wanting to be an "interesting companion" to their children. "I don't want to find myself with nothing but personal service to give my children." They are elite in relation to other women but below the exceptional women in *Who's Who* in terms of education: 43 percent had earned B.A.'s; 8 percent had Ph.D.'s. Ninety percent had special or professional training of some sort before marriage. Thirty percent were doing work which they had *not* trained for and engaged in before marriage. Would this statistic encourage or dishearten the untrained older woman thinking about her future? Most of the women lived in New York or Boston or a college town. What if the untrained older women came from a small town in the Midwest or the South? Forty-two percent had another income to rely on when they began working. [35]

By reading Collier's study from the point of view we are interested in, we can derive some sense of the conditions of life for a working woman professional in mid-adulthood. We have to guess at their ages: 20 percent had children ten years and over; one proud husband "referred to a combination of marriage, work, home and children that has weathered fifteen years," and one woman had an eighteen-year-old daughter. Thirty-six percent had suffered what they, or Collier, called "undue breaks" caused by marriage and children. In the thinking of the time, no doubt influenced by the idea of a male career as seamless, a break from the creative career could be more than "undue"—it could be permanently crippling. Rebecca West expressed this in her hardheaded way. "A woman who has had children in ideal conditions and who was an artist would enjoy therefore a special advantage of which it would be hard to name the equivalent male experience. But it is obvious that the disadvantages of motherhood in this matter go far to outweighing this advantage. It is obvious that during the years spent in child-bearing and child-rearing a woman's mastery of whatever artistic or scientific technique she may have acquired is bound to grow rusty."[36] No doubt there were talented older women who were not writing because they had lost crucial years and could not overcome age discrimination.

Women in the arts, Collier pointed out, were "frequently the ones who can carry on their work at home." Only eleven of those in the arts were working full-time, although 66 percent of all were full-time employees. (Birth control practiced earlier had made this proliferation of careers either possible or easier: women were getting control over "when children may come, how often they come or how many they shall be," as Crystal Eastman set out the ideal.) Thirty-seven percent of Collier's group had only one child, 35 percent only two; only one had six. They had help, sometimes that of husbands but mostly that of paid women of weaker economic standing. A mother of three who had never taken breaks from working said, "Any woman who carries out the combination of work and motherhood, does it by climbing up on the shoulders of another woman." Perhaps another precondition for creativity was (is) a percentage of economically subordinated women available for child care. Whether women went out to work or worked at home, benefiting from more flexible hours, they still had servants, children, spouse, and sometimes other family members to contend with. There was "difficulty concentrating at home" just as there had been for nineteenth-century writers who were mothers, like Frances Trollope. There were years of "an undeniably heavy program for the woman before she was able to earn for herself the proper relief from domestic pressure."[37] We catch here in quiet understatement the constraining realities of the majority of women who did not acquire riches and fame. Yet for these women the obstacles seem no longer of the type that derives from invisible ideology and that gets unconsciously internalized. They no longer refer to women's alleged physiological or mental inaptitude for creativity, not the alleged "egotism" involved in pursuing a writing career. Motherhood and writing indeed conflicted, but the conflicts were practical, and women had plenty of language for discussing them.[38]

The practical, physical toll of this way of life is described when Collier turns briefly to an "older woman, who has been making this combination over a period of years under relentless financial pressure." The particular woman Collier quotes is an experienced survivor, a generous and generative person. Although hard-pressed, she envisions the next generation of daughters also mixing a career with marriage and children. "The older woman . . . invariably sounds a warning to the younger woman of the inevitable cost in health and strength and power. She would not have any other woman attempt as heavy a load as she has carried." One of them spoke emphatically of her own eighteen-year-old daughter: "Of course I want her to have a career, but I want her to have time to recover after her babies are born and I want her to have time to take proper care of herself." And yet, the Columbia professor who admired Collier's study concluded not in sorrow but in admiration: "To experiment knowingly with one's own life to find the Good Life—surely this requires a courage and a genius."[39] "Genius"— the superlative degree of creativity—could by the end of the era be given a new twist and applied to the very lives of this special class of women.

"Thinking Age": A Cultural Critic's Goals

A series of "character" sketches, odd, incongruous, at times contradictory—that is partly what this essay has been drawn into becoming, after initially interrogating an ugly triad of abstractions. In order to think through the meanings of age and aging for any era, in connection with gender and creativity, or sexual orientation, class, race, ethnicity, or any combination of these factors, we can't simply "add age and stir." When we want to understand the belief system of an earlier era, we have to seek out its own concrete representations, and these seem to occur at the intersections it constructed. The obvious benefits of the approach come out when we unearth an era's significant cultural figures, heretofore buried, like the hormone-operation patients, the midlife male protagonist as victim of age-related decline, the postmaternal woman who ought to just pick up a pen and make herself socially useful, the actual older woman writer as an essential cultural worker or a media star. They were new characters in the "cultural imaginary"—the mass of public representations from which, on the whole, we derive our notions of such things as age, gender, and creativity and their intersections.

Partly because these characters are "older"—in mid-adulthood or beyond—historians have rarely noticed them; nor, more importantly, have they been seen in relation to one another, as products of related cultural causes or as counters in ideological games. To find them at all, we have to want to see with the eyes of the not-young, and to admit age as a category useful to cultural studies. (These would constitute psychological and theoretical reorientation of enormous import.) And then, at a practical level, we have to be willing to read the era's newspapers and magazines and census forms, its novels and autobiographies (including its best-sellers) and their reviews, its much-read social science and psychology and sexuality texts, and to look there for the ways in which their authors filled these discourses with age-graded beliefs and prejudices. And what makes these particularly difficult to discover from the first third of the twentieth century is that so many discourses turn out to be mostly about young people, written out of naive admiration for "Youth" or out of unconscious disregard of older people. Then the critic must transform such discoveries (which seem at first like null findings), turning them into evidence of the pervasive youth bias of the culture; and then reread, looking harder for the precious inflections that produced and repeated age attributions and "differences," older "characters," age-related tropes and other cultural formulations.

To understand what it was like to live in another cultural imaginary (even one that has profound influences on our own), we have to drop our own prejudices and values and designs. That means (among the most significant novelties) *not* choosing one voice from the era to "epitomize" it, to "place" as an opening or closing epigraph. In my case, the temptation might be to use the most retrograde male critic, or the most advanced woman genius, to sum up "Creativity, Aging, Gender, 1910–1935." Or perhaps both, the critic *and* the genius. That last choice—warring epigraphs—would suggest that in the cultural arguments of the time, on at least one issue (say, "can women write well?"), there were two sides, more or less equally well armed. Such implications are precisely what we need to eschew. We know, if only from what evidence I've gathered here, that there was a great range of rhetorical positions on the related issues; the air was thick with signals, facts, arguments, and interpretations. There were worlds of prose, worlds of talk; and of course readers from different worlds selectively listening, reading, borrowing, rejecting.

It does feel to me now as if the sides were becoming more equal or overlapping on some of these issues than previously (say in 1890), however lopsided they again became afterwards. One of the qualities of the period that makes it appealing to me personally is that women had better "answers" of all kinds to that particular question, and more public space in which to present them, and that their answers featured older women who had undeniably distinguished careers. A stunningly large, impressive collection of empirical examples may indeed—to answer one question I began with—change the cultural imaginary for those looking for such examples or forced to become aware of them. Some sexist opinions became preposterous to some audiences. By 1935 Havelock Ellis could scarcely have written so forcibly (as he had done in 1902, in *Man and Woman*), "On the whole there can be no doubt whatever that, if we leave out of consideration the interpretive arts, the artistic impulse is vastly more spontaneous, more pronounced, and more widely spread among men than among women." But Dorothy Richardson said in 1925 that art served as one of the last "witnesses for the prosecution in that *cause célèbre,* Man versus Woman," and *Man and Woman* was reprinted as late as 1929. To be sure, some claims about female talent and genius became valid—but again, only to some audiences. Women who had satisfying literary careers and considered themselves feminists frequently told in their autobiographies a historical progress story about women's *collective* progress; their sense of collective movement enhanced the progress each felt she had made over her own life course. Some believed women had fared even better than men in terms of material. "Women have more to tell," asserted American writer Rheta Childe Dorr in *A Woman of Fifty.* "Their world in two generations has changed more amazingly."[40] Were men in their middle years likely to feel that men as they aged had "more to tell"?

And yet, the major ideological factor of the era, for our case, is that as feminism appeared to gain strength, so too did the subversive force of ageism. Aging seen as an unmitigated decline had never started so early in the life course or been made so central to identity and mental accomplishment as in this period—a highly sexualized, biologized, somatized era. This was bad for both men and women writers, and of course for everyone else as well. Early twentieth-century ageism may have been harder on women as they aged, if only because many women did not marry, and celibacy was being condemned as bad for creativity. Yet at this stage of research it is too early to decide whether men or women were in general getting a more bitter representation of aging-into-the-midlife.

Likewise, it is too early to venture to estimate the balance between ageist and sexist forces and forces naturalizing and upgrading the older woman writer. Who—of us or of them—is to say? Can we gauge what the "mass intelligence" believed? Would that be the mass intelligence of 1930? Of 1950, when many of their famous writers had been forgotten, or of now? And would comparative fame or sales be what we wanted to know? Or should we think in terms of individual life stories, but looking harder than biography usually does at the way a woman reads her own aging within the cultural contexts of the time? If so, which older woman writer should we take as normative: Ellen Glasgow and Edna Ferber relishing their mid-life gains, or Willa Cather obliquely lamenting her losses? How should we weigh the relative absence of novels about older women artists against the presence of so many autobiographies by older women artists? Who has standing to decide what issue was (is) decisive, and whether and how it was decided?

Renouncing the erstwhile privileges of the (pretheoretical) historian, I have tried to leave as a residue condensed pictures of their era as it might have been lived then, by some (older) women and men with their own range of values and prejudices about aging, gender, creativity, and genius. Insofar as I've succeeded, the essay will in part work like fiction, enabling its readers to imagine real (older) people of the time in glimpses. A woman of fifty, say, at a dining room table, beginning a cheaply paid article on cheap writing paper—maybe she's black, maybe she's Jewish or Italian; she knows she's neither Virginia Woolf nor Olive Higgins Prouty. A man of fifty closing *Death in Venice* with a personalized sigh and a surreptitious clutch at his heart. A male critic complaining when Pearl Buck got the Nobel Prize that it had not been given to Dreiser, Sandburg, Eliot, or Hemingway; a female critic wondering why it hadn't gone to Wharton, Cather, or Woolf. A woman reader deciding that Ethel Smyth's delightful reminiscences were so endearing. A woman writer of sixty worrying that neither her former novels nor her current autobiography would stabilize her prestige in a youth-oriented cultural climate.[41]

There may be a narrative implied by the order of my juxtapositions, but I want to disclaim that kind of implied narrative. My goal has been to provide material for the use of different readers, ad libitum. General readers and women and men in "age studies" will take what they can use from it. Age studies is my term for a large interdisciplinary zone whose practitioners are becoming increasingly aware of age as a category and increasingly skillful at using it in their very different kinds of work. The zone includes women's studies, gender studies, literary gerontology, life-course studies in developmental psychology, sociology, family and social history, and anthropology. The field should expand; eventually—and the sooner the better—age studies should influence cultural studies, narratology, the history of sexuality.

Looked at one way, the present essay begins with ungendered panic about artistic decay and ends with widespread artistic activity and women's emotions of struggle and achievement. The panic, although suggestive of wider fears, could be seen as countered by reiterated images of older women's competence as producers and (occasional) fearlessness about aging as writers. But for another reader, the fear—since some of it belonged to Thomas Mann, F. Scott Fitzgerald, William Butler Yeats, and Willa Cather—will far outweigh a mass of trivial and ephemeral productions by any number of little-known writers, whether older or younger, male or female. Looked at another way, the essay begins with culturally constructed shame about aging, private pain, and semiprivate decisions, moves on to public performance and public perceptions, and ends with the practical (not the ideological) difficulties in the way of women's writing careers. Or it could be said to begin with time-dated biological "science" and its dogmatic scars and to end with details of heroic problem solving in daily life. And so on, far beyond any list of possible readings I could produce.

If a cultural historian generates material for fiction-making, it's new-fangled open-ended fiction, with a vast cast of characters and many "endings." Cultural studies wants its readers to be empowered—given more new facts, new (midlife) characters with their own dialogue and points of view, new theorizing—and it leaves them free to conclude and appropriate and interpret and add and revise. What might mark this essay for all its readers, however, is its insistence on *age,* the neglected dimension of criticism and theory. Theorists and critics sometimes pay lip service to the need for it but often omit it even from lists of the categories that need to be considered. Up to now, most age studies have ignored the middle years. One of the goals of this essay, and all my work, has been to make that gap seem odd, in need of explanation, and entertainingly remediable. These neglects, the nineties may begin to remedy. This cultural critic ventures to hope that some readers will close her essay impressed with the difference that "thinking age" makes and curious to apply the process in their own work. And once we begin to think age, a more mysterious and intangible project emerges: to discover what our own culture is serving up for us, and what each of us has consumed or resisted.

Notes

Much of the material in this essay derives from my work in progress on the history of the invention of the middle years of life, Midlife Fictions. *I am grateful to Anne Wyatt-Brown for giving me the opportunity to bring "creativity" into relation with my other concerns.*

1. Virginia Woolf's artist in *To The Lighthouse,* Lily Briscoe, finds herself repeating, "Women can't write, women can't paint," a man's summation of female creative potential, in section 17 of "The Window," which is set in the prewar period. Otto Weininger's sharp conclusion from *Sex and Character* is quoted in Anna Garlin Spencer, *Women's Share in Social Culture,* 45.

2. Cf. Norman Jeffares, *William Butler Yeats,* 320, and Richard Ellmann, *Yeats,* 275–76.

3. Gertrude Atherton, *Adventures of a Novelist,* 554, 555, 556.

4. Leonard Williams, *Middle Age and Old Age,* 39; G. Stanley Hall, *Senescence,* 309.

5. Margaret Morganroth Gullette, "The Invention of Male Midlife Sexual Decline," in progress.

6. H. L. Mencken, "Fiction Good and Bad," 379.

7. Havelock Ellis, *Studies in the Psychology of Sex* 3: pt. 1, 181; Blair Bell, *The Sex Complex,* 109; Williams, *Middle Age,* 148–49.

8. Ilia Ilich Metchnikoff, *The Prolongation of Life,* 272; Havelock Ellis, *Man and Woman,* 326; Grete Meisel-Hess, *The Sexual Crisis,* 240; Winifred Holtby, *Women and a Changing Civilization,* 101.

9. William J. Robinson, *Sexual Problems of Today,* 264.

10. Storm Jameson, *Women against Men,* 88.

11. Randolph S. Bourne, *Youth and Life,* 12–13, 16, 18–19, 5, 12.

12. Harriet Monroe, *A Poet's Life,* 400. Pound wrote to Monroe, "My idea of our policy is this: we support American poets—preferably the young ones who have a serious determination to produce master-work" (261). The history of the effect on older writers of mystifying "youth" has yet to be written.

13. Willa Cather, *The Professor's House,* 163; Willa Cather, *A Lost Lady,* 126.

14. Havelock Ellis, *The Psychology of Sex,* 321. On trying to achieve rejuvenation by sexually possessing a child, see Margaret Morganroth Gullette, "The Exile of Adulthood," 215–27, 231.

15. Willa Cather, *The Song of the Lark,* 415, 414, 416.

16. James Woodress, *Willa Cather,* 274.

17. Hermione Lee, *Willa Cather,* 58–59; Sharon O'Brien, *Willa Cather,* 237–40.

18. Harriet Monroe's was titled *A Poet's Life;* Edna Ferber's *A Peculiar Treasure.*

19. See Estelle Jelinek, *Women's Autobiography,* 92.

20. Kathleen Norris, *Noon,* 62.

21. Eachus, "Elinor Glyn," 278; Fred E. H. Schroeder, "Eleanor Hodgman Porter," 3:85; Beatrice K. Hofstadter, "Gene Stratton Porter," 405; Barbara Welter, "Mary Roberts Rinehart," 578; Margaret B. McDowell, "Mary Webb," 282.

22. Carolyn G. Heilbrun, "Edna Ferber," 228; Edna Ferber, *A Peculiar Treasure,* 13, 4; Stanley J. Kunitz and Howard Haycraft, eds., "Temple Bailey," 61.

23. All the information about the Nobel Prize winners in literature comes from Olga S. Opfell, *The Lady Laureates;* the quotation comes from p. 133. *Women of 1924 International,* 207, 208.

24. Gillian Hanscombe and Virginia L. Smyers, *Writing for Their Lives*, 151.

25. Quoted by Jane Marcus, "Introduction" to West, *The Judge*, no pagination given; William Stanley Braithwaite, "The Novels of Jessie Fauset," 24.

26. Editorial, *Vanity Fair*, 15; Cicely Hamilton, *Life Errant*, 60; Alice Beal Parsons, *Woman's Dilemma*, 169. The male critic was Clifton Joseph Furness, ed., writing in his "Introduction" to *The Genteel Female*, xvii. He added: "This is particularly true of literature intended for popular consumption, the great mass of books and papers turned out by publishers frankly to make money."

27. That was Rheta Childe Dorr's metaphor (probably borrowed from Charlotte Perkins Gilman) in *A Woman of Fifty*, 134.

28. Elsie M. Lang knew Mrs. Shute: "Mrs. Shute managed to get her first play produced when she was seventy-three" (*British Women in the Twentieth Century*, 245). Edith Lowry knew Amelia Barr: "Amelia Barr commenced writing when she was fifty and for thirty years afterwards she averaged two books a year" (*The Woman of Forty*, 76). Monroe, *A Poet's Life*, 185; Wharton, *A Backward Glance*, 121; Sylvia Kopald, "Where Are the Female Geniuses?" 108.

29. Ellen Glasgow, *The Woman Within*, 270, 273.

30. Virginia Woolf, *A Room of One's Own*, 113, 114.

31. In the period from 1880 to 1910, when these white older women writers would have been getting an education, black women were handicapped by a heritage of illiteracy and continued discrimination. As late as 1940 only 1.2 percent of black women had completed four years of college (Project on . . . Women, *Minority Women*, 1).

   On, for example, the complicated situation of women in the Harlem Renaissance, see Gloria T. Hull, *Color, Sex, and Poetry*, 7–13; on older women writers who changed their birth years, see ibid., 12–13.

32. Statistics about the growth of the tertiary sector from Alice Echols, "Demise," 16; Bureau of Vocational Information, *Training for the Professions*, 693, 692.

33. Figures for changes between 1910 and 1920, from Lorine Pruette, *Women and Leisure*, 68; statistic about women professionals, from Echols, "Demise," 18; census information, from *Training for the Professions*, 692; Elaine Showalter, *These Modern Women*, 7.

34. On higher education, Echols, "Demise," 18; on women in *Who's Who*, *Women of 1924 International*, 208; Kate L. Gregg, in Showalter, *These Modern Women*, 75.

35. Columbia University professor Leta S. Hollingworth, "The New Woman in the Making," 20; Virginia Collier, *Marriage and Careers*, 24, 70.

36. Collier, *Marriage*, 83; Rebecca West, "Woman as Artist and Thinker," 373.

37. Collier, *Marriage*, 31, 67, 108, 70; Crystal Eastman, *On Women and Revolution*, 48.

38. See Margaret Homans, *Bearing the Word*, 153 et seq.

39. Collier, *Marriage*, 70; Hollingworth, "New Woman," 20.

40. Dorothy Richardson, "Women in the Arts," 47; Dorr, *A Woman of Fifty*, 3.

41. "One thing which has greatly helped to endear [Ethel Smyth] to the English public is the publication of her delightful reminiscences" (Lang, *British Women*, 251). The "woman writer of sixty" is my fictionalization from Jane Marcus's projections about why a small group of women writers whom she studied produced autobiography (Marcus, "Invincible Mediocrity," 119, 122, 124; see also 137).

2

ANNE M. WYATT-BROWN

Another Model of the Aging Writer: Sarton's Politics of Old Age

IN 1990 I was asked to present a paper on May Sarton's *The Education of Harriet Hatfield* (1989) at a meeting which the novelist herself was to attend. Unfortunately, the novel initially disappointed me. Some of Sarton's literary decisions seemed baffling. Why should the novelist, who spent her middle age celebrating the courage of elders, as Kathleen Woodward has demonstrated, suddenly write about a woman more than ten years younger than she?[1] Moreover, the fairy-tale elements of this story undermined the credibility of the plot.

On first reading, Harriet, the sixty-year-old heroine, seemed too good to be true, as this brief plot summary demonstrates. She survives the death of her longtime lover, Victoria Chilton, without much sign of despair. Shortly thereafter she opens a feminist bookstore in Somerville, Massachusetts, a working-class district near Cambridge, an unlikely place for such an enterprise. Despite the sometimes violent behavior of resentful locals, Harriet gathers around her a group of loyal supporters. With their help she manages to discover the identity of the perpetrator of the violence. At the same time her bravery in the face of repeated attacks wins the hearts of her neighbors so that the violent opponent, not Harriet, must eventually depart. In the course of the novel, Harriet becomes the close friend of a homosexual couple, the younger of whom is dying of AIDS. Somewhat earlier, Harriet has announced to a reporter that she is a lesbian, and in response to the subsequent story, her brother confides in her about his own homosexuality. All this suffering convinces Harriet that homophobia must be confronted at every turn, but she urges that bigotry should not be replaced by promiscuity. At the novel's end it is clear that Harriet's bookstore will remain a staple of Somerville life, but some important subplots are left unresolved.

Knowing that Sarton might be present made me hesitate to criticize too harshly. Fortunately, the advice of Peter Elbow, a theorist of writing and pedagogy, suggested a solution to the dilemma. In an appendix to *Writing without Teachers,* he comments wryly on the inability of academics to refrain from criticism. As he puts it, we find the notion of "trying to *believe* . . . heretical and self-indulgent."[2] Equally heretical, I discovered, would be to apply Elbow's technique of responding to student writing to Sarton's novel, to begin by temporarily refraining from arguing with her premises and instead try to reconstruct her point of view as a novelist. Ultimately, I began to realize that the problem was one of expectations. Based on previous experience, I had come to expect that writers in later life would fit one of two patterns, ones that have already been identified by literary gerontologists. But Sarton's novel, rather than fitting already established categories, creates a new one, one which has not yet been discussed. This discovery makes it clear that the task of constructing models of old-age fiction should now begin, in order to expand our understanding of the many ways in which aging artists react to the experiences of growing older. In this chapter three ways are identified by means of which writers adapt their work to their changing status in late middle age and old age. Sarton's novel is discussed in the third category.

The first is broadly speaking a model of continuity, and it can best be explained by referring to Erik Erikson's ideas about identity formation. Erikson's theory of life stages is summarized in a famous chart of the life cycle, in which he describes both the values and challenges of each period in life. These writers in the first group found themselves as individuals—established their identities—in adolescence or early adulthood, as Erikson predicted, and have remained faithful to that vision of themselves, fidelity being the value, according to Erikson, that emerges after adolescents have determined what their roles in life will be. At that time they also discover their compelling identity themes as writers, to borrow a concept from literary critic Norman Holland.[3] The productivity of this group depends largely upon their choice of themes and their capacity to adjust to the changes of midlife and later. Some are able to adapt their themes to accommodate their perceptions of the world, whereas others lack the capacity to redirect their creativity in middle age when their youthful themes no longer seem compelling.

The more fortunate ones are like the Pulitzer Prize–winning poet Richard Eberhart, whose career, according to Carolyn Smith, has consistently made the case for the connection of present self with a past or remembered one. She points out that Eberhart developed an interest in aging and its meaning in his youth but had the necessary "cognitive plasticity" to look for "broad life-span meanings" at every stage of his development. As a result, his view of life has not changed much over time. That is not to say that Eberhart's style has been static, or that he is untouched by suffering. Early in his career he discovered his primary theme, the journey from despair to affirmation, and according to Smith he has re-created that journey repeatedly in "an astonishing variety of images and verse forms." Thus in old age Eberhart has much to write about, and for him poetry is still, as it was earlier in his career, an expression of fundamentally positive feelings. Other examples include Tennyson and Picasso, who, according to Robert Kastenbaum, in youth used their art "to create potential futures" and later on in old age connected "past and future together into a wholeness."[4]

Thematic continuity in itself, however, does not guarantee productivity throughout the life course. In fact, Anglo-American culture abounds with examples of young poets and novelists who died young or lost their urgent need to create sometime in early middle age. As mentioned in the introduction, quantitative studies by Dean Simonton prove that lyric poets peak early and use up their creative potential before they are well into middle age. Until Margaret Gullette's essay in this volume, however, few literary scholars have attempted to analyze systematically so destructive a pattern in light of social forces that shape writers' attitudes toward art.[5]

Scholars will find insights in the field of social psychology. For example, social psychologist Mihály Csikszentmihályi recommends a systems approach for analyzing creativity, in order to conceptualize the complex relationship of artists and their societies. In this model creativity is viewed as "the product of three main shaping forces": the creative "*individual*"; the social institutions that create the "*field,*" and "a stable cultural *domain*" that seeks to "preserve and transmit" what has been created to future generations. Psychologist David Harrington employs a similar analysis to show how ethnocentric creativity can be. He argues convincingly that writers need acceptance and social support from readers and publishers, as well as available themes and genres that fit their particular kind of creative talent.[6] For a variety of reasons some writers do not receive the recognition necessary to sustain their creativity. They seem to have been born either too late or too soon to find an outlet for their particular insights and visions.

This systems approach helps explain why continuity sometimes can lead to lack of productivity in later life. For example, writers like William Wordsworth, E. M. Forster, and Louise Bogan made no radical changes in theme as they aged, but the absence of change had a deleterious effect upon their creativity.[7] Unlike Eberhart's, their works often reflect melancholic feelings of loss or a sense of exclusion from society. They each developed themes that emphasize the intense feelings of childhood and youth at the expense of maturity and old age. One has the sense that they had an over-developed sense of fidelity to their themes, indicating that they paid too high a price to establish their artistic identity. As a result, in midlife when they found it increasingly difficult to continue to tap their well-established sources of creativity, they were unable or unwilling to chart new courses.

A second, more artistically fortunate group consists of those writers who when confronted with the Eriksonian conflict of integrity versus despair in later life, become liberated by the possibility of radical change. These writers include Elizabeth Bowen, Anita Brookner, Penelope Mortimer, and Barbara Pym. As George Vaillant has remarked, individuals often experience depression during transitional phases in their lives, but these moments also offer the opportunity for making one more attempt to solve "old instinctual or interpersonal needs." Like an artist whose career Vaillant followed, these writers use their creativity "to 'affirm the larger meaning of pain.'"[8]

Yet none of this group has experienced this radical change in exactly the same way. For example, Anita Brookner published no fiction in her youth; instead she was a very successful art historian. In late middle age, however, she began writing novels in which she depicts the lives of a variety of isolates, almost as if she were working out her own position in the world. These characters, like Brookner herself, are alone in the world and often find this position difficult to manage. The process of writing and the pleasures of success—she won the Booker Prize for *Hotel du Lac* (1984)—appear to have been salutary for the novelist herself. Her early fiction projects a relentlessly gloomy message, whereas her more recent work offers some modicum of hope to the protagonists. In contrast to Brookner, in early old age Elizabeth Bowen, Barbara Pym, and Penelope Mortimer continued or resumed well-established careers, but each made dramatic changes in her style and focus to meet the personal challenges of that stage of life. The death of Bowen's husband, Pym's stroke, and Mortimer's traumatic divorce forced them to reexamine their lives and to channel their creativity in a different direction. Their later novels directly confront the authors' sense of vulnerability and lack of control over their lives.[9]

These two models are by no means representative of all old-age fiction. A third paradigm is equally significant. It consists of writers in old age whose days of self-exploration appear to be behind them but whose fame guarantees them a larger audience than they once had. This category includes May Sarton, as well as the late Walker Percy. Their most recent novels can both be described as messages in bottles, their legacy for the next generation. These works are not just novels of protest, although one can find elements of remonstrance in them, as well as in much of their earlier fiction. For example, Kathleen Woodward has pointed out that sixteen years earlier Sarton composed *As We Are Now* (1973) primarily to protest "the inhumanity of American society toward the elderly." In old age and ill health, however, both Sarton and Percy (now dead) approach their audience in a somewhat more muted fashion. They do not hesitate to speak their minds, but they adapt the tone of privileged elder giving "a lay sermon," thus fulfilling Erikson's prediction of the "*grand*-generative function" in later life.[10] The writers in this third group are at least a generation removed from their heroes. They use these narratives as a means to pass on their wisdom and experience to those who will follow. Furthermore, they write with the confidence that their readers will listen to and perhaps act upon their messages.

Examining Sarton's latest work from this perspective forces us to confront underlying prejudices about the effect of aging upon literary creativity. Most readers will prefer the qualities of the first two models of late-life fiction, particularly writers, like Elizabeth Bowen, who transcend loss or illness and discover new meanings, no matter how tentative, for the rest of their lives. Obviously this creative activity offers hope for our own problematical futures. Moreover, these swan songs often combine intensity of feeling with a complicated and rich structure. Yet authors can be cantankerous. They write what they want, not what their readers necessarily desire. Sarton's narrative strategies constitute a politics of old age; she uses her fame to impart a message that she hopes will alter social attitudes. In order to understand Sarton's narrative choices, it was necessary to review her earlier career, to try to understand the place of this novel in her life's work.

Besides producing an analysis of Sarton's novels that intrigued and pleased the novelist herself when she heard the paper at the conference, this literature review enhances our appreciation of Sarton's lifelong literary accomplishments. Although one might assume that in old age Sarton would celebrate the lives of the aged, as she does in *Kinds of Love* (1970), a novel that Kathleen Woodward also analyzes in her essay, experienced Sarton readers have learned to expect surprises. Exploring the unexpected has long been her trademark, and the novelist has always been far too adventurous merely to repeat a formula. The death of her parents and moments of depression encouraged her to make loneliness a theme quite early in life. Then, desiring to be honest about her bisexuality, at the age of fifty-three she published a life-review novel, *Mrs. Stevens Hears the Mermaids Sing-*

ing (1965), shortly before she began the first of her well-known journals. Once, however, she had examined her creative life and loves in that novel of midlife, she apparently has felt no particular compunction to repeat the experience.

The one common thread in most of her fiction is Sarton's effort to define the meaning of family. For example, her second novel, *The Bridge of Years* (1946), not only describes a Belgian family she loved dearly but imaginatively creates the life she might have known had her parents stayed in Belgium in 1914 and been lucky enough to have had their two infant sons survive. All that exploration of family life obviously sustained the novelist through the transitions of midlife by offering her what she regarded as secular salvation through art. Writing allowed her to express her sense of loss when her parents died, and her powerful novels, as well as her journals and poems, attracted new friends, many of whom could to some extent substitute for lost family. As George Vaillant has observed, we stop growing when we fail to replace "our human losses"; we need "to acquire new people to care for faster than they die or move away." [11] As a result of her creative efforts, despite a stroke, in old age Sarton's narrative voice is remarkably serene.

Of course we must remember that Sarton is creating fiction in her story of Harriet, not simply retelling her own personal story. Though some of her novelistic energy has a personal source—the plot derives in part from Sarton's musings on the wonders of survival—artistic alchemy transforms this raw material into a folk tale, or perhaps more accurately into a Jungian mythic adventure, like the ones described so movingly by Allan Chinen. Sarton has discovered the truth of Jung's contention that the upheavals of midlife can lead the sufferer into new paths which are potentially regenerative. After all, the novelist left Cambridge, her childhood home, for New Hampshire and then Maine in an effort to put down roots that would be hers alone, not a replication of her parents'. Harriet is about the age that Sarton was when she moved to Maine to finish her quest. At sixty the heroine is a bit older and more vulnerable than many of the powerful empty nesters the psychologist David Gutmann describes, but she still has the energy to seek compensation for what she has lost. [12] Despite the passivity of her past life, her willing submergence in the fabric of Victoria Chilton's life, she discovers unexpected strengths. Like the hero in a Jungian adventure, outsiders help her, in this case friendly bystanders who recall the friendly animals of fairy tales. Harriet is assisted by a most unlikely group of individuals—nuns, a woman who looks like a bag lady but in actual fact is nursing a sick husband, lesbian college students, an artist who is also a battered wife, and a young black professional wife and mother—a mixture much like the one Sarton depicts in her journals.

Sarton willingly bequeaths her resilience to her latest heroine, whose ladylike exterior obscures the steel within. On the first page of the novel Harriet describes her desperate conviction "that I must recreate a self I can live with for the rest of my life" (*HH*, 9), but she quickly discovers that the search is so satisfying that it numbs her pain. Harriet's acute sense of loss becomes retrospective, something she mulls over in private. Like her creator, Harriet survives the loss of her lover because she has the capacity to turn her friends into family substitutes. Sarton makes Harriet relatively young so that telling her story allows the novelist to review the steps by which she became the kind of person she has become in old age. To borrow Margaret Gullette's useful term, the novelist has constructed a midlife progress novel. From Harriet's crisis of early old age, Sarton, like the novelists that Gullette studies, creates "a happier genre," one that celebrates "the existence of heavenly days." [13]

Sarton tells the tale entirely from Harriet's point of view, a narrative decision which unfortunately limits the ways in which Harriet's character can be probed. Restricted to a single perspective, Sarton is reduced to having other characters tell Harriet how wonderful she is, statements that often are not convincing or fresh. Sarton rarely uses the "one-person point of view" narrative in her fiction. *As We Are Now* is the only other novel told entirely in the first person, but in *The Small Room* (1961), she concentrates so intently on her heroine, Lucy Winter, that she creates a claustrophobic atmosphere, much like the one in *The Education of Harriet Hatfield*. In general Sarton prefers to explore the perspective of a variety of characters. The novelist, however, seems almost compelled to free her heroine from bondage, to let her speak for herself. This appears to be at least partly a conscious choice. After all, Sarton is well aware of the problems she faced when using the first person. She once remarked that "the danger of being inside one character alone is special pleading"; she realized that "my talents are, I fear, not dispassionate." [14] By this choice Sarton may lose some of the psychological complexity of her richer characters, but the first-person narration does generate a feeling of urgency from its pared-down prose.

This matter of style is worth further attention because one characteristic of old-age writing can be a new simplicity, prompted by a sense that time cannot be wasted. For example, in her early sixties Barbara Pym focused so intensely on her primary message in a manuscript version of *Quartet in Autumn* (1977) that an editor warned that it was too short to be publishable and friends begged her to add more scenes. [15] Sarton's minimalism took a slightly different form. Although her novel is longer than Pym's, Sarton stripped away the perceptions of other actors in the drama. Harriet tells her story almost laconically; her unadorned prose reinforces the character's insistence that we must seek an acceptance of human difference. Indeed Harriet's honesty about sexual matters is remarkable when Sarton has portrayed her as the sort of woman for whom even saying the word *lesbian* is problematical. One cannot help speculating that Sarton herself must have once felt equally as uncomfortable when she first declared her homosexuality in public.

Didacticism in late-life novels is not uncommon; in Sarton's case, she has long awaited popularity and critical acclaim, and a degree of impatience might be an additional reason to preach. Although Norton has published most of her novels since 1961, it was slow to bring them out in paper. For example, *The Single Hound* (1938), Sarton's first novel, was not reprinted until 1991. Most of her novels appeared in paper ten to fifteen years after their first publication. Few courses in literature have included her novels, and relatively few critics have analyzed her work. In 1977 Sarton complained that she was not in the *Norton Anthology*, "my own publisher's." Comments in her journals emphasize her exasperation at the slowness of this pace. Considering the quality of her best work, one can share her sense of frustration with all this "due deliberate speed." In late life, however, she commands an audience and has a chance to speak frankly about homosexuality to the straight world. For all these reasons, Sarton, like Walker Percy in *The Thanatos Syndrome* (1987), has used this novel to take a stand. We may be shocked by her refusal to write about a frail old woman and be convinced that the author made the wrong choice, like the boy in the "Story of the Shoe Box," who, when fleeing from the Nazis, chose the box with practical objects rather than those of personal value. Yet, as Marc Kaminsky has made clear, what matters is that the boy lived to tell his story and that we in turn tell it to others. For writers the essential point is to maintain "narrative possibility." Thus, sociologist Jaber Gubrium has ample reason to suggest that good luck, good health, and the capacity to use their creativity have allowed certain gifted elders dramatically to postpone or modify the experience of aging itself. In this case, Sarton accomplished through fiction the task of healing which, according to anthropologist Sharon Kaufman, most stroke victims attempt to achieve "by revising and re-creating" their life story so that it reflects what they have learned from their life-threatening illnesses.[16]

Sarton also exemplifies the point that artists often resist being categorized at any point in life—be the classification gender, ethnicity, class, age, or sexual orientation. A close examination of her fictional career suggests that she has always chosen her subjects to meet her own desires rather than seek to satisfy our literary demands. At every point in life, the act of writing has almost literally regenerated and sustained her. Metaphors, like the image of the phoenix arising from its ashes, which Sarton told her audience in Gainesville was her favorite, help to explain the forces that generate creative work and transform, at least for a time, the experience of aging itself.[17] Sarton not only uses her new-won fame to challenge social attitudes but in the process radically undermines the theoretical prejudices of gerontologists, as well. Although *The Education of Harriet Hatfield* is far from her best novel, reviewing Sarton's earlier fiction prepares us for what she has achieved in other, stronger works.

Sarton's case demonstrates that aging theories can offer special insight into the creative process over the life span. Indeed many of the chapters in this volume prove that these ideas sometimes can provide a means of salvaging the reputation of problematical works of art, which otherwise might be dismissed or given a superficial reading. For example, Rembrandt's paintings were not highly valued by his contemporaries. Mihály Csikszentmihályi points out that his " 'creativity' was constructed after his death by art historians" who were able to discern innovations that contemporaries could not see. Moreover, although equating the writer with the product is a fallacy to be avoided, reading literature within the context of the writer's life and prior writing can uncover some of the author's hitherto concealed intentions. At the same time, models merely furnish a shorthand to understanding. Like all schemata they should be used sparingly. Ideally, theory should reveal something that individuals could potentially discover for themselves. Instead, the linguist Deborah Tannen tells us with regret that although the word *schema* should imply a developing pattern, rather than a template, in most work "the notion of constant change has been lost."[18] The best way to evaluate individual difference is to adopt a lifecourse approach to writing. Rather than beginning an analysis of writers' works with the products of middle or old age, one should, whenever possible, review the entire career in order to grasp the meaning of the changes that occur. Then it becomes less tempting to impose a theory of stages upon the lives of writers, or indeed on anyone else. By such means, we gain respect for the complex pattern that individuals create as they react to the vagaries of fate.

Sarton's novel not only defies our easy assumptions about the nature of old-age writing, but its peculiarities demonstrate that desire, not pure chronology, accounts for the unexpected moments of our lives. In contrast, stage theorists analyze the life cycle seeking broadly predictable patterns. These practitioners believe in the overriding importance of chronology in human life, but such a conviction overlooks the timeless and often disruptive nature of desire. For, as Gubrium has speculated, the ability of specially talented elders to hold age at bay subverts all attempts to foretell human behavior. Moreover, Sarton and other writers who appear to transcend their age are hardly unique. The subjects of another study conducted by Kaufman report feeling "ageless" except when ill. Many are well enough to identify themselves as adults rather than old people, until, perhaps, intrusive questions of researchers remind them of the ravages of time. Elders can often maintain their sense of self despite the loss of family members or diminished physical functioning. Even the prospect of their own imminent death can be transcended, as the case of Barbara Pym demonstrates, if the dying perceive the possibility for growth and change in the life that remains. Thus, recognizing the fluidity of actual experience should help gerontologists guard against the temptation to apply any theories too rigidly to their subjects. For example, Erik Erikson, stage theory's grand old man, has modified his famous chart of the life cycle. In *The Life Cycle Completed,* he begins the chart with old age, not infancy, in belated recognition that growing old reshapes one's view of prior experiences.[19]

In sum, as long as literary gerontologists respond honestly to what they read, worries need not arise about the prematurity of theorizing about models of late-life fiction. If we ground our theory carefully in data and record the many different categories of old-age writing that are in the process of emerging, gradually we will be able to illuminate the complex relationship between aging and creativity. No doubt more paradigms will be uncovered as literary gerontologists both find more examples of these preliminary versions and add new varieties to our list. Indeed, a new one is emerging in subsequent chapters in this book: the aging writer as visual sensualist.[20]

Notes

My thanks to Carolyn H. Smith, Gloria G. Fromm, and Bertram Wyatt-Brown, whose helpful suggestions have improved the paper considerably. Earlier formulations of this essay appear in Anne M. Wyatt-Brown, "A Message in the Bottle," and "The Politics of Old Age."

1. Kathleen Woodward, "May Sarton and Fictions of Old Age."
2. Peter Elbow, "The Doubting and the Believing Game," 147.

3. Erik H. Erikson, *Childhood and Society,* 261–63; Norman N. Holland, "Unity Identity Text Self," 815, "Not So Little Hans," 54, and *The Critical I,* 26–27.

4. Carolyn H. Smith, "Richard Eberhart's Poems on Aging," 75–76. Smith quotes the term "cognitive plasticity" from P. B. Baltes and K. W. Schaie, "On the Plasticity of Intelligence in Adulthood and Old Age," *American Psychologist* 31 (1976): 720–25. Robert Kastenbaum, "The Creative Process," 295, points out that both Tennyson and Picasso developed the theme of death early in their work in response to personal crises.

5. Anne M. Wyatt-Brown, Introduction to this volume; Dean Keith Simonton, "Creativity, Aging, and Chance," 407–8; Margaret Morganroth Gullette, "Creativity, Aging, Gender," this volume.

6. Mihály Csikszentmihályi, "Society, Culture, and Person," 325; David M. Harrington, "The Ecology of Human Creativity," 149–50.

7. Anne M. Wyatt-Brown, "A Buried Life"; Marcia Aldrich, "Lethal Brevity," this volume.

8. Erikson, *Childhood,* 268–69; George E. Vaillant, *Adaptation to Life,* 222, 214.

9. Anne M. Wyatt-Brown, "Creativity in Midlife," "Late Style in the Novels of Barbara Pym and Penelope Mortimer," "The Liberation of Mourning in Elizabeth Bowen's *The Little Girls* and *Eva Trout,*" this volume, and *Barbara Pym,* 130–36. In a similar fashion, John Updike, in *Rabbit at Rest* (1990) written after the death of his mother, describes the deterioration of his character Rabbit, whose life he has chronicled for the last thirty years.

10. Woodward, "Sarton," 109; Bertram Wyatt-Brown, "Walker Percy"; Erik H. Erikson, *The Life Cycle Completed,* 63. Marc Kaminsky, "Story of the Shoe Box," 318, notes that "the impassioned tone of the lay sermon" can be traced back to Thoreau and Emerson.

11. May Sarton, *The Bridge of Years;* Vaillant, *Adaptation,* 210, 344. Sarton, *I Knew a Phoenix,* 65–83, 124–27, describes the Belgian house in which she was born and a Belgian family with whom she lived when she was twelve; *A World of Light,* 59, 62, mentions the two brothers who died. Mark Taylor, the protagonist of Sarton's *The Single Hound* (1938), desperately seeks affirmation from the aging poet, Jean Latour, that he too has the makings of a poet.

12. Allan B. Chinen, *In the Ever After* and *Once Upon a Midlife,* has illuminated our understanding of the connection between middle and elder tales and Jungian views of later life. David Gutmann, *Reclaimed Powers,* 208.

13. Margaret Morganroth Gullette, *Safe at Last in the Middle Years,* xii. Gullette, private communication, Nov. 19, 1990, suggested that *HH* is a midlife progress novel. Sarton may well be an example of individuals, who, as Gullette theorizes, are " 'born' into such a hopeful belief and never lose it, despite poverty, lack of education, discrimination, bad luck, even illness." Still, as Gullette makes clear, such optimism "may take considerable energy to maintain" (*Safe,* xiii–xiv).

14. May Sarton, "The Design of a Novel," 31–32, *As We Are Now,* and *The Small Room.* In one of her best novels, *Faithful Are the Wounds* (1955), by using a more omniscient narrator, Sarton has exhibited a remarkable sensitivity to initially unappealing characters like Isabel Ferrier, Edward Cavan's middle-class sister. In the beginning Isabel is a stereotypical Joseph McCarthy supporter, but Sarton's intense ability to understand "the other" does not desert her. Isabel becomes a more complex and troubled figure in the course of the novel. Indeed she ceases to be what Sarton, "Design," 35, calls "a contrived anti-hero" and becomes worthy of her brother. More-

over, Isabel's pain deepens our appreciation of her brother's despair. We can see that Edward has lost a good deal when he stopped talking to her. Sarton teaches us that pain of loss has forced Isabel to construct the empty life to which she clings in the early part of the novel.

15. Anne Wyatt-Brown, *Pym*, 136, 182, n. 28, 29, and "Late Style," 837. Kastenbaum, "Creative Process," 302, calls "concentrated artistic thought" a common characteristic of late style but emphasizes that some older artists are more "expansive."

16. Robin Kaplan and Shelley Neiderbach, "I Live Alone in a Very Beautiful Place," 62; Kaminsky, "Story," 320; Jaber F. Gubrium, "New Thoughts on Identity in the Upward Years"; Sharon Kaufman, "Illness, Biography, and the Interpretation of Self Following a Stroke," 217.

17. May Sarton, poetry reading, March 16, 1990, Gainesville, Fla.

18. Mihály Csikszentmihályi, "The Domain of Creativity," 199; Deborah Tannen, "What's in a Frame," 139. Kastenbaum, "Creative Process," 300, points out that critical judgment is usually subject to revision, making the evaluation of late style especially problematical.

19. Gubrium, "New Thoughts"; Sharon R. Kaufman, *The Ageless Self*, 12–13; Wyatt-Brown, *Pym*, 147–50 (describing how dying affected Pym's final novel); Erikson, *Life Cycle*, 8–9. Other valuable examples of stage theories are: Vaillant, *Adaptation;* Daniel Levinson et al., *Seasons of a Man's Life;* Ramona T. Mercer, Elizabeth G. Nichols, and Glen Caspers Doyle, *Transition in a Woman's Life.*

20. It is impossible to avoid theorizing altogether. The linguist Georgia M. Green, *Pragmatics and Natural Language Understanding*, 152–53, argues that even supposedly value-neutral ethnomethodological empirical studies reflect theories of human behavior, despite their authors' expressed anxiety about indulging in "unverifiable and premature theorizing."

Examples in this volume of visual sensitivity in old age include: Gloria G. Fromm, "Being Old" and Bethany Ladimer, "Colette." See Anne M. Wyatt-Brown, Introduction to this volume.

3

THOMAS C. CARAMAGNO

Suicide and the Illusion of Closure: Aging, Depression, and the Decision to Die

NOTHING invites or defies closure so well as suicide. Self-destruction illustrates the theoretical challenge that biology presents to psycho-biographical readings of an artist's life because many facets of a subject's decision to die resist a "meaningful" analysis. This is especially true of any artist who commits suicide under pressure of age or illness, be it medical or mental. Suicide is at once a personal and an impersonal event, an intended act—at the very least, it is an attempt to escape one's pain—but it is also one that occurs when psychosis, depression, dementia, or any of a number of age-related physical conditions may have undermined the intention-mediating neural circuits in the brain. Here brain and mind intersect and must be evaluated together: how does each affect the other? Unfortunately, psychobiographers tend to look exclusively for a reductionistic, thematic consistency in describing/explaining the last years of their subjects' lives, whether it is the frenetic ambition of Charles Dickens driving himself toward a "fated" stroke or the neurotic compulsion for punishment played out by an amoral Oscar Wilde. Literary conventions require that old age and death be seen as the conclusive final act, not the beginning of a new one, and critics prefer that the protagonist remain in character. But such speculations, made from the safe haven of healthy or young scholarly brains, ignore the very real changes aging or diseased bodies can bring to bear on an individual's mental capacities and desires, even the most basic desire for life itself. Biology plays an important role in how the depressed, impaired, or aged artist faces the end. Yet the body is seldom given significance in psychobiography because it is "antinarrative," an unpleasant intrusion upon the apparent continuity of our psychic lives and our egotistical conviction that we have created ourselves and our destinies out of the "story" of our thoughts. Not so for the artists who lived in those bodies and struggled to cope with physical and mental deterioration intractably independent of character, free will, or desire.

Depression and Suicide

Although my discussion of the connection between depression and suicide is illustrated here for simplicity's sake by one particular case, that of Virginia Woolf, psychobiographers in general need to acquaint themselves with the biological aspects of mood (or "affective") disorders, because a surprisingly large percentage of creative people suffer from them. Although recurrent unipolar (pure) depressions occur in only 5 percent of the general population, and bipolar (manic-depressive illness) in a mere 1 percent, recent studies have shown that a strong association exists between creativity and mood disorders. Such a link has been periodically hypothesized by biographers and psychoanalysts since Lombroso, but recent work has gone beyond rephrasing anecdotal information to support personal notions of insanity. Two researchers, Dr. Kay Redfield Jamison (Johns Hopkins) and Dr. Nancy Andreasen (University of Iowa), both trained in psychiatry but fluent in literary matters, have applied the more rigorous methods of differential diagnosis used today. Jamison surveyed forty-seven accomplished British writers and artists and found that 38 percent had been treated for an affective illness: three-fourths of those treated required drug therapy or hospitalization. Whether or not the disorder caused personal problems, a majority of these subjects felt that it was intimately involved in the creative process: of the forty-seven artists surveyed, 89 percent reported hypomanic (mild mania) states during intense, productive moments, and a third experienced severe mood swings, of which 90 percent were regarded as either integral and necessary (60 percent) or very important (30 percent) to creativity. Andreasen's survey, conducted at the Iowa Writer's Workshop, the most prestigious creative writing program in the United States, revealed that 80 percent of the writers interviewed had had a mood disorder at some time in their lives, 43 percent of which was bipolar. Historically, creativity and affective illness have coincided in such figures as the composers Beethoven, Chopin, Donizetti, Mahler, Rachmaninoff, Schumann, and Hugo Wolf; the painters Jackson Pollock and Van Gogh; and the writers A. C. Benson, Blake, Byron, Chekhov, John Clare, William Collins, Chatterton, Coleridge, Cowper, Dickens, Emerson, Robert Fergusson, Goethe, Hemingway, Thomas Hoccleve, Hopkins, Johnson, R. Lowell, Plath, Poe, Roethke, D. G. Rossetti, Rousseau, Ruskin, Sexton, Shelley, Christopher Smart, and Antonia White. Efforts are already under way to review these cases.[1]

However much mood disorders may be an asset for artists, they can also be fatal. Studies suggest that 95 percent of suicide victims suffer from a psychiatric illness, namely affective disorders, conduct disorders, schizophrenia, and organic brain disorders. Of these four groups, affective disorders (such as depression and manic-depressive illness) account for the largest number of suicides, between 45 and 70 percent, depending on the study. About 25 percent of suicide victims are officially diagnosed as alcoholic, but roughly three-quarters of them also suffer from concurrent major depression. Overall, individuals who are both alcoholics and depressives carry the highest risk for suicide of any group. In the elderly (age sixty-five or over), clinical depression has been reported to be as high as 13 percent; 20 to 35 percent of those with a concurrent medical illness are depressed. Although persons over age sixty-five account for about 11 percent of the U.S. population, they commit 25 percent of the suicides. Suicide rates for men peak between ages eighty and ninety, while for women they peak between fifty and sixty-five. The elderly are usually less impulsive in their decision making and less ambivalent about their wish to die. Although only one in every hundred adolescent attempts at suicide succeeds, one in four attempts among the elderly succeeds because they are more determined and more knowledgeable about the efficacy of lethal methods available. Others decline without overt violence: untreated major depression lowers life expectancy, carries a greater risk of cardiac disease, and often leads to malnourishment, which in turn can cause further medical and psychological difficulties.[2]

In contrast, ignoring the effects of biology tempts biographers to read subjects' lives that end in suicide as miniature morality plays: if only Woolf had been stronger and coped better with her childhood traumas, it is easily assumed, she would have seen that life was good regardless of the cost. We indulge in our private need to have others prove the value of our own lives. Like the readers of a Newgate novel, psychobiographers cannot resist the notion that character and fate are connected and that a woman like Woolf had been courting death ever since childhood. Never mind that the prospect of growing old may have threatened to reduce or impair sensory perception, synthetic thinking, and motor skills—everything that made writing a good book or being alive a joy for her. Disregard the fact that affective disorder changes perception, cognition, and judgment, as can age. Those who are well and younger judge her suicide to be a cowardly, neurotic act.

Such moralistic intrusions upon biography oversimplify the intersection between free will and necessity, between mind and brain. Indeed, discounting the role of the brain leads to unrestricted and biased speculation. Take the most recent explication of Woolf's suicide by Alma H. Bond, which begins: "Who killed Virginia Woolf? What drove her over the brink when so many others were able to survive those difficult years of World War II? Who, if anyone, was chiefly responsible . . . ?"[3] Bond is dissatisfied with Woolf's own reports (suicide notes to her husband, Leonard, and her sister, Vanessa Bell) that no one was to blame:

Tuesday [March 18?, 1941]

Dearest,

I feel certain that I am going mad again: I feel we cant go through another of those terrible times. And I shant recover this time. I begin to hear voices, and cant concentrate. So I am doing what seems the best thing to do. You have given me the greatest possible happiness. You have been in every way all that anyone could be. I dont think two people could have been happier till this terrible disease came. I cant fight it any longer, I know that I am spoiling your life, that without me you could work. And you will I know. You see I cant even write this properly. I cant read. What I want to say is that I owe all the happiness of my life to you. You have been entirely patient with me and incredibly good. I want to say that— everybody knows it. If anybody could have saved me it would have been you. Everything has gone from me but the certainty of your goodness. I cant go on spoiling your life any longer.

I dont think two people could have been happier than we have been.

V.

Sunday [March 23?, 1941]

Dearest,

You cant think how I loved your letter. But I feel that I have gone too far this time to come back again. I am certain now that I am going mad again. It is just as it was the first time, I am always hearing voices, and I know I shant get over it now.

All I want to say is that Leonard has been so astonishingly good, every day, always; I cant imagine that anyone could have done more for me than he has. We have been perfectly happy until the last few weeks, when this horror began. Will you assure him of this? I feel he has so much to do that he will go on, better without me, and you will help him.

I can hardly think clearly any more. If I could I would tell you what you and the children have meant to me. I think you know.

I have fought against it, but I cant any longer.

Virginia[4]

Why should Woolf have felt so vulnerable? In her youth she had suffered and survived extensive metabolic, cognitive, and perceptual distortions;

now she was fifty-nine years old and felt she did not have the strength to endure another protracted episode. But Bond, wishing to assign blame, disregards the impersonal effects of age and biochemistry in order to look for a human culprit. She assumes that Woolf's vulnerability must be psychological, an illusory weakness created by a mind unwilling to gain strength through self-knowledge. Since in her diaries and letters Woolf does not acknowledge a suitably lethal neurotic conflict, Bond has no choice but to supply one and conclude that a "widespread duplicity"[5] has been propagated by Woolf, her family, friends, and subsequent critics to leave unnamed Woolf's real motivation for committing suicide. Bond considers the possible leads as though she were writing a detective novel capable of yielding a solution through clues: the threat of a German invasion, the fear of becoming an inescapable burden to her Jewish husband, the belief that her sister, Vanessa, was withholding her love, the knowledge that her lesbian lover, Vita Sackville-West, was unfaithful, that Leonard Woolf was too domineering, that she might lose the power to write. But none of these has the dramatic power Bond deems necessary to push one over the edge. A Freudian, Bond explains Woolf's vulnerability by privileging (and hypothesizing the existence of) unresolved, unconscious conflicts resulting from early traumas. Invasion, infidelity, loss, diminishing creativity, self-devaluation—all the accumulated guesses made by critics over the years—became more than Woolf could bear, Bond explains, not because they were in themselves unbearable but because they replicated old wounds that never healed: she was weaned too early, her feces were "devalued" by her mother during toilet training, she masochistically wished to surrender to an idealized mother, but she also feared such engulfment and later envied her father's penis. As happens too often in a Freudian landscape, childhood is hell; why else would anyone commit suicide fifty years later?

Discounting all the recent research into biological vulnerability, Bond still relies on Freud's sixty-six-year-old description of psychosis as an unreconciled conflict between the ego and an intolerable reality and on Jacobson's thirty-four-year-old idea that manic-depressives experience pronounced shifts in mood and self-esteem because an immature superego has failed to modulate psychic energy (primarily anger toward parents in mania and anger toward self in depression). Thus, Bond can freely accuse Woolf of "prefer[ring] to experience a depressed mood" rather than face repressed anger, which was the pivotal, the "meaningful" conflict that paralyzed her.[6] Such a theory justifies prolonged psychoanalytic explorations of infantile feelings, some of which Woolf herself did not report, and it underestimates the importance of adult concerns, which she did report in her suicide notes.

As I have shown elsewhere, Virginia Woolf's (indeed, anybody's) bipolar illness was not caused by repressed anger but by a genetically inherited biochemical dysfunction in the brain: some of her breakdowns could have been triggered by stress, either physiological (e.g., influenza) or psychological (e.g., fear of criticism), but the disorder itself was not a symptom or a product of infantile conflict. But even if the subject of a psychobiographical study is not manic-depressive, even if we can show clear evidence of early trauma in a life history that ends in suicide, Bond's skewed approach will serve us poorly because it unduly draws attention away from the problems that the older suicidal person must deal with in the here and now. Clinical studies have not proven the Freudian connection between early traumas and later suicides: some adult suicides experienced early trauma, others did not, so the wise psychotherapist does not neglect the patient's present motives in favor of fecal rejection in early childhood when trying to estimate the patient's potential for suicide. For the most part, the stressful events that precipitate suicide in older adults occur close to the attempt date: the primary fears of the elderly, suicidal or not, relate to the day-to-day problems of living and coping with physical hardship, loneliness, and personal suffering, not necessarily abstract or infantile issues but those encountered in everyday functioning. They fear sensory deprivation (in vision, hearing, smell, and taste), mental decline (especially creative, intellectual abilities), mental illness (especially senility), and segregation from their loved ones. These are realistic concerns though it is impossible to predict who will deteriorate, how much they will deteriorate, or at what age. The majority of the elderly will not suffer serious mental impairment, but fear can magnify even slight changes and inspire suicidal thoughts, especially when worried elders know that dementia can strike individuals younger than themselves.[7]

What brought on Woolf's last attack? Numerous biological factors may have been involved. Studies suggest that manic-depressive relapses increase with age; that depressive episodes in older patients sometimes last longer; that patients who have had more total episodes in their lifetime are at greatest risk for suicide; that people with a history of both severe depression and migraines accompanied by sensations known as auras (as Woolf had) experience a greatly increased likelihood of thinking about and attempting suicide; and that older female depressed patients are more at risk for suicide than younger ones. So perhaps Woolf died for nothing more meaningful than the fact that the biochemical changes in her aging body may have intensified her depression. Or perhaps it was the season: there is a striking increase in the numbers of suicide in May, a rise that begins in March as do the rates of hospital admissions for depression. Affective disorders can also be profoundly influenced by the body's seasonal rhythms; perhaps both age and winter combined to exacerbate Woolf's depression. Another possibility exists: Woolf's last physician, Octavia Wilberforce, suspected in 1940 that her patient might be an alcoholic. If Woolf, like 35 percent of all manic-depressives, medicated herself with alcohol in the last year of her life, the neurochemical changes that result from drinking (such as decreased serotonin levels, which appear to regulate the sleep/wake cycle and mood tone) could have contributed to the severity of her last depression, diminishing impulse control, impairing judgment, and so increasing the risk of suicide.[8]

Although manic-depressives are at high risk for suicide, thirty times more so than the general population, the association between suicide and chemical changes in the brain must be considered in any case of self-destruction. In the near future psychobiographers will have to consider a variety of neurochemical changes that may be detected in their subjects' bodies if they are to avoid the oversimplification we have seen in Woolf's case. As laboratory tests become more available and more refined, and as more suicidal artists receive medical/psychiatric testing and treatment, biographers will find themselves sifting through medical data that has a direct bearing on the subject's state of mind. For instance, low levels of 5-HIAA, a metabolite of the brain neurotransmitter serotonin, found in the cerebrospinal fluid of suicides is "one of the most replicated findings in biological psychiatry today," leading researchers to speculate that "a low 5-HIAA level is correlated with a tendency to act impulsively and violently while in acute emotional or psychiatric turmoil." Although important, 5-HIAA is by no means the only biological factor that will require examination: suicidal states of mind are also associated with elevated levels of urinary 17-hydroxycorticosterone, a plasma cortisol level higher than twenty mcg%, a positive dexamethasone suppression test (revealing an hormone imbalance), a blunted or absent response of thyroid-stimulating hormone, low urinary norepinephrine-epinephrine (like serotonin, a major neurotransmitter in the brain) ratio, low levels of magnesium in cerebrospinal fluid, paroxysmal EEG dysrhythmia, and high monozygotic twin suicide concordance rates (if one twin commits suicide, the other runs an 18 percent chance of committing suicide too; that figure drops to 4.5 percent if the twins are raised apart by adopted parents, but this is still 900 percent higher than the risk of suicide for the general population). Some researchers believe that there may be a genetic factor in suicide independent of the genetic transmission of psychiatric disorders such as manic-depressive illness. This genetic inheritance would, presumably, create the biochemical conditions conducive to suicidal thinking.[9]

Although too late to help us better appreciate Woolf's state of mind in

March 1941, these new findings promise greater understanding for psycho-biographical studies of suicides to come. Until more data come in, we cannot tell whether the chemical changes cited above cause suicidal thoughts or whether the emotional distress of suicidal thoughts causes the brain's chemistry to change; but clearly, whatever the cause-effect relationship at work here, the brain's operating systems are intimately responsive to and involved in such patterns of thinking. Since this is so, we must conclude that any physical condition that impairs the brain's ability to function must be considered if we are to evaluate a patient's decision to die.

Biology has profound personal consequences that invade the most private realms of our souls, our character, our self-insight. When biochemistry falters, the brain's ability to process and evaluate perceptions is diminished. In manic-depressive illness, for instance, interpretations become either predominantly positive or negative, depending upon mood. If they are negative, the self feels impotent and pointless, unable to summon up the strength to survive a future now perceived as grim, just as Woolf was unable to imagine surviving a new breakdown in her suicide note ("I shant recover this time").[10] Reviewing past happiness seldom helps: the depressed brain is unable to integrate the full spectrum of the individual's feelings and desires, past or present, and so overly negativized perceptions feel the most "true," frustrating attempts by the therapist or the family to dissolve their power and reassure the patient that things are not as gloomy as they seem. In her suicide notes Woolf reported remembering the good times, but she could not use them to ameliorate the power of the bad present ("I dont think two people could have been happier till this terrible disease came").

Thinking is further hampered in depression by poor concentration (of which Woolf complained to both her husband and her sister), distractibility, learning deficits, slowed reaction time to stimuli, impaired memory, confusion, "poverty of content" (inadequate content, overabstracted or overconcretized language, repetitive use of ideas without development, or stereotyped thinking), illogicality, and loss of goal (failure to follow a chain of thought through to a conclusion). Depression limits the individual's abilities to deal creatively with new or stressful circumstances: studies show that when depressives are exposed to new material, they are less likely to link novel information to preexisting knowledge, hindering the fundamental, human capacity to recognize significance consistently across time. Their memory of events becomes jumbled, unintegrative habit begins to dominate thought, and they fall back upon uncreative and inflexible routines, which feeds their developing nihilism and pessimism; life does indeed become empty and fragmented for them.[11] Thus, although Woolf remembered that her present despair was "just as it was the first time," she felt that she could not summon up the strength to survive it as she had earlier breakdowns ("I feel that I have gone too far this time to come back again").

Depressed thinking is so skewed toward negative interpretations that psychologists have been able to identify categories of cognitive errors that repeatedly appear in their patients' self-reports. Among these, six errors are paramount in suicidal ruminations, and five occur in Woolf's suicide notes: (1) arbitrary inference: the depressed patient typically draws incorrect conclusions from existing evidence (e.g., "I am always hearing voices, and I know I shant get over it now"); (2) selective abstraction: focusing on a single aspect of a situation instead of looking at the whole (my creative powers must be failing me because my book is "too sketchy"); (3) over-generalization: drawing conclusions from single bits of information (I "cant concentrate. So I am doing what seems the best thing to do"); (4) magnification and minimization ("I owe all the happiness of my life to you. Without me you could work"); (5) personalization ("I cant go on spoiling your life any longer"); (6) absolutist, dichotomous thinking: seeing every experience in absolute terms ("We have been perfectly happy until the last few weeks, when this horror began").[12]

The most dramatic cognitive shift was exhibited in her evaluation of her work. The week before she committed suicide, she asked John Lehmann to return the manuscript of her recently completed novel, *Between the Acts,* claiming that it now seemed "too slight and sketchy," "too silly and trivial," even though Leonard disagreed and her earlier estimate was far more positive. Quentin Bell reports that "never had a novel of hers flowed so rapidly, so effortlessly from her pen; there were no checks, doubts, despairs, struggles or revisions." On November 23, 1940, having just finished the book, Woolf herself wrote: "I am a little triumphant about the book. I think its an interesting attempt in a new method. I think its more quintessential than the others. More milk skimmed off. A richer pat, certainly a fresher than that misery The Years. I've enjoyed writing almost every page." But by March 1941, in the depths of a depression, she drastically revised her opinion: "I didnt realise how bad it was till I read it over."[13]

Such alterations in the manic-depressive's mental functioning can be inconvenient for psychobiographers who are attempting to paint a large canvas encompassing a subject's entire life, but these fluctuations must be recognized and recorded. When not ill, Woolf loved life. Much in her diaries and letters attests to this fact. March 1941 was a hard month, but in December 1940 she was happy and content. Elizabeth Bowen, who visited the Woolfs at Rodmell in mid-February 1941, remembered that Virginia sat "back on her heels and put her head back in a patch of sun, early spring sun, and laughed in this consuming, choking, delightful, hooting way . . . and it has remained with me. So that I get a curious shock when I see people regarding her entirely as a martyred, or a definitely tragic sort of person claimed by the darkness." No matter how happy they are when euthymic (not ill), patients in the throes of severe depression typically misinterpret their chances of surviving the episodes, exhibiting "the delusion of the eternity of the depressed state," the state-bound conviction that a present episode will never end, that they will always suffer ("I shant recover this time"). In Woolf's time such a delusion would have received some corroboration from experience. Before effective antidepressant drug therapy became available in the late 1950s and 1960s, it was common to find patients confined in state mental hospitals for depressive states that literally lasted years.[14] Certainly Woolf knew that her "psychotic" half sister, Laura, spent nearly fifty years in an asylum, and that Laura's grandmother, Isabella Thackeray, remained institutionalized for "post-partum psychosis" for thirty-five years until her death. Furthermore, Virginia's manic-depressive cousin, James Kenneth Stephen, had died in a psychiatric hospital after three years of recurrent episodes. Woolf had reason to fear that the delusion of the eternity of the depressed state might come true.

Woolf was worried that she would never recover, but perhaps she was not just talking about sanity. We have to remember that in older patients, manic anxiety can create severe physiological stress that younger manics are more easily able to survive physically. Depression can reduce food intake, activity, and immune response, which can lead to infection. In a study of the records of 525 psychiatric patients who were hospitalized between 1934 and 1944, Ming T. Tsuang et al. found that older female manics were more significantly at risk of dying from cardiovascular disease than younger patients. In prelithium days in-hospital deaths of manics were not uncommon. In a 1933 study 40 percent of the deaths of hospitalized manic patients were attributed to physical exhaustion, many of these compounded by refusal of food. Woolf certainly remembered what had happened to her cousin James. Upon admission "under emergency order" to St. Andrew's Hospital in 1891, a physically healthy thirty-two-year-old James was described by the attending physician as "tall well built & muscular in good condition (inclined to be stout)." Two and a half months later he was dead; cause of death was listed as "mania, refusal of food, and exhaustion." Manic-depressive illness can take a serious toll on the body, even a young body, and Virginia was nearly twice James's age.[15]

Woolf ran other age-related risks. Before the availability of drug therapy, she had to rely upon sheer willpower to help her withstand the suicidal temptations of short or mild-to-moderate depressive episodes. On July 26, 1940, for instance, in "a battle against depression," she resolved that "this trough of despair shall not, I swear, engulf me." Feeling despondent on March 8, 1941, she wrote her penultimate entry in her diary: "Oh dear yes, I shall conquer this mood. Its a question of being open sleepy, wide eyed at present—letting things come one after another. Now to cook the haddock." When she became so ill that an alarmed Leonard Woolf asked her doctor, Octavia Wilberforce, to examine her, Woolf characteristically put up a brave front and denied being ill, refusing even to discuss it unless Wilberforce promised not to institutionalize her. But willpower depends upon many things, some of them purely physical. Age and each succeeding breakdown can sap the depressive's capacity to hope for recovery. Even when an episode does finally end, the patient may come to dread the next breakdown, fearing that sooner or later depression will triumph. One study suggests that patients become increasingly less tolerant of the pain and disruptions of depression with each new episode, and that the risk of suicide increases with the duration of the illness. Moreover, delusional depressives are five times more likely to commit suicide than nondelusional depressives; psychotic thinking is impaired, and it does not have the same flexibility or integrative creativity that patients need to resolve conflicting feelings about the value of their lives.[16]

Thus, our efforts to second-guess Woolf from the safe position of sanity are doomed to fail. Given the fact that rapid-cycling female manic-depressives (such as Woolf) usually experience more severe depressions more often as they get older, her fear of an increased vulnerability was not unreasonable and may also have been reinforced by a perceived change: Leonard Woolf noted in his memoirs that the first depressive episode (beginning on January 25) in the series that led up to her suicide began in an uncharacteristic way: "For years I had been accustomed to watch for signs of danger in Virginia's mind; and the warning symptoms had come on slowly and unmistakably; the headache, the sleeplessness, the inability to concentrate. . . . but this time there were no warning symptoms of this kind. The depression struck her like a sudden blow." With hindsight, Leonard Woolf remembered that one other episode had also featured an acute turn: it had happened twenty-six years before during the longest manic-depressive breakdown in his wife's life; occurring off and on for nearly two years, it included an unsuccessful suicide attempt.[17] Virginia Woolf may also have made the same connection and arrived at the same conclusion: that her 1941 breakdown would be unusually severe.

Was Woolf delusional in this last illness? Research suggests that a repetition of her earlier major breakdowns (which included delusions and hallucinations, both visual and auditory) would be likely: in a survey of patients suffering from delusional depression, 95 percent had had prior delusional episodes in their lives, whereas only 8 percent of currently nondelusional patients had previous delusional episodes. Moreover, relatives of patients with delusional depression are eight times as likely to suffer delusions themselves as were relatives of patients with nondelusional depression, and James Kenneth Stephen was delusional. In other words, delusional and nondelusional depressions tend to "breed true." The Stephen family doctor, George Savage, certainly believed that insanity ran through family lines. He warned Woolf's manic-depressive cousin that his illness would progressively worsen.[18] No doubt Woolf suspected she, too, ran a significant risk of repeated psychotic illness.

Because manic-depressive illness can significantly alter a patient's perceptions, feelings, and cognition, we cannot judge Woolf's euthymic character by what she said or did when depressed. Even seemingly strong people with a wide range of personal assets may, when depressed, reinterpret those assets as liabilities (e.g., ambition is no longer seen as a positive sign of success but as an empty gesture or rude pushiness or an act of vanity at the expense of others). Suicide itself is not a reliable indicator of one's strength of character or neuroticism or the quality of one's previous life or the support and love of one's family and friends. For some patients, it is the memory of happiness and success once known that makes their present despair seem unendurable.[19] Pointing out a depressive's available resources or opportunities for satisfaction (the love of his family, his potential for success, etc.) may only exacerbate his sense of the internal abyss that separates him from what he feels he needs most.

Aging and Suicide

At some point anyone's willpower or self-control can be contravened by bodily processes. No matter how healthily or wisely they have lived their lives, aging individuals are at increased risk for depression. Older brains and bodies lose some of their neurohormonal tone. Take, for example, Winston Churchill, who suffered from cyclothymia (a mild, nonpsychotic form of manic-depressive illness) for most of his life. His intense energy and confidence inspired his embattled nation during World War II, but he succumbed to an unremitting and debilitating depression in the last five years of his life. Cerebral arteriosclerosis restricted blood flow to his brain, exacerbating his lifelong biochemical predisposition for mood swings. As psychiatrist Anthony Storr has recently argued, Churchill fought his tendency toward depressions by engaging in great enterprises, dreaming of victory when all seemed lost, and fighting external embodiments of his blackest moods, such as Adolf Hitler, rather than giving in to them. When he could conquer these enemies, he felt reassured that he had the willpower to survive "the black dog" of depression that followed him throughout his life. Yet in his old age arteriosclerosis sapped his will by undermining the very organ that mediates intention, that organizes and executes what we experience as "moral fiber," our character. Churchill fell into a "state of apathy and indifference"; he "gave up reading, seldom spoke, and sat for hours before the fire in what must have amounted to a depressive stupor." [20] Nothing he did or desired or thought had so drastic an effect as the "unmeaningful" constriction of blood vessels. The body counts; it is what aging and illness teach us.

Even without the complication of manic-depressive illness, old age is always accompanied by profound modifications in the central nervous system. Older brains decrease in size, weight, and volume. Many studies have shown that the brain loses 5 percent of its weight by age seventy, 10 percent by eighty, and 20 percent by ninety. Levels of neurotransmitters decrease, cell death increases, and many individual neurons diminish in size. Senile plaques and neurofibrillary degeneration impair neuronal function. Now that the average life expectancy has increased in the twentieth century by more than twenty-five years (from forty-seven years in 1900 to seventy-five years in 1980 for North Americans), psychobiographers must become more aware of what physiological changes occur in the brains of increasingly aging writers if they are accurately to assess their accomplishments and their limitations.[21]

The very first difficulty in making such assessments is that psychobiographers should never apply a stereotypical "aged" profile of a general decline to their subjects without specific corroborating evidence. Some brain changes result in cognitive impairment, others do not, and it is important to remember that age-related declines are not uniform from individual to individual: some people seem to age more quickly than others, some experience only minor impairments as they grow older, and specific cognitive disabilities vary greatly. For instance, on the average, skills involving language production, syntax, vocabulary, comprehension, information retention, seeing similarities between objects or situations, and arithmetic show little or no decline until the mid-seventies. Similarly, tests show that sustained attention (the ability to focus on a task without losing track of its goal) and selective attention (ability to ignore irrelevant information) remain intact.

Neither sensory memory (e.g., identifying a single letter from the alphabet when it is shown to them) nor primary memory (e.g., remembering a series of words or numbers) deteriorates with age in healthy brains, but secondary memory—the ability to retain relatively large amounts of information over long periods of time—begins showing significant impairment at age fifty.[22] Older individuals tend to have difficulty with the semantic aspects of word retrieval: the most common error committed in naming items appears in choosing a semantically related associate, such as saying "dice" when shown dominoes. Verbal fluency declines, such as when elderly subjects are asked to name as many examples of a category (e.g., animals or vegetables) as they can or when asked to draw inferences from statements made to them. Cognitive deficits can even extend to purely visual tasks; the elderly are less able to handle complex visual tasks: for instance, they have more difficulty identifying incomplete figures and embedded figures than do younger subjects. They are also impaired in depicting and perceiving three-dimensional drawings.

But such impairments are probably not a problem of storage capacity, as is popularly believed: the forgetting rate of healthy older subjects is roughly the same as in younger persons, so age-related declines in secondary memory are thought to be the result of inadequate encoding or retrieval of the material to be remembered. The young seem to be more adept at using encoding strategies (e.g., categories into which the new information readily fits) to organize and retrieve what they learn. Thus, in studies where elderly subjects are given the strategies that younger subjects provide for themselves, differences in scores are minimized.[23] So some aged writers may do poorly in unstructured activities (for example, departing from a habitual style or subject in a novel way) but well with more structured projects (such as maintaining their habitual style or translating/editing literary works organized by someone else).

However, age often brings with it increased susceptibility to disease, and here mental functioning can be significantly affected. It is estimated that 15 percent of those over age sixty-five suffer from some form of dementia (impairment or loss of mental powers), and 1 to 2 percent are severely impaired. In Alzheimer's disease, for instance, individual neurons are destroyed by clumplike deposits and tangled neural elements; several neurotransmitters—the chemicals that brain cells use to communicate with each other—are lost; the brain's utilization of glucose and oxygen declines significantly. Alzheimer's disease not only affects memory, verbal fluency, and abstract thinking but also frequently produces psychiatric symptoms, such as hallucinations, delusions, and depression, which psychobiographers should not confuse with schizophrenia or manic-depressive illness. Furthermore, we must recognize that the rate of progression for Alzheimer's disease varies enormously: some patients become moderately impaired after only two years, while others remain only mildly impaired after six years. Both severe cardiac disease and atherosclerosis (hardening of the arteries of the brain) can restrict blood flow by as much as half and so reduce the oxygenation of cells; if complicated by other factors, such as small strokes, dementia may result, mental ability will deteriorate, and even personality can change. Severe obstruction of a blood vessel can produce an infarct, the death of brain cells; but even an infarct may be so limited in area that its effect on the patient's cognitive skills or personality may be too subtle for anyone to notice until a series of infarcts have occurred. All of these changes, however subtle, can affect the way our subjects write books, view life, or approach death.[24]

Some psychiatric symptoms are complications of seemingly unrelated medical problems, and for these psychobiographers must be particularly alert and careful. Depressive symptoms, for instance, can be triggered or caused by influenza, viral hepatitis, infectious mononucleosis, vitamin B_{12} deficiency, general paresis (in the last stage of syphilis), tuberculosis, cirrhosis, AIDS (HIV), Cushing's disease, Addison's disease, hypothyroidism, occult abdominal malignancies, systemic lupus erythematosis, multiple sclerosis, cerebral tumors, sleep apnea, dementia, Parkinson's disease, nondominant temporal lobe lesions, pernicious anemia, pellagra, antihypertensive drugs, alcohol, sedative-hypnotics, female hormone supplements, corticosteroids, and amphetamine, barbiturate, or cocaine withdrawal. Anxiety can be linked to hyperthyroidism, and dementia to Parkinson's disease or vitamin B_{12} deficiency; both can result from cardiovascular problems. Besides B_{12}, thiamine and folic acid deficiencies can also cause intellectual dysfunction. Physicians must look for any chronic illness that reduces food intake (e.g., alcoholism, depression, dementia), and they must remember that elderly patients may not benefit from standard dosages of oral vitamin supplements: one study of 226 elderly subjects showed that almost 40 percent had vitamin levels that were two standard deviations below the mean obtained by younger subjects who took the same dosage.[25] The physical well-being of our subjects is as important to psychobiography as their personalities.

Woolf's food intake, for instance, which was often reduced by a depression-induced anorexia, was further diminished in the last year of her life by government-ordered rationing. She claimed in her diary that "our ration of margarine is so small that I cant think of any pudding save milk pudding.

We have no sugar to make sugar puddings: no pastry, unless I buy it ready made. The shops don't fill till midday. Things are bought fast. In the afternoon they are often gone. Meat ration diminishes this week. Milk is so cut that we have to consider even the cats saucer." [26] When she received a pound of butter from Vita Sackville-West in November 1940, Woolf wrote back a rhapsodic letter detailing the glories of its taste and consistency. A month before her suicide, she noted that "food becomes an obsession. I grudge giving away a spice bun. Curious—age, or the war?" [27] How much of a role did malnutrition (perhaps complicated by increased alcohol intake) play in her last depression and her increased sense of vulnerability?

Mental functioning in the elderly can be affected by numerous physical conditions, especially when they occur in combination. In one study, a diagnosis of acute confusional states (ACS) accounted for 26 percent of geriatric patients; accompanied by any of a number of symptoms—attention deficits, disorientation, sleep disturbances, incoherent speech, delusions, hallucinations, or paranoia—ACS can result from a variety of factors: cardiovascular disorders, infection (ranging from mild urinary tract infections to pneumonia) or fever, drug intoxication, metabolic and nutritional disorders, neurological disorders, sleep loss, or excessive or deficient sensory input. The multifactorial nature of ACS has led some researchers to hypothesize that age-related changes in the brain and other organs reduce the functional reserve of the elderly to withstand assaults that younger patients endure without cognitive impairment. And since roughly 85 percent of the aged have a chronic disease or disability, repercussions can be common. Psychological difficulties can also arise from lack of sleep; it is estimated that 25 to 40 percent of the elderly experience sleep disturbances (insomnia, interrupted sleep, sleep apnea) that appear to increase with age.[28]

Drugs and alcohol are a significant problem for the elderly because older bodies metabolize differently. Excretion of drugs from the body is slowed. Kidney function drops 50 percent between the ages of thirty and eighty, which means that more of the drug remains in the system longer. Body water levels may decrease from 25 percent to 18 percent from age twenty to sixty, whereas total body fat may increase from 10 percent to 50 percent. With less muscle and more fat per pound, the older body absorbs a greater amount of fat-soluble drugs in proportion to the body mass. Serum albumin (a plasma protein) levels are reduced by 15 to 25 percent in the elderly, and since many psychotropic drugs bind to albumin, reduced binding frees up greater amounts of these drugs for absorption into body tissues. In some cases elderly patients require only one-tenth the dosage a younger patient would need for the same effect. In older brains neurons usually become more sensitive to drugs; this seems especially true for drugs that depress the central nervous system. Thus, drugs and alcohol that produce few disturbing side effects in the young (and so are overlooked by family members as well as by the family doctor) can create serious problems in mental functioning for the elderly, especially since they are by far the largest users of sedative-hypnotics and tranquilizers, and perhaps as many as 10 percent of adults over sixty years of age abuse alcohol. Woolf did take sedative-hypnotics to alleviate insomnia and manic excitement through the years, specifically chloral hydrate, veronal, trional, medinal, adalin, sodium bromide, and potassium bromide, all of which can be addictive and cause central nervous system depression. Prolonged intake of potassium bromide can even cause mental deterioration. Leonard Woolf's early notations of what medicines his wife took show that she used them cautiously—minimal doses only as long as mood-induced insomnia persisted, usually a matter of a few days—but he stopped recording this information in 1922, so we do not know which drugs or what dosages she may have taken in the last year of her life.[29] Our ignorance at least should caution us to approach her decision to die with more humility and uncertainty than Freudian theory admits.

Although studies suggest that the elderly exhibit no changes in their personality scores (indeed, older subjects score slightly lower in neuroticism compared to younger), a psychiatric illness is more likely to produce serious cognitive changes in the elderly than in the young, and it is probable that their increased vulnerability is related to the substantial neurological changes that occur with age. Even though not morally or psychologically merited, major depression afflicts the elderly in areas in which they are already suffering deficits and so can magnify their sense of vulnerability. Motor performance deteriorates, and some aspects of secondary memory, attention, motivation, and drive are impaired. As psychiatric patients age, personality traits that in the past may have helped them cope with life's stresses and strains can become exaggerated or defensive under the additional stress of a biologically induced psychiatric disorder. Pessimism that once helped individuals detect and critically scrutinize unrealistic ideas in their youth may, in old age, produce such a gloomy and nihilistic outlook upon life that suicide can seem a preferable option. Loss of visual, auditory, and olfactory acuity, as well as loss of mobility, may so isolate older persons that their previous hypersensitivity and suspiciousness (which once might have served to protect them from others' aggression) can be exacerbated into a paranoia that denies them comfort and aid when they need them most. Perfectionistic tendencies that in the past drove individuals to do their best work may become so rigid and inhibiting that they interfere with productivity and decision making. Loss of mobility and energy may undermine the fragile sense of self-esteem of narcissist personalities if they coped by physically seeking out support from others.[30]

Even "normal" persons must reorganize their previous coping mechanisms when they age: high-energy solutions for stressful events (e.g., working overtime to earn more money) must be replaced by low-energy solutions (e.g., spending less), or perhaps even resignation to and acceptance of inescapable limitations. Low-energy individuals may either find their old coping styles inadequate, or they may exaggerate their passivity if old age reinforces dependency. Some may get so desperate about not being able to solve their problems quickly that they act impulsively beyond their physical endurance or their judicious control. Frustration may diminish the elder's self-esteem; this in turn can exacerbate a fear of future stressful events, making them much worse than they really are. All these factors may also increase the risk of suicide. But whatever coping measures are applied, aging gradually reduces the number of options we can choose from, and individuals vary enormously in their beliefs about what options are acceptable to them.[31] Environmental pressures can combine with biological ones: the impact of multiple personal losses, loss of mobility, social isolation, drops in income, and loss of status can be magnified by a reduced capacity to deal with trauma.

In the end, we cannot explain Woolf's suicide by means of the events in her life. Depression alters the patient's perception and evaluation of the "story line" and significance of those events, aging can increase one's vulnerability to depression's insidious whisper, and it would be a matter of blind luck if we could empathize so completely as to see her death with her eyes. It is tempting to approach psychotic or suicidal thinking as if it were just a matter of conflicted thinking resolvable by therapeutic insight. But such a perspective obliterates the troubling difference of insanity, as A. Alvarez concludes:

> To the extent that suicide is logical, it is also unreal: too simple, too convincing, too total, like one of those paranoid systems . . . by which madmen explain the whole universe. The logic of suicide is different. It is like the unanswerable logic of a nightmare . . . : everything makes sense and follows its own strict rules; yet, at the same time, everything is also different, perverted, upside down. Once a man decides to take his own life he enters a shut-off, impregnable but wholly convincing world where every detail fits and each incident reinforces his decision.[32]

If suicides cannot see any other way out, shouldn't we be more worried about our own motivations when we arbitrarily reconstruct their intentions by cloaking them in the word *unconscious?* As George Howe Colt reminds us, survivors of suicides typically feel two things: an intense need to find out "why" their loved ones decided to end their life and "guilt" that they and their wisdom were not there to prevent tragedy. "Guilt," Colt concludes, "is a way of bringing control back into a situation that seems out of control." It becomes part of the motivation to explain the "why" we think we are discovering. Are we not acting from an unconscious guilt when we try to rearrange Woolf's felt options or to moralize on her lack of self-control? And what other unexamined emotions or cultural attitudes drive us? Historically, suicides generally have elicited considerable fear and anger. Although the Greeks and Romans considered it an honorable and even rational act under proper circumstances (such as painful illness or intolerable constraint), in Christian Europe the bodies of suicides were degraded, hanged by the feet, dragged through the streets, burned and thrown on the public garbage heap, their hands cut off. In England an unsuccessful suicide was imprisoned as a felon as late as 1961. Why should there be such intense, emotional reactions to someone else's private despair? Suicide, as Wittgenstein reasoned, is the primal challenge to all ethical systems because it undermines the general consensus that life is good, just as psychosis challenges our notions of rationality and free will.[33] More to the point, loss of self-control, which both affective illness and aging can impose upon us without our permission, is so fearful that we blame suicides (or their parents, family, spouses, lovers, etc., the alleged "killers" of Virginia Woolf) for their failure to conquer what we ourselves find so easy to deny.

Notes

1. Kay Redfield Jamison, "Mood Disorders and Patterns of Creativity in British Writers and Artists"; Nancy C. Andreasen, "Creativity and Mental Illness: Prevalence Rates in Writers and Their First-Degree Relatives." On historical figures, see Frederick K. Goodwin and Kay Redfield Jamison, *Manic-Depressive Illness,* 332–49; Gordon Claridge, Ruth Pryor, and Gwen Watkins, *Sounds from the Bell Jar.*

2. Susan J. Blumenthal and David J. Kupfer, eds., *Suicide over the Life Cycle,* 7–8, 26–29; Marilyn S. Albert and Mark B. Moss, eds., *Geriatric Neuropsychology,* 126; Albert and Moss, *Geriatric,* 115. These figures are based upon H. Resnick and J. Cantor's essay, "Gerifacts," in *Geriatrics* 22 (1967): 68.

3. Alma H. Bond, *Who Killed Virginia Woolf?* 15.

4. Virginia Woolf, *The Letters of Virginia Woolf* 6:481, 485.

5. Bond, *Woolf,* 15.

6. Ibid., 30–36, 34.

7. Thomas C. Caramagno, *The Flight of the Mind;* Thomas C. Caramagno,

"Manic-Depressive Psychosis and Critical Approaches to Virginia Woolf's Life and Work"; Blumenthal and Kupfer, *Suicide*, 67–70; P. S. Fry, *Depression, Stress, and Adaptations in the Elderly*, 21–24.

8. Goodwin and Jamison, *Manic-Depressive*, 136, 243; Anastasios Georgotas and Robert Cancro, *Depression and Mania*, 72, 337; Peter P. Roy-Byrne et al., "Suicide and Course of Illness in Major Affective Disorder"; B. M. Barraclough and D. J. Pallis, "Depression Followed by Suicide: A Comparison of Depressed Suicides with Living Depressives"; Naomi Breslau, "Migraine, Suicidal Ideation, and Suicide Attempts"; Octavia Wilberforce, *Octavia Wilberforce*, 178; Goodwin and Jamison, *Manic-Depressive*, 213, 242, 765–77; Ronald Maris, *Biology of Suicide*, 173–74.

Breslau reports that migraines heralded by aura symptoms, such as ringing in the ears, nausea, blurred vision, or extreme sensitivity to light, boost the already elevated risk of suicide among severely depressed individuals. Abnormalities in the brain's chemical messenger serotonin have been found in all three conditions (migraines, depression, and suicide), and these abnormalities are more pronounced in migraines with aura than in migraine without aura.

9. Goodwin and Jamison, *Manic-Depressive*, 493; Maris, *Biology*, passim; Blumenthal and Kupfer, *Suicide*, 128–29; George Howe Colt, *The Enigma of Suicide*, 202.

10. P. Blaney, "Affect and Memory: A Review"; Georgotas and Cancro, *Depression*, 70.

11. Dewey G. Cornell et al., "Psychomotor Retardation in Melancholic and Non-melancholic Depression: Cognitive and Motor Components"; Goodwin and Jamison, *Manic-Depressive*, 38, 270; Peter C. Whybrow et al., *Mood Disorders*, 9.

12. Fry, *Depression*, 302.

13. Woolf, *Letters* 6:482, 486; Quentin Bell, *Virginia Woolf* 2:222; Virginia Woolf, *The Diary of Virginia Woolf* 5:340.

14. Bell, *Woolf* 2:224; Georgotas and Cancro, *Depression*, 68, 72.

15. Fry, *Depression*, 187; Ming T. Tsuang et al., "Causes of Death in Schizophrenia and Manic-Depression"; Irving M. Derby, "Manic-Depressive 'Exhaustion' Deaths"; Caramagno, *Flight of the Mind*, 101–3. Quotations from J. K. Stephen's medical records were made available by Dr. J. H. Henderson, the current Medical Director of St. Andrew's Hospital.

16. Woolf, *Diary* 5:354, 358; Goodwin and Jamison, *Manic-Depressive*, 239, 241; Georgotas and Cancro, *Depression*, 82.

17. Leonard Woolf, *The Journey Not the Arrival Matters*, 79.

18. Georgotas and Cancro, *Depression*, 80–81; Jane Marcus, "Virginia Woolf and Her Violin: Mothering, Madness and Music," 35; Stephen Trombley, *All That Summer She Was Mad*, 137; Michael Harrison, *Clarence*, 243.

19. Goodwin and Jamison, *Manic-Depressive*, 771; Kay Redfield Jamison, "Psychotherapeutic Issues and Suicide Prevention in the Treatment of Bipolar Disorders," 116; Goodwin and Jamison, *Manic-Depressive*, 236.

20. *Churchill's Black Dog, Kafka's Mice, and Other Phenomena of the Human Mind*, 49.

21. Diego de Leo and Rene F. W. Diekstra, *Depression and Suicide in Late Life*, 53–68; Floyd E. Bloom and Arlyne Lazerson, *Brain, Mind, and Behavior*, 81; Albert and Moss, *Geriatric*, 3.

22. Bloom and Lazerson, *Brain*, 82; Albert and Moss, *Geriatric*, 40–41.

23. Albert and Moss, *Geriatric*, 38–47.

24. Ibid., 145, 147–48, 153–56, 199; Bloom and Lazerson, *Brain*, 82–83.

25. Whybrow et al., *Mood,* 176; Goodwin and Jamison, *Manic-Depressive,* 112; Lawrence D. Breslau and Marie R. Haug, *Depression and Aging,* 11; Albert and Moss, *Geriatrics,* 86, 110.

26. Woolf, *Diary* 5 : 344.

27. Woolf, *Letters* 6 : 448; Woolf, *Diary* 5 : 357.

28. Albert and Moss, *Geriatric,* 106–11; Breslau and Haug, *Depression,* 116.

29. Albert and Moss, *Geriatric,* 121–22, 88–89; Fry, *Depression,* 408–9; Martha Windholz et al., *The Merck Index: An Encyclopedia of Chemicals, Drugs, and Biologicals;* Leonard Woolf, Monks House Papers, collection of unpublished diaries and letters housed in the University of Sussex Library.

30. Albert and Moss, *Geriatric,* 83; Fry, *Depression,* 131, 18–19.

31. Fry, *Depression,* 180–86.

32. A. Alvarez, *The Savage God,* 116.

33. Colt, *Enigma,* 447–49; Alvarez, *Savage,* 58, 58, 45–46, 212.

4

KATHLEEN WOODWARD

Late Theory, Late Style:
Loss and Renewal in Freud and Barthes

OLD AGE is more often than not associated in our culture with loneliness and loss. Consider, for example, the results of a recent survey
of attitudes toward aging and death that was reported in the *New York
Times:* almost 80 percent of those who were interviewed feared a slow descent toward death in a nursing home more than they did dying rapidly of
a disease. What predominates is anxiety over the loss of function, over the
loss of family and friends through death, over the loss of one's home, over
a slow . . . loss.[1]

We find this expression of a pessimism about old age, particularly aging
as it is refracted through the prism of loss, in theoretical texts as well. The
psychoanalyst Gregory Rochlin's *Griefs and Discontents: The Forces of
Change* is a case in point.[2] Rochlin admirably extends Freud's theory of
mourning over the entire course of life, arguing that our lives are shaped
and reshaped by losses which are succeeded by restitution. As the subtitle
of his book declares, loss can be a force for change—this is a theme of my
essay also. But Rochlin goes on to argue that in old age our strength for
change is almost invariably diminished. The invigorating cycle of loss and
restitution that he believes characterizes the rest of the life course comes to
a dead end. In Rochlin's view loss yields only impoverishment, not renewal.
In old age mourning is blocked; melancholia (depression) results.

Although Rochlin's formula accurately describes in psychoanalytic
terms the experience of some people in old age, his portrait of the psychodynamics of old age itself reinforces the prevalent and dark view of old
age as a period of inevitable and crippling losses. His negative expectation
about aging, like other theories of aging as loss, can have the unfortunate

effect of fulfilling its own prophecy of aging as decline. But loss can continue to be transformative throughout old age as well as in other times of our lives. Grief can continue to be a force for change.

In this essay I focus on the dynamics of aging, loss, and creativity through the theorization of mourning itself (my example is the work of Freud) and through the expression of grief in writing, however disguised it may at first appear as criticism (my example here is Roland Barthes's *Camera Lucida*). I read Barthes's text as a countertext to Freud; at the same time I read both of their late texts as love stories, as stories of loss which are transformed into what are also stories of writing. Our lives can be broken by the loss through death of someone we loved. That is true, and I would be foolish to deny it. But they can also be impelled forward by such a loss. As we will see, Freud in old age continued his investigation of mourning in a creative way, and Barthes continued to radically invent a writing self.

How do we come to terms with the death of someone we love? This is the question Freud explored in "Mourning and Melancholia" (1917), a text which has been central to the development of research since.[3] But if "Mourning and Melancholia" is a founding text, it has also been a puzzlingly constraining text. Although the bibliography of psychoanalytic investigations of mourning has grown rather lengthy, for the most part discussions of mourning have not developed in a particularly fertile way theoretically. My disappointment with previous work on mourning, however, has not only to do with the paucity of theoretical elaboration about it. I have wished for a discourse about mourning more expressive than that provided by psychoanalysis, for writing that would combine the affective dimension of the experience of mourning (that is, the emotions associated with mourning) with theoretical descriptions of mourning as a psychological process. As Kathleen Kirby has written, "It seems that even in psychoanalysis, grief is that which is not or cannot be expressed."[4] This is certainly in great part because in psychoanalysis itself the emotions are something to be eliminated, to be unearthed and discharged, to be gotten rid of, not something to be cultivated. To this point I will return.

Three intertwined assumptions, all of which work to differentiate Freud's general model of mourning as described in "Mourning and Melancholia," guide my discussion. It is important to stress that none of them informed Freud's initial speculations on mourning (although some research since has proceeded in these directions). First is the assumption that we respond differently to the deaths of people to whom we are intimately bound at various times in our lives. Much research, for instance, on loss in childhood and adolescence turns on whether mourning is in fact even possible for a young child. My second assumption is that our responses to the death of figures who play different roles in our lives (our parents, our children, our husbands, our wives, our sisters and brothers, our friends) will depend in great part on whether that person can in some measure and in due time be "replaced." Third is the assumption that the process of mourning grows both increasingly more difficult and yet paradoxically more familiar to us as we grow older, as losses inevitably accumulate around us and as we find ourselves coming closer to death ourselves.[5] (Who has not heard the seemingly desultory conversations of friends in their seventies who, reunited after several years, talk almost casually of the lives, which may well be the deaths, of their mutual acquaintances and friends? And what of . . . ? He died last year. Death has become a common occurrence.)

Finally and most importantly I am prompted by these assumptions to suggest that mourning itself, then, may be theorized differently at various times in our lives and that we must take special care to examine closely the context in which such theories are developed, so deeply implicated can we be in the very process of mourning itself.[6] We now commonly speak of an author's or artist's late style—this very volume, in fact, stands as testimony to the generative power of that notion. Similarly, we might think in terms of late theory, placing the development of theory in the context of a person's investigation and experience (intellectual and otherwise) over the course of his or her life and privileging, for the moment, the theoretical work of the later years. But I do not mean to include all theory here. Rather I am concerned with theories about life events and processes in which the investigator's own life experiences must inevitably play a part. Thus in theorizing about the life course we must self-consciously attend to our place in it as we do so. It is the same with mourning—all the more so for the purposes of this essay where loss, grief, and late life intersect.

Can we make any generalizations about late theory? Does the very fact that theoretical questions are "invented" in, say, the final third of one's life inflect them in any way? I cannot answer these questions. But I can say with some assurance that Freud's very theorization of the emotions he associated with mourning changed radically over time and that his theoretical creativity persisted throughout his final years, a long period which was permeated with loss, physical suffering, and psychic pain.

Freud's purpose in "Mourning and Melancholia," he tells us, was to investigate not mourning but melancholia. He wanted to use the process of mourning as a foil to understand melancholia: "Dreams having served us as the prototype in normal life of narcissistic disorders, we shall now try to throw some light on the nature of melancholia by comparing it with the normal affect of mourning" (*SE* 14:243). Freud casts the difference between mourning and melancholia in clear-cut binary terms, and this false opposition has paralyzed discussions of mourning ever since. Mourning is defined as "normal." It is psychic work which has a precise purpose and goal—to "free" ourselves from the emotional bonds which have tied us to the person we loved so that we may "invest" that energy elsewhere, to "detach" ourselves so that we may be "uninhibited." Mourning is "necessary." It denotes a process which takes place over a long period of time. It is slow, infinitesimally so, as we simultaneously psychically cling to what has been lost and "test" reality only to discover that the person we loved is no longer there.

By "reality" Freud means primarily that we compare our memories with what exists in actuality, now. He portrays the process of mourning as a passionate or hyperremembering of all the memories bound up with the person we have lost. Mourning is represented as a dizzying phantasmagoria of memory. Every memory must be tested. But not only the past is at stake. Also involved is what one had imagined the future might bring. And each of those phantasies of the future must be remembered as well. As Freud wrote in his hyperterminological way: "Each single one of the memories and expectations in which the libido is bound to the object is brought up and hypercathected, and detachment of the libido is accomplished in respect of it" (*SE* 14:245). While there is something compelling about Freud's idea of the meticulous and exhaustive memory work of mourning, there is also something vague about it. And this is all that Freud could say in this particular essay about the mysterious process of mourning other than it proceeds little by little as we withdraw our psychic investment from the person we loved. How does mourning "work"? Freud cannot tell us. His explanation is that in the passage of time mourning is "accomplished": "In mourning time is needed for the command of reality-testing to be carried out in detail" (252).

For Freud the most important aspect of this work of mourning is that it must come to an end. As he wrote, "We rely upon its being overcome after a certain lapse in time" (244). Or as he expressed it in the confident little essay "On Transience" (1916), "Mourning as we know, however painful it may be, comes to a spontaneous end" (*SE* 14:307). Thus Freud defined mourning as a way of divesting ourselves of the pain of grief, of getting it over and done with. If we speak of a person as being in mourning, what inevitably we have in mind in classical Freudian terms is that at some time in the future she, or he, will be out of mourning, done with grief.

For Freud, melancholia by contrast is pathological. It is characterized primarily as a state, not a process. It is denial of the reality of loss. It is a "disorder," a "disease." Melancholia is ultimately failed, or unsuccessful, mourning. In this unequivocal distinction I find a peculiar kind of piety, an almost ethical injunction to kill the dead and to adjust ourselves to "reality." Cutting the distinction between mourning and melancholia too sharply, Freud leaves us here with no room for another place, one between a crippling melancholia and the end of mourning.

But my complaint with Freud's essay is, as I have already suggested, not only theoretical. I chafe against its clinical tone. To me his text does not seem sufficiently informed by an understanding of the experience of mourning, of the affective dimensions of grief. I do not mean to indict Freud here. But I do want to foreground the personal context in which he wrote "Mourning and Melancholia"—at the time he was interested in the dynamics of depression and the traumas associated with World War I. More generally, I want to insist here that we take a person's age and experience into critical account when we entertain their formulations of life's events.

Indeed Freud's own confessed experience and commentary confirm that the experience of grief *and* our thoughts about mourning can be subtly differentiated over the life course. Freud wrote "Mourning and Melancholia" when he was fifty-nine. What if he had written it earlier, during the period of his father's debilitating illness and death? Instead he wrote *The Interpretation of Dreams* (1900), which he later said was his "reaction" to his father's death, concluding then that for a son the death of his father "is the most important event, the most poignant loss, in a man's life" (*SE* 4:xxvi).[7] It is the word "poignant" which strikes me as inapt, as lacking the complexity and charge of ambivalence. For we know that soon after *The Interpretation of Dreams,* which testifies to Freud's hostility toward his father, Freud articulated fully what was only latent in the dream book. He developed his now famous theory of the Oedipus complex, a theory of desire and aggressivity which is rooted in particular moments in the life course for both the son and the father: the young son wants to take the place of the middle-aged father. For the middle-aged son, in other words, mourning for the father was associated with a complex of ambivalent emotions which were understood to be a reactivation of feelings experienced long ago. Perhaps, however, the opposite was the case. Perhaps the middle-aged Freud projected his feelings at the time back on earlier childhood experiences.

Or what if Freud had written "Mourning and Melancholia" not when he was in his late fifties but during his advanced old age? I think of the many losses he had to bear throughout his life. One he felt he could not. It was the loss of a four-and-a-half-year-old, his grandson Heinerle, who died in 1923 when Freud was sixty-seven. When this child died it was as if for Freud the generations collapsed together and he had lost his own son. Only a year earlier, in fact, his daughter Sophie, Heinerle's mother, had died at the age of twenty-six. But it was the loss of the (boy) child who was still small which devastated him. It has been said that this was the only time in Freud's life when he cried. Soon after Heinerle's death Freud wrote, "I don't think I have ever experienced such grief. . . . I work out of sheer necessity; fundamentally everything has lost its meaning for me."[8] Two years later he wrote to Marie Bonaparte that he no longer loved anyone. Was it not the death of his small grandson rather than the death of his father that was the most "poignant" event in his life? And his response in old age? Not aggressivity, or at least not that I can see. Rather we hear in his words his exhausted resignation, his deadening pain which was contained by his attachment to the discipline of work.

Three years after the death of his grandson Freud published *Inhibitions, Symptoms and Anxiety* (1926). He was seventy years old at the time. Under the pressure of the discontents of his own aging body, under the pressure of the loss of the grandson he loved so much, Freud turned his attention to what was virtually a new subject for him—anxiety and its relation to separation (not to castration). As John Bowlby has astutely observed, it was only in Freud's late years and in the "revolutionary late work" that is *Inhibitions, Symptoms and Anxiety* that Freud brought his theorizations of anxiety and defense into relation with his theorization of mourning. It was not until this text that Freud understood—it was for him a discovery of momentous proportions—that the "key to an understanding of anxiety" is "missing someone who is loved and longed for" (*SE* 20:134, 136). In a brilliantly clear reading of the trajectory of Freud's thought over the course of his life, Bowlby argues that in this text Freud "was struggling to free himself of the perspective" of his thought as it had developed over his long life in theory and that he succeeded, magnificently, in positing "a new vantage point" from which to see.[9] What did Freud see? He saw the figure of the mother (in Bowlby's terms, our first attachment figure). The mother, of course, is the great missing figure of Freud's work over his long life (and much of psychoanalysis since then has been devoted to elaborating precisely the figure of the mother). I might add that interestingly enough it was precisely during this period that Freud was concerned with losing his mother through death (his mother died in 1930 at the age of ninety-five; Freud was seventy-four at the time).[10]

Six years before the publication of *Inhibitions, Symptoms and Anxiety*

Freud had dealt in *Beyond the Pleasure Principle* (1920) with what I will call separation anxiety in a now famous passage that has come to be referred to simply as the *fort-da*. Recalling his little grandson playing with a wooden spool, calling *fort* ("gone") as he cast it out and *da* ("there") as he reeled it back in, Freud theorized that we learn to master loss by rehearsing it and, importantly for my purposes, by inventing compensation for that loss. Such an exercise is, I would argue, a pedagogy of the emotions, a workout in mastering both anxiety and grief, so difficult is it in this paradigmatic situation to distinguish the two emotions from each other. The child, writes Freud, "compensated himself" for the absence of his mother "by himself staging the disappearance and return of the objects within his reach" (*SE* 18:15). What the child rehearses in play, those of us older often rehearse in fantasy. What if my child were to die? My wife? My husband never to return home? Are these fantasies preparatory? Anticipatory? Do they serve the same function, do they provide compensation in the way that Freud suggests the cultural play of the *fort-da* does? I would say no. Such fantasies may even increase anxiety and anticipatory grief. But this is not my major point. What I want to underscore is that even in the scenario of the *fort-da* Freud is approving strategies for finding a way to give up (if only momentarily) the person to whom one is attached, to be independent, not dependent, an emphasis which is anticipated, as we have seen, in "Mourning and Melancholia." Indeed, as Jessica Benjamin has so astutely pointed out, the emphasis in Freudian psychoanalysis is on detaching ourselves from others, on severing the bonds of love.[11] As such it is consonant with the dominant Western tradition of valuing individualism and independence over filiation and interdependence, and as such, it should be interrogated.

But in *Inhibitions, Symptoms and Anxiety* Freud comes to a different conclusion. Representation of loss is, as it were, a lie; the experience of loss itself is of another order altogether, inexplicable in its pain. In this late work Freud seeks to understand the differences between anxiety, fear, and pain. It is, to echo John Bowlby's word, a struggle. It is as if Freud is seeking to name the unnameable, that which he cannot explain. Anxiety, Freud concludes, "has an unmistakable relation to *expectation:* it is anxiety *about* something. It has a quality of *indefiniteness and lack of object*" (*SE* 20:166). Fear is related to a definite danger. And pain? In an addendum to *Inhibitions, Symptoms and Anxiety* Freud asks a stunning question: "When does separation from an object produce anxiety, when does it produce mourning, and when does it produce, it may be, only pain?" (*SE* 20:169). Freud cannot give a satisfactory answer to his rhetorical question—that is part of the point. But the question itself serves to introduce a new category, that of pain, a pain which is irreducible, which is not assuaged by the process of mourning and the protocols of grief, a theorization of the very pain, perhaps, which he felt with the death of his grandson.

Freud had earlier remarked that "every affect . . . is only a reminiscence of an event."[12] In the case of hysteria, for example, he had argued that the disagreeable event, which had been repressed, must be remembered and, along with it, the accompanying disagreeable emotion revived. The goal of therapy was to extirpate the distressing emotion and return to a state of equilibrium, or calm. In this respect Freud's general theory of the emotions is in accordance with his view of mourning as articulated in "Mourning and Melancholia" and repeated in *Inhibitions, Symptoms and Anxiety*. The aim is to "undo the ties that bind" the bereaved person to the person he (or she) has loved and lost during "the reproduction of situations" (*SE* 20:172)— this reminds us, of course, of the *fort-da*. But Freud had now also concluded that there was another possibility altogether: that of the experience of pain, only pain. In earlier defining mourning as synonymous with our giving up of the dead, Freud had not understood or foreseen the psychic pain that could be entailed in loss—and the degree to which he could not give up his pain, the degree to which mourning as he had earlier described it was not set in motion in all cases.

Yet that very pain, I am also suggesting, contributed to Freud's continuing to revise and rethink the theoretical structures he had created throughout his life.[13] Thus I do not read Freud's late theorization of pain, in other words, in the light of Rochlin's view of the dead end of old age when loss yields only impoverishment. Rather Freud continued—to me it is thrilling—to build his life in theory.

As if in answer to the Freud who had seventy-five years earlier asserted that the death of the father is the most poignant event in a man's life, Barthes in *Camera Lucida* mourns not the father but the mother whom he adored. I read Barthes's self-portrait of his bereavement for his mother as a figure and performance of interminable grief. For me this haunting text, defined as its contents and as a tangible object (the book itself), represents the possibility of a response to loss that situates itself between mourning and melancholia. The book itself embodies a resistance to mourning which entails a kind of willed refusal to relinquish pain. Rejecting our conventional notion of mourning as it has come to us from Freud's essay on mourning and melancholia, Barthes, uncannily echoing the late theory of Freud, makes a subtle distinction between pain and emotion: "It is said that mourning, by its gradual labor, slowly erases pain; I could not, I cannot believe this; because for me, Time eliminates the emotion of loss (I do not weep), that is all. For the rest everything has remained motionless" (*CL,* 75). Over time, Barthes believes, what subsides are the emotions of grief, its wild flourishes (those associated with *Hamlet*'s Laertes, for example).[14] The emotions (what were they? despair? a sense of abandonment? Barthes does not tell us) have emptied themselves out, leaving him vacant and hollow and numbed. He has come to a dead stop: "For the rest everything has remained motionless." Does this not recall Freud's response to the death of his grandson?

Barthes insists on the particularity, the concreteness, of his loss. He refuses to assimilate his loss to an abstraction, a generality, or even to the family structure. What he has lost, he writes, is "not a Figure (the Mother), but a being" (*CL,* 75). He will not even say here *his mother.* What he has lost is "not a being, but a *quality* (a soul): not the indispensable, but the irreplaceable. I could live without the Mother (as we all do, sooner or later); but what life remained would be absolutely and entirely *unqualifiable* (without quality)" (*CL,* 75). Even when he will have survived her death, he imagines that his life will nonetheless remain impoverished.

In *Camera Lucida* Barthes seeks to understand subjectivity in terms of a person's relation to a photograph. It is as if he is exploring the possibility of sustaining the in-between of mourning and melancholia.[15] A photograph is motionless, he says, like his pain. Yet Barthes also locates the very quickening of feeling in a photograph that holds a particular emotional power for him. Unlike the Freud of "Mourning and Melancholia," he does not want his grief to subside. On the contrary, he wants those very feelings to be sustained. Affect, he writes, "was what I didn't want to reduce; being irreducible, it was thereby what I wanted, what I ought to reduce the Photograph *to;* but could I retain an affective intentionality, a view of the object which was immediately steeped in desire, revulsion, nostalgia, euphoria?" (*CL,* 21). He imagines that there must exist a photograph that will renew his numbing pain over his mother's death.

But which photograph? How can Barthes sustain "an affective intentionality"? In one of *Camera Lucida*'s few novelistic scenes we see Barthes alone at night in the rooms where his mother had died, sifting through photographs of her, looking for the one photograph which will express the quality he insists is unique to her: "the assertion of a gentleness" (*CL,* 69). We see him slowly moving back in time with her. The goal of this "gradual labor" (Freud) is not to come to the end of mourning but to maintain it. The finding of the photograph (it is a photograph of his mother taken in a garden) and his writing of that scene do not serve to sublimate his pain but to seal it. This is what he wants. He asks us to imagine him alone, gazing at the photograph of his mother: "The circle is closed, there is no escape. I suffer motionless. . . . I cannot *transform* my grief" (*CL*, 90). Nor does he wish to.

What photograph does Barthes imagine will sustain his grief? Barthes chooses from the heap of images a photograph of his mother taken years before he himself was born, when she was only five years old (just a little older, it occurs to me, than was Freud's grandson Heinerle when he died). The poignancy of youth and of old age are thus for him doubled in this photograph which represents, paradoxically, the vanishing of an appearance. Barthes selects a photograph which represents abstractly his memory of her. It is a stunning choice. The photograph (he calls it the winter garden photograph) does not serve to restore to his memory a specific event or experience he had with his mother. In *Camera Lucida* grieving is not represented in terms of a Freudian hypercathexis of memories of the person lost to death. Barthes writes, "The Photograph does not call up the past (nothing Proustian in a photograph)" (*CL*, 82). "Not only is the photograph never, in essence, a memory . . . but it actually blocks memory, quickly becomes a counter-memory" (*CL*, 91). The "essence" of memory then? It is rooted not in the actual but in the imaginary, in fantasy. This particular photograph of his mother is a kind of imaginary afterimage which takes on value in its materialization after death.

This photograph of his mother is not a souvenir, one of whose purposes is, as Susan Stewart has written, to restore the past, most often to "evoke a voluntary memory of childhood." [16] It is neither a transitional object nor a talisman. It does not soothe the child—a man who is now in his sixties—who has lost his mother. It does not function like the Freudian paradigm of *fort-da* to master separation anxiety, to transform his grief. Its purpose is to reinforce his pain. Thus *Camera Lucida* is like a meditative theoretical dream whose purpose is the fulfillment of a wish. If Barthes will not abandon his countermemory of his mother, then in a sense he can't be lost. If there is a dialectic at work in the family structure of parent and child theorized by Freud in his middle age (the Oedipus complex), so too there is represented here a dialectic in the emotions associated with this structure—an oscillation between the indeterminate poles of anxiety and grief, an oscillation which produces, perhaps, "only pain," the pain Freud wrote of so provocatively in his late text *Inhibitions, Symptoms and Anxiety*.

As theorized in psychoanalysis, mourning is a process that takes place unconsciously. As Freud and others have described it, part of the process is the psychic taking into ourselves, the *internalization,* of the figure of the person we mourn. But in Barthes's gesture of *externalizing* the figure of his mother, he undertakes to block the work of mourning. We can read "I cannot transform my grief" as "I will not." Thus my understanding of the representation of mourning in *Camera Lucida* with its emphasis on exteriorization goes counter to Nicholas Abraham and Maria Torok's explanation of the process at work in the inability to mourn. To the process of introjection in so-called normal mourning, they propose the process of incorporation in an impossible mourning. Their suggestive metaphor is that of the split-off crypt located psychically inside the body and containing what cannot be forgotten, or in the words of the French philosopher Jacques Derrida in "Fors," "the very thing that provokes the worst suffering"; what is contained is a "secret" constituted out of "intolerable pain." Of Abraham and Torok's theory of mourning refused, Derrida explains: "I pretend to keep the dead alive, intact, *safe (save) inside me,* but it is only in order to refuse, in a necessarily equivocal way, to love the dead as a living part of me, dead *save in me,* through the process of introjection, as happens in so-called 'normal' mourning. . . . Faced with the impotence of the process of introjection (gradual, slow, laborious, mediated, effective), incorporation is the only choice: fantasmatic, unmediated, instantaneous, magical, sometimes hallucinatory" (71). Cryptic incorporation is a secret process that "marks the effect of impossible or refused mourning" (78). It is hidden from oneself. But Barthes wishes to keep his pain no secret. In concretizing the production of his pain in relation to a photograph (not a fetish, not a transitional object), he seeks to remain in mourning, to retain his psychic pain. J.-B. Pontalis has described psychic pain as referring to a state halfway between anxiety and attachment to others. We may conclude here that it occupies a middle position *in between* mourning and melancholia. Barthes's pain is more akin to sorrow, then, than melancholia (depression), a distinction which the psychoanalyst Joseph Smith can help us to understand. "In sorrow," Smith writes, "the degree of pain expresses the personal value of what has been lost. In depression the degree of pain is a measure of what is thought required to undo the loss, but it is also the pain of not being able to grieve." [17]

Camera Lucida is haunted by a kind of death-work. Barthes makes it painfully clear that this photograph of his mother is a condensation of all deaths across the generations—of the child he never had, of his mother's death, of his own death. As Barthes nursed his mother into her death she became his "feminized child." As he looks at the photograph he thinks, "The only 'thought' I can have is that at the end of this first death, my own death is inscribed" (*CL,* 92–93). If the mother is the mirror for the infant, this photograph of his mother, still a child herself, shows him his death, the death of the man who is not yet born. Not just in the ontological sense that death will come to all of us in due time but in a more literal way. Inscribed in the photograph of his mother is the genetic code of his family, "the truth of lineage" as he puts it (*CL*, 103). Gazing into the photograph of his mother as a young child, Barthes sees into the future which is old age. "The Photograph," he writes, "is like old age: even in its splendor, it disincarnates the face, manifests its genetic essence" (*CL*, 105). In old age we are increasingly dispossessed of our "individual" bodies, even as we are burdened by them. What remains is the idea of that body, an essence of genetic generational memory.

The photograph represents the catastrophe of death, which is its repetition. In an almost Freudian way Barthes forces himself to feel that our bodies carry death in them. "In front of the photograph of my mother as a child," he writes, "I tell myself: she is going to die: I shudder, like Winnicott's psychotic patient, *over a catastrophe which has already occurred*" (*CL*, 96). In the apartment that had belonged to his mother and in the space of his book, Barthes imagines for himself the repetition of the catastrophe, replaying it over and over in his mind, reliving the death which has already occurred, witnessing and producing his own loss.

Barthes surrounds the figuration of his grief with theoretical meditations on photography. He acknowledges his "uneasiness" (he puts it gently) with being "torn between two languages, one expressive, the other critical" (*CL*, 8). He invents awkward and precious terms—the *punctum*, the *pensum*, the *studium*—which distract us from what they are meant to refer to. What I remember of *Camera Lucida* is the tableau of grief. What I consistently forget is Barthes's critical vocabulary of photography. But Barthes can also write movingly of mourning and photography together: "there [is] in every photograph: the return of the dead" (*CL*, 9). Anxiety and grief, endlessly repeated.

To review: as Freud defines mourning in his essay "Mourning and Melancholia," its aim is our adaptation to "reality." The metaphor is that of detaching binding ties, of undoing ties that bind and constrict. "The complex of melancholia," he wrote, "behaves like an open wound" (*SE* 14:253). For Freud, then, the work of mourning is the work of healing a wound. It is a rite of passage out of the shadow of death and into reality. In *Camera Lucida* Barthes explores photography as a "wound," as a way of refusing to allow the wound of his mother's death to heal (21). In *Camera Lucida* Barthes etches his own death with the tones of fatality. "From now on I could do no more than await my total, undialectical Death," he wrote (72).

As we know, in what was to be an uncanny and tragic coincidence

Barthes died in an automobile accident the very year that *Camera Lucida* was published.

We will never know if Barthes would have been able to sustain his grief. Nor would we have necessarily wanted to hold him to his vow. He died soon after his mother died, and he died at a relatively young age—sixty-five. For all that and perhaps because of it, I read the tableau of Barthes in mourning for his mother as representing the limit in old age of coming to terms with our losses. Barthes's *Camera Lucida* does not present us with proof of this, of course. But *Camera Lucida* elegantly presses us to consider this possibility, presenting a challenge to the early (and still commonly held) Freudian notion of grief as something to be purged.

In loss and at the upper limit in old age (which will be different for every person), we very well may not want to "free" ourselves from the emotional bonds which have secured us to others we have loved so that we may "invest" our energy elsewhere. We may not detach ourselves from our losses. Instead we may live with them. And then die with them. If grief is painful, it is also absorbing. Further, it may be sustaining. Even more, it may be transforming—of thought, of style, of life itself. For: some attachments remain binding phantasmatically forever.

As *Camera Lucida* suggests, with some losses mourning may never come to an end—and such mourning need not necessarily signify impoverishment in old age, as Rochlin would have it. We may remain in between mourning and melancholy. I do not mean, of course, that this may be characteristic of grief in advanced old age only. I am thinking also of a parent losing a young child, or perhaps a child of any age. For the Freud of "Mourning and Melancholia" the end of mourning is concurrent with the understanding that our life must be reshaped through new attachments. But Freud had himself once cautioned that mourning was age-specific. In "On Transience" he wrote that when mourning "has renounced everything that has been lost, then it has consumed itself, and our libido is once more free (in so far as we are still young and active) to replace the lost objects by fresh ones equally or still more precious" (*SE* 14:307). In a sense Freud, as we have seen, pursued the implications of these important parenthetical thoughts in *Inhibitions, Symptoms and Anxiety*.

Similarly, if Barthes's wish was to seal his grief forever, to render it immovable, unchangeable, unalterable, immutable, still his writing hand was moving across the page to achieve this effect of motionlessness. His grief was expressed creatively. Significantly, in *Camera Lucida* the sixty-five-year-old Barthes turned to what was for him a new kind of writing (just as in *Inhibitions, Symptoms and Anxiety* the seventy-year-old Freud turned to new theoretical questions). There is a surprising risk in Barthes's rhetoric of self-expression and a near self-indulgence (and why not?) in metaphor which earlier in his career he had denied. In the late fall of 1977, just after his mother had died, Barthes astonished his audience at a seminar in Paris by expressing his desire to "escape from the prison house of critical metalanguage" and, in J. Gerald Kennedy's words, "through simpler, more compassionate language to close the gap between private experience and public discourse."[18] *Camera Lucida,* written over a period of some seven weeks during the spring of 1978, represents a definitive break with Barthes's other writing. "Nostalgia, sympathy, and final devotion," "all matters of bourgeois sentiment," as Kennedy puts it, surface on the pages of *Camera Lucida* (390). Barthes insists in *Camera Lucida* that he could not *"transform"* his pain, but his pain radically transfigured his style. There is in addition the stunning strength in Barthes's willful resistance to the teleology of mourning which takes the form of neither denial nor negation. With *Camera Lucida* as our text we may conclude that the refusal to allow mourning to run its so-called normal course can vivify and not impoverish a life.

In "Mourning and Melancholia" Freud did not address the possibility of a creative outcome of loss. But as we have seen, both his late work and that of Barthes testify to just such a possibility. In both cases loss in old age stimulated creativity. Coincidentally, uncannily, in their late years both challenged the then canonical notion—and it was Freud's own invention—that mourning in order to be successful was signaled by the end of grief, the cessation of its pain. Freud posed a new theoretical question, challenging his own earlier formulations. Barthes risked the sentimental in style, insisting in particular on retaining an "affective intentionality" (*CL,* 21). Years earlier Proust, Barthes's historical alter ego, had written, "I had to recapture from the shade that which I had felt, to reconvert it into its psychic equivalent. But the way to do it, the only one I could see, what was it— but to create a work of art." The crucial difference between the Proustian and Barthesian aesthetic is this: Barthes sought not to recapture his feelings of long ago but to sustain his sorrow, to dwell in his pain which was for him not representative of a past "moment of being"—the phrase is Virginia Woolf's—but the locus of his being in the present.[19]

Recently George H. Pollock, a psychoanalyst who has done research in the fields of mourning and aging for many years, has explicitly linked creativity and the process of mourning, insisting that "the successful completion of the mourning process results in creative outcome." "Indeed," he writes, "the creative product may reflect the mourning process in theme, style, form, content, and it may itself stand as a memorial." [20] It is in this light that I understand Freud's *Inhibitions, Symptoms and Anxiety* and Barthes's *Camera Lucida:* as reflections in old age of the creative power of loss and its accompaniments, pain and grief. In their different ways, these texts—the writing itself—are memorials to those losses.

More generally, then, what is the relation of writing about mourning to mourning itself? A memorial serves to keep alive a memory, to sustain it, to preserve it. The connotation is positive: a memorial, a monument, honors our dead, commemorates those we have lost and thus stands as a testament to our pain, our losses. There are times when we either may not be able to or should not detach ourselves from the pain of loss, although the canonical notion of mourning prescribes the opposite, a forgetting.

In *Camera Lucida* a sixty-five-year-old man writes eloquently of his love for his mother, unfashionable though it was at the time in his circle to do so. In my essay I have read Barthes's story of the vanishing of his mother as a story of commemoration and of tribute through writing which contests the traditional Freudian view of mourning. And indeed much recent work on mourning in cultural studies has taken just this form: it suggests that loss through death sets writing in motion, resulting in the declaration or expression of pain and a revision of the theorization of mourning itself.

Thus, for example, the anthropologist Renato Rosaldo has written of the sudden death of his wife, the anthropologist Michelle Rosaldo, while they were doing research together in the Philippines. He tells us of the wholly unexpected force of his grief, which impelled him to understand the experience and practices of the Ilongots otherwise and to undertake his own research differently, research that deals in great part with the expression of grief in everyday life outside of publicly acknowledged rituals and symbolic practices. It is a love story, a death story, a writing story. Similarly the cultural critic and AIDS activist Douglas Crimp, who has lost many of his friends to AIDS, has called into question Freud's opposition between activism and mourning. As we have seen for the Freud of "Mourning and Melancholia," mourning is a long and private affair that takes place in the solitary mise-en-scène of the psyche; it is unconscious work which precludes any interest in the outside world. But for Crimp, the grief of loss and the violence of prejudice encountered daily by members of the gay community have transformed mourning into militancy.[21] The experience of grief and rage (Crimp implies that the two are here inseparable) is the catalyst for politicization which takes the form of mobilizing as a group and also, in Crimp's case, writing. Again, a love story, a death story, a writing story that protests the commonly accepted notion of grief as something to rid oneself of privately. And my own essay? I began my reading about mourning only after I too had lost someone so central to my life that with him I lost my sense of a future: it was unimaginable. My own essay on mourning, then, is also a love story.

In my other versions of this essay (it has been written and rewritten and published in two previous versions before this one), my own experience of grief was latent, not manifest, not written, not expressed. I did not even gesture toward it. I attempted to inflect the emotional dimensions of grief through the stories of other people, not my own. My own story seemed then too personal, too impressionistic perhaps. But I no longer think that. What I see too is that I was not only then following the protocols of the profession of literary criticism but I was also modeling my own writing in part after Freud, continuing the tradition that one should not express emotions but analyze them. This time my essay is, openly, an essay on both mourning and aging—I have a strong attachment to the texts and figures of the late Freud and Barthes, and I was prompted also by the experience of grief and the desire to learn more about mourning.

My guess is that most research on mourning is inspired by the experience of loss itself, by people who have been touched by grief. The model of research on grief, therefore, would be diametrically opposed to that of the "objective observer" who is "detached" from the subject of inquiry. Barthes's *Camera Lucida* thus stands for me as a model for such research. It is a subtle and powerful investigation into the process of mourning while at the same time it is a moving expression of that grief, a writing of loss that is simultaneously an expression of creativity. *Camera Lucida* thus serves as a prototype for human sorrow. Our reading of it would not have the purpose of mastering sadness as implied in Freud's model of the *fort-da* but rather that of preparing ourselves for such an experience and understanding the strength of expressing it in writing. It was long ago I read Simone de Beauvoir's *A Very Easy Death,* an eloquent and searching account of her mother's death by cancer at the American Hospital in Paris. A love story, a death story, a writing story. Years later I held on to that book—I do not mean literally—as I watched Michel Benamou, my companion of seven years, die in that same hospital. That book did not make the pain less; it made it more real. This essay is dedicated to his memory.

Notes

1. "Most Want Long Lives but Fear Dependence," *New York Times,* Nov. 18, 1991 (National edition).
2. Gregory Rochlin, *Griefs and Discontents.*
3. Sigmund Freud, "Mourning and Melancholia," *SE* 14:239–58.
4. Kathleen Kirby (Syracuse University), "Indifferent Boundaries." For an excellent critical review of psychoanalytic literature on mourning up to the mid-sixties, see Lorraine D. Siggens, "Mourning," 14–25. For recent readings of literature in terms of mourning, see Sharon Cameron, "Representing Grief," 15–41 (an essay which strangely avoids psychoanalysis), and Neal L. Tolchin, *Mourning, Gender, and Creativity in the Art of Herman Melville,* which contains a comprehensive bibliography of work (literary and otherwise) on mourning.
5. Anna Freud makes a distinction between *grief* in a child and *mourning* in an adult (Anna Freud, "About Losing and Being Lost," 9–19). For Melanie Klein, on the other hand, mourning is a critical phase in the development of the infant, with melancholia associated with the depressive position (Klein, "Mourning and Its Relation to Manic-Depressive States," 125–53).

The psychoanalyst George H. Pollock has steadily made important contributions to research on mourning. He insists that we should study mourning in relation to the life course and in particular to aging. As he asserts in "Aging or Aged," "My studies of various object losses, notably childhood parent loss, childhood sibling loss, adult spouse loss, and adult loss of a child, convince me that it is necessary to describe the function, role and meaning of the important lost 'object' at different periods of the life course. . . . When viewed on a chronological axis, the significance of that which is 'lost' reveals different meanings and functions during the adult periods. For example, the meaning of a spouse is different when one is in the early twenties, thirties, forties, fifties, sixties, seventies, eighties. In a recent study I described the changing meanings siblings have for each other during the adult years and how these sibling relationships are related to adult friendships. . . . During the adult periods, parents and children change in their meanings for each other. The kinship relationships always remain, but the individuals may have different *significances* for each other at various periods of adult life" (552). See also Pollock's "On Mourning, Immortality, and Utopia," 334–62.

Several empirical studies lend support to this view, of which I note only two here. In "Grief Reactions in Later Life," 289–94, Karl Stern, Gwendolyn M. Williams, and Miguel Prados conclude that in older people mourning is marked less by overt signs of grief and more by actual physical illness. The authors also observe a tendency in older people toward the idealization and glorification of those whom they have lost (this may be the case in Barthes's portrayal of his mother in *Camera Lucida*). More generally, Jerome Grunes and Wendy Wasson make the case that the process of mourning is different in the second half of life—mourning may never be complete—and cite this example of an older woman to make their point succinctly: "Incomplete mourning seems to be the lot for many elderly. An eighty-year-old woman, telephoning for an appointment, said that she was suffering from the loss of her great love. When seen at her first appointment, it was discovered that her husband-lover had passed away ten years before but that the painful aspects of his loss were as fresh as if he had recently died" (Grunes and Wasson "The Significance of Loss and Mourning in the Older Adult," in *The Problem of Loss and Mourning,* 182).
6. Similarly, one may resist a certain theorization of mourning depending upon

one's own experience of mourning. A fascinating instance of such resistance from the history of psychoanalysis itself comes to us from Karl Abraham. In "A Short Study of the Development of the Libido, Viewed in the Light of Mental Disorders" (1924), Abraham reports that when he first read "Mourning and Melancholia" he resisted the idea of the introjection of the figure who has been lost. Only later did he realize, he says, that his resistance was due to the fact that the previous year he had lost his father and in fact had displayed physical signs of the psychological process of introjection, which he did not wish to acknowledge.

7. Freud also wrote in *The Interpretation of Dreams* that "men . . . dream mostly of their father's death and women of their mother's" (*SE* 4:256). To my knowledge this interesting observation, which could be explained on the basis of intergenerational gender identification, has not been explored since. It raises the issue of possible connections between mourning and gender. I do not know of any empirical research that deals with mourning and gender other than studies of the different responses of men and women to the death of their spouses; the difference, however, is only noted, not accounted for theoretically. At the other end of the spectrum, Hélène Cixous has theorized mourning in terms of gender, speculating that women do not mourn (that is, do not come to an end of their suffering) but sustain themselves with pain. I make much the same argument here but not in terms of gender. See Hélène Cixous, "Castration or Decapitation," 41–55; see also Juliana Schiesari, "Appropriating the Work of Women's Mourning."

8. Freud to Katá and Lajos Levy, June 11, 1923, in Ernst L. Freud, ed., *Letters of Sigmund Freud*.

9. John Bowlby, *Separation*, 49–50.

10. What was Freud's reaction to his mother's death? It was radically different, he tells us, from his reaction to his father's death, a difference in the intensities of grief which prompts me to underline, again, that mourning itself must be theorized differently over the course of life. Freud found that his mother's death brought him relief, not pain. He gauged his response. It was "peculiar," he judged. And yet he astutely grasped the meaning of his response. As he wrote to Sandor Ferenczi about his reaction to his mother's death: It "has affected me in a peculiar way, this great event. No pain, no grief, which probably can be explained by the special circumstance—her great age, my pity for her helplessness toward the end; at the same time a feeling of liberation, of release, which I think I also understand. I was not free to die as long as she was alive, and now I am" (Freud to Sandor Ferenczi, Sept. 16, 1930, in Freud, *Letters*, 400).

Freud's mother was certainly of an age to die. For expected deaths, we often prepare ourselves by anticipatory mourning. But for those who die at a very advanced age there may be such a subtly incremental separation from them in expectation of their death that we cannot even call it anticipatory mourning. Perhaps in such cases mourning does not take place either before or after death. The work of mourning is primarily an unconscious process, and perhaps our separation from people of a very advanced age can be effected consciously. I do not mean to say here that Freud did or did not do the work of anticipatory mourning for his mother. But from his own account we may conclude that he consciously felt no grief.

11. Jessica Benjamin, *The Bonds of Love*.

12. "In a discussion before the Vienna Psycho-Analytical Society in 1909, Freud is reported by Jones . . . as having said that 'every affect . . . is only a reminiscence of an event'" (James Strachey, Editor's Introduction to *Inhibitions, Symptoms and Anxiety, SE* 20:84).

13. See Peter Homans, *The Ability to Mourn*. Homans argues that in the life

and work of Freud, mourning works to set individuation and theory in motion. "The process of individuation," he writes, "acquires clarity and concreteness when it is understood in relation to the twin realities of mourning and monuments—the one psychological, the other social structural. It is the creative outcome of mourning, and the outcome of individuation is in turn the creation of meaning, a building up of new structures of appreciation born of loss" (263).

14. What of Lacan's reading of Hamlet's celebrated "inability to mourn"? In "Desire and the Interpretation of Desire in *Hamlet*" (1959), Lacan is concerned with the trajectory of the tragedy toward Hamlet's "act," and thus with the fact that a crime has been committed. Like so many other commentators, he is fascinated with Hamlet's so-called procrastination: "Hamlet just doesn't know what he wants" (26). But if we think of grief (that is, the *state*, not the *process*, of mourning) in terms of not giving something up, then we can understand Hamlet this way: he does not act because he does not want to, not because he can't. The object of Hamlet's desire is double: his own emotions (his own pain), which he wishes to retain so to maintain the conversation with the dead (the Ghost), the father. In his reading of *Hamlet* Lacan stresses mourning in its social appearances, observing that it is through discourse that we as social beings complete the work of mourning: "The work of mourning is accomplished at the level of the *logos*" (38). But from my perspective we can understand Hamlet as purposely not wanting to enter into symbolic rituals. Hamlet does not want to bury the dead, yet we could not describe his grief in terms of the crypt, in Abraham and Torok's sense.

15. I am alluding here to the stimulating notion of the in-between in the work of J.-B. Pontalis. See his *Frontiers in Psychoanalysis.*

16. Susan Stewart, *On Longing*, 145.

17. Jacques Derrida, "Fors," 98, 69; Joseph Smith, "Identificatory Styles in Depression and Grief," 260.

The point I am making here pivots on the distinction between externalization and internalization (introjection, incorporation). Internalizing the lost object as a part of mourning has become something of a theoretical piety which may be born out of the superego. Pontalis has written that the "*work-of-mourning* [is] a complex process that operates no longer on representations but rather on an *object* incorporated into the shell, the container, of the ego; a process, therefore, that is intrapsychic in the strongest sense, and whose teleological purpose has been said to 'kill the dead' " (Pontalis, "On Death-Work in Freud, in the Self, in Culture" [1978], 85). Or as Hans W. Loewald has insisted: "Mourning involves not only the gradual, piecemeal relinquishment of the lost object, but also the internalization, the appropriation of aspects of this object—or rather, of aspects of the relationship between the ego and the lost object which are 'set up in the ego' and become a relationship within the ego system" (Loewald, "Internalization, Separation, Mourning, and the Superego," 493).

Smith also makes the following fascinating point: "In grief one has the courage to take pity on oneself—without shame, and for precisely that for which one hurts. If it be a stubbed toe, as it were, then that is the pain acknowledged. The grieving person does not at that point pridefully substitute some 'major loss' as the rationalization for anguish. The depressive, by denying that which he has lost, is left to wallow in objectless feelings of self-pity. To fall short of grieving the actual loss is to be mired down in such 'unattached' feelings of pity, quiet, emptiness, wrongness, humiliation, and impotent rage" (Smith, "Identificatory Styles in Depression and Grief," 260).

18. See J. Gerald Kennedy, "Roland Barthes, Autobiography, and the End of Writing," 383. Barthes's mother died Oct. 25, 1977.

19. Marcel Proust quoted in Hannah Segal, "A Psychoanalytic Approach to Aesthetics," 196–207; Virginia Woolf, *Moments of Being,* 70.

20. George H. Pollock, "The Mourning Process, the Creative Process, and the Creation," 28.

21. Renato Rosaldo, "Grief and a Headhunter's Rage," 1–21; Douglas Crimp, "Mourning and Militancy," 1–18.

II

Against the Dying of the Light
Death and Creativity

5

MARCIA ALDRICH

Lethal Brevity:
Louise Bogan's Lyric Career

T HE MODERNIST POET Louise Bogan never wrote poetry easily or
voluminously. Over her lifetime she published 105 collected poems,
most of them written while she was in her twenties or thirties. *The Sleeping
Fury,* published in 1937 when Bogan was forty years old, was her last book
of new poems. She wrote no poetry from 1941 to 1949, and the *Collected
Poems, 1923–1953* added but three lyrics to the work gathered in *Poems
and New Poems,* published in 1941. In her twenties Bogan was already contrasting her own writing blocks with Keats's "sitting down every morning
and writing 200 lines, fully and easily" (*Letters,* 7). In middle age she wrote
poetry with still greater difficulty and infrequency, reaching an impasse that
persisted for some thirty years, even while she remained active as a translator and critic until her death in 1970. "The woman who died without
producing an oeuvre" was the harsh epitaph Bogan wrote for herself when
still in her thirties; she was haunted by the possibility that history would
remember her only for what she did not accomplish (*Journey,* 103).[1]

One reason for Bogan's small output, offered by many of those who
have written about her, is strict standards of artistic excellence, which created an anxious perfectionism that approached self-censorship. Bogan felt,
as she herself recognized, "the knife of the perfectionist attitude . . . at
my throat" (*Letters,* 79). But if such standards—based in a modernist,
originally masculine aesthetic of impersonality—help account for Bogan's
limited production overall, they do not in themselves explain the shape of
her creative career, the decline and disappearance of poetry in her middle
and late years. After all, Bogan worked in a modernist idiom from the start.
In *Louise Bogan's Aesthetic of Limitation,* Gloria Bowles provides a more

adequate explanation of the volume of poetry Bogan produced—or did not produce—at different stages of life. Along with the psychoaesthetics of perfectionism, Bowles cites biographical and vocational factors. The "burden" of Bogan's reviewing for the *New Yorker*, "her precarious psychological balance, her perfectionism, her sense of being unappreciated, and her idea of the innate limitations of the woman poet . . . combined to effectively put an end to her art in her early forties." [2] All of these factors are comprised in Bogan's sense of the vocation of the feminine lyric poet, which was shaped by an ideology of youthful romantic love, traditionally both the subject matter of the feminine lyric and the source of the woman poet's inspiration. It is this sense of vocation that most directly enforced change over the course of her career. For what does such a complex of assumptions leave to the middle-aged feminine lyricist?

The Traffic in Pleasure: Early Careers

Bogan was one of a number of women writers of the 1920s, including Sara Teasdale, Elinor Wylie, and Edna St. Vincent Millay, who redefined and modernized the feminine lyric. Their signature was established forms like the sonnet, and they retained the traditional concentration on intense personal feeling. In renewing the feminine lyric, however, they replaced celebrations of religious faith and the domestic sphere, predominant in poetry of the nineteenth century, with powerful sensual experience as the chosen means of transcendence. Bogan and her contemporaries still relied on love, but now it was the engine of physical sensation. Teasdale reported in a letter that she had set up a shrine to Aphrodite and declared, "She is more real to me than the Virgin." Whereas Eliot had advanced a universal, ideal order of European tradition, Bogan and her compatriots acknowledged a specific line of women's poetry leading into their own. Teasdale's anthology of love poetry by women, *The Answering Voice,* distills this tradition as it developed up to World War I, emphasizing idealistic yearning, disappointment, and memory. Although Bogan disdained the exaggerated posturing of sentimental nineteenth-century verse on the subject of love, she credited women with maintaining the line of feeling in American poetry against any exclusive modernist impulse toward irony and impersonality. Bogan identified herself with a lyric of emotion because it derived from the valid foundation of women's art: "Women's feeling, at best, is closely attached to the organic heart of life"; to women belonged the functions of "security, receptivity, enclosure, nurturance." Albeit ambivalently, Bogan accepted the sentimental tradition as one that sustained her own poetry. The headline of her obituary in the *New York Times*—"Louise Bogan, Noted Poet Who Wrote about Love, Dead"—dramatizes the extent to which she was identified with the one subject.[3]

It was not a subject free from impediments. Indeed, Bogan's struggle as a writer was from the outset contingent on the identification of the female poet with heterosexual love, the well of feeling. Remarks in "The Heart and the Lyre," Bogan's evaluation of the female tradition, suggest why. Here she links strength of emotion with the feminine lyric gift: "In women, more than in men, the intensity of their emotions is the key to the treasures of the spirit." How and when could one find special strength of feeling? It was available in moments of crisis, in the throes of romance. Of "Zone," first published in *Poems and New Poems*, Bogan noted, "I wrote a poem . . . which derives directly from emotional crisis, as, I feel, a lyric must" (*Journey*, 118). This belief, too, was an inherited feature of the feminine lyric; Teasdale, for example, placed herself in a tradition based in the inevitability of women's frustration in love. But the conviction that the lyric derives from moments of crisis creates difficulties in composition, for crisis is not a sustainable form of experience. As Malcolm Cowley emphasized, Bogan's theory made it impossible for her to write a great deal.[4] Even in her youth, a reliance upon extreme feeling limited Bogan's opportunities to create poetry.

An aesthetic of romantic crisis does permit a certain production of poetry if one has a supply of crises—such as was provided to Bogan by her biography through her twenties. She was born in 1897 into an Irish Catholic family then residing in Livermore Falls, Maine. After several other shifts, her parents moved to Boston when she was still a young girl. Her mother was, in Bogan's account, a handsome but vain woman who derived her sense of identity through attracting the romantic interest of men, however fleeting and destructive. Her energies were compulsively channeled into a traffic in pleasure—the upkeep of her figure and dress, endless arrangements of liaisons. These sexual adventures dominated Bogan's life as a young girl. On one occasion she suffered an episode of blindness lasting two days; she was never able to recall what scene had precipitated this symptom. She was "the highly charged and neurotically inclined product of an extraordinary childhood and an unfortunate early marriage, into which last state [she] had rushed to escape the first" (*Letters*, 6). Living with her family during her freshman year at Boston College, Bogan won a scholarship to Radcliffe but chose to marry Curt Alexander, a corporal in the army, rather than remain at home and attend college. Shortly after the marriage, Alexander was transferred to the Canal Zone, and Bogan, by this time pregnant, followed. She found the exotic Panamanian landscape "alien and hostile" and the marriage an even stranger threshold: "All we had in common was sex" (*Journey,* xxii). After the birth of their daughter, Alexander refused sexual relations with Bogan, and the marriage quickly deteriorated.

Like many other writers early in the century, Bogan turned cultural and personal disappointment into modernist poetry. Her first book, *Body of This Death,* published in 1923 and dedicated to her mother and daughter, takes as its subject women in the throes of love. The subject is fully traditional, but the results are not promising, for the volume finds that the literary life of feeling is one of depersonalization and disillusionment. *Body of This Death* studies the bourgeois family and marriage; the latter is sought to escape the former, but it proves an equivalent entrapment. Figures who seek to detach themselves from family through romantic passion discover that it provides no ultimate remedy. The mother's power over the daughter's fate frames many of her attempted escapes, and marital rites of passage fail. Women are identified with beautiful, often aestheticized, objects—stones, marble girls who hear "no echo save their own." The volume builds a spiral of betrayals, each ending in an image of arrest.

> To love never in this manner!
> To be quiet in the fern
> Like a thing gone dead and still.
> ("Men Loved Wholly beyond Wisdom") [5]

Female destiny is the experience of "being trapped—of being used, of being made an object" (*Journey,* 126).

Body of This Death begins on a note of hope. Heterosexual consummation, romantic love, would be the means to Bogan's self-creation; sexual love and fertility would empower her. The book's lead-off poem, "A Tale," expresses a longing for love as a means of control, as well as transcendence in the manner of the feminine lyric. Bogan, in the person of the poem's youthful protagonist, hopes for "a land of change" away from the suffocatingly familiar props of her New England childhood. Outwardly she succeeds in severing ties to her family, breaking apart what had shut her in "as lock upon lock." But the allegiance to passion under conditions of inequality, what amounts to women's objectification in male desire, can be debilitating and cruel. The body, for all its sensory power, betrays women who are conventionally young and desirable in a man's world.

> nothing dares
> To be enduring, save where, south

of hidden deserts, torn fire glares
On beauty with a rusted mouth.
Where something dreadful and another
Look quietly upon each other.
     ("A Tale")

The metonymy of the mouth, rusted and partial, paves the way to the subjects of the last couplet. There the dehumanized "something and another"
figure the depersonalizing effect of the youth's fate. "A Tale" initiates the
pattern of sexual quest and failed release in *Body of This Death*. In the
dramatic disappointment of Bogan's journey's end, we find the source of
the projected landscapes:

Here I could well devise the journey to nothing,
At night getting down from the wagon by the black barns,
The zenith a point of darkness, breaking to bits,
Showering motionless stars over the houses.
Scenes relentless—the black and white grooves of a woodcut.
     ("A Letter," *Journey*, 70–71)

The "withered arbor" in "Statue and Birds" is another sample of disillusionment, the statue representing the results of the transformation of
strong experience into the lyric, the essence of Bogan's sense of her poetic
process.

Here, in the withered arbor, like the arrested wind,
Straight sides, carven knees,
Stands the statue, with hands flung out in alarm
Or remonstrances.

Over the lintel sway the woven bracts of the vine
In a pattern of angles.
The quill of the fountain falters, woods rake on the sky
Their brusque tangles.

The birds walk by slowly, circling the marble girl,
The golden quails,
The pheasants, closed up in their arrowy wings,
Dragging their sharp tails.

The inquietudes of the sap and of the blood are spent.
What is forsaken will rest.
But her heel is lifted,—she would flee,—the whistle of the birds
Fails on her breast.

The marble girl occupies the center of the arbor, around which the birds slowly circle and from which they depart. Their motion is opposed to the marble girl's stasis; art as static perfection opposed to the freedom of the birds. Against their natural movements we can measure the girl's beautiful but frozen gesture.

The emphasis on "Here" suggests that the text we read, the poem, is also an arbor of sorts. It, too, is a sanctuary, a shady recess enshrining the female statue. But in the poem's process, the statue erodes as statue. It becomes "the marble girl" and finally the "she" of the closing stanza. This final pronoun is a composite of the statue and the depersonalized poet. The walls soften with the poet's late discovery of herself within them. Thus Bogan places her own female beauty in a withered arbor, suggesting an unnatural enervation, the loss of freedom for and by the figuration of art. Enshrinement in an artificial recess becomes another entrapment. The female statue suggests the aesthetic imperatives of Keats's Grecian urn: to attain final perfection, the marble girl must become "an object, in the double sense of being dead and also an object for aesthetic contemplation."[6] In the marble girl's arrested form, Bogan encodes her own self-defeat and complicity within the tradition that objectifies women.

The persistence of the subject of love in the feminine lyric, whether in the traditional moods or with Boganian bitterness, exemplifies a dependence common among women on youthful heterosexual ties for self-definition. The rite of passage theme in "Betrothed" shows how thoroughly the conventional female of Bogan's period was still defined by heterosexual love relationships. The betrothal song, as a set piece of nineteenth-century poetry, celebrates a young woman's passage into marriage. Bogan represents the young woman as an elegiac figure of feminine dismay.

> You have put your two hands upon me, and your mouth,
> You have said my name as a prayer.
> Here where trees are planted by the water
> I have watched your eyes, cleansed from regret,
> And your lips, closed over all that love cannot say.
>
> My mother remembers the agony of her womb
> And long years that seemed to promise more than this.
> She says, "You do not want me,
> You will go away."
>
> In the country whereto I go
> I shall not see the face of my friend

Nor her hair the color of sunburnt grasses;
Together we shall not find
The land on whose hills bends the new moon
In air traversed of birds.

The lover's hands and mouth, placed or imposed on the female, silence rather than caress, and this imposed silence seems linked to the daughter's failure to deliver herself cleanly from her mother's womb. The "you" of "Betrothed" makes proprietary claims upon the female, wrenching possession from the mother. Thus the poem emphasizes the continuity of possession from mother to husband, from daughter to wife, "lock upon lock." It is through relationship with the husband that Bogan discovers the crucial fact about women's sexual identity: they are defined by their relations with others. The female's identity never stands alone, cut free from the mother's claims of birth or from the husband's future rights.

If love as subject connects Bogan's lyric to the nineteenth century, it is still possible to distinguish women's relationships during the period of Bogan's first publications from those prevailing in the nineteenth century. The poems in *Body of This Death* define a possessive love between unequal lovers. Although the woman is often absorbed and transformed by such love, she must give up friends, family, home, and landscape, even her prior sense of self, to achieve her exaltation. The 1920s, when Bogan's volume was published, saw a shift away from a greater identification of women with women in the nineteenth century. The invention of the category of homosexuality late in the nineteenth century stands as a watershed between the two periods, creating that which is proscribed. A contemporary indicator of this shift is a group of essays compiled in the *Nation* under the title *These Modern Women.*[7] Attempting to ascertain what distinguished contemporary women's experiences, the essays describe a reorientation away from the homosocial ties of girlhood toward heterosexual relationships.

Perhaps the most economical means to sketch the cultural pressures prevailing in the 1920s is to show that the female lyric poet responded to what produced like results in two great contemporary film actresses, Greta Garbo and Louise Brooks. Their appeal to the film audience—by means of beauty, passion, and suffering—resembled the specifications for the desired and desiring female in the lyric. Garbo personified glamour, sensual expression, and inaccessibility to the general audience, a version of the closed poem encoding sexual appetite. Her film characters sacrificed themselves— to one man, for love. Brooks, on the other hand, exemplified the unbridled pleasure principle. In critical tributes her acting is a matter of instinctual physicality: she "needed no directing, but could move across the screen causing the work of art to be born by her mere presence." Directors made similar observations about Garbo, believing she embodied what Roland Barthes in "The Face of Garbo" called the "lyricism of women."[8] The impulse is to locate the basis of the actress's art in her youthful desirability. The same impulse exhibits itself in the critical response to lyric poets, whose art was the gesture of overflowing emotion. Their reception in the 1920s was not generally a matter of analysis; instead it was suffused in romance and infatuation. Many were celebrated beauties whose photographs accompanied their poems in print. Millay cut a romantic figure, rising to notice through public readings that captivated numbers of men, intensifying the propensity to collapse distinctions between poet and poetry. Wylie's much-publicized romantic life, in combination with the austere form of her beauty, was a considerable factor in the reception of her poems. In reviews, descriptions of her physical appearance and of her poems overlap.

Of course the most obvious ideal of physical beauty for women in this century has been youthfulness. As Lois Banner remarks, "An unlined face, hair neither gray nor white, a slim body with good muscle tone have been the signs of beauty achieved." After the 1920s the focus on youth came to include sophistication, glamour, and experience; however, a deepening of sensual experience was still contained within a paradigm of youth and beauty. Garbo quit the screen at age thirty-seven; Brooks's career began before she was twenty-one and lasted but thirteen years. Withdrawal from the public eye was necessary for the actresses to preserve their images from the revisions that would have accompanied their aging. They grew older behind closed doors and sunglasses. The assumption that the aging body is, in Kathleen Woodward's phrase, the "sign of deformation" links these retirements to Bogan's career.[9] In her medium Bogan was as deeply immersed in a process of youthful passion, a romantic objectification of women. The lyric, in the hands of young women, embodied qualities of youth—compression, intensity, passion, and longing—without the marks of decline associated with old age.

The allotted role of women poets, a concern with romantic love, satisfied Bogan's youthful sense of the kind of poetry she aspired to write, even if the outcome of love, as represented in *Body of This Death*, was destructive. Many writers embraced their identification with love, youth, and desirability because of the opportunities offered but never imagined their fate when they no longer were young. In Western culture, certain forms of power pass swiftly from the old to the young. Marketability in the positions historically open to women, from waitressing to acting, depends upon youthfulness. Women experience anxiety in aging because, quite simply, they may be superseded; women poets were troubled by the process of aging because it seemed to deny them their subject—passion. Valuing love, women poets of the period simultaneously valued youth. When Bogan arrived in middle age, she was faced with alternative prospects: to change the focus and process of her writing or to retire from poetry.

The Catalpa Tree: Autumns

In her thirties Bogan suffered several emotional breakdowns requiring hospitalization. She separated from and then divorced her second husband, survived her mother's death, and set up housekeeping as a single parent. The death of her mother, whom Bogan held responsible for her emotional turmoil, left much festering within the poet. At the same time, with her divorce Bogan relinquished once and for all the intensely inspiring yet potentially destructive romantic basis of her life. In the aftermath of her breakdowns and the dissolution of her two most crucial relationships, Bogan made concerted efforts on all fronts to establish her life on steadier, more cautious footing. In the words of "After the Persian": "I do not wish to know / The depths of your terrible jungle . . . / I am the dweller on the temperate threshold." She was a pensioner in the house of love no more.

> I said out of sleeping:
> Passion, farewell.
>   ("Second Song")

Gone would be ecstasy; gone, too, despair. Bogan hoped that the emergence of what she called her "new personality," based on emotional stability and restraint, would lead to an increase in creative vitality. In stepping past the youthful framework of crisis, Bogan stepped into uncharted territory.

If woman's proper subject in the traditional lyric was love, what then was she to write about when she no longer loved? What is most interesting about Bogan's response is that she was so conscious of her position as a woman. She knew that women who wrote compressed lyrics suffered in comparison to male poets who kept writing into old age and produced large oeuvres. She keenly felt the contrast between Yeats's body of work and her own small group of poems. The male poet managed to write into late life, Bogan suggested, because he had a wider range of acceptable material and experience upon which to draw; he was not wed to young love. Rilke and Yeats achieved long and successful careers because "they drew to themselves more and more experience; their work never dried up at the source or bloated into empty orotundity" (*Journey,* 116). But the course for older women poets was uncertain. Reviewing Millay's *Huntsman, What Quarry?* in 1939, Bogan broached the subject of the modernist woman poet's dilemma in relinquishing the youthful basis of her art: "It is difficult to say what a woman poet should concern herself with as she grows older, because women who have produced an impressively bulky body of work are few. But is there any reason to believe that a woman's spiritual fibre is less sturdy than a man's? Is it not possible for a woman to come to terms with herself, if not with the world . . . ?" (*Journey,* 116–17). In this passage Bogan expresses doubt about the subjects possible for the woman poet writing after the period of youthful love. Perhaps she could draw more and more experience to herself; the matter is here left undecided. Bogan's uncertain tone—her inability to answer the question—shows that she was grappling with a new orientation in her career and a new basis to her poetry. She could conceptualize the necessity, but she could not specify new sources for her poetry.

There was a second problem in Bogan's passing the stage of romantic passion. Love was not just the subject of the feminine lyric; it was also poetry's inspiration. Bogan's reference to coming to terms with oneself suggests that a sturdy maturity of outlook might have taken the place of passionate love in the inspiration of poetry. But her work appears to have "dried up at the source" instead. This last image becomes a significant one in again comparing the woman's range to the man's. The endurance of male poets was related to the contemporary (but also ancient) belief in the conjunction of artistic and sexual energies. Bogan herself fused these two distinguishable energies by linking the sensations of romantic love, "the letting go, the swoon, the suffused eyes, the loose hand, the constriction in the throat, the abasement, the feeling of release," with what she called "le souffle du génie—the breath of inspiration" (*Journey,* 74, 119). Sexuality was further equated with the reproductive years, tying a woman's sexual life closely to childbearing. The end of the childbearing years was then construed as the withering of sexual desire, and men were thought to experience longer sexual lives than women, an assumption not widely questioned until the 1970s. If Bogan accepted these cultural presumptions, that women's procreative and creative lives were one and the same, then her career as a poet was linked to the reproductive aspects of female heterosexual life.

The drying up at the source, then, was menopause. The subject was itself taboo for Bogan and never broached directly; she referred to it obliquely or in jest. But from the comment made to her editor—"A woman writes with her ovaries"—and to Theodore Roethke—that women poets dry up at forty—it is clear that Bogan associated the onset of menopause with her inability to write poetry. The treatment of menopause by contemporary medical and psychoanalytic theorists as the breakdown of the sexual system must have affected the way she saw her sexuality at this stage of life. In medical and popular texts, menopause was represented as a pathological state, describing the "breakdown of a system of authority," a process of failure and decline.[10] This analysis depended on an emphasis on sexual production, beginning with the production of eggs, as women's physiological purpose. Under the common understanding, menopause deprived women of their purpose.

Each woman experiences menopause in her own way,[11] but at the beginning of menopause, Bogan experienced the series of personal losses mentioned in the beginning of this section. Thus her experience of a diminished sexual drive eroded the grounds of her authorship. Bogan was living alone, and her creative writing had slowed to a trickle. She possessed a premature sense of aging without fulfillments. She felt old—there is no other word for it. Journal entries from the period are a mournful testimony to how painfully Bogan felt time's passing. In reading them, one is continually shocked to realize they were written by a forty-year-old woman, for they seem the fearful meditations of someone much older. Bogan's career suggests that a system that ties creativity to reproductive capacity prevents a woman poet from growing throughout her life. Her response to middle life may be seen in "The Catalpa Tree," published in 1941 when Bogan was forty-four. In the poem, Bogan is greeted by a weakened voice of the ghost of her former self:

> Words do not come to the old prayer,—only the rung names and the
>   pauses.
> An autumn I remember only by the pods of the catalpa tree that did
>   not fall.
> Tears were shed, sobbed to wild herbs in a field, whatever their causes,
> And a house had a wall like a web of thorns about it. I remember that
>   wall.
>
> Only the long pods remained; the tree was drained like a sieve.
> Perhaps the secret voice you hear under your mouth was all I could
>   keep:
> The burnished pods not claimed by a wizened month once said I should
>   live.
> They hang in my song of another autumn, in this hour stolen from
>   sleep.[12]

The failure of the invocation is clear, a full contrast to the authoritative onset of earlier poems ("Women have no wilderness in them"). The invocation associated with inspired writing now produces an empty litany of names. Even the natural details of the psychic landscape resist the poet's attention. Memory has been reduced to a failed talisman, "the pods of the catalpa tree that did not fall." What Bogan recalls are tears, unanchored to circumstances that confer meaning. She remembers feminine nurturance and the security of the house, the root of strength in women's art and lives, which appears as a protective enclosure. But the house has undergone a frightening transformation. The "web of thorns about it" joins the barrenness of autumn with the crown of martyrdom.

The second stanza develops the plot of declining powers. The speaker becomes a body part, the mouth of the "secret" and more authentic former poet, whose gifts have been buried. Traces of Bogan's old will to write survive in the pods spared from time, yet she cannot deploy them against loss. They seem saturated in an earlier season: "They hang in my song of another autumn." Sadness suffuses the scene and cannot be dispelled, and the impasse drains whatever energy the poem marshaled at the outset: "The tree was drained like a sieve." The present, an "hour stolen from sleep," suggests that Bogan's writing in midlife is a brief aberration from the narcotic of her days. The moment of life in poetry is now a rare and elegiac gift.

Bogan's response to the middle time of life was not the only one possible. But given the social conventions, the medical theories, and the literary portraits of middle-aged menopausal women prevalent in the first half of the twentieth century, she was primed to view her own experience as a withering loss of sexuality and as an eroding of already narrowed creative impulses. She might have turned to a more forthright biographical style or the aesthetics of radical personal transformation averred by H.D. But the example of her lyric peers suggested a different course. Women like Millay peaked in their twenties. Millay's astounding early success took shape in love sonnets, and when she turned to social issues, for example the poem from 1927 on Sacco and Vanzetti, "Justice Denied in Massachusetts," critical estimation of her poetry sank. *The Buck in the Snow,* another departure from her earlier sonnets on love, was indifferently received. When she returned to the kind of poetry that made her reputation with *Fatal Interview* in 1931, the public was again happy.[13]

Handicapped by the absence of a tradition of women lyric poets who had successfully negotiated the passage into middle life, Bogan had nothing to offset her self- or culturally imposed limits. The absence of an alternate tradition in women's poetry made it difficult for her and for other lyric poets of her generation to develop a late style. Having defined her inspiration as romantic love, an eroticism of physical sensation depending on male dominance and female abasement, Bogan found she could no longer fulfill that role. Sometime between 1932 and 1937, when she was in her late thirties, Bogan wrote: "Today it seemed as though nothing would ever happen again. Saw my real, half-withered, silly face in a shop mirror in the street, under the bald light of an evening shower, and shuddered. The woman who died without producing an oeuvre. The woman who ran away" (*Journey*, 103).

"The Woman Who Died without Producing an Oeuvre"

During her period of creative silence, Bogan's professional life expanded into wider possibilities of teaching, lecturing, editing, and translating. She was the respected poetry critic for the *New Yorker* from 1936 until a few years before her death. In 1942 she became a Fellow in American Letters at the Library of Congress, and in 1944 she held visiting teaching positions at the University of Washington and the University of Chicago. Yet these increased possibilities did not revitalize what Bogan considered to be her real writing. She found herself split between a varied world of work, in which she was moderately mobile, and a private world that resisted change or new relationships. Even in the social, literary realm, Bogan had a relatively small number of close friends and correspondents, and over the course of her life few new friends were admitted. Nor did her tastes in writing or her views on the role of politics, for example, undergo much revision. Her personal life and her life as a poet both stalled.

Bogan was very conscious of herself as a writer of a particular age. After one of her breakdowns, Bogan remarked that "perhaps, in the main, the process of partial disintegration is salutary, and even necessary, when sensitive people reach their middle thirties. A good look into that abyss described by so many—Pascal, Dante, Sophocles, Dostoevsky, to name a few. . . . It's just as well to know that the ninth circle has an icy floor by experience: by having laid the living hand on it" (*Journey*, 90). But Bogan's circumscribed conception of the shape of the lyric poet's career did not allow her to reshape her career in midlife. The female poet's career closely follows the conventionally constructed span of a woman's beauty and sexuality: "apprenticeship, a period of full flowering, and a gradual decline of creative energy" (*Journey*, 121). In a passage I have already quoted, Bogan writes, "It is difficult to say what a woman poet should concern herself with as she grows older." In these remarks, Bogan expresses a sense of aging as a passage beyond productive youth. Absent is any conception of this time of life as a middle, a distinct period of creation. By contrast, a strong sense of a middle is given in the opening lines of Dante's *Inferno: Nel mezzo del cammin di nostra vita / mi ritrovai per una selva oscura* ("Midway in the journey of our life I found myself in a dark wood"). If beset by its own terrors, middle age can still be conceived as a period of creation perhaps more powerful than youth: *ma per trattar del be ch'i' vi trovai, / diro de l'altre cose ch'i' v'ho scorte'* ("But, to treat of the good that I found in it, I will tell of the other things I saw there").[14]

There are, of course, many historical, aesthetic, religious, and personal factors that prevented Bogan from conceiving her career in the fashion of the medieval, Catholic, male, epic poet. Bogan's dilemma as a poet was aggravated by the circumstances of her life and by the purity of her aesthetic beliefs. The brevity of Bogan's active career shows us that a woman trying to come to terms with herself and with the world may not be aided by the recognized models of female aging. Like too many others, Bogan felt obliged to conform to cultural presumptions that denigrated her role in late life. When Bogan's romantic life diminished and a stage of her physiological life passed, she was prepared to believe that her creative life was ending too. Bogan's less frequent production after 1938 stemmed, at least in part, from her inability to circumvent the limitations of the female lyric poet as she understood her. In October 1938, after the publication of *The Sleeping Fury*, Bogan wrote, "I don't think I will write very much more" (*Letters*, 138). And she did not.

In the second half of the twentieth century, a resistance to presumed decline in middle age becomes more likely for the female lyricist, yet it still demands a struggle against the conventions of waning passion. A prime example is Louise Glück, who has published several books of acclaimed poetry, among them *The House on Marshland*. This volume, from 1975, includes "To Autumn," a lyric in the great tradition of seasonal meditations on the poet's career. Glück writes from the vantage of one no longer young. But she offers a construction of survival into middle age counter to the phenomena of loss that prevail in "The Catalpa Tree." Glück confronts the conventional plot of a woman poet's middle age as a time of exhaustion and decline. She revises the division of a woman poet's career into youth, as the period of the most perfect expression, and age, as the emptying out into silence. To base a poet's development in seasonal structures suggests that a poet's career follows the cycles of growth and decay. But "To Autumn" refuses to reproduce the script that consigns women poets to silent hiding after the youth and beauty of their spring has subsided.

> Morning quivers in the thorns; above the budded snowdrops
> caked with dew like little virgins, the azalea bush
> ejects its first leaves, and it is spring again.

The willow waits its turn, the coast
is coated with a faint green fuzz, anticipating
mold. Only I
do not collaborate, having
flowered earlier. I am no longer young. What
of it? Summer approaches, and the long
decaying days of autumn when I shall begin
the great poems of my middle period.[15]

After the long, gentle lines evoking the first unfoldings of spring, Glück
interjects herself into the scene. This rough cutting-in marks resistance: she
will not follow the seasonal development as it is given to her. Glück does
not labor with nature to produce its flowering. Instead she offers a developmental map of aging as a series of multiple locations through which she
moves at will. At the start of what in the traditional lyric would be decline, Glück stakes her new beginning: "the long / decaying days of autumn
when I shall begin / the great poems of my middle period." The poems of
youth tantalize with delicacy, but the ripening of those powers in middle
age results in great poems.

Unlike natural production, the endless reproducing of itself, a woman
has a finite capacity for spring. A natural grid laid upon her life precludes
her coming to terms with the processes of aging. Such an imposition reads
a woman's creativity solely in terms of sexual reproduction. Therefore, the
erotic life of nature cannot provide an adequate model for women's creative
life in all its manifestations. Glück extends Keats's example of bestowing
to autumn its own songs. But unlike Keats, she can claim the powers of
autumn even during the spring. The woman poet produces in autumn and
spring.

Born twenty years after the publication of Bogan's first book of poems,
Glück must still overcome strictures on the feminine poet in order to write
the lyric into middle age. She is able to refuse to internalize the customary attitude toward aging that stopped Bogan. But the very refusal evinces
the endurance of residual assumptions about the shape of a woman poet's
career.

Notes

1. The irony is that Bogan as critic was herself involved in writing a historical
account that would diminish the value of her own work. Unlike Adrienne Rich, for
example, whose historical and critical work provides an essential apparatus for her

poetry, Bogan's criticism is often of little use—sometimes even deceptive—in reading her poetry.

2. Gloria Bowles, *Louise Bogan's Aesthetic of Limitation*, 126.

3. William Drake, *Sara Teasdale*, 25; Louise Bogan, *Achievement In American Poetry*, 19, and *Journey*, 140; "Louise Bogan, Noted Poet Who Wrote About Love, Dead," 39.

For an account of the transformation of women's lyrics, see Alicia Suskin Ostriker, *Stealing the Language*. Ostriker numbers Bogan in the group of women "who composed the first substantial body of [women's] lyric poetry" (46).

Bogan's opinion on sentimental nineteenth-century verse should be distinguished from her opinion of Emily Dickinson, who possessed genuine gifts of mystical and poetic revelation.

4. Louise Bogan, *Poet's Alphabet*, 428; Malcolm Cowley, "Three Poets," 58. As a further difficulty, the strong passions behind the feminine lyric were, in Bogan's synthesis of sentiment and the modernist vogue, to be given carefully confined expression; Yvor Winters called Bogan's poems "insulated units" ("The Poetry of Louise Bogan," 32). Wylie remarked that her own stanzas were contrived like musical snuffboxes or small jeweled receptacles for gilded birds (Celeste Turner Wright, "Elinor Wylie," 159). In a review published in 1954, Leonie Adams described Bogan's poetry as an "art of limits, the limits of the inner occasion and of the recognized mode" (quoted in Bowles, *Bozan's Aesthetic*, 40). The "recognized mode" is a lyric form with a romantic content; these together marked the limits accorded to and accepted by Bogan and her contemporaries.

5. Louise Bogan, *The Blue Estuaries*. Subsequent references to Bogan's poetry are to this volume unless otherwise noted.

6. Margaret Homans, *Women Writers and Poetic Identity*, 221. Bogan was not alone in her image of herself as artifact, fixed for an instant, "under the eye of eternity"—Theodore Roethke's description of Bogan's artistic aspirations ("The Poetry of Louise Bogan," 88). Elinor Wylie wrote a series of poems and novels about the firing of girls into porcelain artifacts. Edith Wharton's Lily in *The House of Mirth* suggests how closely death is implicated in standards of female beauty.

7. Elaine Showalter, ed., *These Modern Women*.

8. Kenneth Tynan, *Show People*, 267; Barthes quoted in Betsy Erkkila, "Greta Garbo," 597.

9. Lois Banner, *American Beauty*, 278; Kathleen Woodward, *Aging and Its Discontents*, 10.

10. Elizabeth Frank, *Louise Bogan*, 328; Emily Martin, *The Woman in the Body*, 42.

11. Margaret Mead referred to her "post-menopausal zest" (quoted in Lois Banner, "The Meaning of Menopause," 9).

12. Louise Bogan, "The Catalpa Tree," 8.

13. Debra Fried, "Andromeda Unbound," 1–22.

14. Dante Alighiere, *Inferno*.

15. Louise Glück, *The House on Marshland*.

6

M. M. LALLY

The Virgin and the Gipsy:
Rewriting the Pain

Thou shalt not covet thy neighbor's wife.
—Exodus 20:17

Look! We Have Come Through!
—Title of D. H. Lawrence poem

IT IS highly ironic that two of the works of D. H. Lawrence having the most to do with home and children, "The Rocking-Horse Winner" and the poem "Piano," are so frequently anthologized—in that nothing could so fail of representing, overall, his canon and spirit. For throughout all of Lawrence's own life and throughout his fiction, the innocent face of childhood is to be found within a surreal context of adult passions and pain.

When, in 1912, Frieda Weekley joined D. H. Lawrence on the Continent, having decided to accept his love and share his "rotten chances," the couple's new life began as a celebration, a triumph. But it was not long before Lawrence realized that his paradise would never be clear of the shadows of Frieda's three young children, abandoned to their father and his hurt and anger, with all that that would inevitably come to mean.

To this most eminent of adored sons, the shock was devastating. He who had been a veritable paradigm of the oedipal victor—gaining the ascendancy over his own father and carrying into life from that first battle the ultimate strength and confidence—now found his days rent by terrible scenes with Frieda. His new life rested on a fault of guilt and pain; he knew that her distant children—silent and powerless though they might seem to be—could at any time displace him. He lived for years angry, fearful, and powerless.

Often Lawrence, never in robust health, reflected bitterly upon the price he had paid for his wife: he was exhausted, drained. In time, for whatever reason—punishment, guilt, fear, a desire to keep Frieda's grief at bay, or, perhaps, some reason unknown even to himself—he ceased altogether creating children like the Morels and Anna Brangwen, his vivid, psychologically complex children, who lived and grew in unforgettable ways inside their homes and families. He never did comment upon this decision; perhaps no one ever asked. But in 1926, four years before the end of his brief life, he wrote the rather shrill and enigmatic novella *The Virgin and the Gipsy,* turning over and over in his mind, at the last, love's triangle and all that it can do, to the one life and the many.

Clearly, and sadly, in abandoning what Jessie Chambers called "the little world," Lawrence abandoned not only what was to be his position at the vanguard of the greatest movement in twentieth-century literature but the most essential, powerful materials of his own genius. And while the dimensions of his genius were such that we hardly notice, feeling none the poorer for his decision—and while critics provide many convincing reasons for Lawrence's years of travel and provide, as well, probing discussions of his later works—it is not inconsistent with the substantial body of negative criticism on his later novels to hold that, leaving home and children behind, he proceeded on a course that led, ultimately, to self-imposed isolation and aesthetic decline.

Over the years, a number of critics have noted that in the Lawrencean scheme of things there exists a great and crucial void. The question has been rendered with special cogency by several of Lawrence's early critics, in works which preceded or converged with the sexual revolution of recent decades and the accompanying explosion and fallout of new respect for this unorthodox author. No less a defender of Lawrence than F. R. Leavis detected something seriously amiss in the writer's grand design:

> Though his sense of the finality of [Aaron Sisson's] marriage, the permanence of the tie that holds him to his wife, is insisted on, he has no feelings at all, it would seem, about his children. It is surely a significant inadvertence, a significant default of imagination, on Lawrence's part. And it has its relevance in a critical consideration of his wisdom, or doctrine (not to shirk the word). For to insist that the relation between a man and a woman is the supremely important one, to insist that the marriage for life is the relation necessary for the fulfillment of the "deeper desires," and yet to be to this tune blank about the family—it is surely very odd.[1]

What troubled Leavis has troubled others as well. Graham Hough, "Father Tiverton," and Eliseo Vivas all have faulted Lawrence for his gigantic blind spot; they differ only in their choices of a cause to which the omission might be ascribed. Hough sees Lawrence to have been, in his life, naturally cold to the idea of fatherhood, and he sees him paying in his work the penalty of a "yawning incompleteness in his sexual doctrine." He reflects: "Though [Lawrence] spends a great deal of energy on the relations between parents and children, it is nearly always on its perversions, and there is scarcely an instance in his novels of normal parental love."[2]

Tiverton concurs with this view; he observes, "It is significant, I think, that Lawrence was so insistent on disentangling the phallic reality from any mere utilitarian purpose that he goes to the opposite extreme of excluding the reproductive instinct from it altogether."[3]

Vivas is the most adamant. He sees the void in Lawrence's work to be representative of a profound deficiency in the man himself and in his vision; he declares that "the love [Lawrence] craves is eros and never agape. Of the latter he knew nothing, and what he thought he knew about it made him loathe it." Lawrence's, he says, was "a psychology incapable of love. It is useless to try to deny it."[4]

Yet this was the same Lawrence who created the fresh exuberance of William Morel at the wakes; his simple love and zest for the world around him triumph for the moment over Annie's whining and his mother's sober thoughts:

> [William] pulled from his pocket two egg-cups, with pink moss-roses on them.
>
> "I got these from that stall where y'ave ter get them marbles in them holes. An' I got these two in two goes—'aepenny a go—they've got moss-roses on, look here. I wanted these."
>
> She knew he wanted them for her.
>
> "H'm!" she said, pleased. "They *are* pretty!"
>
> "Shall you carry em, 'cause I'm frightened o' breakin' em?"
>
> He was tipful of excitement now she had come, led her about the ground, showed her everything. Then, at the peepshow, she explained the pictures, in a sort of story, to which he listened as if spellbound. He would not leave her. All the time he stuck close to her, bristling with a small boy's pride of her. For no other woman looked such a lady as she did, in her little black bonnet and her cloak. (*S&L*, 15)

And this is the same Lawrence who wrote to May Holbrook in 1909 describing the little girl in whose parents' home he lived: "Indoors Hilda Mary is hanging onto my legs, laughing up at me. She has brilliant hazel eyes, so round and daring. Soon I shall take her and get her to sleep. She does not like to go to bed, but I am a good 'dustman.' I hold her tight and sing—roar away at the noisiest songs. This subdues her, she tucks her face in my neck and toddles off to 'bo' [bed] while her hair tickles my nose to a frenzy" (*L*, 115).

Hilda Mary and her kind were to burst into life in fiction thanks to Lawrence. But there came a time when these images would fade and disappear, when Lawrence would not only omit all mention of—or regard for—the young but would actively flee from them, in both his life and his art. *The Rainbow*'s Anna Lensky is the only child in a Lawrencean novel to stand in happiness between two parents who love both the child and each other; in the Lawrence novels which follow, the homes are all wrong. In *Women in Love* the drowned child, Diana Crich, is a distant malevolence, frozen in a posture of desperate and everlasting need. In the leadership novels, following 1921, after the Sisson children are left and forgotten, Ramon's sons (in *The Plumed Serpent*) have learned to despise him, and the children in *Kangaroo* lay claim to only two paragraphs.

Lawrence looked at children as long as he could bear to, but on December 29, 1912, when his world turned upside down, he wrote Edward Garnett: "[Frieda and I] sort of forgot about its being Christmas. It didn't go off with much of a bang here—owing to other Christmases looking so forlornly over the years at us—blast them. So I didn't send you greetings as I might have done if I'd had any decency" (*L*, 496).

Many years later, his writing suggests that he may have bitterly resented the intervening Christmases, which surely looked at him and Frieda with not only forlornness but with irremediable pain and rancor. In *Aaron's Rod* he creates the life of children and home one last perfect time, but in a way that is as savage as it is sensitive: ten years after the first of his battles with domestic love, he creates home only so that he may kill it off at last. In the opening scenes of the novel, the children break the old Christmas ornament, the blue ball, and Aaron abandons his family on Christmas Eve. "The Blue Ball," home, children, families, Christmas: he has, indeed, to use his own word, "blasted" all of them. One can only wonder whether he was aware that he was, in the process, blasting his own art.

The progressive distortion of the children's images in the works of Lawrence and their eventual banishment, standing alone, allow for various interpretations of the direction taken by Lawrence's art over the years; yet Lawrence's and Frieda's letters and the accounts written by their friends provide a privileged insight into just how deep this trouble ran in the author's heart and home. The overall picture of the Lawrences together reveals two people in an essentially strong though often hysterical and violent marriage. But on one point all their friends agreed: when the scenes were the most fierce, it was almost always because Frieda—or someone else—had mentioned her children. A few words then could unleash in Lawrence a torrent of rage that would mean horrified guests, smashed tea things and furniture, physical thrashings, and open threats of murder. Frieda and everyone else involved were paying dearly for her decision.

David Garnett witnessed the events of this period, and his memories provide an uncanny preview of what lay ahead. He remembers the trouble between Lawrence and Frieda and says that it "kept flaring out in Lawrence's behaviour." Reflecting on the depth and inevitability of a mother's love for her children, Garnett says: "Any kind-hearted man would have felt an added tenderness and sympathy for her. But there was a streak of cruelty in Lawrence; he was jealous of the children and angry with Frieda, because she could not forget them. Now that she had come back to England, she was longing to see them, and the spiteful, ill-conditioned, ungenerous side of Lawrence's character was constantly breaking out in different ways. He lacked what are called 'the instincts of a gentleman'—and he most certainly wasn't one."

Nor did Garnett find Lawrence "any more attractive" for his blaming Frieda for all of these difficulties while exonerating himself; in fact, Garnett's so-ardent sympathy for Frieda almost tints the page as he observes that the suffering Frieda was "as painful to watch as an animal in a trap," that she was like "a lioness or a puma" who cannot forget her cubs, and that her nature is entirely "noble."[5]

From the very beginning Lawrence was aware that he would not pass through this fire unscathed, unchanged. He recognized early that he, too, was paying a price; ironically, his letters of 1912 and 1913 prophesy the nature of that price. Newly entered upon his life with Frieda, he observes to Arthur McLeod, on December 17, 1912, that he finds himself always "resisting" Weekley and all that he represents; he complains that "the tragedy there is in keeping Frieda" has already forced him to adopt the stance and spirit of a businessman rather than that of the poet, the openhearted artist (L, 488). Again and again, he and Frieda recount to their friends the difficulties and even deceptions forced upon them by this wearing conflict.[6]

On December 17, 1912, Lawrence writes to Edward Garnett of Weekley's ultimatum to Frieda: he will divorce her if she renounces all claim to her children. (Lawrence—years younger and blinded by hope, egocentrism, or naïveté—refuses to believe that Weekley means what he says.) But he is becoming increasingly aware of the kind of strain and fatigue that accompany such a battle: " 'Constant dropping will wear away a stone,' as my mother used to say. But, by the Lord, I'm dead tired inside—fit to drop. It's just the strain of resisting, of seven months resistance. I feel as if I canna do no more—the rest's got to come" (*L*, 489).

Tellingly, it is on Christmas Day of that year that he finds himself writing Sallie Hopkin: "We've had such a hard time, pegging through this autumn—the children, Weekley, and ourselves. If two people start clean of trouble, without children and other husbands between 'em, it's hard for them to get simple and close to each other—but when it's like this—oh Lord, it takes it out of you" (*L*, 492). Devoted and steadfast though he is and intends to be, he nonetheless ruefully tells Edward Garnett, "If ever you know anybody who is tempted to run away with another man's wife, warn him to be very sure of himself. There come such ghastly times, such ghastly letters from England. But I don't regret it one jot or tittle. Only it's hard that the other folk are so much hurt" (*L*, 434).

Indeed there has been much hurt. Beyond the separation itself and Frieda's flight to Lawrence—beyond the letters, tears, and threats—there was one more wound, profound in its implications and consequences. Lawrence writes Sallie Hopkin: "Things have been hard, and worth it. There has been some sickening misery. Prof. W[eekley] wanted F[rieda] back, and thought she would come. Also, he was furious, and raved. He is breaking up the Nottingham home, taking the three children to live with himself and his old parents in Chiswick. . . . It has been rather ghastly, that part of the affair. If only one didn't hurt so many people" (*L*, 440).

As an adult, Barbara Weekley Barr, Frieda's youngest child, would recall this forbidden glimpse of her mother, from whom she had been instructed to run away: "I remember scampering along in fear and excitement to the safety of Miss Dollman's School at the sight of Frieda's disquieting, solitary figure. Then, looking over my shoulder, I would see that she was still smiling in a bewildered way, not wishing, perhaps, to leave any sting."[7]

The pain lasted through the years. John Middleton Murry recalled it from another perspective:

Katherine and I had been invited to a supper of roast veal. Everything had gone well; the crocks and the saucepans had been thoroughly well washed, and we were talking gaily enough, when there was a mention of Frieda's children, and Frieda burst into tears. Lawrence went pale. In a moment, there was a fearful outburst. Ominously, there was no physical violence. Lawrence, though passionately angry, had kept control; and it was the more frightening. He had had enough, he said; she must go, she was draining the life out of him. She must go, she must go now. She knew what money he had; he would give her her share—more than her share. He went upstairs, and came down again, and counted out on the table to me sixteen sovereigns. Frieda was standing by the door, crying, with her hat and coat on, ready to go—but where?[8]

After many long years Frieda sat with Mabel Dodge Luhan in the isolation of New Mexico, her grief by no means abated. Later Mabel wrote: "Frieda had to mask her interest and affection for her children from Lawrence. He couldn't stand having her even speak of them. He had taken her away from them and she had to go through that separation by herself—with no help from him."[9]

Since the Lawrences even opened each other's mail and spent almost every moment together, there must have been a miserable but inviolate understanding between them: There are to be no children in our world. So Frieda gave up the children of her life, and Lawrence sacrificed the children in his art. The irony is that eventually Frieda would be able to reestablish contact with her daughters; Lawrence, on the other hand, lost an entire natural world when he turned his face away from home and children, the only real life he had ever known before he married.

The wealthy Luhan, who had given the Lawrences the use of her Taos cabin, was (although newly remarried) intensely preoccupied with the many moods and movements of Lawrence the man. Indeed, it was she who would one day make off with the writer's ashes—necessitating Frieda's having to have them cemented in place.

Nevertheless, despite the troubled undercurrents which existed between them at the time, the two women were capable of some rare occasions of "momentary sympathy," and remembering one of them, Luhan recalls the riveting poignancy of Frieda: "She missed their little clothes, she said. She had spent so many hours making little dresses and underclothes for the girls! Now her hands were empty."[10]

The Danish painter Knud Merrild and his friend Kai Gotzsche also lived in Taos during the time Lawrence was there, and they came to know him fairly well. For the most part, theirs was a mutual friendship; perhaps no other of Lawrence's friends was as kindly disposed toward him as Merrild, who seems, from his account of those New Mexico days, to be an even-tempered man and a credible narrator.

Still, though Merrild could, on the one hand, reflect, not without amusement, upon Lawrence's irrepressible didacticism, he could also bolt in alarm, seeing Lawrence in one of his torrential moments. He recalls the raging afternoon when Lawrence chased his little dog Pips (Bibbles) all through his cabin and outside it, pummmeling and kicking it all the while, and finally hurling it into the air with all his strength, to land on snow or rocks.[11]

Merrild's impression of Frieda is presented with kindness and understanding:

Frieda took me into her confidence and said, "Merrild, you probably know that I have been married before and have three children with my former husband. When we were divorced, he forbade me ever to see my children again or write to them. And so did Lawrence. He won't let me talk about them, or even mention their names. At times, it becomes unbearable for me."

"I think I can understand how a mother must feel," I said. I felt a deep sympathy for her and asked how old the children were and if they were well.

"That is just what I don't know," she said. "I haven't had any news about them for ages. My friends in England have been keeping me informed, but I haven't heard anything for a long time and am very worried. And when they do write, and Lawrence sees the letters, he becomes infuriated. Then we have endless quarrels, which I wouldn't mind so much if I only knew that my children were well." [12]

Merrild is appalled and confused:

I thought it was rather petty of Lawrence to forbid his wife to seek news about the welfare of her children; I thought it rather egotistical and cruel. I tried to analyse his behaviour. I thought he was pretty small about this, but I also knew he was big, so I concluded that perhaps he was being wise. . . .

But I couldn't make it come out right. I still thought he was pretty small with Frieda about her cigarettes and her children. He let his inner self rule, and his better self was overpowered by these other forces. [13]

Of particular interest among the grim and sketchy child-figures of the later years are Ramon's Christian sons in *The Plumed Serpent* (1926). They confront their father in sullen, accusatory defiance, aghast at his proclaimed pagan inclinations; they will be, henceforward, the standard-bearers of their mother, martyred in love and deprived of life:

"Never," said the young Cyprian, his eyes flashing, "never can we love you, Papa. You are our enemy. You killed our mother." . . .

"Mama loved you much, much, much!" cried Cyprian, the tears rising to his eyes. "Always she loved you and prayed for you—" He began to cry.

"And I, my son?" said Ramon.

"You hated her and killed her! Oh Mama! Mama! Oh Mama! I want my mother!" he wept.

"Come to me, little one!" said Ramon softly, holding out his hands.

"No!" cried Cyprian, stamping his foot and flashing his eyes through his tears. "No! No!"

The elder boy hung his head and was crying too. (*PS*, 354)

The parallel with Frieda's son Monty is painfully obvious here. As Luhan recalls many years after Frieda's separation from her children:

> The girls asked [for a visit with Frieda], but the oldest one, the boy, couldn't forgive her. He went completely English and blotted out of himself his German blood. When she tried to see him, during the war, he answered, saying that his mother was the enemy:
>
> "Every time one of those bombing planes circle over London, I know it is my mother. . . ."
>
> Poor Frieda suffered over her children more than Lawrence ever knew. He would not know it. He must be everything to her: the child, the son, as well as the lover. He couldn't admit any rivals.[14]

The landscape has been altered, the genders transposed, but the emotions are, alas, not alien enough. Ramon's bitter son had a living antecedent in Weekley's home.

For his part, in those rare instances in Lawrence's work when he appears at all, the Weekley-character is a long-suffering blend of father, saint, and cuckold. In Lawrence's poem "The Ballad of the Willful Woman," he is St. Joseph abandoned; in *The Virgin and the Gipsy*, so many years later, he is a vicar abandoned—but by this time he has earned a face; it reveals that he has deep passions of his own. In this late work Lawrence attempts to satirize the love-martyred husband, who is given to a litany of recitations of all he has suffered at the hands of "She-Who-Was-Cynthia."

But this novella is, in many ways, odd, and it has a curious history. Lawrence completed the holograph in January 1926, after what must surely have been one of the most terrible years of his life. In February of the preceding year, he had contracted malaria in Mexico and had almost died. The following month, in Mexico City, his condition was positively diagnosed as tuberculosis (which, only fifteen years earlier, had been the leading cause of death in the United States). He was given only a year or two to live.[15]

The photographs taken of Lawrence during this period underscore the meaning of this grim information, and Keith Sagar says, "After a two-day fight and after putting rouge on his cheeks, Lawrence got across the border at El Paso and arrived in Santa Fe [on the] 29[th of March]." This knowledge marked a change in Lawrence's attitude; his words increasingly betray fatigue and a growing contempt for mankind, and he seems to dwell upon the fact that he is now forty years old and wants to enjoy his life.[16]

This confrontation with his own mortality leads him to create a beautiful story, called *The Flying Fish,* which he reads aloud to the Brewsters, but which he declares he will never finish, so intimate a part is it of his encounter with death. At the same time, he has resolved never again to write a novel—and yet he quietly completes the holograph of his long work *The Virgin and the Gipsy* with what appears to be a kind of secret efficiency.[17] In time, he will violate his own plan, allowing a short story to grow into the oft-rewritten *Lady Chatterley's Lover,* while *The Virgin and the Gipsy* lingers in need of revision and joins *The Flying Fish* in a kind of limbo, unusual for the works of Lawrence.

It does not matter that in *The Virgin and the Gipsy* he mocks Weekley, costuming him in a religious role, that he cartoons Weekley's family in the caricatures of Granny and the housekeeping "Aunt Cissy," who is "over forty, pale, pious, and gnawed by an inward worm" (*V&G,* 705). What matters are the canyons of emotion over which Lawrence casts his fading light, with an offhand manner miserably at odds with the subject matter of the novella and the realities that had so deeply scarred him.

> When the vicar's wife went off with a young and penniless man the scandal knew no bounds. Her two little girls were only seven and nine years old respectively. And the vicar was such a good husband. True, his hair was grey. But his moustache was dark, he was handsome, and still full of furtive passion for his unrestrained and beautiful wife. Why did she go? Why did she burst away with such an *éclat* of revulsion, like a touch of madness?
>
> Nobody gave any answer. Only the pious said she was a bad woman. While some of the good women kept silent. They knew.
>
> The two little girls never knew. Wounded, they decided that it was because their mother found them negligible. (*V&G,* 705)

Poor Lawrence. No matter how hard he might try, no one will laugh. This is not the stuff of humor, especially when it is the dying statement of that same penniless young man. We recognize this patchwork home; we recognize this suffering father and husband; what we do not recognize is the soulless humor.

Nor can Lawrence hope to amuse us when he confides that the rector "had displayed an intense and not very dignified grief after the flight of his wife" and that "sympathetic ladies had stayed him from suicide." Even he, in his own early letters, seemed to find nothing entertaining in these actual events.

Below its surface *The Virgin and the Gipsy* exists as a kind of conundrum, a puzzle made out of the pieces of Lawrence's life, which are being constantly arranged and rearranged, their variables being slightly adjusted throughout. Three couples, all of whom are involved in adulterous love triangles, are set into motion; in all three situations young children are (or have been) caught up in the struggle. As the fiction turns kaleidoscopically, each of the three love triangles represents different shades of the problem and a different resolution of the war between desire and responsibility.

The vicar (a "somewhat distinguished essayist and controversialist") is clearly drawn from the living Weekley, the cast-off member of Lawrence's own triad. Eventually, it is implied, his rancorous maundering will drag him down into the insular miseries and comic celibacy of his sister Cissy, who survives on a single boiled potato at dinner and chocolates the rest of the time. So far beyond sexual redemption is she that she must share her very sleeping hours with the lonely and petulant Granny: "So Aunt Cissy slept with Granny. And she hated it. She said *she* could never sleep. And she grew greyer and greyer, and the food in the house got worse, and Aunt Cissy had to have an operation" (*V&G*, 711).

At the opposite extreme from the horrific breakup of the Weekleys is that of "the Eastwoods"—actually, Major Eastwood and his married fiancée, Mrs. Fawcett, whom Lawrence perversely insists upon hammering with the label "the Jewess": "[She] was taking her wealth away from the well-known engineer and transferring it to the penniless, sporting young Major Eastwood, who must be five or six years younger than she. Rather intriguing."[18]

With the Eastwoods, Lawrence adjusts the story somewhat, toward compromise and agreement all around. Mrs. Fawcett is to have a far easier time of her divorce than She-Who-Was-Cynthia (-Frieda) did. As luck would have it, her children are both teenagers, and her husband has agreed to give them both up to his rival and his wife directly after their marriage (*V&G*, 739).

In reality, of course, betrayed spouses so soon alchemized out of bitterness were surely as rare as gypsy wives who vanished conveniently at the right moment out of love's triangle, leaving other women to tend their children and feed their husbands—and still others, far more appealing, to take meals with them.

Yet we wonder if Lawrence is not turning over and over in his mind the various factors and conversations that came to make all the difference in his life and Frieda's: Could they have found a peaceful solution, if—as with the Eastwoods—there had been only two children, or if the children had been older? If Weekley had been a different kind of man, or if he—or the affair—had been dealt with in some other way?

The third couple represents, interestingly, a hint of the next generation, those who ought not be condemned to repeat such life-consuming history. Lawrence, Merrild said, was always much given to teaching and preaching, and in his novella-parable, he places Frieda's daughter Barby in the role of the focal character, Yvette. She inherits the very dilemma that had once been Lawrence's own in loving her mother. Again, of course, in the fictional world, the genders are transposed: a young woman (not a man), has fallen in love with a married man (not woman), the parent (still) of very young children. Her friends counsel her toward a clandestine interlude, away from deep trouble.

As Yvette reflects that only this one man has made her feel "different," the "tiny Jewess" exclaims indignantly that the gypsy had no right to look at her with desire in his eyes. At this moment, Major Eastwood, who has until now remained private and silent, draws the distinction between mere "appetite" and desire, suggesting that Yvette learn to appreciate how irreplaceable and rare is the latter.

Meanwhile, at home, the rector furiously describes the Eastwoods as he sees them: "A young sponge going off with a woman older than himself, so that he can live on her money! The woman leaving her home and her children!" (*V&G*, 745). To him, they are unspeakable, depraved—and perhaps Yvette is truly like her mother, their kind and not his own.

One is not left long to wonder whether in his depths Lawrence shared somehow in this judgment upon his own life. Indeed, his vision is exactly, here, what Vivas saw it to be: utterly without agape. The family and its need for cohesiveness is not in any way represented, through so much as one syllable or glimpse of a face, by the innocent children of the gypsy or of Mrs. Fawcett; rather, Lawrence evades that issue totally, forcing upon us instead the image of the looming, toadlike, and flatulent Granny. "[Yvette] forgot the Eastwoods again. After all, what was the revolt of the little Jewess, compared to Granny and the Saywell bunch! A husband was never more than a semi-casual thing! But a family!—an awful, smelly family that would never disperse, stuck half dead round the base of a fungoid old woman! How was one to cope with that?" (*V&G*, 748)

Not one sentence of this novella concerns itself with those for whom marriage exists as a haven and shelter during life's urgent, vulnerable years; instead, Lawrence turns marital loyalty and running off with a lover into a question of who is "free-born," and who "base-born"—whatever that may mean. Weekley is one who was "born cowed," while Yvette sees Eastwood as a "simple, straightforward man" (746).

It is Lawrence's hieratic narrator who censes the text with these dark and random blessings; one can only wonder, given his self-involvement, how Lawrence himself would have behaved in Weekley's place, contending, in that era, with such appalling and irrevocable rejection and shame and with the condemnation to long years of intense and unrelieved responsibility. But empathy, like agape, is not an emotion we associate with Lawrence.

Indeed, Jerome Buckley is certainly correct in seeing in the writer's work, as early as Paul Morel, signs of the nature of "a true egoist, in the Meredithian sense": tortured sensibilities, demonstrations of histrionics, "moodiness, sentimentality, arrogance, and rage"—and, tellingly, a temperament "seldom touched by the comic spirit."[19] (In fact, his 1912 "comedy in four parts," *The Fight for Barbara,* which tells in great detail how Lawrence and Frieda held firm against the pathetic and distracted Weekley and against Frieda's parents at the time of the separation, is not only shamelessly unfunny but curiously forgetful of the fact that Frieda and Weekley—now translated into Barbara and Frederic Tressider—are parents [CPL 269– 319]. It also raises real questions as to the sincerity of his letters at the time.)

With the vicar and his unnamed rival existing as antipodal elements, only Eastwood and Fawcett seem reasonable and triumphant; still, Fawcett has, after all, lost his children. His only triumph is over rage and bitterness, and for that his only reward may well be the fool's cap, since no one can promise that Eastwood will honestly welcome his stepchildren or provide them with a good life.

Ultimately, the very conflict that Yvette has read in the life of the Eastwoods—unseen responsibility versus overwhelming desire—comes to invade her own life as well. The gypsy, the father of five children, looks at her as he should not; she is young, innocent, and vague, but she becomes increasingly haunted by his image.

Interestingly, the outcome of this fantasy is far different from Lawrence's own reality: as Yvette wavers on the brink, a flood as deus ex machina brings about, at once, proof of shared love, a peaceful resolution, and relief from all her emotional and moral burdens. Granny and the pious sanctum over which she has so long presided are simply washed away; Yvette is warmed to life, briefly and virtuously, by the gypsy's body, and the gypsy, without any clear motivation, removes the decision from her shoulders and departs—quietly, fondly, and responsibly—with his family: "And Yvette, lying in bed, moaned in her heart: 'Oh, I love him! I love him! I love him!' The grief over him kept her prostrate. Yet practically she too was acquiescent in the fact of his disappearance. Her young soul knew the wisdom of it" (V&G, 758).[20]

Lawrence's final statement is intriguing and deeply puzzling. In the final analysis the surface sarcasm of *The Virgin and the Gipsy* cannot cry down the substance, Yvette's legacy of longing and loss, and that most un-Lawrencean resolution of her sexual conflict. Lawrence simply takes the flood in his hands as a giant eraser and wipes all the trouble away.

What are we to make of it? (The fortune-teller had, after all, told Yvette that life would go on, that she would one day be happy in marriage with children of her own.)

Clearly, this is no act of contrition. Lawrence believes as he always has in the primacy of Eros, in the power of the male-female relation and its centrality in life. But this is a vision that has, obviously, been altered by pain; even as we see with what relish Lawrence seems to effect the hideous death of the despised Granny—carried off, wedding ring and all, to a watery grave—we see, at the same time, that he and his gypsy have chosen to set her granddaughter utterly free (*V&G*, 753). The gentle, unknowing Barby will not, after all, become enmeshed and "tangled too much in the skein of guilt / Caught, when [her] heart would leap, in a net of lives" (*CP*, 884–85). Nor will Mellors, who has had no such heavy net cast over his life or Connie Chatterley's.

Adultery is a tangle which has fascinated Lawrence since the days so many years ago when Helen Corke confided in him the story of her married lover and his suicide, moving him to write *The Trespasser* and his poem "Red" (from which the preceding lines are taken). Perhaps he has learned, over the years, what an indomitable power the family actually is.

For his part, from the war between desire and responsibility the vicar has come away with only a pyrrhic victory: in his family, tension and damage will never end. On the other hand, the Eastwoods, together, and Yvette and the gypsy, apart, have won much more. The pivotal element seems to be an almost uncanny wisdom on the part of the married lover, an ability to see, for the sake of all whom he or she loves, where—if anywhere—lies peace. In this sense, the gypsy is indeed wise: it is not only his wife who can read the future. Unfortunately, few are gifted with such clairvoyance.

More important than this, however, is the strand that runs through so many of the novels and tales. Again and again, a Lawrencean man stalks into the moral and social garden and plainly seizes (or does away with) whatever he wants, echoing, through his actions, Lawrence's own declaration, "With 'should' and 'ought' I have nothing to do." Jerome Buckley is certainly correct: he is, indeed, the "true egoist," with no interest in—or talent for—agape. His is the Nietzschean vision, prevalent in the time, of natural power and right triumphing over cowed meekness and servitude. He carries within himself an emotional wildness and an ethical wilderness, and—be he Aaron Sisson, Ramon, Eastwood, Mellors, or Lawrence himself—he sees the established order merely as something that must yield to his imperatives, ultimately rearranging itself around him.

And yet, Lawrence–Paul Morel had once been the prince of his own household, and he had been a loving, generous, and transcendently sensitive figure within that realm. It may have been the harshness of life afterward that caused him to turn his artistic vision away forever from the warmth and brightness of the hearth—the fresh table laid before sunrise, the spindly bicycle careering down the dirt path, the beloved mother dressed in dark frock and bonnet for Sunday services. And he may have done so in the leaden awareness that if all of that radiance and love inside the home was Gertrude Morel and Lydia Lawrence, it had once been and could so easily be again—Frieda Weekley.

A more grim hypothesis, however, is that within that childhood home, Lawrence-Paul learned, on some level, that it was he who was loved most by his mother, however inappropriate and damaging that love might have been. It follows, then, that a man who has vanquished his own father will have nothing to fear, in later years, either from what appears to be the facade of authority or from other men. And if, as Wordsworth says, the child is the father of the man, it is the young, triumphant, and utterly ruined Paul Morel–D. H. Lawrence who has given life to those later insouciant and self-assured interlopers, Eastwood and Mellors, who care so little for other men and their pain.

It is no wonder that the homes in D. H. Lawrence represent only the perversions of family life, and it is no wonder that *The Virgin and the Gipsy* comes, emotionally, to almost no ending at all. Perhaps, indeed, it cannot. For it may well be that *The Virgin and the Gipsy,* with its congeries of haunting memories, is something much beyond a mere unrevised novella. It may have been, actually, the literary manifestation of Lawrence's own life review—a phenomenon precipitated by his attempt to come to terms with his own impending death. Robert N. Butler has studied these universal reminiscences in the aged and has recognized in them "the resurgence of unresolved conflicts." They are, he says, "prompted by the realization of approaching dissolution and death, and the inability to maintain one's sense of personal invulnerability." Importantly, it is not only the aged, Butler points out, who look backward over their lives; so, too, do younger persons—"for example, the fatally ill or the condemned."[21]

Among those for whom this process is most painful, he says, are "those who have consciously exercised the human capacity to injure others" and those who are "characterologically arrogant and prideful"[22]—those, then, whose narcissism must find the specter of death as astonishing as it is appalling. For all of these reasons and in all of these ways, *The Virgin and the Gipsy* seems to exist apart from the other major works of Lawrence: it seems to pit life's sexual imperatives against conscience in a way no other of them does.

The choices and events of Lawrence's life wounded him in the very heart of his genius. The delicate and unique mechanism that had made him what he was was taken apart, year by year, until, in *The Virgin and the Gipsy,* the parts lay strewn about the man, and he cast one final, uncomprehending look over them. How interesting it is, then, that what he made of his pain—this small, strange, uneven work—resonates with the steady tones of its author's contempt for Weekley, his love for Frieda, and a certain unutterable wistfulness.

And so we wonder: does not this novella betray, after all, some slight shudder of guilt and regret in Lawrence? And if it does, did he, in all the physical and psychic pain of that eleventh hour, find it only the more malignant and intolerable?[23] Whatever the answer, he left the work in need of revision and went on to write, instead, the various versions of *Lady Chatterley's Lover*—perpetuating, to the death, the battle between those inner and better selves.

Notes

This chapter is the revision of a paper presented at The International Conference on D. H. Lawrence in Montpellier, France, in June 1990.

1. F. R. Leavis, *D. H. Lawrence*, 38.
2. Graham Hough, *Dark Sun*, 232.
3. Father William Tiverton [Martin Jarrett-Kerr], *D. H. Lawrence and Human Existence*, 94. The consequence of Lawrence's focusing as he does, Tiverton maintains, is "an unreal insulation of the sex act from the total natural scheme" and a failure to produce the whole man and the whole woman.
4. Eliseo Vivas, *D. H. Lawrence*, 42, 103. Vivas also observes: "Whatever the explanation of the frustration of his social instinct, the fact itself leads at once to Lawrence's tragedy—and not only the tragedy of the man but that of the artist also. For it is no doubt this radical alienation that denies his vision of the world the love (in the sense of agape) that would have placed his work at the level which, with his gifts, it could have easily attained. His work is the product of high talent, and it is overburdened with beauty. His novels probe aspects of human experience no other novelist of his age except Proust dares examine. But the world he forges is incomplete, it is not a fully human world. Lawrence, because of his incapacity to love, remained throughout his life, a marginal man" (114).
5. David Garnett, *The Golden Echo*, 254–55.

6. See Lawrence to Edward Garnett, Oct. 15, Dec. 17, 1912, May 19, 1913, to David Garnett, Feb. 27, 1913, *L*, 463, 489, 551, 521.

7. Barbara Weekley Barr, "Memoir of D. H. Lawrence," 9.

8. John Middleton Murry, *Between Two Worlds*, 305.

9. Mabel Dodge Luhan, *Lorenzo in Taos*, 103.

10. Ibid., 104.

11. Knud Merrild, *With D. H. Lawrence in New Mexico*, 172–74.

12. Ibid., 138–39.

13. Ibid., 140.

14. Luhan, *Lorenzo*, 104–5.

15. Keith Sagar, *D. H. Lawrence*, 142–43. See also Jeffrey Meyers's excellent discussion of these events ("Tuberculosis, 1925"), *D. H. Lawrence*, 324–35.

16. See, for example, Sagar, *Lawrence*, 149, 152–57, 161–63, 164–65. Sagar quotes Lawrence from Harry T. Moore, ed., *The Collected Letters of D. H. Lawrence*, 923, "I haven't done any of the Etruscan book yet: and shan't do it, unless the mood changes. Why write books for the swine, unless one absolutely must!"

17. Sagar, *Lawrence*, 143, cites Earl and Achsah Brewster, *D. H. Lawrence*, 288. See also Sagar, *Lawrence*, 149.

18. Lawrence's treatment of Mrs. Fawcett is as febrile and shortsighted as his crippling of Clifford Chatterly; he robs her of her name, calling her, no fewer than eighteen times in three pages, "the Jewess," a "little Jewess," a "tiny Jewess," a "spoilt Jewess," a "bourgeois Jewess," with the "curious ways of a Jewess" (*V&G*, 736–38).

There is a clear resemblance here to the situation of a penniless young Lawrence, just so much younger than Frieda, and to her aristocratic background and similarly passionate decision on his behalf. This is only one, of course, of a network of autobiographical elements in the work, which are not at all uncommon in Lawrence.

19. Jerome H. Buckley, *Season of Youth*, 220–23.

20. I am not unaware of the venerable debate over this issue—over, that is, whether or not Yvette and the Gipsy are in this scene intimate beyond nakedness. It is my own belief that the story's conclusion is far more subtle and provocative if they are not. And, after all, Yvette has just witnessed, mere moments before, the horrible death of her own grandmother.

21. Robert N. Butler, "The Life Review," 66–67. Jeffrey Meyers, *D. H. Lawrence*, 73–75, calls tuberculosis "the dreaded word that [Lawrence] would scarcely mention [all] his life." When he had, in 1913, coughed up bright arterial blood, he had insisted only that his lungs were "crocky": "I am not really afraid of consumption. I don't know why—I don't think I shall ever die of *that*." His end, then, must have seemed not only a betrayal of body but of intuition.

22. Butler, "Life Review," 70.

23. Ibid., 73–74, raises powerful questions about the uncharted relationship between guilt and the life review.

III

The Origins of Late Style

7

BRIAN A. CONNERY

Self-Representation and Memorials in the Late Poetry of Swift

IN HIS "Thoughts on Various Subjects," Jonathan Swift observed that "every Man desires to live long; but no Man would be old" (*PW* 4:243). Subsequently, of course, he vividly illustrated this principle in the third book of *Gulliver's Travels,* and had he written nothing else, the pathetically immortal Struldbruggs alone would have associated Swift forever with literary representations of aging: "They were not only opinionative, peevish, covetous, morose, vain, talkative, but uncapable of friendship, and dead to all natural affection, which never descended below their grandchildren. Envy and impotent desire are their prevailing passions" (*PW* 11:212). In fact, Swift's concern with aging appears to have been virtually lifelong; in 1699, at thirty-two, Swift composed a list of resolutions headed "When I come to be old," the language of which is echoed almost thirty years later in the description of the Struldbruggs. The resolutions include "Not to be peevish or morose, or suspicious . . . Not to tell the same Story over and over to the same People . . . Not to talk much, nor of myself . . . Not to be positive or opinionatre," and the list concludes, in typical Swiftian fashion, "Not to sett up for observing all these Rules, for fear I should observe none" (*PW* 1:xxxvi).

As these writings indicate, Swift's antipathy toward aging seems not to partake of a fear of death but is associated instead with a fear of mental and emotional deterioration and social mortification. Upon hearing of Swift's suffering a stroke, one of his young friends, Lord Orrery, wrote that his own melancholy at the thought of Swift's condition was intensified by remembering the times the Dean had depicted "persons in that condition, with a liveliness and a horror, that in this late occasion have recalled to me his very word."[1] Swift's fears, thus, were prophetic, and both his contemporaries and his subsequent biographers and critics have found varying degrees of irony in the pathos of his final years. Samuel Johnson's cautionary depiction of him as a "driv'ler and a show" is but the most famous of many representations of Swift in his decline.

Most such accounts seem influenced by their authors' assumptions about or definitions of old age, as well as by assumptions about the life cycle as narrative. Irvin Ehrenpreis, Swift's most current authoritative biographer, seems to imply by his chapter headings that "old age" is synonymous with incapacity, for according to his account Swift's stroke marks his passage into the ranks of the aged. Indeed, in considering the biographies of Swift and their accounts of his final years, one may be prompted to wonder whether the Aristotelian plot constitutes a reflection of the life cycle or whether biographers tend to impose an Aristotelian plot upon the lives of their subjects. One might wonder further about the degree to which the Aristotelian plot therefore colors our interpretation of aging, making the final years always seem catastrophic. The construction of the literary "author" Swift has proven remarkably adaptable to those who wish to find in his later years either confirmation of his misanthropy or mental instability or confirmation of their own views of the relation between middle adulthood and old age.

The present essay offers an account of Swift's experience of aging as it appears in four groups of his poems after his final return to Ireland in 1728. The cheerful poems at Market Hill, the normative poems on Dr. Delany, the scatological poems, and the paradoxical poems on his own death indicate a sequence of concerns and illustrate developing rhetorical strategies that are highly suggestive of Swift's experience of the latter portion of his life. Though Swift's disappointment in the failure of his political ambitions in England in 1714 was certainly both a crisis and a turning point in his life, the poems at Market Hill sixteen years later show us a Swift who has adapted to the vicissitudes of his life, moving toward the achievement of an Eriksonian integrity. The scatological poems reflect Swift's experience of the mortification inherent in the aging physical body. On the other hand, the poems on Dr. Delany and those on his own death show us Swift engaged in representing the possibility of virtue while mythicizing his own life, simultaneously attempting to control the delivery of his name and work to posterity and acknowledging the power of his readers to shape him to their own will.

Aging and Absence

To consider the effects of aging upon Swift requires consideration of several puzzling circumstances. Even as a relatively young poet in the 1690s, he displays the stereotypical traits of the grumpy curmudgeon. Conversely, in *Gulliver's Travels,* written in his fifties, and in some late poems written in his sixties, critics have discerned without much trouble more than a trace of infantilism. In fact, the entire question of the nature of aging in the late seventeenth and early eighteenth century remains problematical. While age itself is a biological phenomena, the meaning of aging is certainly determined socially and culturally. While the average life expectancy at birth in Swift's lifetime is generally given as thirty-five years, this figure is misleading: 20 percent of infants died before reaching one year of age. Peter Laslett reports, surprisingly, that in 1695, one in ten members of the population was over the age of sixty-five.[2] The aged were, then, less rare in Britain than the Struldbruggs in Lagado. Among Swift's friends, many lived to impressive ages: Dr. Arbuthnot to sixty-eight, Francis Atterbury to seventy, Sir William Temple to seventy-one, Lord Carteret and Patrick Delany to seventy-three, George Faulkner to seventy-six, and Mrs. Dingley and Mrs. Whiteway to seventy-eight. Still, Swift's intimates tended not to be of his own generation, so that, for example, Temple, Swift's mentor, died when Swift was thirty-two, and Mrs. Whiteway outlived Swift by twenty-three years. Many others, although within Swift's generational cohort, like Atterbury and Bolingbroke, were exiled in France in the 1720s, or like Arbuthnot were left behind when Swift returned to Ireland. Still others died relatively young, like Esther Johnson at forty-seven and Alexander Pope at fifty-six. In his later years, then, Swift repeatedly experienced not only the real deaths of some of his friends and contemporaries but the metaphorical deaths of friends who were irretrievably absent. Thus, Swift did contend with the experience of isolation that is so often a component of the social experience of aging.

The question of Swift's experience of aging is complicated further by his lack of family relationships, which so often serve to define life roles and transitions as the individual proceeds from the role of child to those of spouse, parent, and grandparent. Swift's life was erratic. He was born after the death of his father, then kidnapped to England by his nursemaid for three years during his infancy, and spent no more than a year subsequently with his mother before going to a boarding elementary school. He never married, though he developed intimate and affectionate relations with a sequence of younger women throughout his life. Consequently, he lived and died childless. All this makes Swift's transitional phases and crises difficult to discern. The one continuity in his life was the experience of absence. Still, Swift's entry in his account book in 1710, upon receiving news of his mother's death, indicates his sensitivity to the interrelation between family and the experience of aging: "I have now lost my barrier between me and death; God grant I may live to be as well prepared for it as I confidently believe her to have been!"[3] Throughout his lifetime Swift adopted friends in roles that we might consider as surrogate fathers (Sir William Temple, Archbishop King), mothers (Mrs. Whiteway), sons (Matthew Pilkington, William Harrison), and daughters (Laetitia Pilkington, Mrs. Barber, Lady Acheson), but the degree to which these relations are susceptible to accurate contemporary psychoanalytic interpretation is, in my view, questionable. Still, the death of his father and his childhood removals from his mother and subsequently from his nurse and again from his mother constitute a series of losses which were to be recapitulated in the deaths, exiles, and absences of many of his closest friends in adulthood. Thus, some psychoanalytic speculation may be in order in the examination of Swift's final years.

According to psychological theory, of course, just as mothers and others constitute mirrors for infants, necessary in the development of both the psychic senses of identity with and separation from the other, so the disappearances and absences of these figures must subject the infants to questioning regarding their own continuity. When the mother or nurse with whom the child identifies disappears, the child must wonder who has died—the mother or child or both. As both Freud and Lacan have suggested, the infant's resolution of the crisis comes from imagination and language—the imaginative reconstitution of the absent figure in the present "da" of the child's language.

The problem of continuity in spite of absence appears central to Swift's late work. In the mature Swift disappearances of friends and loved ones in death or in England and France may constitute a recapitulation of his early crises. Moreover, in Swift the deterioration of memory in his final decade creates a parallel crisis. Memory loss makes it difficult and perhaps impossible to reconstitute the past satisfactorily in the present and thus simultaneously undermines the sense of the possibility of continuity. Swift's solutions to both problems lie in language: in poetry he reconstitutes not only his past but his present and future selves in order to create a sense of secure, coherent, continuing identity. At the same time, knowing the vicissitudes of language and readers, to both of which he must trust for his continuity after death, Swift questions the possibility of the success of the project—and ultimately acknowledges that in re-creating himself in language he makes himself subject to the reading, and thus the will, of others.

Disappointment and Integrity

Biographers of Swift are certainly correct in identifying Swift's return to Ireland after the death of Queen Anne as a turning point in his sense of his relation to society. In a poem, "In Sickness," written on the journey in 1714, Swift laments the possibility of his death in Ireland: "why should I repine / To see my life so fast decline? / But, why obscurely here alone? / Where I am neither loved nor known."[4] The despair felt by Swift over the failure of the Harley administration and his disappointment in his own failure to secure preferment in England prompt him here, inspired by his illness, to welcome the possibility of death; his dissatisfaction springs not from the possibility of his death but the possibility of dying *obscurely*. Eighteen years later, in a letter to Bolingbroke, Swift links his return to Ireland with the beginning of his reckoning with death: "I was 47 years old when I began to think of death; and the reflections upon it now begin when I wake in the morning, and end when I am going to sleep." Thus, the poem is sincere, and the return to Ireland was undeniably a crisis; Swift clearly believed that his chances for greatness were concluded and that the return marked the end of his political and social eminence. But to suggest, as so many biographers have done, that he felt the same twenty years later is to suppose a radical inability to adjust, an incapacity to work toward the "integrity" which Erik Erikson postulates as the last stage of the life cycle and which he defines as "the acceptance of one's one and only life cycle and of the people who have become significant to it as something that had to be and that, by necessity, permitted of no substitution."[5]

The lament we hear in "In Sickness" certainly could not have continued after Swift's successes with both the Drapier letters (1724–25) and *Gulliver's Travels* (1726). During the final nineteen years of his life, he was a beloved celebrity in Dublin. In 1726 it appears that he refused to apply to friends to seek the position of bishop of Cloyne in England; in 1732 he refused an almost sure ecclesiastical living in England offered by Bolingbroke; and in 1733 he could write to Pope of his life in Ireland with some apparent satisfaction: "I walk the streets in peace without being justled, nor even without a thousand blessings from my friends the vulgar."[6]

However, in spite of Swift's satisfaction in overcoming the obscurity he had dreaded, the years 1727–33 must have brought a renewed sense of his mortality. He brought to a close his last visit to England by visiting his family house in Goodrich and there designing a memorial for his grandfather, the Reverend Thomas Swift. Throughout these five years many of Swift's intimates passed away, beginning with his beloved Esther Johnson in 1727, followed by Archbishop King in 1729 and Gay in 1732. Although no longer ignored by the public, Swift surely continued to sense the imminent possibility of extinction and its attendant obscurity.

Swift's final birthday poem for Esther Johnson, "To Stella," in 1727, when he himself was sixty and she was failing in health at forty-six, demonstrates his continuing efforts to contend with the process of aging: "This day then, let us not be told / That you are sick, and I grown old, / Nor think on our approaching ills, / And talk of spectacles and pills. / Tomorrow will be time enough / To hear such mortifying stuff" (3–8). As Louise Barnett has suggested, virtually all of Swift's birthday poems for Stella show his coming to terms with aging. Here Swift articulates a distinction recently made by Kathleen Woodward between living in prospective time (looking forward to future events as the source of meaning or significance) and living in retrospective time by looking to the past for meaning and significance.[7] Swift appears to have made the shift, here, to retrospective time, and, as will become apparent, this shift will prompt a greater concern in his work as well as in his correspondence with memory, both public and private.

Yet the period after Stella's death, while Swift was in his early sixties, is marked also by the beginning of a burst of writing about the present, initiated for the most part upon Swift's developing friendship with Sir Arthur and Lady Acheson and his long visit with them at their country estate at Market Hill. If we may trust Swift's advice to his circle of poetical protégés in the early 1730s ("Health and good humour are two ingredients absolutely necessary in the poetical trade"), then Swift's domestic life with the Achesons must have been almost as cheerful as he depicts it in the poems. In them appear traces of most of the themes and strategies which Swift was to use throughout his subsequent writing. First, Swift produces in the Market Hill poems a number of self-portraits in the third person. These lead to the implicit self-portraits in the scatological poems as well as the explicit self-portraits in the poems on Dr. Delany and in his "Verses on the Death of Dr. Swift." The concern with the scatological itself becomes manifest in the last poem of the Market Hill series, "A Panegyric on the Dean," itself a self-portrait.[8]

The Market Hill poems offer, then, a counterpoint to Swift's self-pitying self-portrait in "In Sickness." As previously, he depicts himself in retirement, cut off both from England and power and conscious of the imminence of death. But the mood is cheerful, for Swift has found pleasurable ways of passing his time in his adopted family. In "To Dean Swift," written in the person of Sir Arthur, Swift presents himself as an anomaly in the Irish countryside—but a cheerful one. He celebrates his salvation from obscurity in his status of national hero (and scourge of the English) as the Drapier:

> Good cause have I to sing and vapour,
> For I am landlord to the Drapier:
> He, that of every ear's the charmer,
> Now condescends to be my farmer,
> And grace my villa with his strains;
> Lives such a bard on British plains? (1–6)

The final question here points to Swift's continuing sense of his injured merit in his forced removal to Ireland—but significantly this time he renders the situation as England's loss more than his own.

Swift considered purchasing property adjacent to the Achesons', presumably where he would live out his days. His next poem, "Drapier's Hill," envisages this retirement property as his final memorial and thus initiates the theme of the vanity and vicissitudes of memorialization. The poem is based upon Swift's economics of nostalgia in which land is the only stable value. The hill, according to this poem, will endure as a very local sign and reminder of Swift's life and work:

> That when the nation long enslaved,
> Forgets by whom it once was saved;
> When none the Drapier's praise shall sing;
> His signs aloft no longer swing;
> His medals and his prints forgotten,
> And all his handkerchiefs are rotten;
> His famous *Letters* made waste paper;
> This hill may keep the name of Drapier:
> In spite of envy flourish still,
> And Drapier's vie with Cooper's Hill. (11–20)

Swift is certainly susceptible to charges of pride here, as he catalogues the tributes of the Irish to his success as the Drapier. It is quite clear that his political and literary success as the Drapier is the achievement of which he is most proud. He had simultaneously engaged in a literary tour de force, enraged the political powers of England toward whom he felt such antipathy, effected lasting political change, and earned both fame and gratitude from the Irish. Significantly, it is the character or persona of the Dean and

Drapier—not that of the angry, misanthropic Gulliver—that dominates the rest of his work. Of the memorials catalogued in this poem, only the Drapier's *Letters* themselves are Swift's own production. What Swift values most are the tributes from others—the praise, the signs, the medals, the prints, and the handkerchiefs (which were made with devices in honor of the author) which proliferated after the Drapier's success. Unfortunately, these signifiers of his life and his success are subject to deterioration: they will not last, and thus he wants his name attached to the more permanent hill. Yet the hill, as it becomes part of the poem, becomes itself a literary product. The closing couplet produces a peculiar paradox, as Swift compares his own potentially real real estate to the poetic real estate of John Denham in the popular poem "Cooper's Hill." The poem thus asserts the value of both the physical Drapier's Hill and the poetic "Drapier Hill," simultaneously pro-claiming and denying the value of Swift's literary productions. Poetry can offer immortality—as attested by Denham's achievement—but writing has also previously been associated in the poem with "waste." The distinction between poetry and waste is to be made ultimately by the audience—not the poet—and thus even as Swift's gratitude for the tributes of others and his longing for continued memorialization are apparent, his mistrust of the security of this fame is also clear. All of his work may be reduced to a name ("This hill may keep the name of Drapier"), a signifier potentially without a signified.

Swift associates himself and his works with waste again in "A Pane-gyric on the Dean" (1730), the last of the Market Hill poems, written in the persona of Lady Acheson. The poem's depiction of Swift as an inept but energetic countryman closes with approximately 150 lines of ironic, mock georgic description of Swift's memorable achievement during his stay at Market Hill: the construction of two privies. The section is introduced by a depiction of Swift at the butter churn, which leads in turn to a depiction of Swift writing poetry, showing the analogous flurry of activity and paucity of product in the two pastimes:

> Nor is your skill, or labour less,
> When bent upon some smart lampoon,
> You toss and turn your brain till noon;
> Which, in its jumblings round the skull,
> Dilates, and makes the vessel full,
> While nothing comes but froth at first
> You think your giddy head will burst. (197–204)

The passage is significant in its linking of Swift's vertigo, his "giddy head," with composing. Like churning butter, writing poetry for Swift—perhaps any engagement with language—is a frenzy of mental motion with no stability, no center, and frequently no stable product or meaning, nothing but froth and discomfort. A year earlier Swift had similarly linked his giddiness to the reading of bad poetry in "On Burning a Dull Poem" (1729): "I found my head began to swim, / A numbness crept through every limb: / In haste, with imprecations dire, / I threw the volume in the fire" (9–12). Language, like identity, like psychic reality, and like Swift's own body and sense of balance, is not only unstable but destabilizing. Moreover, as the subsequent segue to Swift's privies in "A Panegyric on the Dean" makes clear, writing may produce only waste, poetry being, potentially, as Swift's early fable of the spider and the bee in *The Battle of the Books* suggests, a form of excrescence, and thus here, like a privy, a tomb or shrine to waste.

The associations in the "Panegyric" among poetry, women (Lady Acheson), waste, and, importantly, Swift himself seem to contain the germs of the subsequent poems, so much discussed and analyzed, generally referred to simply as the "scatological poems," also probably written during his early sixties. These works, whatever else they may tell us about the character of Swift, tell us much about his experience of aging. The basic strategy of the poems is to present, through the viewpoint of pastoral convention or romantic lover, the idealized body of woman and then either to dismantle and disfigure that body physically ("A Young Nymph Going to Bed") or to besmirch that body through attention to its wastes ("Strephon and Chloe," "Cassinus and Peter"). Ruth Salvaggio's recent discussion of the poems from a feminist perspective seems largely accurate, as she claims that Swift "continues to figure his dissatisfaction with and alienation from the world in terms of the body . . . [but] now it is his own body as well, his own physical link to the world of decay, waste, and decomposing material that takes him to 'nothingness' and 'absence.'"[9] While Salvaggio is concerned primarily with Swift's attitudes toward women and his use of woman as sign, her comment linking Swift's women in the poems with death, decay, and nothingness is apt here. As previously remarked, Swift's birthday poems to Stella, the true love of his life, were consistently engagements with the onset of age and thus the impermanence of and possible betrayal by the body. In these earlier poems, then, Swift had linked woman with age and physical mortality. Indeed, for many of the Augustan writers, the woman's toilette was no more than a sign for the vain attempt to arrest age and mortality.

These associations are made more explicit in the scatological poems. "Strephon and Chloe," in which each of the two lovers, after marriage, reconcile themselves to the bodily functions of the other, seems not so much to be about the unloveliness of the digestive tract as about mortality itself as it is metaphorically rendered in the poems. Strephon's disillusionment is consistently presented in terms of his mistaken belief that his beloved is nonmortal and thus not subject to the mortification of the body. As the poem begins, we see, through his eyes, Chloe and her transcendence of physicality: "You'd swear that so divine a creature / Felt no necessities of nature" (19–20). Strephon's anxiety about the wedding night is a product of his apparently burdensome sense of his own physicality: "Strephon had long perplexed his brains, / How with so high a nymph he might / Demean himself the wedding night: / For, as he viewed his person round, / Mere mortal flesh was all he found" (71–76). His overriding question is, "Can such a deity endure / A mortal human touch impure?" (89–90). Ultimately, Chloe's urination and flatulence prove not so much her nauseating nature as her mortality: "He found her, while the scent increased, / As *mortal* as himself at least" (185–86; italics are Swift's). And while the poem does offer dietary injunctions for future brides, its closing lines underscore the concern with mortality, as well as Swift's normative presentation of the abiding pleasures which last into old age:

On sense and wit your passion found,
By decency cemented round;
Let prudence with good nature strive,
To keep esteem and love alive.
Then come old age whene'er it will,
Your friendship shall continue still:
And thus a mutual gentle fire,
Shall never but with life expire. (307–13)

In psychoanalytic terms, then, these poems trace the triumph of Thanatos over Eros, the recognition and acceptance of death, represented by the body and its wastes, and the consequent extinction of desire. More generally, the relation between male psyche and female body throughout the scatological poems is analogous to the relation between human psyche and human body, Swift's psyche and Swift's body, which humbles him through its refusal to submit to his imagination and idealization.

In spite of the betrayal and mortification by the body, the conclusion of "Strephon and Chloe" suggests that both virtue and contentment are possible, and Swift throughout his work offers examples of the ideals to which he aspired. Increasingly, in his later poems, and especially in "Verses on the Death of Dr. Swift," Swift unites these virtues with his portraits of himself, offering a mythical Swift to his readers. At the same time that he was writing these mortifying implicit self-portraits in the scatological poems, he was developing in other poems idealized portraits, of both himself and others.

The Swiftian conception of the heroic was made clear in Gulliver's trip to Glubbdubdrib where he summons Brutus, Junius, Socrates, Epaminondas, Cato the younger, and Sir Thomas More, "a *sextumvirate* to which all the age of the world cannot add a seventh" (*PW* 11:196). As these six examples indicate, the Swiftian hero is the *vir bonus,* the one just man among fools and knaves, who does not truckle to power or to an authority which is itself a product of corruption. In a series of poems written between the Market Hill poems and the scatological poems, on the occasion of Swift's friend Dr. Delany's pursuit through poetry of the patronage and preferment of Carteret, the lord lieutenant of Ireland, Swift sketches out his disapproval of the search for preferment in a corrupt world—and thereby, by ironic implication, celebrates his own lack of preferment. In "A Libel on the Reverend Dr. Delany," Swift portrays himself as an old man who has learned through experience: "But I, in politics grown old, / Whose thoughts are of a different mould, / Who, from my soul, sincerely hate / Both kings and ministers of state" (171–74). As in Pope's "To Augustus" and his own "On Poetry, a Rapsody," Swift presents a corrupt world in which only corruption can succeed. Pointing to himself as an example for his conclusion, Swift represents himself as a martyr for the cause of good poetry and politics. In the inverted world assumed by the poem, praise is blame and blame is praise: "On me, when dunces are satiric, / I take it for a panegyric. / 'Hated by fools, and fools to hate,' / Be that my motto, and my fate" (169–72). Swift seems here already to be playing with ideas for his epitaph. Depending upon one's view, these lines offer either a rationalization for the failure of Swift's youthful ambition or a glimpse of Eriksonian integrity, "the acceptance of one's one and only life cycle." Or perhaps both. In Swift's ironic view, his apparent worldly failure is embraced as a sign of his moral success.

As an example of dull satire amounting to panegyric, among the poems on Dr. Delany, Swift extends his practice of portraying himself through the mouths of Lord and Lady Acheson, in an ironic piece upon himself, "An Answer to Dr. Delany's Fable of the Pheasant and the Lark" in which the speaker of the poem is a government Whig who scorns Swift and his talents as "So dull, that but for spleen and spite, / We ne'er should know that he could write: / Who thinks the nation always erred, / Because himself is not preferred" (70–73). This clearly anticipates Swift's use of a hostile speaker in "The Life and Genuine Character of Dr. Swift," and the strategy here is important. Irony depends not only upon the reader's recognition of a situation contrary to fact but upon the reader's assent to the ironically implied countertruth. In presenting ironically false portraits of himself, Swift enlists the cooperation of the reader in correcting the falsehoods and in substituting for them a contrasting (and therefore panegyrical) true picture. The lines cited are particularly problematical to the reader because they are so close to the truth. Yet the ironic use of a hostile speaker induces the reader to reason that the truth must lie elsewhere. As Louise Barnett points out, "By playing all the roles Swift exercises control over the negative as well as the positive versions of self." [10] This is certainly Swift's strategy— the poems are by no means dialogical. Still, there are limits to the control the poet can exert, limits of which Swift seems fully aware. The strategy implies both Swift's apparent desire for control and his sense of the difficulty of controlling a reader.

As Barnett has pointed out, the problem confronting Swift is one he recognized even in his earliest writings, his odes. In the "Ode to the Athenian Society" (1691), Swift argues like Foucault that the author is a fiction created by readers, perhaps having little or nothing to do with the writer:

> Because, alas when we all die
> Careless and ignorant posterity,
> Although they praise the learning and the wit,
>   And though the title seems to show
> The name and man, by whom the book was writ,
>   Yet how shall they be brought to know
> Whether that very name was he, or you, or I? (162–68)

The arbitrary relation between signifier ("name") and signified ("the man") clearly troubles Swift. The reader's ultimate control of the author's own language—and thus the author's identity—is vexing. The poem's conclusion solves the problem through an ironic paradox: "Men, who lived and died without a name, / Are the chief heroes in the sacred list of fame" (306–7). Fame depends upon namelessness and is ultimately democratic, independent of the author's self-affirming *sum* and *fiat* in language. Even though language appears to fix identity as it substitutes presence for absence, in its function as intersubjective medium it ultimately gestures only to the future. Jacques Lacan suggests that as we create ourselves in language which must then be understood by readers or auditors, our self-created identity refers not to the past but to the future: "In order to be recognized by the other, I utter what was only in view of what will be. . . . What is realized in my history is not the past definite of what was, since it is no more, or even the present perfect of what has been in what I am, but the future anterior of what I shall have been for what I am in the process of becoming." [11] The poet's "I am," the constitution of the self in language, becomes the reader's "You are" and subsequently "You will be," as the poet him/herself becomes the object of the reader's subjectivity. Thus, as Swift attempts to re-create himself and to establish his identity in language, he is constantly aware of the instability of such an identity and of his inevitable reliance upon his readers for affirmation.

The problem of identity, while posited as an adolescent crisis in the Eriksonian model of the life cycle, clearly seems to reemerge with a difference in old age. In Swift the task of constructing and maintaining identity is undertaken publicly. The idea of authorial identity continued to tease Swift. His habitual use of personae and pseudonyms may certainly be explained in part by his fear of legal and political backlashes to his writing. But one has to wonder why he declined, for instance, during the mid-1730s to have his name appear on any of the volumes of his collected works. Volume 1 attributes the works to "J.S., D.D., D.S.P.D.," and the subsequent volumes refer simply to "the author." Certainly, no reader at this point in Swift's career would have any doubts, for instance, as to who the author of *Gulliver's Travels* might be. Swift is incapable of reachieving the air of mystery that marked the original publication of many of his works—and the political issues addressed in these works were now of no immediate consequence and thus unlikely to bestir legal action.[12] Why, then, in what is clearly an effort to assert his identity and to memorialize himself as an author does Swift not attach his name to his work?

In conjunction with Swift's musings about nameless immortality in his early ode, two incidents in the 1730s help to elucidate what is going on here. In the first, one Francis Grant writes to Swift, seeking his support for a project to promote the fishing industry of Ireland. Swift responds ironically that the idea is a good one and therefore doomed to fail. He excuses himself from active promotion of the scheme by noting his age—but also offers an extended description of his service to Ireland as the Drapier and concludes that he now "can do no more." Curiously, the letter is unsigned but followed by a postscript: "I would have subscribed my name, if I had not a very bad one; so I leave you to guess it."[13] Swift here employs overtly the same strategy for inducing reader cooperation just mentioned in reference to his ironic self-panegyrics. Indeed, in another usage, this is a standard satiric device: leaving the identity of satiric victims blank or encoded so that the reader must fill in the blanks and thus become complicit in the satire by identifying the victims and articulating their names. In this case, however, Swift wants his reader's complicity not in identifying his victims but in recognizing his own merit—exactly the strategy of the ironic self-portraits in which Swift expects readers to recognize and correct ironic falsehoods. Francis Grant is made responsible for recognizing the merit and supplying the name of the author of the letter.

In an episode which offers an exact counterpoint to this letter, Swift demands inscription of his name. In 1737 the City of Dublin meant to honor Swift's service to Ireland by offering him the freedom of the city in a silver box. In a fit of pique, he returns the box to the city, complaining that the reasons for the honor should be made explicit. Moreover, he objects: "As to the silver box, there is not so much as my name upon it. . . . Therefore, I have sent back the box and instrument of freedom . . . leaving to your choice, whether to insert the reasons for which you were pleased to give me my freedom, or bestow the box upon some worthy person whom you may have an intention to honor because it will equally fit everybody." [14] The echo of the sense of Swift's ode is inescapable: "How shall they be brought to know / Whether that very name was he, or you, or I?" In this case, unlike his letter to Francis Grant, Swift demands his name in print—and printed in metal, not just on paper. The difference can only be, again, that although he will not write his own name, he wants *others* to articulate both who he is and what he has achieved. Just as he leaves Francis Grant "to guess it," he is here "leaving to your choice" whether or not to write his name and achievement. For him to write his own name is plainly self-promotion. For others to write his name is an affirmation of who he aspires to be—indeed, it is the completion by the reader of Swift's construction of self.

Kathleen Woodward's speculations about the possibility of a "mirror stage of old age" illuminates the dynamics between author and reader in Swift's writing here: "If the mirror stage of infancy is distinguished by the perception of binary opposition, the mirror stage of old age is . . . inherently triangular, involving the gaze of others as well as two images of oneself." [15] The gaze of others confirms or denies the self-created image of Swift, negotiating between his subjective "I" and his self-constructed "me."

Indeed, it seems possible to argue that the final ten years of Swift's competency in poetry were devoted to his efforts to evoke such affirmations and thus to induce others to create memorials to himself. Like King Lear, Swift seems to have been implicitly crying out, "Who is it who can tell me who I am?" Throughout his career as writer, Swift had recognized that self-perception is always suspect: indeed, his mission as satirist was to allow people to glimpse themselves accurately in his mirror of satire. A sermon generally attributed to Swift (though not without controversy), "On the Difficulty of Knowing One's Self," argues for the necessity of some sort of reflective device in the process of achieving and maintaining self-knowledge: "A Man can no more know his own Heart than he can know his own Face, any other Way than by Reflection: He may as well tell over every feature of the smaller Portions of his Face without Help of a Looking-Glass, as he can tell all the inward Bents and Tendencies of the Soul" (*PW* 9 : 355). Given such assumptions, the desire to control one's memorialization becomes metaphorically a desire to manipulate the mirror. Swift's desire to appear reflected in the poetry of Pope, for instance, is evident throughout his letters in the 1730s: "My happiness is . . . the ages to come will celebrate me, and know you are a friend who loved and esteemed me, although I died the object of court and party hatred." [16] Swift here outlines the dynamics of his concern: he can attain posthumous identity only through the reflection of his image by others.

Memory and Identity

If the problems of identity and self-knowledge have a renewed urgency in old age, they are compounded by the problem of forgetfulness. As early as 1734 at age sixty-seven, Swift is concerned with the growing failure of his memory: "I have lost by these diseases [his vertigo] much of my memory, which makes me commit many blunders, in my common actions at home, by mistaking one thing for another particularly in writing, when I make a hundred literal errors." [17] Here, the failure of memory makes the relation between signified and signifier ever more slippery, and it introduces gaps in the continuity of both the world and the self. Significantly, the failure of memory, for Swift, is evident "particularly" in writing, the locus of value for Swift.

Memory is, of course, one of the great pleasures and one of the keenest anxieties of old age. In Swift's last poem to Stella, he had offered memory as a compensation for the difficulties of old age, recommending the reflection on past virtuous actions as

> Some lasting pleasure in the mind;
> Which by remembrance will assuage,
> Grief, sickness, poverty, and age;
> And strongly shoot a radiant dart,
> To shine through life's declining part. (30–34)

But the decline of memory creates even more absences in the life of the aging subject, including absences of the self: metaphorical deaths of past selves who are now rendered incapable of imaginative resurrection. In his "Thoughts on Various Subjects," Swift had remarked that "Observation is an old Man's Memory" (*PW* 4:251). As memory fails, one may live increasingly in the present—and the present may thus be rendered absurd by its discontinuousness, its lack of narrational continuity.

The deterioration of memory thus challenges the sense of self-continuity and necessitates the daily reestablishment of fictions of self-coherence. Writing of his patients with Korsakov's syndrome, which involves complete breakdown of memory (and is thus far more debilitating than Swift's own condition), Oliver Sacks is so eloquent as to deserve quotation at length: "We have, each of us, a life-story, an inner narrative—whose continuity, whose sense, *is* our lives. It might be said that each of us constructs and lives a 'narrative,' and that this narrative *is* us, our identities." A victim of Korsakov's syndrome, thus, is "deprived . . . of a quiet continuous narrative, and driven to a sort of narrational frenzy," driven to "creating a world and self" in place of what he can no longer recall. Thus, a patient must "literally make himself and his world up every moment." Sacks says, then, that the patient must "seek meaning, *make* meaning, in a desperate way, continually inventing, throwing bridges of meaning over abysses of meaninglessness, the chaos that yawns continually beneath him."[18]

In the aging subject, more than narrative coherence is wanted. Robert Butler's work on reminiscence in the elderly indicates that what is wanted is significance. In a subsequent study, particularly relevant to Swift, Virginia Revere and Sheldon S. Tobin observe that the narrative of life reminiscence by the elderly becomes mythicized as the subject attempts to justify the life lived.[19] As we retell our stories, we make heroes of ourselves and thus give our pasts significance which thereby justifies our lives.

In light of these clinical observations on aging and memory, Swift's self-portrait in the "Verses on the Death of Dr. Swift" becomes particularly poignant:

> That old vertigo in his head
> Will never leave him, till he's dead:
> Besides, his memory decays,
> He recollects not what he says;
> He cannot call his friends to mind;
> Forgets the place where last he dined:
> Plies you with stories o'er and o'er,
> He told them fifty times before. (83–90)

Swift's solution to the problem of absent memory seems the same as his solution to other problems of absence: language. Fortunately, Swift had compiled a vast repository of language—his works, both published and unpublished—which he could use to re-create the narrative of himself as author. Even here, however, memory sometimes thwarts him, as is indicated in the semicomic, semipathetic correspondence related to his manuscript of *Directions to Servants,* which he remembers having written but cannot locate.[20]

Swift's attention turns therefore toward a review of his works. From 1734 to 1738 he is active in reviewing the materials for Faulkner's edition.

Particularly important to Swift was his plan to publish *A History of the Four Last Years*, his account of the Harley ministry. Swift's purpose in its publication is made quite clear in letters to the young earl of Oxford, in which he argues, reflecting his fear of "careless posterity," that history is being falsified at the hands of the Whigs. The publication of his history, thus, will serve "for the information of posterity, and to control the most impudent falsehoods."[21] But the history was to serve as a memorial to Swift himself as well, as he suggests in his unfinished memoirs, where he characterizes the piece as "an entertainment to those who will have any personal regard for me or my memory" (*PW* 8:107). Writing, then, is a repository for memory; the individual's memory transformed into writing can outlast forgetfulness and can then be transformed through reading into collective memory.

Perhaps even more significant within the same letter is Swift's self-portrait: "I have been many months the shadow of the shadow of the shadow of etc. etc. of Dr. Swift. Age, giddiness, deafness, loss of memory, rage and rancour against persons and proceedings—I have not recounted the twentieth part." Less than three months previously, Swift had described himself in similar terms in another letter: "I am grown an entire ghost of what I was."[22] Swift's sense of himself as disappearing, receding, fading, is clear here—and this surely reflects his experience of aging and memory loss, the impetus for the "narrational frenzy" of this period.

The urge to memorialize himself (and thus to stabilize his identity) and be memorialized is, perhaps, the largest theme of Swift's work. In his early odes to men out of power, in his politics and economics of nostalgia, in his satires which hold up modern humanity for comparison to the ancients or to lost ideals, he is concerned always with re-creating presence out of absence, compelling readers to remember the thing that is no longer. Lacan reminds us that the symbol originates in the play between desire and death;[23] Swift, more mundanely, remarks that most people are reluctant and unwilling to be forgotten, observing that even "the Vulgar" put up grave markers (*PW* 4:244).

Indeed, just as the poems of his last ten years and his work on the publication of older works serve as means for self-memorial, within these poems an explicit concern for memorialization recurs. In the scatological poem "Cassinus and Peter," Cassinus, fearing his own imminent death from his confrontation with Celia's mortality, pleads for a memorial:

> Yet, kind Arcadians, on my urn
> These elegies and sonnets burn,
> And on the marble grave these rhymes,

A monument to after-times:
"Here Cassy lies, by Celia slain,
And dying, never told his pain." (73–78)

Here again is Swift's sense of the impermanence of writing: the poetry of Cassinus will be burned. And here too is his longing for a more permanent inscription, the rhymes engraved in marble. Like Swift's "Verses" on his own death, Cassy's epitaph declares Cassy speechless even as he speaks through it.

Swift's most famous late poem is, of course, the eulogy and epitaph for himself, "Verses on the Death of Dr. Swift." In it, as has been demonstrated in a little-noticed article by Philip Anderson, Swift once again traces the ravages of the process of dissemination.[24] He looks ahead to what will happen to his writings (and, consequently, since he now lives only in words, to himself) after his death: "Now Curll his shop from rubbish drains; / Three genuine tomes of Swift's remains. / And then to make them pass the glibber, / Revised by Tibbald, Moore, and Cibber" (197–200). Having been deformed at the hands of the Whig scribblers he despised, his works (and himself, and his name) will eventually be erased. A year after his death, his works will be obscure:

Some country squire to Lintot goes,
Inquiring for Swift in verse and prose:
Says Lintot, 'I have heard the name.
He died a year ago.' The same.
He searcheth all his shop in vain. (252–57)

Both passages quoted above emphasize Swift's existence only in words ("Swift in verse and prose"), and the second passage marks the beginning of his linguistic death. Even his written words exist no more, for he has deteriorated into oral speech. Lintot has "heard the name," but the printed words can no longer be found.

Swift's final eulogy within the poem, then, is an oral one, given by a Whig at the Rose Tavern. Here Swift recognizes the inevitability of his lapsing into oral speech and of his consequent deformation. Yet in a wonderful feat of Swiftian control, he reaches out of the grave as author of the poem to reconvert the oral speech into writing, simultaneously controlling the language and acknowledging the limits of his control. As in the ironic self-panegyrics, he renders his self-portrait in the mouth of an potentially hostile speaker, relying upon the reader to distinguish truth and falsehood. In so doing, he acknowledges the reader's ultimate autonomy.

A less famous prior version of "Verses" makes overtly clear what Swift is doing here, the presentation of a pseudodialogical representation of self. In "The Life and Genuine Character of Dr. Swift," as in the scenes throughout "Verses," a variety of characters' attitudes toward Swift are juxtaposed, creating both contradictions and complements, from which the reader must derive and re-create the "genuine" character:

> What money was behind him found?
> 'I hear about two thousand pound—
> 'Tis owned he was a man of wit—'
> Yet many a foolish thing he writ;
> 'And sure he must be deeply learned!'
> That's more than ever I discerned. (73–78)

It becomes more clear here that Swift, even as he constructs himself in the fictionalized language of others, betrays his sense of alienation from himself. Swift's incessant self-portraits create a process similar to that of the analysand described by Lacan: "He ends up by recognizing that this being [i.e., his self, established in the course of analysis] has never been anything more than his construct in the imaginary and that this construct disappoints all his certainties. For in this labour which he undertakes to reconstruct *for another,* he rediscovers the fundamental alienation that made him construct it *like another,* and which has always destined it to be taken from him *by another.*" [25] Such alienation in Swift's works is demonstrated by the continuous felt tension created by his simultaneous efforts at constructing and controlling his self in language and his acknowledgment of the futility of those efforts, indicated by his representing the distortion of himself which he attributes to others.

So too, the "Verses" show a posthumous proliferation of different Swifts as he is taken from himself by others: "Now Grub Street wits are all employed; / With elegies the town is cloyed: / Some paragraph in every paper, / To curse the Dean or bless the Drapier" (165–68). But even for this process, Swift attempted to prepare. Both "Verses" and "The Life" are offered as examples to the public of how to and how not to commemorate him. Recognizing that as author he is the product not only of his words but of the reader as well, Swift attempts to teach the Irish how to honor and so to preserve him. In "Traulus" (1730), he had portrayed himself as "the people's favourite" (10), and subsequently, in the voice of the people he had made himself their hero: "Yet still the Dean on freedom raves. / His spirit always strives with slaves. / 'Tis time at last to spare his ink. / And let them rot, or hang, or sink" (95–102). Similarly, in 1734 Swift composed a

satire against lawyer Richard Bettesworth with a title summarizing his ultimate wish fulfillment, "The Yahoo's Overthrow," in which he uses the most
popular of verse forms, the ballad, to imitate the voice of the public singing
his praise and damning his enemy: "The Dean and his merits we every one
know, / But this skip of a lawyer, where the de'il did he grow? / Knock
him down, down, down, knock him down" (6–10). Swift here represents
himself in language in order to re-create himself, a re-creation necessitated
not only by his deteriorating memory but also by his sense of imminent
demise. At the same time he recognizes the futility of such representation
and knows that "Swift" can survive not in his own repetition of himself
in language but only in the public's repetition of himself in language, and
consequently he instructs the public on the ways to re-create and preserve
himself.

What is even more extraordinary is the extent to which he succeeded.
In 1738 the *Dublin Journal* published a tribute to Swift, punning on his
name and thereby calling attention to the slippery identity between signified
and signifier upon which Swift trusts for his immortality, as well as calling
attention to the double meaning of the signifier, the multiple and unstable
meaning of Swift:

> If DEATH denotes to be at rest
> Of SWIFT he'll never be Possess'd;
> As Sure as Water's in the Ocean
> While SWIFT is SWIFT, he is in motion;
> Then while in motion 'tis confess'd;
> That SWIFT will never be at rest:
> What's SWIFT is QUICK, then on this head,
> SWIFT can't at once be QUICK and DEAD. [26]

Swift himself was famously attentive to his own will and epitaph. His
arrangements for his funeral are exact, and he did, of course, compose his
own epitaph. He stipulates that he will be buried in St. Patrick's three days
after his decease, "as privately as possible," at midnight. Like his Cassinus, he requests a black marble monument, inscribed, "HIC DEPOSITUM EST
CORPUS JONATHAN SWIFT, S.T.D. HUJUS ECCLESIAE CATHEDRALIS DECANI,
UBI SAEVA INDIGNATIO ULTERIUS COR LACERARE NEQUIT. ABI VIATOR, ET
IMITARE, SI POTERIS, STRENUUM PRO VIRILI LIBERTATIS VINDICATOREM"
(*PW* 13:149).[27]

While the epitaph emphasizes that the tomb contains the *body* ("hic est
depositum corpus") of Swift, that is, the mortal remains of the physicality
which was always mortifying to him, it also marks in and of itself Swift's

final transformation of self into language, and his final surrender to the process of dissemination. Having no children, his words are his only progeny. Born of an absent father and raised in a series of absences, he reproduces himself in the family tradition. In his will, his final attempt at control of his public identity, he successfully commands the way in which others will inscribe his name.

Notes

I am grateful for the cheerful assistance of the editors, Janice Rossen and Anne Wyatt-Brown, throughout the course of writing this essay.

1. Lord Orrery to Dean Swift, Dec. 4, 1742, *The Correspondence of Jonathan Swift* 5:208.

2. For the social construction of aging, see Tamara Hareven, "The Last Stage." For information on aging and life expectancy in the eighteenth century in Britain, see Peter Laslett, *The World We Have Lost*, 103.

3. See Irvin Ehrenpreis, *Swift: The Man, His Works, and the Age.* The bulk of the biographical details I have summarized are based upon Ehrenpreis's account of Swift's early life.

4. Jonathan Swift, "In Sickness," in *Jonathan Swift: The Complete Poems.* All quotations from Swift's poetry are from this edition. Subsequent quotations are cited by line numbers in the text.

5. Swift to Bolingbroke, Oct. 31, 1729, *Correspondence* 3:354; Erik Erikson, *Childhood and Society*, 232.

6. Ehrenpreis recounts Swift's rejections of the two posts in England (*Swift* 3:487, 727). The letter to Pope (July 8, 1733) is from *Correspondence* 4:171. There is, of course, contrary evidence which testifies to Swift's continuing dissatisfaction, particularly his letters which describe his antipathy toward the Irish. In 1734, for instance, he writes to Bolingbroke: "I must be content to die among such a people, with whom it may however be said it is better to die than live," evoking simultaneously Bolingbroke's sympathy for Swift's misfortune and antipathy toward the Irish. But Swift continues, revealing a political purpose: "But what is all this to your Lordship or to England? It is a great deal to the latter, for your wealth is completed by your tyranny and oppression here. You see my old murmurings are not yet ceased, but it is the same as if they were, because I am now grown desperate, and having nothing to do but rail with a very few friends in a safe corner of the house" (ibid., 4:249–50). In typical Swiftian fashion, Swift claims obscurity while remaining the most public man in Dublin and claims quietness while speaking his mind. I believe therefore that Irvin Ehrenpreis is generally accurate in his suggestion that Swift's seeming antipathy to Ireland is more rhetorical than actual.

7. Louise Barnett, *Swift's Poetic Worlds*, 94; Kathleen Woodward, "Reminiscence and the Life Review," 155.

8. Swift to Mrs. Caesar, July 30, 1733, *Correspondence* 4:184. Similarly, the duchess of Queensbury writes to Swift, "I remember you once told me always to sit down to write when I was in good health and good humour" (March 4, 1734, ibid., 4:223–24).

Robert Uphaus has written convincingly on the continuity between the Market Hill poems, the Delany poems, and Swift's verses on his death, in "Swift's 'Whole Character.'"

9. Ruth Salvaggio, *Enlightened Absence*, 96. I do not here intend to imply that attention to the factor of aging leads to an authoritative reading of the scatological poems. Abler critics than I have attempted analyses of these poems in psychoanalytic and other terms. Within the context of this ongoing discussion, I hope that my own comments indicate that Swift clearly identifies as much with the female figures within the poems as he does with the male voyeurs, and that if these poems express an animosity toward women, as Swift figures women as representatives of both romantic and realistic images of the body, they express an equal animosity toward himself, his works, and his own body. For other discussions of the poems, the reader is advised to consult one or more of the following: Jae Num Lee, *Swift and Scatological Satire;* Peter J. Schakel, *The Poetry of Jonathan Swift;* Thomas B. Gilmore Jr., "The Comedy of Swift's Scatological Poems."

10. Barnett, *Swift's Poetic Worlds*, 83.

11. Jacques Lacan, "The Function and Field of Speech and Language," 86. The theme of dissemination is continued both in *Tale of a Tub*, in which the father's will is misinterpreted by the three sons, and in the third section of *Gulliver's Travels*, in which Gulliver discovers that original authors do not recognize themselves in their commentators.

12. It is worthy of remark, in this light, that Swift did put his name to an Irish political pamphlet during this period: *Consideration of Two Bills* (1733). In this case, as Irvin Ehrenpreis argues, he must have believed that his name would give the pamphlet greater rhetorical power: "An important part of his strategy is the lack of a mask. Swift had passed beyond the status in which caution dictated a pseudonym. He could now assume no disguise that would give his reasoning more authority than his true title" (*Swift* 3:718).

13. Swift to Frances Grant, March 23, 1734, *Correspondence* 4:229–31.

14. Swift to the Corporation of Cork, Aug. 15, 1737, ibid., 5:67–8.

15. Kathleen Woodward, *Aging and Its Discontents*, 69.

16. Swift to Pope, May 31, 1737, *Correspondence* 5:42.

17. Swift to Pope, Nov. 1, 1734, ibid., 4:262.

18. Oliver Sacks, "A Matter of Identity," 105–6.

19. See Robert Butler, "The Life Review," and Virginia Revere and Sheldon S. Tobin, "Myth and Reality."

20. *Directions to Servants* probably was begun in 1702 (see Herbert Davis's comments in *PW* 13:xxi). In 1738 Swift began to think of publishing it. On Aug. 31, 1738, Swift writes to his publisher that Mrs. Ridgeway has just found one half of the manuscript, and he inquires as to whether Faulkner knows where the other half is (*Correspondence* 5:121). More than a year later, in December 1739, Swift seems to have forgotten where any of the manuscript might be and writes again to Faulkner for information (ibid., 5:172).

21. Swift to the Earl of Oxford, June 14, 1737, *Correspondence* 4:262.

22. Swift to Orrery, Feb. 2, 1738, ibid., 5:46.

23. Lacan, "Function," 104.

24. See Philip Anderson, "Transformations of 'Swift' and the Development of Swift's Satiric Vision in *Verses on the Death of Dr. Swift*." John Irwin Fischer has also noted the ways in which the process of dissemination in "Verses" parallels the

corruption of the body after death; see *On Swift's Poetry,* 158. Of the many other discussions of the poem, the most consonant with the current essay is David Vieth's reader-response–oriented essay, "The Mystery of Personal Identity: Swift's Verses on His Own Death."

25. Lacan, "Function," 42.

26. Quoted by Herbert Davis in the preface to *PW* 13:xxxvi.

27. Yeats's translation is the most famous: "Swift has sailed unto his rest; / Savage indignation there / Cannot lacerate his breast. / Imitate him if you dare, / World besotted traveller; he / Served human liberty."

8

ANNE M. WYATT-BROWN

The Liberation of Mourning in Elizabeth Bowen's
The Little Girls and Eva Trout

S INCE HER DEATH in 1973, Elizabeth Bowen's formidable novels have not received much attention from theoretically inclined academics. As a result, no one has noted that her final two works, *The Little Girls* and *Eva Trout,* move the novel in the direction of postmodern experimentation. The innovations of the Anglo-Irish novelist have been ignored for several reasons. As Howard Moss explained in 1979, "The wrong reputation can be as deadly as none." For some time the academy has denigrated works belonging in the tradition of the comedy of manners. Such efforts seem snobbish in our egalitarian and ethnically conscious society. Unless evidence of subversion or overtly feminist undertones appears among the social nuances, writers like Bowen are not taken seriously. Her generally conservative political and social attitudes, as John Hildebidle reports, can be inferred by "the frequency and judgmental force with which the word 'vulgar' enters into her fiction." Moreover, those modern critics who do not object to her upper-class prejudices have little understanding of the effect of aging upon her choice of material and style. As a result, they find it difficult to interpret her least traditional fiction.[1]

Bowen's fiction resists superficial reading. In particular her final two experimental novels, *The Little Girls* and *Eva Trout,* which should have attracted the attention of theorists, are so complex that they bewilder even the wariest of readers. One often has the uneasy feeling of being an intruder into Bowen's private world, lost without a guide. Prior critics have attempted to sort out the confusing strains in Bowen's early fiction with some success but have generally have left the later works alone.[2]

164

Throughout Bowen's career, the dominant themes in her fiction involve the interaction of marriage and society, the subjects of the comedy of manners. Yet at no point is Bowen's fiction merely conservative or old-fashioned. For example, Hildebidle stresses the conservative, "unmistakable consistency" of her writing but also concludes quite accurately that the novelist's suffering caused her to convert the conventions of social comedy from a comedy of manners to a "modern *tragedy* of manners." Bowen's fiction contains at least two contradictory strands: she juxtaposes the asocial and psychotic with the everyday and the ordinary. Like the American novelist Walker Percy, whose middle-class, highly educated characters are "lost in the cosmos"—to borrow the title of one of his books—most of Bowen's adolescents and sensitive adults feel the same way. Indeed, in common with most of the imaginative and innovative practitioners of social comedy in this century—E. M. Forster, Barbara Pym, Molly Keane, Anita Brookner, and Elizabeth Jolley—Bowen concentrates on revealing the fissures in society. Rather than seeking to uphold the status quo, she writes out of a profound sense of her own alienation, an estrangement which can be traced to the losses of her early childhood. Nicholas Royle goes so far as to insist that Bowen's novels are not social at all but "concern the asocial and psychotic." Drawing on the psychoanalytic work of Nicolas Abraham and Maria Torok, he argues that one can find traces of "refused or impossible mourning, unspeakable secrets, and transgenerational hauntings" in all her novels, even in the apparently lighthearted *A World of Love*.[3] As she grew older, Bowen's sense of isolation increased. In consequence, the experimental features of her final novels seem to threaten the existence of social comedy altogether.

The first step toward understanding Bowen's contributions to narrative form is to recognize that particularly her last two novels represent a transitional genre, what Roger Salomon calls "desperate storytelling." Like the writers in the mock-heroic tradition whose work he examines, Bowen also felt that she was "living beyond or 'post' any cultural period" appropriate for the conventions of her chosen genre, traditional social comedy. Yet, for personal reasons, she "still remained committed in some fashion to the values generated by such narrative."[4] Events in her later life encouraged her to transform the conservative conventions of comedy almost beyond recognition.

In view of the complexity of Bowen's work and the effect of aging upon her writing, an interdisciplinary approach is needed to illuminate the final novels. By linking a psychodynamic understanding of depression with the theoretical perspectives of biography and literary gerontology, one can interpret Bowen's experimental novels in a much more favorable light than do critics like Hermione Lee, without losing sight of the author's intricate texture. Although aging, ill health, and depression played an important role in shaping Bowen's later fiction, Lee misses the point when she claims these novels merely illustrate the novelist's "late *malaise*" and should be dismissed as "symptoms of a predicament," the result of the "rather unhappy circumstances of Elizabeth Bowen's old age."[5]

Instead, Amir Cohen-Shalev recently has suggested that the last works of aging artists (and by implication writers) often arouse inflated expectations in the viewer/critic. When these final works, he suggests, are "too elusive for unequivocal delivery in an established code," they are often rejected as a symptom of decline. Moreover, Spencer Curtis Brown, Bowen's close friend and literary executor, testifies that in her last years the writer "deliberately sought new techniques and all the excitement of learning to express her own individual music on a new instrument." She attempted to remove as much of the omniscient narrator as possible, allowing the characters to talk and act without her interpretation. He asserts that the challenge kept her writing vigorous and experimental. Although she wrote about a fallen world, one radically changed from her girlhood, he notes that "her sense of comedy . . . irradiated the later books even more than the earlier." Psychiatrist George Vaillant puts the issue well when he says that "anxiety and depression, like blisters and fractures, become the price of a venturesome life."[6]

Seen from this perspective, *Eva Trout* and *The Little Girls* represent a new direction in Bowen's fiction. They can rightly be seen as the development of a late style rather than as a symptom of malaise. In fact, we can read these final novels as part of Bowen's search for identity, a pursuit one scarcely would expect from a novelist writing in her early sixties. Nonetheless, this is a quest which the critic can share by attempting—as Norman Holland put it—to "develop continuities through both . . . life and . . . writing." Such a reading suggests that Bowen's swan songs have much to teach us about courage near the end of life.[7]

In order to understand Bowen's accomplishments, one must reassess the very real problems that she faced at several critical points in her personal and professional life. From the beginning to the end, Bowen's experiences blended an unusual mixture of aristocratic privilege and emotional deprivation. When she was young, both her family and her country were besieged by events beyond their control. She descended from an Anglo-Irish family, which had built Bowen's Court in 1775 (*BC*, 161). Neither social prestige, however, nor family inheritance could save her from feeling unprotected as a child. During her youth Ireland itself was torn asunder in the conflict between the indigenous Roman Catholic inhabitants and their Protestant landholders. Bowen's Court survived the Troubles intact. Yet guerrilla tactics shook the confidence of the landed aristocracy, and the Bowens had many an uneasy moment (*BC,* 439–40).

Moreover, Bowen's personal family life was unmanageably precarious. Henry Bowen, her father, went mad when she was five (*BC,* 409) and eventually was institutionalized for some years. Her mother was so determinedly oblivious to his state that relatives had to warn her of her husband's increasingly demented condition. Things deteriorated to such an extreme that Bowen found it necessary at the age of six to pursue a "campaign of not noticing" troublesome events around her (*BC,* 416). Eventually, after two years of reacting to Henry Bowen's illness, Mrs. Bowen decided to move with her daughter to the coast of Kent, where they lived near the mother's "network" of relatives (*EB,* 24). Despite frequent moves from one "fantasy home" to another—much like the ones Eva Trout attempts to build for her adopted son Jeremy—Bowen and her mother were able to create what the novelist called "pavilions of love" (*P&C,* 29).

According to Bowen it was at Kent—the scene where the novel *The Little Girls* takes place—that she began to discover her sensitivity to and love of landscape (*P&C,* 7–9), an affection which eventually provided some compensation for the discomfort of the disruptions of her life. Furthermore, in time her father's mental health started to improve, allowing him to visit them. Then in 1912 when Bowen was thirteen, her mother developed cancer and died (*BC,* 424–25). The girl had no chance to bid her mother farewell. She had been farmed out to a neighbor, a decision that made the child feel superfluous. No doubt the elders thought they were protecting her from the ravages of grief, but the isolation meant that she could not mourn naturally. She cried the first night, but on the day of the funeral, which she was not allowed to attend, she "gave way to an excess of high spirits," reported the friend with whom she was staying (*EB,* 27). Afterwards, for many years Bowen "could not remember her [mother], think of her, speak of her or suffer to hear her spoken of" (*P&C,* 48).

Bowen, Victoria Glendinning asserts, transcended rather than repressed those things that puzzled her.[8] According to the biographer, by closing her eyes to the problems around her, she managed to survive her father's hospitalization, subsequent moves, and her mother's death without developing debilitating emotional scars. Indeed, Bowen herself believed that her early life taught her to love places and things more than people. The dreamlike atmosphere of her early life, she thought, explained why she had fewer early memories than most people, a characteristic she shares with her heroine Eva

Trout as well. Glendinning claimed that Bowen's methods of managing her feelings were largely successful, agreeing with the novelist that a lifelong stammer remained her only significant disability (*EB*, 22–23; *P&C*, 12).

In contrast, I would argue that Bowen found the reality of her mother's death, in conjunction with her father's mental illness and the uprooting from her ancestral home, too much to face. Much later the writer discussed how at the age of eight she had refused to let herself think of her lost home, Bowen's Court, saying, "Perhaps children are sterner than grown-up people in their refusal to suffer, in their refusal, even, to feel at all" (*BC*, 418–19). George Pollock in "Mourning and Adaptation," has argued that the loss of a parent inhibits a child's capacity to mature emotionally. In his judgment "a sudden unexpected death" is far more traumatic than "a chronic loss due to institutionalization." Bowen experienced both kinds of losses at particularly vulnerable times in her childhood. As Pollock has demonstrated, the degree of suffering depends partly upon the age and the psychosexual stage of the survivor. Henry Bowen's illness began when his daughter was five and lasted until she was eleven (*BC*, 409). Thus, she had little opportunity to work through her oedipal feelings for him. Then Mrs. Bowen died when her daughter was thirteen and about to enter puberty, a time when girls tend to be especially dependent upon their mothers (*BC*, 425). No wonder Bowen, like one of George Pollock's patients, attempted to "defend herself against . . . feelings of 'nothingness and emptiness.' "[9] When one considers that Bowen's grief was blocked, it is not surprising that her entire oeuvre is full of references to orphans and bereavement—indicating how affected she was by that loss. Yet not until she began writing *The Little Girls* in her early sixties could she make use of the details of those final days in Kent.

It seems likely that the trauma of loss forced Bowen to employ what Abraham and Torok call "preservative repression," in which the past is preserved in such a repressed form that no part of it can be undone or expiated for. Becoming an orphan made Bowen preternaturally aware of what Nicholas Rand calls "the gaps or 'silences' left within the living by the secrets of others." Writing fiction, however, provided Bowen the opportunity to relive old hurts and name the unnameable. She never became an hysteric or a *cryptophore*—a person who is obsessed by dark secrets—but, as Royle has noted, her fiction contains many metaphors of secrets, crimes, accomplices, and tombs, all of which clearly had personal significance to her.[10] As she grew older, Bowen gained considerable insight into madness. Indeed her later novels are dedicated to the principle that the line between sanity and madness is permeable; aberrant behavior has recognizable origins. Especially in later life, Bowen wrote fluently about individuals who threaten to cross the barrier between sane and insane, without losing sympathy for their situation.

Although Bowen's resilience and understanding of the etiology of madness are impressive, her behavior resembled her mother's habit of denial. For many years the novelist, like her mother, avoided facing uncomfortable truths, although she never carried the habit to the same pathological extent. Instead, her imagination compensated her for occasional parental neglect. Bowen recalled that her parents "ruled their private kingdoms of thought, and inside it, I, their first child, began to set up my own" (*SW*, 9). By such means, Glendinning observes, Bowen effectively avoided psychic unhappiness, while leading a reasonably normal life and beginning a remarkable career as a novelist and short-story writer (*EB*, 22–23).

Bowen's method of repressing emotional dilemmas appeared to work effectively for some years. Art offered an arena for displacing personal conflict, a domain to explore her own feelings at a considerable remove without violating the kind of detachment she prized. In youth, some aspects of the disturbances that she had knowingly suppressed became the raw material of her fictional world. Bowen's orphaned state made her especially sensitive to the plight of vulnerable or unwanted progeny. Her early novels feature young people who are powerless to protect themselves against the vagaries and diffidence of their caretakers. In them Bowen re-created the conspiratorial atmosphere of her childhood. At times her characters react to the dishonesty of their elders. Her juveniles are rarely passive; thus, many of them become disruptive forces in their households. By the time she wrote her final novel, however, she realized that violence might be unleashed if successive generations disregarded the welfare of their offspring. In *Eva Trout* Eva's young son, the deaf and dumb Jeremy, appears to be indifferent to what his adopted mother Eva might be doing. In the end, though, he explodes destructively, shooting his mother with a revolver.

In novel after novel Bowen returned obsessively to the same themes, a repetition which suggests that art by itself is not an effective therapy. Instead, like most individuals for whom writing provides an outlet for powerful feelings, devising scenes of orphans and neglected children temporarily relieved Bowen's anguish but did not permanently resolve her deep sense of deprivation and loss. Her bereavement also had a powerful influence on the choices she made early in life, and those choices in turn continued to affect her selection of subject matter in fiction. Although the benign interest of her extended family spared her the worst effects of social isolation, nonetheless Bowen craved a more personal, familial, and romantic love. In 1921 at twenty, shortly after her father's remarriage in 1918 (*EB*, 38), she announced an engagement, but the whole matter ended so abruptly that in time it almost seemed to have been a dream. Glendinning describes Bowen's condition during that period as "heightened" and reports that from the start her aunt was "sceptical." Glendinning dismisses the subject with the purely social observation that ultimately "nothing worked out. . . . It wouldn't have done" (*EB,* 40).

Yet the writer was haunted by recollections of that event, with its uncomfortable but absurd mixture of desire and social control. More than forty years later, on the first page of *Eva Trout,* the heroine refers to a newly broken engagement (*ET,* 11). Of course Eva does not represent the novelist directly, nor can we infer Bowen's feelings from Eva's reactions. The heroine has no "sceptical" relatives to challenge her fantasy although privately her friends disparage her story. Also, unlike the novelist who years later could still recapture the confusion that surrounded her own failed engagement, Eva abandons her painful recollection more easily. Sometime later in the novel when the memory has faded, Eva readily admits that the whole matter was a hoax (*ET,* 89). But when one considers the sexual charades with which the novel abounds—a supposed pregnancy that is really an illegal adoption and the fake wedding journey that Eva tries to stage at the end with her beloved Henry—that broken engagement and its attendant commotion had clearly left its imprint on Bowen's imagination.

At twenty-four the aspiring young writer, who had just published her first volume of stories, married Alan Cameron, despite the warning signs that he might lack sexual interest in her. At thirty Cameron was living a comfortable bachelor's existence with his mother and a clergyman, who, years later, became the prototype of Father Tony Clavering-Haight in *Eva Trout.* Glendinning interprets Bowen's marriage to the older Cameron as happy but admittedly celibate. At the same time, the biographer suggests that Bowen became a compulsive writer partly to compensate for her lack of sexual satisfaction.[11] In 1933, three years after her father's death (*EB,* 69), Bowen began to satisfy her emotional needs by taking a series of much younger men as lovers, the first of whom was an Oxford don, Humphrey House (*EB,* 86). He later told his wife that Bowen had been a virgin when their affair began (*EB,* 88). Far more important and long-lasting in Bowen's life than House, however, was Charles Ritchie, a Canadian. Yet in the end he was as elusive as her father Henry Bowen had been. Although Ritchie was unfailingly devoted, Bowen never had the satisfaction of marrying him, even when she was free to do so. In 1948, just four years before Cameron's death, Ritchie married his cousin, thereby effectively removing himself from the list of eligible bachelors (*EB,* 182).

Bowen's frustrated longing for the much younger Ritchie helps explain why her heroine, Eva Trout, suffers from unrequited love for Henry Dancey, who at the novel's beginning is only twelve years old. Several reasons point to Henry Dancey being a parodic version of Charles Ritchie. Ritchie, who was seven years younger than Bowen, was the great love of her life, just as Henry is, even though he is twelve years younger than Eva. Further, Henry assists Eva in her ill-fated attempt to sell her Jaguar and leave the Arbles without a trace. Bowen, who herself felt like an "outsider-insider" in England, thanks to her Anglo-Irish heritage, sensed that Canadian Ritchie shared her anomalous position in England, as well as her occasional moments of feeling like a spy (*EB*, 139). Both Henry and Ritchie also played the role of younger brother to an admired older sister. In view of Henry's and Eva's oedipal, indeed almost incestuous, devotion, Bowen chose to name young Dancey for her father Henry Bowen rather than for Ritchie, to whom she dedicated the novel.

At this point one must remember that Bowen was capable of salvaging situations that another less talented person might have found devastating. For example, odd though her sexless marriage seems in our hypersexual age, Alan Cameron apparently met her most important emotional needs, by providing a replacement for her parents.[12] He managed their business affairs, selected her wardrobe, and provided a necessary stability to their lives. He conducted his affairs—whatever they were—so discreetly that Glendinning makes no mention of any liaison, making only a few references to a longtime married friend and colleague Eric Gillett. Most observers agree that Bowen loved Cameron, and ample evidence suggests that she was emotionally dependent upon him, but after he died signs of tension in their relationship appear in *Eva Trout*. In that novel Bowen wittily portrays the interaction of several homosexual and celibate men, Constantine Ormeau, Willy Trout, and Father Clavering-Haight. To some extent, the novelist sits in judgment. Eva has clearly been the victim of her father's neglect; all his attention went to his fickle lover, Constantine.

Still no matter how inadequate Cameron may have been as a lover, when he died, from alcoholism and heart and eye trouble, Bowen at fifty-three felt that her world had vanished. Her elaborate defenses collapsed. For some time she found it difficult to write at all. Circumstances made a mockery of her attempt to imitate her mother by "not noticing." In the ensuing depression she found it impossible to manage her financial affairs and ended by selling Bowen's Court in 1959 to a man who promptly tore it down (*BC*, 459). Not only did Bowen feel the loss of her reliable guide and support, but Cameron's death rekindled the feelings of grief that she had repressed at her mother's untimely death. Studies of mourning indicate how complex that phenomenon can be. Early evidence suggested that in some cases a second bereavement in adulthood can trigger what John Bowlby calls "a belated reaction" to an earlier loss that was never mourned. In 1968 Felix Brown, an English psychiatrist, noted that as early as 1926 Mapother had pointed out that when individuals who are orphaned early in life lose a spouse later on, the depression they experience shows "a regression to events in early life tinged with the same emotion, suggesting that it is a kind of reactivation of some previous experience." Brown also reports Anthony's 1940 findings that the death of a parent often arouses feelings of guilt in children between the ages of eight and twelve—Bowen was just thirteen. Bowlby's 1980 study of depression further confirms such findings, while George Pollock reported in 1981 that "empirical findings from individuals who lost parents or siblings in childhood" indicate that they are predisposed to "a severe reaction to a later life change or loss." [13]

The upheavals of Bowen's fifties and sixties suggest that her husband's death set off a belated crisis of mourning for her long-dead mother. Fortunately, she had the means to overcome her difficulties. At first, however, the amount of work she produced diminished, as she restlessly moved about the United States taking up one writer-in-residence post after another (*EB*, 206). Her literary agent, Curtis Brown, reports that she had "a bad breakdown of health" after she sold Bowen's Court, exacerbated by "guilt that she had failed her ancestry by failing to pass on her inheritance." Fortunately her novelistic gifts, he says, distracted her from her troubles and allowed her "to keep her life creatively and satisfyingly full." [14] Bowen managed to write only three novels in the twenty years after Cameron's death, whereas in the previous twenty she had written seven. Still, her last two novels eventually provided a battleground where she could struggle with her unruly emotions. They contain some of her most probing and powerful material; at long last she confronted more openly than before her suppressed feelings about her mother and her often mixed emotions about her husband.

The Little Girls, published when Bowen was sixty-four, provided the initial turning point in her later career. Its protagonist, Dinah Delacroix, battles her unacknowledged sense of loss by means of an unconventional life review, in which Bowen participated by proxy. In his landmark 1963 essay, "The Life Review," Robert Butler describes four main aspects of that moment when an individual finds it necessary to survey his or her past. Looking backwards at some point in a conscious fashion and reviewing one's life, he notes, are universal traits. The elderly, whose futures are short, tend to reminisce more than the young. In some cases this scrutiny can contribute to the occurrence of "late-life disorders" such as depression, which it does in Dinah's case. Finally, those elderly whose life review has a positive outcome may develop "candor, serenity, and wisdom." He also believes that individuals initiate a life review "as a general response to crisis of various types," of which death is the most obvious example. Although Dinah is not in a state of crisis before she initiates the life review, Bowen certainly was.[15]

Thematically, as the Bowen critics have pointed out, the novel deals with the insatiable desire of those growing older to recapture the past. The main character Dinah is an exceptionally attractive woman in her late fifties; in fact, her youthful appearance suggests that life has not quite touched her. Yet she has been married and widowed and is now the mother of two sons, as well as a grandmother. She is prone to enthusiasms which make little sense to her friends. Most recently, she has been burying objects in a cave, so that future generations will be able to reconstruct her society from those remnants. Suddenly, she is sent into a fugue state by the juxtaposition of a chance question, "Who's going to seal it up?" and the sight of an uneven swing (*LT*, 16, 20).[16] Then, realizing that she is repeating an experience from her girlhood, she becomes obsessed with desire to find her long-lost schoolmates, whom she last saw in 1914. At age eleven they had all scattered when World War I broke out. Impulsively Dinah sends out nearly £100 worth of newspaper advertisements until the two women respond. The old friends feel that their settled lives are in jeopardy when they are summoned by this voice from the past. Clare, the woman for whom Dinah has the most elaborate feelings, is particularly uncomfortable with Dinah's intensity.

Bowen's new way of writing "externally" without interpreting her characters' thoughts and feelings makes this beginning read like a play with inadequate stage directions. Why should a crooked swing and an unsealed cave start Dinah upon her quest? Yet for Bowen the answer is simple; like the clinician Jean Baker Miller, she perceives the importance of relationships in women's lives, especially those developed in latency. As a result, Dinah comes to life as a character for the first time in the marvelously vital scenes of reunion with her friends. These encounters also demonstrate the truth of Carol Gilligan's observation that women feel bonded to the lives of their friends. Even though the three women have been separated for many years, they quickly recapture their old selves and interact with all their accustomed eccentricities, in what is almost a private code.[17] The very ease with which they resume their more assertive and engaged girlhood behavior suggests that they had lost or left behind an important segment of themselves when they parted from their friends many years before. Thus, Bowen implies that adult behavior is a mask which can disintegrate when one is reunited with old friends.

The middle section consists of a flashback to 1914. It takes place largely at St. Agatha's, during the summer when Dinah and her friends were eleven, at the end of latency. The reconstruction not only captures the essence of this time in their lives but provides the information necessary to understand what is happening in the present. The little girls play like puppy dogs, sexual differences being irrelevant. The little boys who hang on the periphery of their world are treated like brothers or cousins. Parents are people whose commands must be slyly circumvented. Outward rebellion is not possible, but the girls are experts at obeying the letter rather than the spirit of the law. Their irreverent behavior reminds us that Bowen as a girl was accused of being "bumptious" (*BC*, 420) and participated enthusiastically in her cousin's rows (*P&C*, 17). The world Bowen describes is an Edenic one, captured just before the snake of self-consciousness enters the garden.

The three girls, Dinah, Clare, and Sheila—a.k.a. Dicey, Mumbo, and Sheikie—are best friends and partners in crime. Dinah and Clare, however, have a special bond that exceeds their emotional understanding.[18] Dinah's mother and Clare's father are in love but are entirely too honorable to disrupt their families by having an affair. Mrs. Piggott, Dinah's mother, is a widow; her husband committed suicide before Dinah was born (*LG*, 193). The two eleven-year-olds are caught up in the world of adult emotions that they can only dimly fathom. In spite of the undercurrent of adult emotions, the girls are entirely childlike and convincing in their reactions.

Bowen is a master at evoking the comic atmosphere of the school life of girls. In a BBC interview of 1959, three years before she began *The Little Girls,* she described writing in language that echoes D. W. Winnicott's location of creativity in an intermediate space "between the dream and the reality, that which is called the cultural life." Bowen declared that composing is "an extension . . . of the imaginative play thing a child has—that life isn't amusing enough, so you build it up with imagination of your own" (*EB*, 31). Thus, one incident from girlhood appeared in her novel. Shortly after her mother's death, Bowen instigated a "burying ritual" at her school, Harpenden Hall (*P&C*, 57). Glendinning, reflecting Bowen's view of the matter, emphasizes that the girls merely buried "a biscuit tin containing some cryptic writing" (*EB*, 29). She misses the point that Bowen was seeking a means to handle her anxieties about her mother's death and burial. Sensitive children who are not allowed to see the dead body sometimes worry that the corpse is not truly dead and will wake up later on in the grave. As a result, much attention in *The Little Girls* is given to whether the coffer the girls bury still contains the objects they had placed in it. Furthermore, much of this section is devoted to the details of purchasing accoutrements for the burial and making plans—exactly the stages from which Bowen had been excluded when her mother died. The attention devoted to the details of the burial suggests that the episode in some strange way compensated for that exclusion, by allowing the adult writer the opportunity to explore her early anxieties about death.[19] Knowing something of Bowen's personal history explains why Dinah regresses when years later she discovers that the items have been removed from the coffer.

The middle section ends on July 23, 1914, with a picnic, the sort of ritual set piece found in Jane Austen and other writers of social comedy. But this picnic, like the one in E. M. Forster's *A Passage to India* (1924), marks the disruption of normal social intercourse, the unleashing of evil. It begins innocently enough as a celebration of one child's birthday and the end of summer term. It would have been a time of temporary leave-taking had not the war broken out early the next month. As it happened the goodbyes were to be unexpectedly permanent, just as Mrs. Bowen's death had been for her daughter. Frustration marks the farewells. Major Burkin-Jones is forced to speak to his lady love, Mrs. Piggott, in a sort of code, lest the attentive Dinah realize their intense attachment. Feeling excluded, Dinah runs to bid Clare farewell, but Clare refuses to greet her properly. She drives off triumphantly with her father, leaving Dinah screaming her name at the top of her lungs like an angry infant deprived of her mother.

As a result of the rupture, emotional moments continue to reverberate, much as the mysterious sound in the Marabar Caves echoes for Miss Quested and Mrs. Moore in Forster's *A Passage to India*. In contrast, however, Forster's characters cannot escape the resounding echo. They are forced to reevaluate their lives. But Bowen's characters, like their creator, adeptly bury their misery. Therefore, when Dinah sees Clare in adulthood, she has no idea why she is troubled by Clare's presence. The two women brief each other on their parents' deaths quite calmly, but very gradually a dim memory of that long-ago parting works its way to the surface of Dinah's mind, making her feel as if she had been recently bereaved.

The final section of the novel returns to the present. Dinah feels compelled to complete the unfinished business of the past. She instigates the digging up of the coffer, which turns out to be empty, indicating the impossibility of reconstructing the past as it once was. Feeling devastated by her discovery, she turns to Clare for comfort. Clare, however, is loath to respond; Dinah reminds her too much of Mrs. Piggott, whom Clare had loved years ago with a child's helpless intensity. In one key scene Dinah asks her if she is a lesbian (*LG*, 197). Clare refuses to answer, but clearly she is afraid of the feelings that Dinah arouses. As a result, Clare deserts Dinah one Sunday night, leaving her friend in a distracted state.

Dinah's accident and reaction are very like Miss Quested's hysterical adventure in the Marabar Caves in Forster's novel. She has a mysterious collapse, which Glendinning suggests has earmarks of the madness of Bowen's father (*EB*, 220). At this point Dinah's children and grandchildren close ranks. Dinah's sons display their resilience, as well as their comic obtuseness. They tell Sheila Artworth that their forceful mother is "as a rule . . . so very placid" (*LG*, 232). (Sheila feels compelled to divert herself from reacting by playing with her finger bowl.) Still Bowen is not as despairing about the survival of the family as is Forster. Dinah is a widow like her mother, but the two boys have had each other—and various cousins—for moral support. Clare and Dinah may suffer from "the non-sins of our fathers— and mothers" as Dinah suggests (*LG*, 186), yet Dinah's children are exempt from the curse. The family as a whole can survive the disintegration of one individual. Therefore Dinah's granddaughters sit complacently in the living room cutting pictures out of magazines, safe in their childish world while the adults agonize around them. Rumors of trouble have reached them but do not penetrate their defenses.

Moreover, friendship triumphs at last. Gradually the story is reconstructed, by combining all possible tellers with all available listeners. The psychoanalyst Winnicott understood the therapeutic value of such reconstructions and emphasized how important the empathic listener can be to the process of healing.[20] Even the peripheral Sheila Artworth finds some comfort from the renewed friendship. She tells the story of her lost love to Clare (*LG*, 229–30) and, without stirring up any animosity or disgust, admits to Dinah's sons that she had deposited in the coffer her sixth toe, a congenital anomaly which had shamed her in girlhood. She had never told her friends about that toe. Her obsessive dancing, Bowen hints, with its exhibitionist elements compensated her for feeling deformed (*LG*, 234–35). In contrast, Clare and Dinah take longer to sort out their misunderstandings. Eventually Clare realizes that Dinah merely wants to be consoled for the losses of her childhood, rather than to take Mrs. Piggott's place as an unconscious temptress. Then, at last, she comforts the needy Dinah. In the very last scene, Clare finally remembers the picnic in 1914 when she failed to bid her distraught friend farewell. In recompense she says goodbye to Dinah "for now and for then." Dinah wakes as if from a bad dream, saying, "Clare, Clare, where have you been?" (*LG*, 236–37), and the novel ends on the redemptive recognition of loss and the hope for some restitution in the future.

The message of the novel is mixed. Reconstructing the past is a disturbing experience, which may at least temporarily put the protagonist at risk. Hildebidle argues that such journeys into the past represent "death threats to the self." Indeed, Bowen emphasizes that the journey of remembrance is full of risk; depression is the inevitable outcome if one expects to be able to bring back the past completely. Yet Dinah's story demonstrates that some recollection is absolutely necessary when events in the present have reawakened unacknowledged grief from the past. Bowen's narrative also makes the case for the importance of latency and the friendships of that period in the life of a woman. In fact, she hints that unless one re-enters the past and recaptures at least a trace of one's old self, one may be doomed to sleepwalk through life. Therefore the novel ends on an affirmative note. Dinah and Clare are able to repair some of the damage that the uprooting had caused. Bowen herself experienced a cathartic effect from completing the novel, similar to the relief of insight that George Pollock's patients feel after regaining their memory of past events.[21] After *The Little Girls* was published, Bowen bought a house in the town where her mother had died. As her biographer has commented, that action completed "her return journey" (*EB*, 221).

Although fiction offered Bowen an opportunity to view her sense of displacement at some remove, the actual drafting of the novel took its toll. She had difficulty concluding *The Little Girls* and needed more than the usual amount of help and moral support from her agent, Curtis Brown.[22] The novel's conceptual problems resulted from its emotionally charged content. Not only was her heroine, Dinah Delacroix, attempting to reconstruct the severed strands of her past life experience and to understand her own emotions, but the author was engaged in the same task as well. As a result she could not be confident about the direction that the work should take. In its complicated plot, Bowen reconstructs the fragments of her early life with her mother, in those last days before Mrs. Bowen's untimely death. (Although Bowen had described those last years in *Bowen's Court* [1942], at that time she made no attempt to recapture her feelings for her beloved mother.) The abrupt ending to that happy interlude had made Bowen feel for many years that relationships with houses and with people were too fragile to be recaptured once they were ruptured, a point she later repeats in *Eva Trout* (*ET*, 163, 254). Finishing *The Little Girls*, however, temporarily released Bowen from that limiting belief in her personal life.

The lessons of insight, however, do not last forever. *Eva Trout or Changing Scenes* (1969), written in her late sixties, a few years before she died of lung cancer, continues Bowen's effort to probe her past and explore her vision of the future. Although critics like Hermione Lee have condemned it, this novel is intuitive, detached, and honest in its pessimism. Because Bowen better understood and accepted her own mixed feelings, she accurately captured the irrational strength of all of her characters' desires. Having successfully confronted the profound sense of loss caused by her mother's death in *The Little Girls,* Bowen could examine her own deeply submerged love for and disappointment in the men and the places in her life, past and present. Her recent loss aroused an old sense of being orphaned; thus she exhibited, as George Vaillant claims the "unloved" often do, "a special capacity to identify and to empathize with the pain and suffering in the world."[23] At the same time she exhibited considerable control by constructing a narrative of Olympian detachment in which to consider these painful feelings. The novel's disjointed structure—once again Bowen moves through time and space without providing any guides—challenges the reader to follow the abrupt shifts in time and place. The plot consists of a series of "changing scenes," a pattern that Bowen reinforces by means of the novel's subtitle. Although several scenes of vicarage life—based on the author's girlhood recollections of having lessons with a nearby rector's family (*P&C,* 16–17)—appear in the early chapters, other elements undermine this familiar convention of social comedy. As the author herself hints in the text, the novel is a black comedy (*ET,* 239).

This time the aging writer creates what Glendinning calls an "eponymous heroine . . . an orphaned heiress, unloved, clumsy, 'left unfinished', innocent with that damaging innocence so deep-lodged in Elizabeth's mythology" (*EB,* 225). Eva's remarkable mix of complete vulnerability and mythic forcefulness represents some elements of the writer herself. Losing Bowen's Court had destroyed some of the writer's confidence, thereby creating a dilemma which she converts into a metaphor for Eva's predicament. One senses that Eva's unsettled childhood, during which she moved constantly following her father and his lover, Constantine, provides an objective correlative for Bowen's feelings of dislocation, which had been exacerbated by the author's violent reaction to losing her ancestral home. In the novel the ruined castle, which Eva and the Danceys visit first in chapter 1, represents Bowen's late, lamented family estate. The castle is no longer habitable. Seeing it awakens Eva's desperate need for love, but even she realizes that it is not a place to realize these dreams. This novel, however, is by no means completely autobiographical, despite the echoes from Bowen's life and the presence of some familiar people. Eva is an artistic creation.[24] She is what Bowen thought she might have become had she been less fortunate or had less talent, and, of course, Eva's situation is far more dire than Bowen's ever was. In contrast to the author, Eva never learns to mourn her lost mother nor understands how damaged she has been by such a childhood.

The plot unfolds inexorably following the logic of a Greek tragedy. It abounds with many hints of impending doom, and its protagonist is as blind to their meaning as Oedipus is to Tiresias's warnings. This time, however, Bowen constructs her fatalism on psychological insight rather than on repression. She carefully describes the way in which well-meaning and successful families for generation after generation inadvertently damage their children until one of their offspring finally wreaks a terrible revenge. The plot's gyrations also parody the uprooted nature of contemporary life, by exaggerating the many moves Bowen herself had experienced. Eva, the heiress, is unleashed upon an unsuspecting world with too much money and too little sense of what it means to be a member of a family. Her answer to any frustration is to go into hiding somewhere else, thus frightening and hurting the feelings of those who feel responsible for her.[25] The novel's disrupted chronology represents the difficulties of reconstructing the character of Eva's past.

Unlike Dinah Delacroix and her friends, Eva has no confidant, no one who has shared her life. Instead her story is pieced together by bit players, who have little empathy for her plight. Her shallow parents provide no example of mature love. Thus Eva can experience desire but does not develop any sense of responsibility for her beloved. Her mother dies in an airplane crash, while absconding with a young lover. Her father, a financier of world renown named Willy Trout, reserves his deepest affections for his lover, the perfidious Constantine, while he finds servants and schools willing to watch over the orphaned Eva. Willy never notices that his daughter can neither talk clearly nor cry. As a result Eva seems hardly human. Unlike Bowen, whose maternal aunts took charge of her, none of Eva's relatives fills the gap. At the novel's end, Eva is depressed and angered when family members who answer her invitation to see her off at Victoria Station fail even to recognize her. She complains to Constantine, "Those were my people; they *should* have known me" (*ET,* 264).

Eva's life consists of a series of melodramatic events, similar to those found in many soap operas, but which are transformed by Bowen's ability to combine a comic sensibility with real feelings drawn from her own past. The narrative shifts ground periodically, forcing the reader to struggle to assimilate a kaleidoscope of conflicting perspectives. For example, the disruptions of early childhood are followed by a marvelously comic episode at an experimental school. Housed in the famous castle, the school is financed by Willy Trout and stocked with renegade teachers and delinquent children, who are psychologically well-informed and old beyond their years. They set "an Oedipus-trap" for one of the teachers "by arranging an effigy of his mother in his bed" (*ET,* 51). The children's behavior is so outrageous that Mrs. Stote, a local cleaner, calls the institution "a Home for afflicted children" and ponders why Eva "had to be put away" when her only sin was being "a little dull" (*ET,* 53). The school closed its doors at the end of term when Eva's roommate, named Elsinore after Hamlet's castle, nearly dies from complications following a suicide attempt. Yet despite the absurd name, Elsinore awakens Eva's desire for love. Watching Elsinore be rescued by her mother encourages Eva to seek a substitute for her own dead one.

Thus, Eva insists on being transferred to a conventional boarding school, a more likely hunting ground. There she encounters a gifted teacher, Iseult Smith, who undertakes to humanize the girl. She, however, abruptly abandons Eva when the mother-hungry girl recites a Metaphysical poem, one which reveals her intense love for her teacher (*ET,* 65–66). Eva loves Iseult much as the child Clare loves Mrs. Piggott in *The Little Girls.* Like the grown-up Clare, Miss Smith rejects her pupil's overtures to avoid the temptation of succumbing to Eva's appeal. Motivated partly by a desire for revenge, some years later, after her father's suicide, Eva decides to move into her teacher's house—Miss Smith having in the meantime married Eric Arble. This time the monstrous young woman proceeds to destroy their marriage by enticing the susceptible Eric.

Meantime, the Danceys, the vicar's family in the Arbles' village, try to provide Eva with a taste of normal family life. This episode is based on one of Bowen's girlhood recollections. During the years when Bowen was living in exile with her mother, someone arranged for her to take lessons with the Salmons, the family of a nearby clergyman. Unfortunately, their intimate family life intensified the child's feelings of being an outsider (*P&C,* 14–19), and like Eva she asserted her supremacy whenever possible. Not surprisingly, the Danceys' intervention is equally doomed to failure. Instead of attaching herself to the parents, Eva singles out Henry, aged twelve, to be her savior. Henry attracts her for several reasons. He is the most intelligent and best-looking of his family, and instead of being afraid of Eva, he treats her "as he might an astray moose which when too overpowering could be shooed away" (*ET,* 14). Of course, he needs to grow up quickly if he is to play the required role of consort. Needless to say, he is entranced by the twenty-four-year-old young woman. She beguiles him with tales of a broken engagement, a view of the deserted castle where the honeymoon was to have taken place, and with what Iseult Arble calls "those consuming eyes and that shoving Jaguar" (*ET,* 92).

At this point, Eva increases the tension by running away and later hinting to Iseult that she was going to bear Eric Arble's child. She then departs to America where she buys a child, Jeremy, in an illegal adoption. For all her great wealth, however, she receives what Henry Dancey later calls "a pup" (*ET*, 152), damaged goods, for the child can neither hear nor talk.[26] Henry mistakenly assumes that no one could love a child like that, but Eva, who for most of her life has felt far more defective, adores the boy. For a number of years Eva voluntarily stays in exile in America, re-creating Bowen's "pavilions of love" with her mother by excluding the outside world from her symbiotic relationship with Jeremy. When, however, the time comes for the boy to be educated, the basis of their connection disintegrates. Eva, whose desire for romantic love knows no bounds, returns to England where she once again visits Henry Dancey. She ends by turning her son over to the Bonnards, French doctors and educators, while she pursues Henry, who at twenty is almost old enough to marry.

Despite the twists and turns of the plot, Bowen's presentation of male characters and of grieving families represents new emotional dimensions in her work. Men play a minor role in *The Little Girls* but display a greater range of feeling in *Eva Trout*. For example, Constantine begins as a sly villain. He manipulates Eva and the Arbles, as he had once juggled lovers while keeping a firm grasp on the affections of Willy Trout. By the end of the novel, however, he seems dazzled by Eva, almost obsequious in his expressed desire to give her whatever aid she needs. Mr. Dancey, Henry's father, becomes increasingly important as the plot progresses. He was based partly on Bowen's recollection of Mr. Salmon, the clergyman father whom she had "continued to idolise" in girlhood, even when the lessons she was having with his daughters went badly (*P&C*, 18). Although Mr. Dancey's perpetual hay fever provides a leitmotiv for him, much as it does for Forster's Wilcoxes in *Howards End* (1910), Dancey, unlike the Wilcoxes, is capable of a full range of human emotion. He wrestles with complex feelings of love and concern for his unruly son, while he ministers impressively to his congregation. Moreover, he and his wife stoically bear witness to their grief after the death of their younger daughter, Louise. Unlike Eva's relatives, who do not even recognize her when they appear at the station, moments before her death, the Danceys provide an impressive example of deep feelings and love for a daughter. Surely Bowen could not have written such poignant and direct scenes in the years before she completed *The Little Girls*.

Surprisingly, Henry, cast in the heroic role far before his time, nearly lives up to Eva's emotional investment in him. Somehow he makes convincing rather than absurd the thirty-two-year-old Eva's love for him. Despite the incestuous dimension of their love—both of them are seeking to replace lost family members—almost by accident he teaches Eva to express her loving feelings. Yet Henry, unlike his parents, has great difficulty in telling anyone about Louise's death, for his sister was especially dear to him. In a moment of heightened emotion, he calls Eva "my love, my sister" (*ET,* 264), indicating that he hopes that Eva will take Louise's place in his heart. For her part, Eva hopes that Henry will compensate for all the missing relationships in her life, a tall order that is doomed to failure. Both of them are clearly replacing or "refinding" lost objects of desire. (According to Freud, all later love objects are replacements for the lost breast of infancy; "the finding of an object is in fact the refinding of it.")[27] Still, we cannot help but respond to the vision of Eva weeping. For the first time in her life she sheds what Henry calls "those extraordinary tears!" (*ET,* 267), when he promises to make her fake wedding journey a real one.

Eva's apotheosis turns out to be cruelly short, for she has ignored the Bonnards' dire warnings about Jeremy's feelings. In following her heart, she, like Willy Trout, has attempted to abandon her child, but the boy refuses to play the role of passive victim. True to his American origin and upbringing, Jeremy finds a gun, which has been hidden among Eva's household effects by Iseult Arble. He arrives at Victoria Station, the scene of the start of Eva's wedding journey. He looks so much like a "child star" that the other participants assume that they have accidentally wandered onto a set and try not to obstruct "the rigged-up cameras which . . . they took to be present and in action, or soon in action—for, how should there *not* be cameras?" (*ET,* 265). Jeremy, who fancies himself an avenger like Orestes, shoots his mother. All the participants are stunned by Eva's demise: "a woman bystander to whom nothing was anything" is the only person capable of action. When Jeremy cannot stop running, "she snatched him back before he could fall over the dead body" (*ET,* 268). The novel ends with these words as if to indicate the uselessness of any further comment.

The novel's shattering violence and its depiction of sexual confusion surely reflected the cultural climate of the 1960s, the time in which it was written. The period was one of radical social and political upheaval, in which normal family values were challenged on every front. It was a particularly difficult time to endure for a politically conservative older woman, who was also mourning the loss of her husband and her family house. Yet Bowen created grim comic drama out of instability and upheaval. Writing about the demise of the Trouts made it easier to accept that she had no child to continue her own family line. Instead of privately mourning the end of the house of Bowen, she created a fictional memorial in the fall of the house of Trout. Rather than clinging to outworn conventions, as the novelist Barbara Pym had done during the same period, Bowen redesigned her novel to fit the changing mood that she sensed.[28]

In these final works the novelist used her fiction to begin the task of re-creating her identity in old age. She constructed a discourse that moves toward the postmodern; she converted her disequilibrium into plots that quite literally mirror her sense of emptiness and fear of loss of control. Indeed, Bowen's final novels are remarkable testaments to the way in which art can transform unhappiness and abandonment into experimental forms. Although Bowen snatches tragedy out of the jaws of comedy in *Eva Trout*, nonetheless, her final novels are marked by the qualities of candor, serenity, and wisdom that Robert Butler sees as characteristic of most elderly individuals who successfully complete a life review, the serenity in *Eva Trout* being that of tragic catharsis. Bowen's art teaches us that these attributes in late life are neither static virtues nor cause for smugness. Indeed they assimilate pain, and at a cost. One senses that she learned to accept the uncertainty of her existence and almost to welcome the fluxes of her emotional life. Like the psychoanalyst Winnicott, who made no effort to cut short the "preliminary chaos" of the early days of treatment, for they were "the first phase of the creative process," Bowen discovered that her creativity thrived on chaos. Although Anna Freud does not include writing comic fiction as one of the ways the ego defends itself in her famous *The Ego and the Mechanisms of Defence,* Bowen's example demonstrates that the creative process offers some artists a way of making effective use of their depression, so that, as Kathleen Woodward has pointed out, their art creates a space between mourning and melancholia.[29]

These last two novels are an artistic and personal triumph for Bowen, but at the same time they make disturbing reading. They offer no easy compensation for the psychological losses the characters experience. Nonetheless, they represent a breakthrough in understanding the psychological forces that shape our lives. Throughout her literary career Elizabeth Bowen enjoyed enormous success with both literary critics and the general public. In fact, she had almost achieved the status of a literary icon by the time she wrote her last two novels. What we must recognize is that she risked this standing by making a bold departure from the well-established pattern that had brought her recognition. Rather than deplore, as Hermione Lee does, the uncertainty that permeates these novels, we should marvel that an acclaimed novelist chose to write so honestly and vulnerably about the insecurity that she experienced at the end of her life. Feeling confident in her own artistry, Bowen refused to offer easy conclusions. Unlike Constantine who even at the novel's end claims he has "nothing to declare" (*ET*, 264), Bowen was completely engaged in her world. By accepting her own agony and making the most of her hard-earned lessons she bequeathed us two stunning novels as a legacy.

Notes

The phrase "liberation of mourning" is adapted from George H. Pollock, "Aging or Aged," 570, who argues that "the mourning-liberation process . . . has a creative outcome." Earlier versions of parts of this essay appear in "Life Review in the Novels of Molly Keane, Elizabeth Bowen, and Peter Taylor" and "Eva Trout and the Return of the Repressed."
R. B. Kershner made helpful comments and suggestions about this chapter. Nicholas Royle not only gave trenchant but useful criticisms of my chapter but brought theoretical essays on the crypt by Rand and Abraham and Torok to my attention.

1. Howard Moss, "Elizabeth Bowen," 224; John Hildebidle, *Five Irish Writers,* 124. According to the most recent listings in the *Journal of Modern Literature,* Annual Review nos. 9–16 (Dec. 1982–89), besides the items cited in this chapter, work on Bowen includes six articles, six chapters in books, three dissertations, and nine chapters of thematic dissertations. Very little of a theoretical nature has appeared. At the same time Bowen's reputation among writers still remains strong.

2. Full-length studies of Bowen include: Victoria Glendinning's biography, *EB;* Hermione Lee, *Elizabeth Bowen;* Patricia Craig, *Elizabeth Bowen;* Phyllis Lassner, *Elizabeth Bowen.*

3. Hildebidle, *Irish Writers,* 92, 128; Nicholas Royle, "Crypts in London." An expanded and revised version of Royle's essay also will appear in Andrew Bennett and Nicholas Royle, *Still Lives.* R. B. Kershner, Jr., "Bowen's Oneiric *House in Paris,*" also reveals the dark side of Bowen's comedy.

4. Roger B. Salomon, *Desperate Storytelling,* 3. Kathleen Woodward, "Late Theory, Late Style," this volume, calls similar products of depression "love stories."

5. Lee, *EB,* 190–91, 206.

6. Amir Cohen-Shalev, "Old Age Style," 28; Spencer Curtis Brown, Foreword to *PC,* xxxvii–xxxviii; George E. Vaillant, *Adaptation to Life,* 370.

7. Norman Holland, *The Brain of Robert Frost,* 40. Holland recommends that we learn to become "more comfortable in one's own skin" (41) but does not describe how aging writers like Bowen struggle to piece together the missing fragments of their identity late in life.
Eva Trout is Bowen's last completed novel. "The Move-In" is the first chapter of her final fragment. It consists of the unexpected and unwanted arrival of three young people at a country house, which they mistakenly believe to be owned by the aunt of a young man they once met casually on a bus. It has a comically eerie quality but is too fragmentary to suggests what direction Bowen would have taken.

8. Glendinning's biography now seems overly protective of the writer, for she accepts without question Bowen's interpretation of events. At the time of writing, Glendinning had to contend with Bowen's admirers, who were still under the spell of the novelist's powerful presence. Robert Liddell expressed his disapproval of Glendinning's biography, claiming that it was far too soon after Bowen's death for personal revelations or critical reevaluation of her work (Liddell to Barbara Pym, May 27, Oct. 1, 1978, Pym MS 154, fols. 123, 129). Still, Glendinning's rejection of psychological analysis kept her from showing Bowen triumphing over depression through the innovations of her art.

9. George H. Pollock, "Mourning and Adaptation," 349, 353–54.

10. Nicolas Abraham and Maria Torok, "The Topography of Reality," 64–

65; Nicholas Rand, "Psychoanalysis with Literature," 60. Royle, "Crypts in London," finds Abraham and Torok's theory of the crypt or phantom useful in analyzing Bowen's work but fears that applying such an analysis to her life would result in a "crypto-analysis."

11. Although Bowen had several affairs with men, according to May Sarton at least two were with women (Sarton, *A World of Light,* 195–97; Glendinning, *EB,* 192–93). Craig, *EB,* 128, says there is no evidence to support Sarton's allegation that she had a short "affair" with Bowen. Sarton wrote about the incident with considerable sensitivity, acknowledging that Bowen's behavior was uncharacteristic. Bowen certainly understood the feelings that generated lesbian relationships. Her mother's death left her with a sympathy for the intensity that women sometimes show each other, for at thirteen losing her mother had seemed catastrophic. Moss, "EB," 229, comments that "the Bowen preoccupation (but not obsession)" with love begins with "the missing mother."

12. B. Bloom, *Developing Talent in Young Children* (New York: Ballantine, 1985), cited by Mihály Csikszentmihályi, "Society, Culture, and Person," 338, has shown that gifted children require an "extensive support system" of parents and teachers if they are to reach their full potential. Alan Cameron clearly provided the kind of assistance that Bowen's parents had been unable to provide their daughter.

13. John Bowlby, *Attachment and Loss* 3:159; E. Mapother and S. Anthony, cited by Felix Brown, "Bereavement and Lack of a Parent in Childhood," 436; Pollock, "Aging," 571. More recent studies, however, suggest that—depending on the abruptness of the death—the individual may or may not experience real distress in normal mourning. Those who are psychologically strong may "go through mourning relatively unshaken" (Daniel Goleman, "New Studies Find Many Myths about Mourning," 17). Bowen clearly was affected by her loss; otherwise she would not have chosen the sort of husband that she did.

14. Curtis Brown, Foreword, xxxvi. Craig, *EB,* 117–18, points out that *The Heat of the Day,* Bowen's wartime novel, also presented a literary challenge, but not primarily an emotional one.

15. Robert N. Butler, "The Life Review," 65, 67. Barbara Pym also created characters for whom she created a life review, rather than attempting to reexamine her own life (Anne M. Wyatt-Brown, *Barbara Pym,* 128–29).

16. Dinah has much in common with Ursula Vernon, a neighbor at Bowen's Court and contemporary, who seemed agelessly beautiful to Bowen. Lady Ursula's childhood had been as disrupted as Bowen's. Lady Ursula was equally "haunted"; the two became conspirators and enjoyed "rioting around" together, Lady Ursula's husband being in a wheelchair. Bowen dedicated *LG* to her (*EB,* 195–96, 220).

In Walker Percy's *The Last Gentleman,* 18, Will Barrett suffers from fugue states. Will periodically "wandered around . . . sunk in thought" when buried emotions from the past threaten to overpower him.

17. Jean Baker Miller, *Toward a New Psychology for Women,* 83; Carol Gilligan, *In a Different Voice,* 35. Hildebidle, *Irish Writers,* 99, n. 6, emphasizes the "theatrical" element in Bowen's work, her use of "clear stage-settings." Miller theorizes that for many women even "the threat of disruption of connections is perceived not just a loss of a relationship but as something closer to a total loss of self" (83). *LG* also demonstrates the "intensely social and also moral nature of the young child's relation with others" (Carol Gilligan, "Adolescent Development Reconsidered," ix). In that essay Gilligan cites John Mordecai Gottman's monograph ("How Children Become

Friends," *Society for Research in Child Development Monograph* 48, no. 3 [1983])
that demonstrates children have the ability to remember their friends even after long
separations. Finally, Dinah's frantic pursuit also suggests the truth of Gilligan's observation ("Remapping the Moral Domain," 11) that "attachments—located in time and
arising from mutual engagement—are by definition irreplaceable."

18. Clare herself bears some resemblance to the author: she wore large costume
jewelry, which was Bowen's trademark, and adored Mrs. Piggott, Dinah's mother, just
as Bowen had worshiped her own mother.

19. D. W. Winnicott, "Ego Distortion in Terms of True and False Self," 150. For
further discussion, see Winnicott, "Transitional Objects and Transitional Phenomena."
Nicholas Royle (pers. com., March 1, 1992) argues that the burial of a biscuit tin is
equivalent to the packet of love letters in *A World of Love* (1955), but the burying
ritual in *LG* refers directly to the death of Bowen's mother and the letters do not.

20. D. W. Winnicott, "Child Department Consultations," 82, points out that reconstructing the story of a child's emotional development provides part of the cure.
He emphasizes the paradox that the story is only complete when the analyst's reaction
offers "the true recognition that all the pieces do weld together into a whole."

21. Hildebidle, *Irish Writers,* 102; Pollock, "Aging," 575.

22. Curtis Brown, Foreword, xxxix, describes the ensuing difficulty that Bowen's
technical experiment caused her in composition.

23. Vaillant, *Adaptation,* 294.

24. Glendinning, *EB,* 95, reports that "the physical model for Eva Trout was
glimpsed at an airport."

25. Eva's early life has been as "rootless and declassé" as Portia's in *The Death
of the Heart* (Ann Ashworth, " 'But Why Was She Called Portia?' " 160). Ashworth
reports that when Portia is sent to live with her brother, she regards it as an exile, a
place that offers the young girl no "means of attracting any but the most inappropriate matrimonial prospects." Eva feels even more desperate at the Arbles; in Bowen's
judgment her emotional deprivation is beyond repair.

26. Eva's and Jeremy's problems with speech are symptomatic of their bereft
situation. Bowen suggests that Eva's inept use of language is the result of parental neglect. At the time Bowen wrote the novel she probably had in mind her own stammer,
or perhaps her occasionally tortured syntax, which may have been the written equivalent of a stutter. Ironically, a few years after she completed *ET,* Bowen lost her voice
completely from cancer of the lungs (*EB,* 238).

27. Sigmund Freud, "The Transformations of Puberty," 88.

28. See Wyatt-Brown, *Pym,* 106–7. George H. Pollock, "Mourning and Memorialization through Music," 424, argues that when creative people suffer grievous
losses, "the direction of musical creativity and creativity in general will be influenced
by intrapsychic processes of mourning and memorialization."

29. Marion Milner, *The Suppressed Madness of Sane Men,* 247, describes Winnicott's behavior. Anna Freud, *The Ego and the Mechanisms of Defence;* Woodward,
Aging, chap. 6.

9

JOSEPHINE V. ARNOLD

Montherlant and the Problem of the Aging Pederast

HENRY DE MONTHERLANT'S published works, which span half a century, constitute an outstanding example of literature of the life cycle. Born in 1895 and dead by his own hand in 1972, this celebrated French author lived long enough to address the concerns of the seven ages of man. The writings of his early and middle years, most of which spoke to the interests and preoccupations of adolescent, young adult, and middle-aged males, earned him enormous popularity among readers of both sexes as well as high acclaim from critics. His reputation rested solidly on two pillars: machismo and misogyny. Men applauded his unabashed affirmation of masculine values. Women enjoyed the publicity that fell to their lot after the publication of his four-volume best-seller, *Les Jeunes Filles* (*The Girls*) in the years just before World War II. Although this novel is possibly the most flagrant example of misogyny in French or any other literature, it consolidated Montherlant's reputation as a man's man. Male readers relished the misogynistic pronouncements to which they inwardly subscribed. Female readers, living at a time when Frenchwomen did not have the vote and were still under the tutelage of their husbands, were more flattered by the limelight than outraged by the insults.

When Montherlant turned from the novel and the essay to the drama, during the German occupation of France in World War II, his literary stock rose higher than ever. In his plays Montherlant, now approaching fifty, provided his compatriots with portrayals of elderly, powerful, dignified men who were regarded by audiences as symbols of France's former grandeur. Unfortunately, one of the last old men he created for the stage failed mightily to please. Those who went to the theater expecting to see a Don Juan of heroic dimensions were confronted with what appeared to be a ridiculous old buffoon. Montherlant transformed the dashing, legendary lover into a "dirty old man," compulsively cruising the streets in search of any young creature, no matter how repugnant, who could be induced to respond to his advances. Montherlant's version of this sixty-six-year-old gallant is capable of waiting for hours under a broiling sun for a likely prospect to appear. The townspeople dump the contents of their chamber pots all over him, and still he fails to move from his post. Nothing can deter him from his appointed rounds.

The spectacle of an old man's obsession with youth, sex, and ever-changing partners repelled theatergoers and critics alike. According to Gabriel Matzneff, who attended the premier of *Don Juan* on November 4, 1958, numbers of spectators walked out in the middle of the performance. The play was withdrawn a little more than a week later as a result of both critical disparagement and public indignation (*MFT*, 7).

Not everyone disliked the play. Matzneff, a writer and personal friend of Montherlant, admired it, as did Dominique Fernandez, now a well-known author, then a young theater critic for the *Nouvelle Revue Française*. Significantly, the former is an avowed pedophile and the latter is openly gay. Montherlant, a closet pederast for most of his long life, was able, through this play, to communicate to these two individuals a pained sensibility that was incomprehensible to a wider, largely heterosexual audience. Nearly thirty years after reviewing the play, Fernandez declared that in 1958 a homosexual playwright could only portray homosexual anguish on stage by disguising it as a fear of aging.[1] This is a provocative observation deserving of further exploration. The insurmountable difference between youth and age is at the very heart of this play. However, in order to arrive at a deeper understanding of Don Juan's dilemma, we must make the distinction cautiously not clarified by Matzneff and Fernandez. Montherlant was not a homosexual, or lover of men. He was a pederast with an unvarying attraction to prepubertal boys. His Don Juan character is ostensibly a lover of young females, but the heterosexual veneer is thin. The use, wherever possible, of nouns that are not gender-specific in Don Juan's references to objects of sexual desire creates an intentional ambiguity.

If spectators in 1958 were repelled by an old satyr's relentless quest for young girls, they would doubtless have expressed far stronger reactions to an undisguised portrayal of man-boy love. In Montherlant's lifetime theater audiences were not yet ready to confront explicit representations of any type of homosexuality. The ambiguous nature of the author's point of view in *Don Juan* proved harmful to the play, but greater explicitness would have been out of the question. There is no disputing the fact that until recently society placed severe limitations on theatrical representations of any kind of homosexuality, regardless of age or gender. Fernandez notes that Jean Genet, so outspoken in his novels on the subject of homosexuality, was far more restrained in his plays.[2]

Throughout his career Montherlant was unable to deal openly with the subject of pederasty, despite the fact that it was the governing principle of his entire life, according to Roger Peyrefitte, the sometime confidant and companion of Montherlant's sexual escapades.[3] He lived in constant fear of discovery because sex with a minor was against the law in France. In fact, he had an extensive police record as a molester of youths, although his fame as a writer helped him to avoid public exposure and imprisonment. Later on, as a member of the French Academy, he enjoyed complete immunity from prosecution, despite the fact that law enforcement officials in Paris and Marseille had detailed knowledge of his pederastic activities.

In 1940 Montherlant's secret was known officially by only a handful of people. As time wore on, such friends as Jean Cocteau and Colette were able to guess the nature of Montherlant's sexuality but never dared to broach the subject in his presence. A mere hint would have sufficed to destroy the friendship. How it would have confounded him to learn that by the end of his life the secret was a secret no longer to the literary and journalistic establishment in Paris. It was not until 1977, with the publication of Roger Peyrefitte's *Propos secrets,* that the public at large was apprised of Montherlant's pederastic activities.

The ever-present fear of discovery was the reason for Montherlant's heterosexual mask. However, as his youth began to recede, the mask began to slip. The anguish of the aging pederast came into conflict with the earlier macho pose so familiar to admirers and detractors alike. The need to give expression, somehow, to the pain caused by the widening gulf between the older male and the perpetually youthful objects of his desire was a determining force in his writing for the theater. The playwright's own words, spoken by actors for an audience of real people, provided a necessary outlet for Montherlant's sexuality. Although the lines and situations were properly grasped by a mere handful of initiates, the plays constituted at one and the same time a private joke and a public confession.

The use of the mask in *Don Juan* illustrates the fundamental conflict between the need for love and the fear of death. The protagonist puts on a real mask every day in order to avoid unpleasant consequences resulting from his licentiousness. As time goes on, it becomes clear that our hero also hopes that the mask will conceal his advancing age. In act 1, scene 2 he approaches a young girl without his mask and she finds him distasteful. He then dons the mask, at which point her reaction is one of fear. Despite the offer of a bribe, his attempts at seduction are unsuccessful. His everyday mask is of no further use. His age can no longer be concealed. He continues to wear the mask in the hope that death will not recognize him. But death is not so easily duped. In the last scene of the play Don Juan's customary mask is suddenly transformed into a death's head. It cannot be removed. The mask of death and his mortal flesh have become one. The fear of aging and the fear of dying have melded with the undiminished need to make fresh conquests, thereby creating a walking death's head.

Don Juan and his new face gallop off to Seville in search of new loves as the curtain falls. But the glory days are over. The Don Juan of old is no more. In his place is death who walks the streets in search of one more trick. The author confirmed the significance of this image by changing the title of the play in 1972 to *La Mort qui fait le trottoir* (Death, the streetwalker).

Montherlant ended his own life when age and infirmity made it increasingly difficult to cruise the streets of Paris. For him a life without the love of boys was inconceivable and unendurable. In a conversation with Guy Dumur, the noted theater critic for the weekly French magazine the *Nouvel Observateur,* in June 1988, I learned that Montherlant in his last years had become an unkempt and pathetic old man, still looking for boys on the streets and in the movie theaters. He had already lost the sight in one eye and had been subject for some years to dizziness and falls. The problem with balance was the result of a sunstroke incurred at the Tuileries Gardens, while he cruised for too long on an unusually hot afternoon. In writing about the sunstroke he never mentioned what he was doing in the heat of the day. Later on, he blamed the injury to his eye on a fall in his bathroom. According to Roger Peyrefitte, Montherlant was badly beaten by the brother and friends of a young boy whom he had attempted to molest in a movie theater.[4]

For Montherlant, the inveterate pederast, old age had become a cruel joke. He had loved young boys from the time he himself was an adolescent. At that age his love was returned, more completely than it would be ever again, by a fourteen-year-old schoolmate. That affair ended brutally and abruptly when Montherlant was expelled from school on the grounds of improper conduct. From that point on, he became fixated on boys of the age of his beloved, give or take a year or two. The tragedy for Montherlant lay in the fact that the object of his desire never aged; while he, of course, could not do otherwise. Rabbi ben Ezra's exhortation to his loved one to grow old along with him because "the best is yet to be" is a comforting prospect forever denied the pederast. Such a man can never know what it is like to age apace with the beloved or to "love the sorrows of [a] changing face," be it his own or anyone else's.

For Montherlant the aging of the male body was a nasty trick of fate, leading to ridicule, violence, and, ultimately, suicide. Nonetheless, this same trick of fate nurtured and sustained his creativity as nothing else could have done. His Don Juan is essentially a trickster. As an old man who cannot be loved for what he is, Don Juan feels obliged to dupe every female he meets. He conceals his age with a mask or other artificial means. In the very first scene he tries to make himself look younger by biting his lips and curling his mustache, not unlike Aschenbach's attempt to attract Tadzio through similar means in Thomas Mann's *Death in Venice*. Montherlant's indefatigable sexagenarian asks his son, Alcacer, to refer to him in front of young girls as a man of forty-five. He is capable of saying or doing anything to obtain sexual gratification. Only the intensity of sexual pleasure can help him forget the imminence of death. At the same time Don Juan claims that he never lies to women because he means what he says when he says it. Thus the trickster tricks himself into believing that he has a code of personal conduct that is idiosyncratic but not dishonorable.

According to the legend, Don Juan was never able to stay with one woman. He always had to move on to someone else. Many theories have been propounded concerning the underlying reasons for his behavior, including impotence, search for the mother, hatred for women, quest for an ideal, to name only a few. This ultimate seducer was the perfect choice for expressing the exigencies of Montherlant's own sexual identity. A pederast must ceaselessly search for new love objects. The period directly preceding puberty is fleeting. Once a boy began to grow hair on his face, Montherlant found him unappealing because he was fixated on prepubertal physiological characteristics. Over and over again in his work the author describes adult males as ugly. He never could understand how women managed to sleep with them. This incomprehension did not in the least increase his respect for the ladies.

Even more abhorrent to Montherlant was the very idea that two grown, hairy men could take pleasure in one another's bodies. His homophobia was intense and virtually a reflex whenever homoerotic subjects were evoked or even remotely alluded to. Once, when Roger Peyrefitte asked him if he had ever had anal sex with a woman, Montherlant replied indignantly in the negative, claiming that to have done so would have caused the woman to take him for a homosexual.[5]

Although Montherlant affirmed to Peyrefitte that he did have some sexual experience with women in order to be able to write knowledgeably about them, his libidinal ideal was the prepubertal male child. We know from the Montherlant-Peyrefitte correspondence that "child" actually meant "boy." However, in *Les Olympiques* (The Olympians), he expressed a marked admiration for athletic young women who appeared to be neither male nor female but examples of what he called a "third sex." He was also of the opinion that young boys, who were neither men nor women, belonged to this "third sex" as well. By removing young boys from their usual sexual classification, Montherlant could trick himself into believing that his love for them was acceptable. After all, what he liked most about them was their soft, beardless, and therefore feminine aspect.

This reasoning appears specious to say the least; particularly since those soft, beardless creatures known as women were anathema to him. However, this exercise in self-justification seems to have been necessary in order for Montherlant to continue to write about the subject that haunted the greater part of his life: aging men and their affective relations to children. The word *enfant* (child) is woven throughout the variegated tapestry of the writer's work. The reader or spectator who can recognize and follow this subtle thread will find it in many unexpected places. Both in French and in English the words *enfant* and *child* may designate a being of either sex. They are also used to describe a very young person, without specifying age, who is not, in one way or another, a full-fledged adult. To say that he or she is just a child does not, in either tongue, necessarily mean that the individual in question is sexually immature. Thanks to this fortuitous ambiguity of language, Montherlant was able to indulge in covertly expressing his sexual penchant without offending his heterosexual admirers. In fact, the use of *enfant* in erotic situations served to reinforce the image of masculine dominance that the public had come to expect in his work. His reputation for machismo and misogyny was so notorious that audiences were not disposed to make more subtle interpretations.

In his plays children are frequently introduced, at times in a seemingly gratuitous manner. However, the stage is not as propitious a medium for the vagaries of gender as is the written word. When a child appears on stage in one of Montherlant's dramas, it is usually a very young boy who has to interact in some way with the aging hero of the play. In one of his most famous plays, *La Reine morte* (*Queen after Death*), we find a telling example of this type of encounter between youth and age. This play marks the beginning of Montherlant's theatrical successes. It is based on a seventeenth-century Spanish drama entitled *Reinar despues de morir* (To reign after dying), by Luis Velez de Guevara. Montherlant was originally supposed to translate this play for the Comédie-Française. After reading and much reflection, he gradually transformed the Spanish work into a play of his own, modifying it as he saw fit. Significantly, according to his own description of how *La Reine morte* came into being, he greatly expanded the role of the seventy-year-old King Ferrante and invented the character of the young page, Dino del Moro (*RM*, 180–82).

In the last scene the dying king selects Dino out of all his entourage and clasps him to his breast in the hope that the child's innocence will somehow wash away his sins. The function of the page in this scene might well be questioned by spectators who barely have had occasion to notice this minor character. Yet the scene is entirely in keeping with the king's dilemma concerning children, and the author's as well. For Ferrante and his creator, children are a source of salvation and perdition, pleasure and anguish, hope and disappointment, but most of all fear. The king orders the death of his pregnant daughter-in-law, Doña Inès, because his son, Don Pedro, married her against his father's wishes. Having just destroyed one innocent child, the dying monarch hopes to be saved by the innocence of another. This is a vain hope indeed because it is obvious that Dino cannot help him. In the final scene of the play the young page, who is the last and only courtier to linger near the dead king's body, finally abandons it in order to kneel before the corpse of Inès. Her husband places a crown not on her head but on her belly. The object of veneration is not the dead woman but the dead child.

The need to revere and the need to destroy the ever-present child is an insoluble dilemma, manifesting itself repeatedly in the works of Montherlant. For the pederast the child is the forbidden fruit, heart of all desire, source of all danger. In play after play, youthful characters are evoked and then obliterated, physically or emotionally, by an older male protagonist who is then himself destroyed by his own conflicting needs. In *Demain il fera jour* (*Tomorrow the Dawn*) a father's disappointment in his son is the unwitting cause of the boy's death. *Le Maître de Santiago* (*The Master of Santiago*) portrays an old man who sacrifices his daughter to a set of outmoded principles that serve no one, including himself. The hero of *Brocéliande*, Persilès, becomes the victim of long-dead fathers. He commits suicide when, after having prided himself on descending from King Louis XII (Saint Louis), he learns to his great chagrin that he is only one of thousands of descendants. For the unique to become commonplace proves unendurable.

Montherlant was to pay dearly for a love that was unique yet punished in a bleakly commonplace manner. To be expelled from the school where he came into daily contact with the boy who was to provide the one fundamental love experience of his life was like being shut out of the Garden of Eden. The deep love that he felt for the lad he would name Serge in his theater and fiction would revive again in dreams that recurred off and on till the end of his days.

Writing of this experience not long after its occurrence, Montherlant continued to draft different versions of a novel on the subject, repeatedly deferring its termination and publication for fear of exposing his secret. In 1951 he published a play based on the schoolboy episode entitled *La Ville dont le prince est un enfant* (literally The city whose prince is a child), published in English as *The Fire That Consumes*. No public performance was given until 1967, five years before Montherlant's death, and two years before the publication of an expurgated edition of a novel on the same subject, *Les Garçons* (*The Boys*).

The earlier published edition of the play enjoyed considerable success in bookstores and among critics. Both the selection committee of the Comédie-Française and the celebrated acting team of Jean-Louis Barrault and Madeleine Renaud wanted to produce the play in their respective theaters. After some hesitation the author consulted the archbishop of Paris on the propriety of a public performance of what must be called a love triangle in a Catholic school, involving two teen-age boys and a priest in his thirties. On receiving a negative response from the archbishop, Montherlant declined the aforementioned offers.

Why did he both seek and accept the advice of a highly placed cleric, when he had long since ceased to be a believer? His ostensible reason was that he did not wish to put into question the values of Catholic education. The probable reason is not difficult to surmise. In 1951 Montherlant was not yet ready to reveal his secret to a live audience. A book was safe; the theater was not. This play, which was close to his heart, did not constitute a private joke perpetrated on an unsuspecting public. There was no disguise, no mask, no legendary hero or historical personage to hide behind.

In his notes to the 1967 production Montherlant made it clear that the dramatic situation depicted in *La Ville dont le prince est un enfant* was based on his personal experiences. The play was eminently successful. By 1967 the times were beginning to change with respect to differences in sexual orientation. Furthermore, Montherlant was then seventy-two and feeling the weight of his years and physical infirmities. He could not make his permanent exit without leaving some trace of what had been the most profound experience of his life. Although his fear of exposure never left him, his advanced age made it possible for him to give to the world two works based on the great passion and trauma of his youth. The passing decades had created not only the physical but also the aesthetic distance necessary for his creativity. He could finally cast off the heterosexual trappings of his earlier writings, while simultaneously allowing that the events depicted belonged to a phase in life common to many, yet usually relinquished on reaching adulthood.

Montherlant did not completely abandon his habit of concealment with the publication of *Les Garçons* in 1969, since this edition contains many cuts. The unexpurgated version did not appear until 1973, the year after his death. He made arrangements for the publication in a limited edition and carefully prepared the text before committing suicide. The novel did not share the same critical destiny as its companion piece, *La Ville dont le prince est un enfant*. It created scarcely a ripple in Parisian literary circles. After the famous student uprisings in 1968, which left their mark on every French person one talks to, nobody cared any longer about sexual escapades in a boys' school in the days before World War I. After all, the same subject had already been dealt with by Roger Peyrefitte in 1944 in a novel entitled *Les Amitiés particulières* (*Special Friendships*) with a fair amount of success. In fact, Montherlant accused his friend Peyrefitte of stealing the idea from him.[6] Peyrefitte was able to execute what was indeed Montherlant's idea because the former, a novice writer at the time, was far less troubled by his sexual identity and its exposure than was the latter, an already famous author with an established reputation to protect.

By the late 1960s Montherlant may have felt that he had nothing to lose by finally publishing works on the subject of pederasty. He had lived long enough to see the waning of his immense popularity. He had made it a point of honor to avoid all literary coteries and "isms." He was a stranger to the fashions of literary discourse and remained to the end a maverick and a loner, with but a handful of friends. Without heirs or acolytes, he believed that his reputation would not long survive his death. With only a few years left to live, he cast the die, so to speak, and awaited the consequences. There were scarcely any at all.

What might have been viewed as an act of potential self-destruction can now be interpreted as one of self-preservation—the self at the very core of his being. Both *La Ville dont le prince est un enfant* and *Les Garçons* show us the love of two individuals, one an accomplished youth of sixteen, the other an adult priest, for a clumsy yet appealing fourteen-year-old boy. In the play we see only the affective side of the conflict. In the novel the author reveals the physical aspect within a broader, specifically sexual context. In neither work does the author suggest even remotely that the Abbé de Pradts has sexual designs on the younger boy, Serge. Nevertheless, the turning point in both works occurs when the priest discovers Alban, the elder, alone with Serge in a place where they could only have met for clandestine purposes. The suspicion of misconduct, even without actual proof, was enough to transform the abbé's jealousy into an unalterable drive toward revenge.

Although Alban is the hero of the novel and the play and our sympathies rest with him at all times, it is impossible to blame de Pradts for instigating Alban's expulsion. The older man knows that he cannot compete with his youthful rival. Serge sees the abbé as an old fogey who insists on discipline and hard work, when all the fourteen-year-old wants to do is go out and play with the other boys. Alban, an older, brilliant student, awakens first admiration then love in the heart of young Serge. De Pradts is duty and dreariness incarnate. He knows all too well that the boy finds him old and unattractive. Although only thirty-three, his baldness makes him look older to Serge. There is nothing about him, reflects the abbé, that can capture the interest or attention of his protégé, for he brings no promise of laughter and exuberance. As the boy's mentor, de Pradts does not feel free to indulge; he can only restrict, restrain, repress. His love for Serge is hopeless indeed.

Alban's expulsion from school proves disastrous not only for him but also for his more powerful rival. The head of the school, the Abbé Pradeau de la Halle, not unaware of the unspoken reasons for his colleague's actions, decides to send Serge away also. Attempting to console de Pradts, his superior asssures him that some day he will find Serge again. This scene, occurring at the very end of the play, reveals a despairing de Pradts who knows that no such consolation is possible. He will never find Serge again because that fourteen-year-old boy will have ceased to exist. At this point Montherlant's personal anguish is transferred from Alban to his persecutor. The author has split himself in two and shown us the pain of thwarted pederastic love in both its formative and culminating phases. The play ends on a fatalistic note, with each member of the triangle forever lost to the other. The conclusion of the novel, on the other hand, is a return to the private ironies discerned in the theatrical texts, most notably *Don Juan*.

In the last chapter of *Les Garçons* the reader is treated to a sequel of sorts that might well be entitled "Whatever Happened to the Abbé de Pradts?" The first part of the novel, dealing with Alban's school days, bears the title *Au paradis des enfants* (*A Children's Paradise*). If the text begins with a child's paradise, it ends with an old man's fantasy. De Pradts has overcome his grief and has managed to obtain pastoral assignments that bring him in close contact with many delectable local boys, who are invariably quite fond of him. As he lies on his deathbed, the last sounds he hears are the happy shouts of boys playing soccer and the tapping of a ball against the wall of his room. The youthful cries and the joyous memories they evoke are the only benediction he requires. *La Ville dont le prince est un enfant* and *Les Garçons,* taken together, are an elegy to youth and its passing. Montherlant has told us in no uncertain terms that the price a pederast pays for fidelity to his primary love object is to become a "dirty old man."

Montherlant's notion of what constitutes an old man is a complex one. In novels written in the nineteen thirties when the author was barely forty, his male protagonists express on more than one occasion the opinion that males become physically repulsive by the age of eighteen and, moreover, that most faces of twenty-year-olds are just as disgusting as those of elderly men. Even the best twenty- or thirty-year-old male body is not as good as that of any fourteen- or fifteen-year-old.

These opinions may seem a bit extreme; but for a lover of boys, puberty is the great divide. After that appalling metamorphosis, all men become hairy brutes who, he firmly believes, are unattractive to everyone. The author's notorious misogyny rests far less on a genuine dislike for women than on a bewilderment, strongly laced with contempt, for a sex that is not only willing but eager to have commerce with distinctly unpalatable creatures. Women must be really hard up, muses Guiscart, another of his Don Juanesque protagonists, to love a man with a two-day growth of beard and pimples on his neck (*RS,* 402).

Montherlant's compulsion to conceal his sexual orientation forced him to write much more about women than he wanted to. This sad but unavoidable necessity of saying "girl" when he meant "boy" played no small part in his antagonism toward women. His misogyny, which reached its zenith in his mid-forties, earned him many admirers, but many detractors as well. Readers who did not respond to the author's flagrant machismo were perplexed by the evidence of a sensuality that somehow did not ring true.

This disturbingly false note in the early and mid-life writings gradually diminished with time. As the advancing years made it both more difficult and more dangerous to pursue the objects of his desire, Montherlant's tone became less strident and more poignant. In one of his last volumes of essays, *Va jouer avec cette poussière* (Go play with this dust), he asserts that a person's perspective on life depends entirely on his or her age. This sort of pronouncement may seem overly facile, he maintains; but the fact remains that no one ever talks about it (*VJP,* 35). As a pederast, he had to think about age and age differences every day of his life. In this late essay he permits himself to raise the issue but not to dwell on it in detail. Instead, he gives us a sly peek behind his mask by informing us that there are all sorts of experiences he might have written about yet chose to withhold for diverse reasons. Any writer at all, according to Montherlant, is capable of unfolding secret tales that could enrich our knowledge and understanding of the world. When he or she deliberately refrains from doing so, it is out of fear of social ostracism.

Since there are a host of other reasons why authors feel compelled to keep silent on topics that could create problems for them, Montherlant concludes that the literary output of a lifetime represents only the smallest, most insignificant part of what the writers might have wished to communicate. He is distressed by the realization that authors are judged only on what they have allowed themselves to publish. No one knows what they really thought and felt but could not bring themselves to reveal.

It was left to Montherlant's biographer Pierre Sipriot and his former friend and correspondent Roger Peyrefitte to make public that which was largely private. They did Montherlant no disservice. By removing the mask, it became possible for the discerning reader and critic to follow the pederastic subtext that underlies all the works from early youth to advanced age. Despite the misgivings expressed in *Va jouer avec cette poussière,* Montherlant did indeed enrich our knowledge of life and the world, of love in a real and special form.

Nevertheless, the concept of an aging pederast has been and continues to be a problem for many of us, most especially for parents of young children. Pederasty and pedophilia are generally regarded as aberrant forms of sexuality, requiring some sort of explanation, be it psychological, medical, or both. Examined from each of these perspectives, Montherlant's case becomes doubly fascinating. In his long life pederasty was the indestructible link between childhood and old age. Its psychological origins can be attributed to an unusual family situation created by the circumstances of his birth. His mother had been a pretty, popular, fun-loving twenty-year-old at the time of her marriage to Comte Joseph Millon de Montherlant. For this young woman, the immediate result of marriage was pregnancy, followed by a delivery that nearly cost her her life. The child grew up knowing that he had been born in a sea of blood. His mother spent her remaining two decades as an invalid, living for and through her only son. Her social existence ended with the birth of Henry, as did her sexual relations with her husband. The young boy, a daily witness to his mother's invalidism and his father's aloofness, could not but conclude that the consequences of marriage were disastrous.

Henry, the only felicitous result of an otherwise dismal union, became the exclusive object of his mother's love and maternal grandmother's adoration. In a play from his midlife period, *Celles qu'on prend dans ses bras*

(The ones we embrace), Montherlant emphasizes the belief that a child can never know any love as great as that lavished upon him by a mother and a grandmother. Nothing else will ever measure up to that love, and no other object will be worthy of it. It is not difficult to see how this overvaluation of the boy-child by the women of his household was to influence the rest of Montherlant's life.

As the young Henry grew into adolescence, he continued to get along well with his grandmother but began to chafe against his mother's possessiveness. Mme de Montherlant's obsessive love for her son translated itself into the youth's own obsession with a younger schoolmate. His extreme misogyny, as manifested in virtually all of his literary works, may be traced in part to the women who had helped to focus his libido on objects deemed unsuitable by a heterosexual society.

The author's misogyny and concomitant machismo developed as by-products of the necessity to conceal his proclivities. To deflect suspicion, he had to be a supermale. In order to come to terms with his erotic needs he had to condemn women at every turn. He hated them for giving birth to the very children whom he loved but hated himself for loving. In one of his letters to Roger Peyrefitte he opened with the bitter observation that he was writing that day from the gutter.[7] Montherlant blamed women for existing. If there were no women and, therefore, no heterosexuality, no need would arise for concealment. He despised the heterosexual couple. If we all belonged to the third sex he was so fond of, love and harmony would surely prevail. In a posthumously published novel entitled *Thrasylle*, Montherlant created a pastoral idyll, set in ancient Greece, that illustrated just such a world. In it women and most adult males are conspicuously absent, leaving a society composed mainly of playful, laughing, loving boys, free to follow their desires.

While proclaiming the primacy of sensual gratification in most of his works, Montherlant knew that he was a driven man in the search for pleasure. He was afraid of being found out yet continued to thrive on that fear. Danger was part of the thrill. The link between danger and eroticism is quite evident in Montherlant's well-known love of bullfights. He attended his first corrida at the age of fourteen and became an instant aficionado. This intense interest was supported by an earlier fascination, at age nine, with the novel *Quo Vadis*, by Henryk Sienkiewicz. In this widely read book the interaction of eroticism and mortal danger occurs most vividly in a Roman arena, where the life of Lygia, naked and tied to the horns of an aurochs, depends on the brute strength of the devoted Ursus.

The fact that Montherlant was incapable of putting a stop to his cruising, despite intervals of self-hatred and threats to life, limb, and reputation, definitely places him in the category of a paraphile, as described by the noted sexologist Dr. John Money. His book *Gay, Straight, and In-Between* gives detailed clinical descriptions of what a paraphile is, as well as the number and types of existing paraphilias. Money defines paraphilia "as a condition occurring in men and women of being compulsively responsive to, and for optimal initiation and maintenance of sexuoerotic arousal and the facilitation or attainment of orgasm, obligatively fixated and dependent on an unusual, personally or socially unacceptable stimulus either perceived directly, or in the imagery or ideation of fantasy."[8]

Money has so far compiled a list of more than forty paraphilias. The one that applies to Montherlant is pedophilia. All paraphilias involve obsessive-compulsive behavior, often characterized by a fugue or trancelike state. This was true of Montherlant, who in later life was observed in such a state, while cruising, by acquaintances privy to his secret. Paraphiles do not choose their condition and are unable to change it. There were days when the author, in a desperate effort to confine himself to his apartment, would refuse to shave. Since he was fastidious in his person and did not like to appear unkempt in public, he hoped this lack of grooming would help to keep him off the streets. Because there is nothing voluntary about a paraphilia, he inevitably found himself back in his old haunts.

The subject of this study presents an almost perfect clinical illustration of Money's theories. Paraphilias develop in early childhood. They may result from punishment for sexual behavior, as was the case with the young Henry when he was expelled from his beloved school for improper conduct with another boy. A paraphilia may have either a prenatal or postnatal connection with the limbic brain, evidence for which is the characteristic trancelike state. Money goes on to describe chronophilia, or age disparity, of which one aspect is pedophilia. He tells us how the pedophile requires juveniles to satisfy lust and how, therefore, the duration of the relationship is necessarily limited. "The partner's eligibility is abolished by the odors and maturational changes of puberty."[9]

It is Money's conviction that "pedophilia has its phyletic origins in parentalism. What happens developmentally is that parentalism becomes paraphylically diverted into the service of lust. Parent-child pairbonding and lover-lover pairbonding become merged together, as do parental love and erotic love."[10] We know from Montherlant's own statements that he often acted in loco parentis toward many of the boys he knew.

In another study of paraphilias, *Lovemaps*, Money is at pains to point out that a person's sexuality is as individual and distinctive as a thumbprint. To attack or criticize our sexuality is to threaten our very concept of self. The paraphile offers a particularly forceful resistance to this type of personal assault. He will strongly condemn those who condemn him. Montherlant's contempt for women and for heterosexual couples is precisely the type of reaction described in *Lovemaps*. Without going much further into clinical detail, I must include Money's description of what he calls an "affectionate pedophile." He wants his readers to become aware that a pedophile must not be stereotyped as a "sexual degenerate whose degeneracy will inexorably lead to sadistic depravity and lust murder." There is no proof, Money affirms, to substantiate such a conclusion, and he proceeds to inform us that "affectionate pedophilia, which lacks violence or killing, is not the same paraphilia as lust murder directed toward children [erotophonophilia]. Nor is it the same as rape (biastophilia) directed toward children. Typically, these paraphilias do not co-exist in the same person, nor does one convert into the other." [11] As far as Montherlant is concerned, there is no evidence to suggest that he ever used coercion. The lads were free to accept or reject his advances. Moreover, two of the boys who were his protégés during the early years of World War II assured Montherlant that all the boys in their school engaged in sexual activity with one another. In a word, they were neither novices nor unwilling participants in their relationship with the older man. That sexual experimentation was widespread in both boy's and girl's schools during Montherlant's lifetime is confirmed by such prominent French authors as Roger Martin du Gard in *Le Lieutenant-Colonel de Maumort* and Violette Leduc in *Thérèse et Isabelle*.

The aforementioned observations are not intended to serve as excuses but rather as clarifications of behavior that is subject to virtually universal condemnation. In working with sex offenders Money has become convinced that paraphilias are manifestations of an illness that should be treated medically, not legally. He does not believe that pedophiles or other paraphiles should be incarcerated, since imprisonment will not change their behavior. Money strongly recommends treatment in clinics specializing in sexual disorders. There a sexually dysfunctional individual will be able to receive the therapy and/or medication required to control his condition.

In Montherlant's day not much in the way of treatment would have been available, except for a rudimentary type of psychoanalysis. It is fascinating to note that his very last novel directly confronts the issue of psychoanalysis, its uses and abuses. In *Un Assassin est mon maître* (An assassin is my master) the protagonist, a librarian named Exupère, makes the great discovery of his life when he first reads Freud's *Introduction à la psychoanalyse* (Introduction to psychoanalysis). This book becomes the basis for all his subsequent conduct and beliefs. Psychoanalysis in this novel functions as a religion. Like many systems of belief, it has its dark side and proves to be the hero's undoing. Montherlant mocks Freud and all his works by creating a character who obsessively misapplies the teachings derived from the master, thereby precipitating his own destruction.

This final work of fiction is a cry in the wilderness, a call for help, in the full knowledge that help would dismantle the self Montherlant had nurtured for seven decades. For him to find peace as a man, the artist, as we know him, could not have survived. It may be argued that hundreds, if not thousands, of young boys paid the price for Montherlant's creativity. However one wishes to decide on this issue, the author himself believed that he had been helpful to the boys he knew by providing material assistance, as well as the guidance and affection of a parent. Many of these boys kept in touch with him over the years to apprise him of their jobs, marriages, and offspring. In effect Montherlant has informed us that his protégés grew up to lead "normal," heterosexual lives, something he was never able to achieve.

Montherlant did make two serious attempts to live like the majority. He actually became engaged to two different women, once in the twenties and once in the early thirties. Each time he broke off the relationship because he could not face the prospect of spending the rest of his life in such close proximity with a female. The circumstances surrounding the second engagement formed the basis for the great tetralogy of *Les Jeunes Filles*. A Montherlant reformed and neutralized, or neutered, by psychotherapy would not have left us the significant body of work that has enriched both French and world literature of the twentieth century.

In conclusion I wish to state that it has not been my intention to condone child molestation or any other kind of unwelcome sexual encroachment on the right of privacy. I hope to have demonstrated that the problems of the aging Montherlant were caused by the insatiable child within himself, to whom only the author's death could bring appeasement. Perhaps this glimpse into a pederast's painful pleasures will broaden our understanding of what may well be regarded as one of the last taboos.

Notes

1. Dominique Fernandez, *Le Rapt de Ganymède*, 337.
2. Ibid.
3. Roger Peyrefitte, *Propos secrets*, 68–69.
4. Ibid., 55–56.

5. Ibid., 314.
6. Peyrefitte, *Propos*, 68–69.
7. Henry de Montherlant and Roger Peyrefitte, *Correspondance*, 66.
8. John Money, *Gay, Straight, and In-Between*, 133.
9. Ibid., 133, 137.
10. Ibid., 138.
11. John Money, *Lovemaps*, 7, 72, 73.

CONSTANCE ROOKE

Oh What a Paradise It Seems:
John Cheever's Swan Song

Swan Song: The Last Text of a Great Writer

Oh What a Paradise It Seems was published in 1982, just four months
before the death of its author. It was written as the corruption of
cancer spread, in the knowledge that in all likelihood this brief novel would
be John Cheever's final sustained utterance, his last word and testament.
The title of Cheever's last work distills the "message" of his life text and
is echoed at the writer's last "hour" (the final page of the text) when the
voice of Cheever's narrator records a "feeling" ascribed to Lemuel Sears,
the aged protagonist:

> The thought of stars contributed to the power of his feeling. What
> moved him was a sense of those worlds around us, our knowledge how-
> ever imperfect of their nature, our sense of their possessing some grain
> of our past and of our lives to come. It was that most powerful sense of
> our being alive on the planet. It was that most powerful sense of how
> singular, in the vastness of creation, is the richness of our opportunity.
> The sense of that hour was of an exquisite privilege, the great benefice of
> living here and renewing ourselves with love. What a paradise it seemed!
> (*Paradise*, 105)

Hélène Cixous, the distinguished and still youthful French literary theorist, could "dream" this feeling, which she ascribes specifically to the last
day of the writer:

> I have always dreamed about the last text of a great writer. A text writ-
> ten with final energies, the last breath. On the last day before death,
> the author sits on the edge of the earth, feet light in the infinite air, and
> looks at the stars. Tomorrow the author will be a star among the stars,

a molecule among all the molecules. The last day is beautiful for those who know how to live it, it is one of the most beautiful days of life. On that particular day (I should say days, for the last days can be several days) one sees the world with the eye of the Gods: I am finally going to become a part of the worldly mysteries. Sitting on the edge of the earth the author is already almost no one. . . . Before the imminence of the starred silence, they [the phrases] hasten, assemble, and say the essential. They are a sublime farewell to life: not mourning, but acknowledgement. How beautiful you are, O life, they say. ("EF," 9)

Cixous goes on to say that "the ultimate works are short and burning like the fire which reaches towards the stars" and to discuss the last work of a great Brazilian writer, Clarice Lispector: "This book was written by a weary and passionate hand. In a way Clarice had already ceased to be an author, to be a writer. It is the last text, the one that comes *after*. After all books. After time. After the self. It belongs to eternity" ("EF," 9–10).

The applicability of Cixous's lyrical theory of last texts to the case of John Cheever is striking. We have the resonance of Cheever's apostrophe ("How beautiful you are, O life"), the stars, the brevity of *Oh What a Paradise It Seems,* the weariness of which Cheever speaks in his journals, and the passionate acknowledgment—the paean to life—which is the text itself. More strikingly, though, through Cixous's attention to the ontology of the writer at the point of death ("the author is already almost no one") we may approach an explanation for the extraordinarily strange and potent voice of Cheever's swan song. This is the voice of the author who is already almost no one, a voice poised between worlds, between the particular and the universal.

Writer as Exemplar: The Meditative Mode

Kathleen Woodward, in her remarkable study of the late poems of T. S. Eliot, Ezra Pound, Wallace Stevens, and William Carlos Williams, uses the category of "wisdom"—identified by Erik Erikson as the strength that is particular to the last stage of the life cycle—to describe the achievement of these poems. Like Woodward, I find that Erikson's model for old age is especially compelling as a description of what Woodward calls the "meditative mode" of writers in old age. This meditative mode, says Woodward, "is characterized by a quiet openness to the primal realities of human experience which allows them simply to *be*, to disclose themselves before the gaze of the whole mind" (*AL*, 12). Because the writer is so often cast as one who precedes the rest of us, who goes before and through the power of imagination points the way, we may find it natural to regard the old writer as the exemplar of Erikson's final stage. Or we may find both this view of the writer and Erikson's association of wisdom and old age suspiciously romantic. Still, the art of old age does often express or enact the wisdom of which Erikson speaks. There—if not in our own lives, or in the extratextual life of the writer—we may find it, and so take heart.

The meditative mode is especially pronounced in the aged writer for an obvious reason: the writer's task has always required the exercise of the meditative faculty, and this increases in old age because old age has a tendency to augment that faculty or disposition in us all. Woodward argues that the writer who achieves "an ecological balance between mind and world" (*AL,* 170) does so through a cumulative process that Gregory Bateson calls "calibration." Each experience of "working with a material, meeting its resistances with one's own ideas" is a learning experience; each creative engagement with "a particular form, a certain theme" feeds into and enriches the next (*AL,* 169). This description of the aesthetic endeavor over time is roughly analogous to Erikson's idea that each phase of the life cycle feeds into the next and requires us to revisit and reintegrate the conflicts of all previous stages. In the course of a long career, a writer like John Cheever returns again and again to the old obsessions—but with a calibrated difference.

From "a long life of working with images"—or potent images, I would argue, which necessarily embody both the idea and its resistances—the exceptional writer (whom Cixous calls the great writer) may at last attain "some form of mystical experience." The depth psychologist Erich Neumann, in his essay "Art and Time," cited by Woodward, defines the mystical as "an encounter [that] occurs between ego and nonego in which the contradictions of the world, ego, and self are suspended" (*AL,* 20). This, I think, is the experience that is communicated to us in Cheever's *Paradise* and that is described in Cixous's theory of last texts.

"Wisdom," Erikson says, "is detached concern with life itself, in the face of death itself," while integrity and despair are the "two seemingly contrary dispositions" which must be balanced if wisdom is to be achieved.[1] As these dispositions are manifest in Cheever's last text, integrity means the integration of diverse aspects of the self and the "resistances" of experience (for the integration of self necessarily involves the integration of self and world), while despair arises not only (as Erikson suggests) from the imminence of death but also from a fear that is intimately related to that, since death necessarily involves dissolution; this fear is that "integrity" itself is an illusion. Wisdom, then, must involve a letting go and an embrace. It is

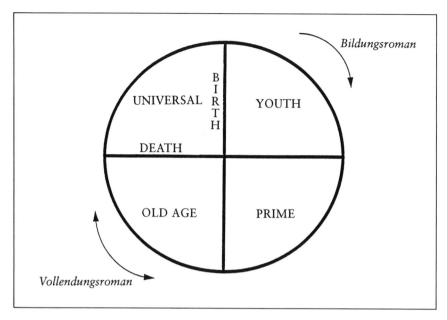

Fig. 1. Model of human life

an act of faith which knows the risk of illusion, as Cheever's emblematic title makes clear: *Oh What a Paradise It Seems.*

Vollendungsroman, Metafiction, and Last-Text Consciousness

Part of my intention in this essay is to situate Cheever's last novel within the context of a genre that I have called the *Vollendungsroman,* the novel of old age. This coinage, taken from a German verb meaning "to wind up," together with the word for "novel," is modeled on the term *Bildungsroman,* widely used by literary scholars to refer to the novel of youth or growing up. Figure 1 shows the model of human life that I have used in studying the *Vollendungsroman.*

The quadrant marked "Universal" is the raison d'être of this diagram. Again and again, I have found that it is relevant to the sense of human life that informs the novel of old age. In the particular life story of the aged protagonist, ego is gradually constructed and then begins to be deconstructed. The universal (which is both the first and the last quadrant) is the zone we cannot construct, cannot particularize; it is before and after ego, beyond our control. Yet it persists beneath consciousness and is always in some way real to our imaginations, as primal memory and anticipation, as origin and goal—and is particularly strong in the *Vollendungsroman*. Cheever's last text is of great interest because it attempts to speak to us from that zone: "It is the last text, the one that comes *after*. After all the books. After time. After the self. It belongs to eternity" ("EF," 10).

I have argued elsewhere that a special intensity characterizes the *Vollendungsroman*, an intensity resulting from the felt proximity of death.[2] The imagination of the writer is challenged by the invention of an aged protagonist; the writer's responsibility (assumed on behalf of the character) is to seize some affirmation out of the jaws of death, to discover meaning in the face of nothingness. Cheever's *Vollendungsroman* is a special case, however, for in addition to being in some sense about old age, *Oh What a Paradise It Seems* is a novel written by an old and dying writer. What difference does it make if the writer is old and nearing death? Should we assume that an even greater intensity obtains in this case, now that the writer's own life is on the line? Because of my faith in the power of imagination—borne out by such intensely empathic novels of old age written in youth as Margaret Laurence's *The Stone Angel* and David Malouf's *An Imaginary Life,* as well as by the fact that Hélène Cixous can "dream" with such intensity the condition of Clarice Lispector—I am reluctant to make this claim.

Nevertheless, I am interested in the relationship of Cheever's old age and the imminence of his death to the nature of his text. Last novels or novels written in old age are not always or even usually about old age, and *Vollendungsromane* are not always or even usually written by old writers. Cheever, then, in producing a superb *Vollendungsroman* in old age, and a novel that he knew would be his last, is in fairly select company. And what we find in this particular case is not only that the intensity of the *Vollendungsroman* combines with an Eriksonian detachment—which is common enough—but also that the difference arising from the author's own extratextual situation invades the text in a specific way, as last-text consciousness is paradoxically embodied in its disembodied narrative voice. Scott Donaldson, Cheever's biographer, says of a tape recording made when Cheever had sent off the galleys of *Paradise* that the author "spoke with satisfaction . . . as if completing that chore had somehow qualified him for last things."[3] My own sense, however, is that the text itself is the "last thing"; and I will argue that the text is permeated and to a large degree determined by Cheever's (and subsequently by our own) awareness of that fact.

To claim this is to claim that *Oh What a Paradise It Seems* is a metafictional work. In contrast to realistic fiction, which asks the reader quite simply to regard the fictive world as real, metafiction calls the reader's attention to the fictive nature of the text. Typically, it is also concerned with the fictive (unreal or story-making) nature of reality; it plays with and seeks to problematize the line that separates the world we live in from the world of fiction. Paradoxically, metafiction asserts and denies the force of that line. (This line, because it problematizes the location of the real, is analogous to the one that is drawn at the point of death.) The contemporary *Vollendungsroman* can be either realistic or metafictional. But surprisingly common even in the realistic *Vollendungsroman*, where gestures toward the fictionality of the text have no place, is the suggestion that human life has a fictional quality.

One dimension of this fictionality is the Platonic suggestion that the real is located elsewhere, in the zone I have called the universal. Another dimension of the fictionality of life is suggested by the analogy between living and writing a life story. The elderly protagonist is often cast as a person looking back on (or reading) the "story" that he or she has written and continues to write in life. In selecting, shaping, and evaluating the data of memory, the protagonist (as author and critic) creates once more a sense of identity (the protagonist as fictional character). *Oh What a Paradise It Seems* is an unusual case, because here the life-review model has been partly displaced from the protagonist to the author. The identities of Lemuel Sears, the narrator, and John Cheever are merged—so that most profoundly the text is seen as belonging to the figure of Cheever, who subsumes the other two as their creator. It is a daring and a dazzling move.

The particular life story of Lemuel Sears is smaller than the story of the text as a whole. For this reason, I think, Sears is not directly engaged in a process of life review; and the narrator, though he performs this function for Sears in a fragmented and muted way, is also engaged in the larger process that I would like to call Cheever's "life-text review." I use this term "life text" to describe the body of work that a writer inhabits and creates, as we all inhabit and create our lives. The effect of a life-text review is achieved by metafictional gestures and by the myriad echoes (which I cannot rehearse here) of earlier work by Cheever that resonate throughout the text. *Paradise* is the last text, and a reprise of all previous texts, in the same way that the aged protagonist of the *Vollendungsroman* is the last version of the self, and a reprise of all previous versions.

But the aged protagonist of *Paradise* is more than the last version of the man Lemuel Sears: he is also the last fictional construct. The figure of Sears contains Cheever's previous fictional avatars of the self, as this last text contains the texts that have gone before. In proffering and dissolving metafictively the identity of Lemuel Sears, and in gesturing through life-text review toward what Bateson calls the "calibration" of art (*AL*, 169),

Cheever tries to suggest that the wisdom of the text and the wisdom of the author cannot finally be distinguished from one another. On the brink of the silence that will follow his death, he points to these words—and stakes his life or his chance of immortality upon them.

Clearly, the first gesture, the first sentence, of Cheever's swan song— "This is a story to be read in bed in an old house on a rainy night" (*Paradise*, 1)—alerts us to a metafictional element in the text we are about to read. Much less clear, presumably, since reviewers and critics have overlooked it, is the specific thrust of Cheever's metafictional gambit. Cheever is aware, and is asking his readers to be aware, not only that *Oh What a Paradise It Seems* is "a story to be read" but also that this is the last story to be written by a real man called John Cheever. And he can ask this within the text, because he has with great subtlety and force challenged its boundaries.

The failure to recognize that last-text consciousness is inscribed within the text may account for the very mixed reception of Cheever's last novel. One senses in many of the reviews a reluctance to be hard on this peculiar, cryptic novel, precisely because the reviewers have extratextual knowledge that a famous writer is nearing the end of his life. The most scathing review sets such considerations aside, asserting that *Paradise* is "by any and every standard a bad book." But the most positive reviews seem conscious of the novel's metafictive reach. Thus, one reviewer says that "few swan-songs from any important writer of fiction can have been as well-tuned as . . . [this] epitaph to [Cheever's] working life." Another, who calls it "one of the most accomplished novels I have ever read," notes that "the rug of the plot . . . is gradually and brilliantly pulled from under our feet. For who is the narrator?"[4] My reply, the thesis of this essay, is that the narrator— who speaks of Lemuel Sears in the third person—is Lemuel Sears, and that he is also Cheever, addressing us "on the last day before death" from the perspective of a man who is already dead.

The Plot

One of the curiosities of this text is the apparent absurdity of Cheever's plot—in its weird details, its repeated and jarring interruption of the several plot lines, and its seemingly gratuitous and abrupt introduction and dismissal of characters. While thematic connections may help us to make some sense of its odd design, *Paradise* cannot ultimately satisfy readers who are unattuned to the role of the narrative voice—for voice in this text is like the choreographer of a performance on skates, which converts technical risk and bravado into a thing of beauty. Here, then—nearly stripped of the vital contribution made by voice—is Cheever's slippery plot.

Lemuel Sears, an old man who is still vaguely active in the computer business, loves to skate on Beasley's Pond (in the village of Janice) and is alarmed by its intentional devastation. The Mafia, we eventually learn, is behind the move to fill the pond with hazardous waste; and it is hiding behind a pretense that "the sole purpose" of this exercise (as perhaps of Cheever's exercise) is to build on the site "a monument to the forgotten dead" (*Paradise*, 91). Sears asks his lawyer to investigate; soon we are told casually that this lawyer has been murdered. Sears hires an environmentalist named Chisholm to pursue the investigation, and later in the novel he, too, is murdered. (This curious discretion, the refusal to give more than cursory attention to these murders, seems related to Cheever's ambiguous acceptance/rejection of his own imminent death.)

But in the meantime, the narrative has veered off to pursue the affair of the insistently virile protagonist with Renée, an elusive and much younger woman who tells him repeatedly that he doesn't understand the first thing about women. When Renée ends the affair without explanation, Sears is launched into a sexual encounter with Eduardo, the elevator man in Renée's building. He goes immediately to a psychiatrist and tells him that "I did enjoy myself with the elevator man and if I should have to declare myself a homosexual it would be the end of my life" (*Paradise*, 55). Later, Sears and Eduardo drive off very happily on a fishing expedition, but that water, too, turns out to be polluted. We guess that there is some connection between the impurity of water and the supposed life-destroying corruption of homosexuality, and that this links the two plots. But we are also made aware that this liaison is miraculously free of the taint of possession, that it is honest and tender. In both relationships, then, Sears's ability to understand in life the love that he affirms beyond the grave is denied. (And this signals a recognition that is characteristic of the *Vollendungsroman*: Reason is insufficient finally to resolve the contradictions, and the act of completion or winding up is always incomplete without some gesture of transcendence.)

This sexual narrative is interrupted periodically by the story of Betsy, who eventually saves the pond. Betsy enters the novel first through her next-door neighbors, the Salazzos. Betsy witnesses the assassination of his family dog, Buster, by Sam Cellos who has been enraged by his wife's decision to buy dogfood instead of dinner; Maria Cellos then uses her Mafia connections to get her husband a lucrative job supervising the ruination of the pond. (Nature, we may conclude, whether in the form of pond or dog, must take second place to human greed.) Betsy then has a fight with Maria over self-interest versus the common good when Maria tries to take too many groceries through the express lane of the Buy Brite supermarket. Like the pond, the express lane gets clogged by greed; but the other shoppers throw their support to Betsy, and one old man tells Maria that "people like you cause wars" (*Paradise*, 51). Betsy leaves with a bottle of teriyaki sauce, which at the end of the novel she will return to the Buy Brite, laced with poison and tagged with a warning: "Stop poisoning Beasley's Pond or I will poison the food in all 28 Buy Brites" (*Paradise*, 98). Betsy will be moved to rouse the population once again, partly because her "nostalgia for a destiny, a calling, would outlast all sorts of satiation" (*Paradise*, 100). This unwillingness to be satiated by the love of husband and children (by the success of one's own particular life) is a mystery, the narrator says. And it is clearly one that he approves.

In Betsy we see that family love (in common with the failure of family love) can lead to a more all-embracing concern for the human family. Driving home from a lovely day at the beach, Betsy and Henry stop to switch drivers—and Henry leaves the baby by the side of the highway. Chisholm, the lonely environmentalist hired by Sears, comes along and finds Binxie, thus restoring to wholeness this one small human family. Betsy then crosses parochial family lines to kiss Chisholm and welcome this sad man into her home, where they dine sacramentally on green noodles. She says, "We don't know how to thank you for saving Binxie's life," and Chisholm replies, "Do whatever you can to save Beasley's Pond" (*Paradise*, 85)—so when Chisholm is murdered after the town meeting, Betsy takes up the torch.

At this meeting Lemuel Sears's appeal for salvation on aesthetic grounds, his claim that Beasley's Pond must be saved so that human beings can skate upon it, is regarded as annoyingly trivial by almost everyone. Chisholm is killed, Betsy poisons the teriyaki sauce three times, the news of a "POISONED FAMILY IN SATISFACTORY CONDITION" (*Paradise*, 100) hits the headlines, and the dumping in Beasley's Pond is stopped. Sears then establishes the Beasley Foundation to restore the pond through the miracles of human technology, which he expounds at length. Sears's enthusiasm for the language of this technology, we are told, "sprang from the fact that he had found some sameness in the search for love and the search for potable water" (*Paradise*, 104). Particularly interesting here is the fact that Betsy, rather than Sears—who is Cheever's more immediate avatar—saves the pond; yet she, too, is his creation, and she is set on the path by Chisholm, who is Sears's employee. A continuum is implied, which allows Cheever simultaneously to carry and to pass along his torch. This continuum also makes clear the final irrelevance of the success or failure of the particular human life story to the task of concern, since both Chisholm and Betsy carry the torch. (And this too is characteristic of the *Vollendungsroman*: it is through our commitment to the ideal that actual failures lose their power to erode the quality of affirmation.)

The novel ends with Sears recalling the mortal beauty of Renée and "the utter delight of loving . . . [which] seemed, in his case, to involve some clumsiness, as if he carried a heavy trunk up a staircase with a turning." This curious image—a stairway on which Sears climbs still carrying the baggage of his life—is revealed as a stairway to the stars by the "turning" of the next and penultimate paragraph of the text, where "the thought of stars" leads to the exclamation "What a Paradise it seemed!" (*Paradise*, 105). Sears is clumsy now, I feel, because he has begun the metamorphosis from life to death, and because this heavy trunk (not the essence of love that it contains, but the experience of it as a burden) is alien to the extraterrestrial lover of this planet that he is in the process of becoming. He is also merging here with the narrator and with the author who, Hélène Cixous suggests, is finally relieved of his burden: "On the last day before death, the author sits on the edge of the earth, feet light in the infinite air, and looks at the stars" ("EF," 9). Symbolically, this is the moment of Sears's death.

Narrative Voice: A Bridge between Worlds

I have suggested that the narrator is a ghostly version of both Lemuel Sears and John Cheever, and I will supply evidence for this claim in a moment. But first we might consider why Cheever chose for his last text a dead narrator who points in both directions at once, to the protagonist within the text and the author outside of it. What are the psychological advantages to Cheever of the continuum that is established by this means? To establish via the narrator an identity with Sears might well be appealing to a dying man, who has himself passed beyond the vigor of old age that he assigns to the character. "One would not have to help him across the street" (*Paradise*, 3), the narrator says—while Cheever himself did require such help. At the same time, we know from Donaldson's biography and from Cheever's journals that his extraordinary sex drive could withstand almost to the last hour even the foes of chemotherapy and cancer. Thus, through Sears he can claim a vigor that he is proud still to possess and a vigor that he has lost. To choose a dead narrator (and to identify himself with that narrator) allows Cheever to project himself imaginatively into the hereafter. And what is the hereafter for a writer? It is the reader picking up his tale on a rainy night, the immortality of art.

By projecting himself into both Sears and the dead narrator, Cheever is able to leap over the frailty and pain of his life's end, creating in his text a bridge from one place to the other. By this means he spans the gap between art and life and the gap between life and death. The identity established with Sears via the narrator also allows Cheever to assert the writer's stake in his character: a fictional construct which is both self and other, which he loves and to which he is responsible because it is both self and other. Cheever reveals and obscures the fact that Sears is the narrator because he wants both things, identity and separation. This combined identity and separation of narrator and protagonist points to the crucial identity/separation of Cheever and his fictional world, or even perhaps of Cheever the writer and Cheever the man. For at the point of death, two things must happen: the man dissolves into the writer (whose work alone survives), and the writer dissolves into the man—whose life is intensely loved at this juncture, who can write no more, who will become in Cixous's words "a molecule among all the molecules" ("EF," 9).

The novel begins with the statement that "this is a story to be read in an old house on a rainy night." And the next sentences refer to the rainy night in which we are meant to be reading—thus, for example, "The rain is gentle and needed but not needed with any desperation" (*Paradise*, 1). But imperceptibly the setting in which we are meant to read merges with the village of Janice, the setting we read about. The effect of this is first to install us in the time about which the narrator is writing, and so to emphasize that he is in the future. Second, I think, because a tale read on a rainy night in an old house should be an old tale, we are also carried forward into a future in which we and the tale will have aged. Then, like the old house, we will have mellowed; and the gentle rain will not be "needed with any desperation." More conspicuously eerie is the blurring of the boundary between the reading/writing experience (the present or future rainy night, where we sit in bed with the book in our hands) and the fictional place, the sleepy village of Janice—where a reference to Unidentified Flying Objects may serve as an omen of worlds to come.

Oh What a Paradise It Seems is written from an unspecified vantage point in time and space. Repeatedly, the narrator connects "the time of which I am writing" with insistently contemporary signposts—water pollution, jogging, superhighways, and so on. The effect of this device on the contemporary reader is to create an eerie sense that the narrator is dead, that he addresses us from beyond the grave; it also decisively casts the narrator as the writer.

Anthropological imagery is used to analyze contemporary society and to connect it with much earlier periods of human history. Thus, for example, the contemporary supermarket is seen as containing still the essential features of an ancient marketplace, and contemporary North American "nomadism" is by the insistent use of that term connected with much earlier and more far-flung versions of that human phenomenon. Behind present scenes and events, older and more distant images are glimpsed—as when Beasley's Pond causes Sears to think of eighteenth- and nineteenth-century skating scenes by Dutch painters, and then of a drawing from "a much earlier period" (*Paradise*, 5), and finally of the claim of a discredited paleontologist—which Sears cherishes nonetheless, as a fictional truth—that the ability to skate gave *Homo sapiens* the velocity required to outstrip Neanderthal man. Similarly, Chisholm greets the baby he finds abandoned by the side of a highway as Moses—so that Route 336 is linked across time and space to the Nile.

The effect of this layering is partly to confirm the contemporary reader's sense that the "now" of Janice is itself or will inevitably become historical. And in the context of present environmental threats, even that is optimistic prophecy. The news is still better if we can accept imaginatively the idea that the narrator speaks to us from a future in which it is possible to say that "in the time of which I am writing most of our great rivers and bodies of water were [and by implication are no longer] in serious danger" (*Paradise*, 101). But I would argue that in choosing this vantage point for his narrator, Cheever is also optimistically making provision for readers who will take up this book a hundred or a thousand years from now. He is addressing those readers, too, in a swan song that he hopes will prove immortal.

The novel's many imaginative forays to such locales as Italy and Eastern Europe, away from the focal site of Janice, have for me the effect of arguing that "Cheever Country" is a larger place than Cheever's critics had supposed—as Cheever glances here at many of the foreign settings employed elsewhere in his fiction. At the same time, the ease and frequency of these geographical leaps (like the narrative leaps from one character to another) imply a distant, almost unearthly perspective. The suggestion that "paradise [is] either mountainous or maritime, depending on one's taste" (*Paradise*, 11) has a similar effect. One feels that Cheever is turning the globe in his hand.

This oddly named village of Janice, coming from a writer who is fond of name play, may suggest Janus, the two-faced Roman god of doorways and beginnings. Janice/Janus and the narration as a whole point in two directions at once: toward Sears and Cheever, death and life, pollution and purity, the contemporary and the historical, the heights of the mountains and the depths of the sea, the author's pride and his humility. Another instance of name play in this text is also Janus-like: the hint of palindrome in the protagonist's names, both "Lemuel" and "Sears." Allusions here also have a kind of metafictional force. Thus, "Lemuel" is Jonathan Swift's Lemuel Gulliver, a traveler into other worlds characterized by dizzying shifts of scale, as well as the kind of Old Testament prophet's name that recurs so frequently in the Cheever family tree. And "Sears," suggesting both the contemporary department store and "seer," may also evoke King Lear. (The strangeness of "Lemuel" and the greater familiarity of "Samuel" may cause us to transpose the first letters of each name—and come up not only with "Lear" but with "Samuel leers"!)

The Janus image also applies to the tone of the novel, which is both skeptical and loving—like Lemuel Sears's daughter or like the sibyl he encounters in a cave, who laughs at the wallet he extends to her, acknowledging that she's on the take, and that her profession involves self-interest and fakery, while at the same time celebrating their mutual and entirely genuine appreciation of "la grande poésie de la vie" (*Paradise*, 60–61). Sears's robust appreciation of the sibyl recalls his pleasure in the bogus yet poetically true suggestion of the paleontologist concerning the critical importance of skating in human history. On both occasions we sense that Lemuel Sears is a poet—or the author—in disguise. Like fiction, the poetry of life is compacted of such polarities as faith and doubt, miracle and chicanery, admiration and disgust—and life itself must (in Cheever's estimation) be loved whole.

Sears's two wives (who are recalled in the scene with the sibyl) serve to characterize his attitude to the supernatural, or to the zone which precedes and follows the particular life story, the zone I have called the universal. With his first wife, Sears felt from the beginning "the authority . . . of familiarity"; here, it seems, the universal authorizes their particular union by an operation of grace. Again, as she lay dying in his arms, he felt that "she was returning to some stratum of existence where they had first met and where they would meet again" (*Paradise*, 57). His second wife represents the failure of grace and the failure of love in and for this world. Estelle, who "felt that the world we see—the world Sears adored—was superficial," is ironically named. (This is clear when, at the end of the novel, the thought of stars leads Sears to a sense of his exquisite privilege as a denizen of this world.) He can only feel the authority of the supernatural when it is grounded in natural love.

Sears rejects Estelle's claim on occult powers for two reasons. It is suspect because "her foresight [unlike Cheever's] was largely pessimistic"— in fact, "he could not remember her having prophesied any triumphs of the spirit" (*Paradise*, 61)—and because "she defended her prescience competitively as if supernatural insights were a field sport" (*Paradise*, 58). He can feel the "authority" of the supernatural only if it is not sought competitively and only if it is joined to a loving acceptance of this world. (This position recalls what Kathleen Woodward refers to as the non-Promethean "state of receptivity" that is essential to wisdom, or the condition in which the natural and the supernatural may converge [*AL*, 12]).

Those critics who emphasize Cheever's profound dissatisfaction with modern life and his nostalgia for a lost and golden era are therefore mistaken. They see his skepticism but not his faith in love, and they neglect his insistence on the "grande poésie" of all that is given in the here and now. Thus, for example, one critic notes as characteristic of Cheever's "stridency" the narrator's reference to "the asininity of the game show" (*Paradise*, 25) that a character watches on television;[5] and he fails to note the balance that Cheever achieves when—in a scene that asserts the communal ideal—he allows other characters (Betsy, Henry, and Chisholm) to complete "the pleasures of the evening" by watching "their particularly favorite shows on television" (*Paradise*, 84). We do not suppose that these shows are more distinguished than the asinine game show; the point here is that Cheever can acknowledge any vessel as capable of sacred use. And the significant critical point to be made about the first reference to television is not that it is a gratuitous jibe but that it is balanced by the second. "To scorn one's world," Sears thinks, "is despicable" (*Paradise*, 67). He rejects the "self-induced autumnal twilight" of his age and dislikes the "disposition to complain," the tune that he hears all around him: "That things had been better was the music, the reprise of his days" (*Paradise*, 33). He has heard this from the young and from his elders, but it is not his music.

A Rifle in Paradise

The voice of the narrator of *Paradise* is disembodied, with the startling exception of a brief, enigmatic scene which reveals that the narrator is both Sears and Cheever. At the beginning of the third chapter, the narrator describes himself as lying in a streambed, concealed with a rifle, "waiting to assassinate a pretender who is expected to come here, fishing for trout" (*Paradise*, 24). Though the pretender is only "expected to come here," he is promptly described as if he were there all along. My explanation for this is that the narrator/writer "expects" him to appear on the page, which he can do without any realistic hullabaloo of arrival. The site (and the meaning) of their prospective encounter is metafictional; both the narrator and the pretender are apparitions. It is not surprising to me that the ghostly narrator should be "concealed" or that he is hiding in a streambed, since water in this text is traditionally construed as the place of death and rebirth.

At the beginning of the novel, there is a curious wartime tableau of

Sears and "the unburied dead" (*Paradise*, 4); he is armed with a rifle, on a beautiful summer's day—and we may recall this when we come to the scene of the assassin and the pretender. But the identification of the dead narrator with Sears is signaled more clearly by a sprig of mint, which functions like the scent of those famous madeleines that trigger a flood of memory in Proust's *The Remembrance of Things Past*. The signal—"The smell of mint is very strong and I hear the music of water" (*Paradise*, 24)—is understood only at the end of the novel, when Sears breaks a leaf of mint between his fingers to release the scent and hears "the sound of water" (*Paradise*, 104). The mint and the sound of water exist at the margin between worlds, as at the end of the novel Sears is returned by these images to a valedictory experience of the mortal beauty of Renée and then led on to the "thought of stars" and "worlds around us" (*Paradise*, 105). In the assassin scene, the narrator (who may be regarded as one of "the unburied dead") descends on the imaginary staircase that Sears climbs at the end of the novel, drawn to the same place by the same trigger of memory—which is Sears's memory because he is Sears.

The narrator begins plaintively, reluctantly: "I wish this story I'm telling began with the fragrance of mint growing along a stream bed where I am lying." And almost imperceptibly, like the pretender, he appears; somewhere between "mint" and "stream bed" the disembodied narrator undergoes his strange metamorphosis and becomes a figure contained within the world of the text ("where I am lying"). But why does he wish the story could begin with the fragrance of mint, as this story in fact does? Apparently because he would rather deal with "such matters" than with the ugly story of Cellos shooting his dog, which is coming up. Like the narrator, we want a paradisaical antidote, in keeping with the smell of mint and the music of water, but what we have instead—the reality of "such matters"—is the ugly tableau of the narrator with a rifle, waiting to assassinate a young man.

Who is this pretender, and why does the narrator want to assassinate him? I have several answers, all necessarily fragile because this is the stuff of dreams, yet potent if we can regard the narrator not only as Sears but also as Cheever himself. In this scene, the old and dying writer seeks bodily form in order to engage once more in his lifelong quarrel with himself. ("We make out of the quarrel with others rhetoric," Yeats wrote, "but out of the quarrels with ourselves poetry.")[6] In effect, he relinquishes the Olympian perspective on the scene in order to deal once more with "matters" that have not yet been finally resolved. The serenity of the wise old man— of Cheever—is disturbed, and this should not be surprising. In old age, as Erikson has argued, we hover between integrity and despair; and wisdom must heed those tremors—the fear of death, the remnants of discordancy—which threaten to disturb the integrity or integration of the self.

If Cheever's quarrel is with himself, the pretender may be seen as a youthful avatar of Cheever: The pretender is a well-favored young man and thinks himself quite alone. There is, he seems to think, some blessedness in fishing trout with flies. He sings while he assembles his rod and looks up at the sky and around at the trees to reassure himself of the naturalness of this garden from which, unknown to him, he is about to be dismissed (*Paradise*, 24).

In this passage we can hear Cheever's bitterness over the loss of youth and his own imminent dismissal from the garden. Like this youth he believed in the "blessedness" of nature as his enduring home; but "unknown to him" he was always "about to be dismissed." Similarly, Sears at a dark moment (when he is made to feel that his sexuality is monstrous, following his dismissal by Renée) feels that "hostility seemed to be his home" (*Paradise*, 45). If the "pretender" is Cheever himself, his real target is the illusion of blessedness; this is why he has summoned this young man to the page and why he calls him the pretender. Yet "the smell of mint seriously challenges the right of this or any other murder" (*Paradise*, 24). The assassination cannot occur now that he is actually back in the garden of this world, because the ghost feels again the pull of love—as mint led Sears to his tender and erotic vision of Renée—which leads once more to the feeling of blessedness. (Hostility only seemed for a dark interval to be his home.)

The wish to assassinate the pretender also recalls the many fratricides of Cheever's fiction, which have often been explained as stemming from an intense love/hate relationship with his own brother. Scott Donaldson says that "Cheever sometimes hinted that he and his brother had become lovers" and also reports that "the love he felt for his brother was, as he said a hundred times, 'the strongest love' of his life." Asked by his daughter Susan whether he had ever wanted to kill his brother, Cheever replied that he had imagined doing so on a "trout fishing" expedition.[7] In any case, there are in Cheever's fiction clear links between the figures of the brother, the homosexual, and the double (or doppelgänger) and fratricide. And for Cheever—as, I think, for Hemingway—trout fishing was a masculine idyll associated with homosexual feeling.

John Cheever was raised to despise homosexuality; but again and again in his fiction, we find that it is regarded as both an earthly abomination and an angelic ideal. The "pretender" in this scene who insists on the "naturalness" of his male paradise (man without woman, alone or with another man) could therefore be the homosexual in himself to whom the narrator (as Cheever's ghost) is still not reconciled. The pretender is an all-purpose figure of male sexuality, who pretends that one orientation or the other is natural. He is also clearly related to Eduardo, whom Sears takes on a fishing trip that is both sacred and a site of pollution, and whom, the psychiatrist claims, Sears has "invented [as] some ghostly surrogate of a lost school friend or a male relation from your early youth" (*Paradise*, 63). Sears, who said that his life would end if he were to declare himself a homosexual, is also the ghostly assassin.

I regard the pretender also as a figure of the artist that Cheever (like Hemingway) feared would succeed and supplant him, mainly because I sense in reading this scene the operation of the myth of the Fisher King. In that myth a kingdom suffers drought (which is comparable in the novel to the lack of potable water) and is restored when a virile young man kills off the old king; his potency is manifested by the assassination of his predecessor. It seems to me that the narrator's phallic rifle is directed with hostility at a pretender to his throne, and that what Cheever demonstrates in this strange scene is the reverse of what Harold Bloom has called the anxiety of influence; he is the old king, experiencing the anxiety of supersession, who wants to shoot first. On a rainy night in the future, Cheever hopes that we will read his book. Because rain (which would end the drought) is insistently portrayed within the novel as conducive to both lovemaking and reading, it seems that Cheever is using the myth behind this scene to link the two areas about which he is experiencing unrest.

In the myth drought is also linked with infertility, and in the novel the contamination of water is thought to have caused the miscarriage of a baby "who looked more like a dog than a human" (*Paradise*, 89). Cheever's mission (via Sears, via Chisholm and Betsy) is to end the contamination of the pond, the salvation of which is linked to "a clean, happy baby" (*Paradise*, 81). Healthy babies, like Moses/Binxie, lead us to the promised land; it is for their sake that pollution must be fought and the promise of an earthly paradise fulfilled. The baby is essential to the health of the kingdom: thus Chisholm, immediately before he discovers the baby, feels that he has "lost his crown, his kingdom" (*Paradise*, 80).

The problem is that Cheever's homosexual desire represents for him a violation of this ideal of cleanliness and generation; it is a threat both to the kingdom and to his right of stewardship. Thus, homosexuality is associated on the level of image with the contamination of the pond. To the extent that the pretender represents his homosexual desire, the wish to shoot the pretender casts the narrator (and the bisexual author) in the role of the insistently virile, heterosexual male who kills the impotent Fisher King and so restores nature to a state of health. And this makes a kind of sense because it was only in old age that Cheever began to declare his sexual interest in men; thus, the young fisherman can be an image both of the youthful object of desire and of Cheever the aged homosexual as Fisher King.

I have suggested that Cheever enters the text as the aged Fisher King who wants to kill the pretender, because the young man threatens to steal his kingdom of life and art, and that the pretender is the Fisher King whom Cheever as the defender of the heterosexual faith would kill in order to restore the kingdom to fertility. Both things are possible in this Janus-like text. To resolve the contradictions and dissipate the hostility, only an un-selfish love will suffice. Thus, the narrator dismisses his intensely personal demons and returns to his disembodied state, to pursue the quest for "the purity of water," which he says is "far more important than dynasties" (*Paradise*, 24).

Humility and Communitas

The word *dynasties* signals precisely the will to power that was involved in the wish to assassinate the pretender. What Cheever turns to instead is an egalitarian ideal of community, through which the hierarchical ego may hope to be reformed. It seems important, therefore, that the pond is not saved by Sears alone. Near the end of the novel, when Sears is relishing his command of the technology that is restoring the pond and his command of technological language (an ironic parallel, I believe, to Cheever's own expertise with language), the narrator makes this comment: "Sears liked to think that the resurrection of Beasley's Pond had taught him some hu-mility, but his humility was not very apparent" (*Paradise*, 102). My point is that Cheever knows both the impediments to humility and the wisdom of humility.

Kathleen Woodward cites the anthropologist Victor Turner on the ideal of " 'communitas,' a condition of social unity (community) characterized by undifferentiated social status (what Martin Buber has termed the 'I-Thou' relationship of the self to the other)." And she speaks of how Ezra Pound found wisdom in a "social bond among marginals" (*AL,* 17). The value of *communitas* is very often asserted in the *Vollendungsroman*, as old age itself confers marginality, and as the elderly protagonist grows in wisdom through learning to dispense with social privilege and through forming a crucial bond with other "marginals." Something like this, I believe, must have happened for John Cheever through homosexual experience. (Age alone could not have had this effect on such a famous writer.) Thus, homosexuals in an airport are "venereal vagrants" (*Paradise*, 46); Eduardo is an elevator man; and Sears tries without avail "to bring to his venereal drives something like the rectitude of Burke's *Peerage* [or] the New York Social Register" (*Paradise*, 46). But the eventual acceptance of a socially despised homosexual love helps this almost aristocratic figure to understand that he is in fact a man of the people.

Sears thinks that "he has never known anyone so honest" (*Paradise*, 71) as Eduardo and finds with him "a union from which jealousy had been leached" (*Paradise*, 65). The honesty he ascribes to Eduardo is a function of his own, for what is happening now seems entirely real, an end to pretense. And his new ability to love without a need to possess is another sign of *communitas*. At the same time, love with Eduardo teaches him something about new "modes of loneliness" (*Paradise*, 63). These two things—*communitas* and loneliness—seem to go together, as a preparation for the elderly protagonist's departure for the universal. They signal the wisdom of a "detached concern with life itself, in the face of death itself."[8] And Sears is transported to this state by the agency of elevator and airport, by the homosexual figure who in Cheever's late fiction is always somehow angelic.

The Music of Water: "The Language of His Nativity"

Perhaps the most common image in the *Vollendungsroman* is water, which generally signifies the flux and open form of nature and is associated with the fear of death and the hope of spiritual renewal. Often it is opposed to the house, which is an image of society as opposed to nature and the protective carapace of a singular identity; typically, the aged protagonist moves away from the particular house and toward the universal water. Water functions most powerfully as a symbol of the universal quadrant from which we came and to which we must return. We may dissolve or drown in water, like the very old people Betsy sees at the beach, who are "so old that if they went swimming they would sink" (*Paradise*, 73–74). But the beauty of water nevertheless beckons and speaks of a blessedness that transfigures all the pain and error that may overwhelm us in old age. It suggests a kind of grace. Thus, one of the old women on the beach mystifies Betsy by saying repeatedly, "Oh what have we done to deserve such a beautiful day!" (*Paradise*, 74).

For Lemuel Sears, water—in particular "a trout stream in a forest, a traverse of potable water"—is a "bridge that spans the mysterious abyss between our spiritual and our carnal selves" (*Paradise*, 89). Water here is its own bridge. Immersion in this world leads paradoxically to transcendence.

Another version of this paradox is seen in the image of Sears skating on the surface of Beasley's Pond, as water (in the form of ice) again creates its own bridge. When Sears is skating on the pond at the beginning of the novel, he hears a young woman cry out, "Isn't it heavenly? I love it, I like it, I like it, I love it," and Sears recalls that he once heard precisely that exclamation while engaged in "erotic acrobatics" with a lover. Skating is both sex and art, the two great loves of John Cheever's life and the two great means of transcendence—which are both paradoxically achieved through immersion in this world. As he skates, Sears feels "the pleasure of fleetness" (*Paradise*, 5), for skating (like sex and art) is a mode of transport that is itself an ecstasy.

In old age Sears is skating on "a long stretch of black ice" (*Paradise*, 5), and what he feels is a sense of "homecoming": "At long last, at the end of a cold, long journey, he was returning to a place where his name was known and loved and lamps burned in the rooms and fires in the hearth" (*Paradise*, 6). This image is an interesting variant of the water/house opposition in the novel of old age. Here, the water also carries Sears toward identity and home, a place where his name (and John Cheever's) would be "known and loved." Again, we may feel how profoundly for Cheever the image of "paradise" is linked to the aspirations of this world, the desire to be made welcome—known and loved—as both an artist and a man.

The water of the trout stream is for Sears "a bridge that spans the mysterious abyss between our spiritual and our carnal selves" (*Paradise*, 89). The word "carnal" here carries something of the force of "lewdness," as on the occasion when "a surge of lewdness" (an experience of desire for Eduardo) convinces Sears that "these caverns of his nature would never enjoy coherence." Yet he experiences this surge also as "nostalgia" (*Paradise*, 71). The carnal self is therefore part of a coherent whole which Sears thinks he cannot achieve in life but for which he yearns, nostalgically. And the serenity of water (the reconciliation of opposites) corresponds paradoxically "to a memory as deep as any he possessed" (*Paradise*, 88), a memory of the dynamic "fountainhead" (*Paradise*, 89). This is Cheever's image of what Kathleen Woodward calls "the still point" (*AL*, 7)—which for T. S. Eliot in "Burnt Norton" is "the still point of the turning world. Neither / flesh nor fleshless; / Neither from nor towards; at the still point, / there the dance is, / But neither arrest nor movement. And do not call / it fixity."

When he was young, water spoke to Sears "in the tongues of men and angels"; again, the point is that water includes the carnal (men) as well as the spiritual (angels). Now he is an old man who speaks "five or six languages—all of them poorly," and what he yearns for is "the sound of water [which] seemed to be the language of his nativity, some tongue he had spoken before his birth." It reminds him of "eavesdropping in some other room than where the party was" (*Paradise*, 89). This last image connects with "some stratum of existence" (*Paradise*, 57) to which Sears's first wife has returned, and where she awaits their blissful reunion. It connects with the "rooms" in which his name is known and loved. And it connects significantly with a voice from the street that Sears overhears when he is agonizing over his possible homosexuality in the psychiatrist's office, the "cheerful voice of a man calling some other man to throw him a ball." He feels deep longing and "nostalgia . . . not only for his youth but for the robustness, simplicity and beauty that life could possess" and for "a feeling of beginning" (*Paradise*, 56).

I would suggest that the language of water speaks to Sears of resolution, something that seems beyond his capacity in the several languages he has attempted in life; it is a language that would grant him a full integration, full acceptance. The sound of water comes from the room where Eliot's dance is, where the party is, and by extension from the street where the men play happily together; at the end of the novel, it returns him in imagination to a woman's bed. Its music suggests that this is all possible, and that his lewdness is not after all "a profound contamination" (*Paradise*, 104). What he wants is an end to exile, which he has experienced in life through shame over the "Mr. Hyde" (*Paradise*, 39) of his insistent sexuality—as when Renée rejects him, and he enters "some Balkans of the spirit" (*Paradise*, 44). Sears is balkanized, split, alienated from himself and others, when he is made to feel that there is an abyss between his "spiritual and . . . carnal selves" (*Paradise*, 89).

Most striking in *Oh What a Paradise It Seems* is Cheever's insistence that "paradise" is not simply a prelapsarian Eden, not only otherworldly, not only spirit. The universal for Cheever, as for any great artist, must exist in a dynamic relationship with the particular. Thus, in his last text we see that Cheever is still struggling with the particulars of his own life. But he has also found—or adumbrated through his ghostly narrator, a man on skates—the still point of the dance. He has found the wisdom and courage of old age: "An aged man is but a paltry thing, a tattered coat upon a stick, unless he sees the bright plumage of the bird called courage—*Cardinalis virginius*, in this case—and oh how his heart leapt" (*Paradise*, 3). In this echo of Yeats, which shades almost imperceptibly into Cheever's own words, he discovers the humility and the pride of the *communitas* of art. He can take comfort in his achievement, and let it go. Though still "unburied" (*Paradise*, 4), Cheever has in fact created in his last text his own "monument," ensuring that he will not be among the "forgotten dead." Yet it is clear that he could not have done so if this were "sole purpose" (*Paradise*, 91). His heart must leap with a love of this world that comes from the "fountainhead" (*Paradise*, 89). And so it does. "After all books. After time. After the self" ("EF," 10). John Cheever in his extraordinary, haunting swan song may be said to have entered "the music of water" (*Paradise*, 24).

Notes

1. Erik H. Erikson, Joan M. Erikson, and Helen Q. Kivnick, *Vital Involvement in Old Age*, 37, 33.
2. Constance Rooke, "Hagar's Old Age," 74.
3. Scott Donaldson, *John Cheever*, 339.
4. Geoffrey Stokes, Robert Ottaway, Bill Greenwell, reviews of *Oh What a Paradise It Seems*.
5. Adam Gussow, "Cheever's Failed Paradise," 103.
6. W. B. Yeats, "Per Amica Silentia Lunae," 331.
7. Donaldson, *Cheever*, 49, 53, 141.
8. Erikson et al., *Vital Involvement in Old Age*, 37.

IV

The Phenomenology of Aging

JUDITH DE LUCE

Quod Temptabam Scribere Versus Erat: Ovid in Exile

IN EXILE at the end of his life, Ovid urges the poet Perilla[1] in Rome to keep writing (*Tr.* 3.7). Youth and beauty will pass, he warns; poetry alone is immortal. For Ovid, writing poetry had always been a way to challenge the inexorable mortality of human affairs. Now he found himself exiled from Rome in part because of his poetry, isolated from family and friends, with no audience for his work. Yet in spite of the considerable hardship under which he lived, Ovid did not abandon his art. His incessant writing from exile was not simply an old man's cry for help; rather, it affirmed the poet's vitality as an artist. In the end, the young man who could write nothing but verse, *quod temptabam scribere versus erat,* became the old man who could do nothing but write verse.

Taken as a whole, the *Tristia* and *Epistulae ex Ponto,* written in exile, highlight the contrast between Ovid's despairing experience of old age and his vigorous creativity in the face of that old age. Throughout these final poems Ovid reflects Roman tradition when he represents his old age in the grimmest terms, yet he never relinquishes his determination to keep writing or his conviction that his verse will survive its author. This chapter examines the dissonance between Ovid's experience as an old man and his enduring confidence as a poet.[2]

The exile poems also remind us that Publius Ovidius Naso (43 B.C.E.– 17 C.E.) had prepared for a lifetime spent writing poetry. In old age Ovid tells us in his autobiography (*Tr.* 4.10) that he was born in Sulmo of equestrian rank and that his father had intended him to follow in his brother's footsteps and to pursue a career in public life. With his brother already embarked on a career in oratory, his father asked Ovid why he pursued so profitless an occupation as writing. Ovid, taking his father's advice, attempted to give up poetry, but no matter how hard he tried, *quod temptabam scribere versus erat* (26), whatever I tried to write was a verse. Ovid continued to write up until his death; age did not impair his productivity. If the *Amores* were written when he was in his twenties, Ovid wrote consistently and published regularly over a forty-year period, producing at least eleven extant works, the lost *Medea,* and perhaps the problematic *Halieutica* in the course of that career. In addition he may have written other lost works hinted at in the *Tristia* and *Epistulae ex Ponto,* the exile poems. Not only did Ovid write continuously, but the extant works alone represent nearly every genre, from the elegiac to the epistolary to the didactic to the narrative.

But at fifty this prolific writer found himself banished from the urbane, sophisticated world he occupied, separated from his family, friends, and literary colleagues, and exiled by the emperor Augustus to Tomis, along the Black Sea, a community utterly alien to him. Nothing recommended Tomis to Ovid: its savage weather was intolerable; the ever-present danger of attack from the neighboring tribes terrified him; the absence of other writers, or critics, or even readers left Ovid still more isolated. The fact that the inhabitants spoke neither Latin nor Greek meant that this most articulate poet was deprived even of conversation. But he was not barred from writing, and write he did, at least the ninety-six poems that we have in the *Tristia,* and the *Epistulae ex Ponto,* and perhaps others as well. If he is indeed the author of the *Halieutica,* then he was engaged in yet a new writing project when he died in 17 C.E.

We still do not know for certain why Ovid was exiled by Augustus. The poet says that it was for a *carmen et error,* a poem and a mistake, but scholars do not agree on the identity of the poem or the nature of the mistake. Some scholars even question whether Ovid went into exile at all, but I will join those scholars who have traditionally assumed, on the basis of the *Tristia* and *Epistulae ex Ponto,* that Ovid actually was in Tomis.[3] Whether or not he was banished to Tomis, however, Ovid certainly regarded exile as a metaphor for old age. In fact, the losses suffered in exile—the severing of ties with family and friends, loss of an occupation, constraints on one's mobility, barriers to intellectual and professional interests, alienation from the familiar—all correspond closely with those losses the Romans identified with old age.

Ovid would have been regarded as old at fifty. As modern readers we need to remember that chronological old age in Greco-Roman antiquity is not comparable to modern assumptions of what it means to be old. In Rome a woman might well be regarded as old at menopause, which physicians usually believed occurred at forty. Since women traditionally are regarded as old some ten to fifteen years earlier than their male contemporaries, by the standards of his day Ovid was an old man when he left Rome.[4]

The Romans regarded old age with considerable ambivalence.[5] On the one hand, they shared the pessimism of the Greek tradition which characterized old age as a time of need, vulnerability, and loss of happiness late in life. Like the Greeks, the Romans recognized various systems of age grading and subscribed to the theory of *tempestivitas,* or seasonableness, the principle that certain behaviors are appropriate for particular ages. In the *Ars Poetica (Epistle* 2.3), written when he was himself an old man, Horace exhorts poets to respect age norms and to "linger over traits that are joined and fitted to the age" (175–76). Thus, according to Horace, a poet ought to describe an old man as overly cautious, acquisitive, irascible, inclined to condemn the young men of the day and prone to praise overmuch his own former youth (169–76). Horace never depicts a younger man so negatively, but only the figure of the old man. Violation of the principle of *tempestivitas* exposed one to ridicule and censure. Old women, for example, are frequently singled out for ridicule for their sexual appetites, which are reviled as unseemly; old fathers in comedy are represented as deceitful, lecherous buffoons. Roman elders may also appear forgetful, miserly, suffering from loss of health and above all loss of sensual pleasure. On the other hand, the Romans did not regard old age with unrelieved pessimism. While Rome was certainly not a gerontocracy, it did, for example, adhere to the principles of seniority. Old men and women could exert considerable influence and were supported in doing so by legal, social, and political institutions.

It could be argued that Cicero's *Cato Maior de senectute* provides a most persuasive case for a vigorous old age filled with ample opportunities to participate in the civic life of Rome and to pursue intellectual and literary interests. Cicero completed the essay when he was sixty-four, during that period when he wrote philosophy to assuage his grief over the death of his daughter, Tullia. He dedicated the essay to his intimate friend Atticus, who was himself sixty-five. Cicero says that he chose to write this essay "to lighten for you and for me our common burden of old age, which, if not already pressing hard upon us, is surely coming on apace" (1.2).

The dramatic time of *De senectute* is 150 B.C.E. when Cato at eighty-four converses with two younger friends, thirty-five-year-old Scipio and thirty-six-year-old Laelius. As he addresses four traditional complaints about old age, Cato argues for the continuity of personality across the life span and for the possibility of a creative, productive, useful old age, even in the face of diminishing health and physical strength. Cato predicates the possibility of a productive old age on the preparations one would have to make in youth. Cato resorts to his own version of *tempestivitas* but without Horace's negativity: "Life's race-course is fixed; Nature has only a single path and that path is run but once, and to each stage of existence has been allotted its own appropriate quality; so that the weakness of childhood, the impetuosity of youth, the seriousness of middle life, the maturity of old age—each bears some of Nature's fruit, which must be garnered in its own season" (10.33).

Throughout the essay Cato characterizes old age as a time of freedom from those sensual pleasures and ambitions which kept him busy in his youth and which threatened to distract him from matters of the mind. Moreover, the proximity of death to old age does not alarm him. He sees his old age as a time when he can exert his influence in the state and when he can teach younger men who can benefit from his skill and experience. When people condemn old age, according to Cato, what they are actually doing is blaming not old age but traits of character. Old age can be a busy time indeed, provided one has prepared for it from youth and provided one has opportunities to remain active.

In spite of the encouraging picture which Cato presents of late age, however, it is also possible that he protests too much and that the essay reflects Cicero's concern for the quality of his own old age. As Harcum has observed, old age for the Romans was a "time to be dreaded rather than hoped for. . . . Even a Cicero could make it only endurable, not desirable."[6]

In some ways, Ovid's old age as he describes it corresponds closely to the more pessimistic Roman perspective, to the very complaints which Cicero confronts. Nonetheless, while Ovid complains about illness, timidity, loneliness, and innumerable losses, the poet never loses his desire to write, nor does he question seriously the power of poetry. Granted, modern critics are often disappointed by the exile poems, complaining of their repetitive dreariness (as the author himself does, in *Pont.* 3.9) and the absence of the wry humor and facile wit of the earlier poems. Such critics have tended to read the *Tristia* and the *Epistulae ex Ponto* without considering the age of their author.[7] Reading these poems with Ovid's age very much in mind, however, helps us understand his choice of genre, the tenor of the poems, and the relationship between the poet and his earliest works and the final poems written from Tomis. Above all, such a reading underscores the very continuity which Cicero's Cato had discussed. Ovid had prepared himself to be a poet as a young man; as an old man he could not cease to be that poet.

Neither old age nor ill health belongs in the world of Ovid's earlier poems. In the *Amores,* for example, there are no sympathetic representatives of elders. If old age has no place here, death has even less. Even the poet's serious reflection on his own mortality is missing from the earlier poems. At this point we may attribute the absence of old age to a variety of factors. Perhaps Ovid, with youth's arrogant assumption of immortality, little considers the possibility of his own old age or death. Perhaps the genre does not allow for any serious or sympathetic inclusion of old age since it is unseemly for elders, as far as Roman popular culture is concerned, to be engaged in affairs of the heart.

In the exile poems Ovid returns to the genre of his earliest work; old age does appear as a motif in these later poems, however, and here it is primarily his own old age that Ovid describes. This is not the comfortable old age of Cephalus in the *Republic*—a time of peace, rich personal associations, opportunities to discuss politics and philosophy and to enjoy the attentions of the young. Neither is it the vigorous old age promised in Cicero's *De senectute.* Cato had argued that reasonable diet, regular exercise, and challenging occupations for the mind contributed to a pleasant old age that need not be feared as a time when youthful vigor gives way to illness, diminished mental alertness, or reduced sources of pleasure. But Cato was not exiled to Tomis.

In Ovid's exile poems we discover a profoundly vulnerable, depressed man, fearful that he will succumb either to illness or to hostile attack by neighboring tribes. In fact, he regards himself as already "dead." In *Tristia* 3.3, addressed to his wife, Ovid equates exile with death and reveals his very real fear of dying in Tomis. Ill and too weak to write, he dictates his poem. He reassures his wife that she should be glad his death will free him from all the misfortunes of his exile: "When I lost my native land, then must you think that I perished, that was my earlier and harder death" (53–54).

But the prospect of physical death in Tomis presents new horrors to him: he envisions dying alone, without his wife's comfort, without the familiar funeral rites. He even wishes that the soul might perish with the body: otherwise, "a Roman will wander among Sarmatian shades, a stranger forever among barbarians. But my bones—see that they are carried home in a little urn: so shall I not be an exile even in death" (63–66).

Not only do the exile poems reflect Ovid's experience of old age, but *Tristia* 4.8 takes old age as its theme and considers the physical, psychological, and social consequences of growing old. "Already my temples are like the plumage of a swan, for white old age is bleaching my dark hair. Already the years of frailty and life's inactive time are stealing upon me, and already 'tis hard for me in my weakness to bear up" (1–4). What a younger Ovid had expected old age would be like does not correspond with its reality. The younger man would have envisioned an old age spent in comfortable leisure, "peacefully growing old in my lady's embrace, among my dear comrades and in my native land" (5–12). This vision is a far cry from Ovid's life in Tomis.

If *Tr.* 4.10 presents us with Ovid's autobiography, *Tr.* 2 to Augustus becomes Ovid's résumé—part apologia, part reflection on the poetic life. After marveling that he could still write at all, since his poetry had incurred the emperor's wrath, Ovid reviews his poetic career and reports that others wrote of love, too, but only he suffered for the writing. He also excuses himself for not having written weightier poems, but this *recusatio,* or demurral, lacks the confidence and humor of such earlier defenses of his choice of genre as *Am.* 2.1. In *Tr.* 2 he insists that he simply does not have the strength for grander themes: "But if thou shouldst bid me sing of the Giants conquered by Jove's lightning, the burden will weaken me in the attempt. Only a rich mind can tell the tale of Caesar's mighty deeds if the theme is not to surpass the work" (333–36).

Again in sharp contrast to the spirit of his earlier poems, Ovid in *Pont.* 3.3 reports a dream in which Amor appeared to him, an Amor quite unrecognizable in the world of the earlier *Amores:* "There stood love, not with the face he used to have, sadly resting his left hand upon the maple post, no necklace on his throat, no ornament in his hair, his locks not carefully arranged as of old" (13–16). This Amor has no reason to laugh. Ovid's Muse has suffered from the hardships of exile and of age.

Ovid's tendency to evoke in his later work the poems he wrote in his youth is intimately connected with the relationship between how he experienced old age and his productivity. Ovid could have made a very different artistic choice as to genre and theme at the end of his life. At one time only the epic was regarded as prestigious enough to conclude a career. Lawrence Lipking has tied the poetic career of another Latin poet, Vergil, to his age, arguing that "as old age comes on, he gathers all his powers for a mighty effort [the *Aeneid*] that epitomizes the collective wisdom of his civilization, the world as it has been and should be."[8]

Unlike Vergil, however, Ovid did not follow the usual course. He had already written an epic of sorts, the *Metamorphoses,* and the effect of exile and of old age suggested a different route for him, a route that would take him back to his start and to the genre of his earliest poems. The exile poems show Ovid engaging in what Robert Butler has called a "life review." According to Butler, this process of reviewing one's life, confronting unresolved conflicts, making amends, assessing one's accomplishments, making peace, may be prompted, among other things, by the realization of the proximity of death. The outcome of the review, moreover, is affected by a number of factors, including "the lifelong unfolding of character."[9] When I first began to study Ovid's creativity in old age, I believed that it was primarily the process of the life review itself which most influenced the poet's final poems. I am now inclined to think that "the lifelong unfolding of character," the continuity of personality from youth to old age, accounts in large measure for the persistence and nature of Ovid's creative impulse throughout his life, even in the face of exile in Tomis. Writing gives voice to that character which the life review discloses and reaffirms.

Butler's theory provides a useful framework within which to study Ovid's exile poetry, where the poet returns to the genre and a number of the themes of his earliest poems. Yet even as he returns or echoes those earlier efforts, Ovid makes some changes. Betty Rose Nagle has argued that Ovid returns to his earlier poems precisely because he is writing from exile and is anxious to point up the differences between the conditions under which he wrote as a young man and the conditions under which he now must write.[10] Yet while his motive may well have been to attract sympathy and aid in changing the conditions of his exile, his age and the proximity of death play an important part in how he writes. Participating in this life review prompts Ovid not only to return to his earlier poems but to come to terms with his life and his poetic career. He emerges from this process still determined to write poetry.

If we compare Ovid with another Latin poet who also wrote from youth into old age, we find that in some ways Ovid's response to and his representation of old age are not atypical. Earlier I referred to Quintus Horatius Flaccus (65 B.C.E.–8 C.E.) as the author of a classic statement on *tempestivitas*. Like Ovid, as he gets older Horace reflects with increasing frequency on the nature of poetry and his role as a poet. Like Ovid, advancing age does not interfere with Horace's art. Unlike Ovid, Horace enjoyed a comfortable old age, a pleasant home, his beloved Sabine farm, the patronage of the emperor Augustus through Maecenas. Although he clearly experienced an old age significantly more pleasant than Ovid's, he is also extremely sensitive to the realities of old age.[11] Horace is perfectly capable, for example, of exuberantly ridiculing elders, particularly women (such as the old witch Canidia) who violate the principle of *tempestivitas*. He even notes his own violation of age norms, although not with the viciousness which he directs at a Canidia.[12]

While still a young man, Horace certainly did not refrain from reflecting upon age or upon the nature and practice of poetry, as in his Soracte

Ode (1.9), for example. Well before the fourth book of *Odes* Horace had talked in traditional terms about the permanence of poetry, as in O. 2.20. Like Ovid, by the time Horace is an old man, reflections on the nature and immortality of poetry and on old age fill the fourth book of *Odes*. In O. 4.1, for example, Horace at fifty begs Venus to go easy with him; in O. 4.2 Horace reflects on his role as poet. In O. 4.11 Horace, following the principle of *tempestivitas,* sets all passion aside except his passion for poetry. He concludes the fourth book by writing that Apollo had stopped him from attempting grander poetic themes by saying that his "sails" were too small for the task. This recalls Ovid who, in his *recusatio* in *Tristia* 2, refers to his talent as a "rowboat" suitable for the small pond of erotic poetry, perhaps, but inappropriate to the seas of more weighty themes.

In his recent reexamination of Horace, David Armstrong refers in passing to this increasing interest in old age and the challenges of a creative life on the part of the poet.[13] For the moment, we should note that Horace, enjoying a comfortable old age, is aware of the limitations of age, yet those limitations do not interfere with his art. He had long been a productive and popular poet and remained so in his old age. If he did in fact engage in the life review which Butler suggests, it was not a painful process. As he returned to the poetic form in which he had written earlier in his career, he could speak with some humor and some insight into what it meant to be old. His poetry, however, does not reflect the pain of Ovid in part because of the enormous disparity between his and Ovid's actual experience with old age.

With Horace as an example of an old man reflecting on his age and on his craft but in a spirit very different from Ovid's, we need to return to the younger poet's perspective on writing poetry. Even as he continues to write at a pace which has hardly slackened since his youth, Ovid tends to represent his creative strength as failing as surely as his physical strength. He apologizes, for example, for the unkempt appearance of his poetry, in *Tr.* 1.1. The exile poems were not written, as their predecessors had been, in the peace of his garden. In fact, he regards the conditions under which he must work as utterly uncongenial to writing poetry. In Tomis he has no audience, no critics, no books, no stimulation, no other poets with whom to talk or exchange poems.

But even if the conditions were conducive to this activity, would he be able to write? In *Tr.* 1.6 he assures his wife that he would make her immortal in his poetry, if only he could manage it: "Alas that great power lies not in my song and my lips cannot match thy merits—if ever in former times I had aught of quickening vigour, all has been extinguished by my long sorrows"

(29–32). In *Pont.* 1.5 Ovid complains: "You see how inactivity spoils an idle body . . . for me, too, whatever skill I had in shaping song is failing" (5–8). "Even this . . . I write forcing it with difficulty from an unwilling hand" (9–10). Even if he can manage to write, he does not revise as he once would have: "When I read it over I am ashamed of my work because I note many a thing that even in my own, the maker's judgment, deserves to be erased. Yet I do not correct it. This is a greater labour than the writing, and my sick mind has not the power to endure anything hard" (15–18).

Whether or not his poetic powers are actually failing, Ovid continues to write even when doing so reopens old wounds. Like Juvenal but for different reasons, he cannot not write. He recognizes that in spite of the fact that it was his Muse that precipitated his exile, he cannot live without her. Furthermore, writing occupies his time, keeps his mind active, and sometimes allows him respite from his grief. Yet the most poignant reason he gives for writing is not the need for distraction or solace but the need to speak and to be heard: "An exile's voice is this: letters furnish me a tongue, and if I may not write, I shall be dumb" (*Pont.* 2.6. 3–4).

Writing poetry gives Ovid a voice, allows him to speak in a situation in which he must otherwise remain silent. Perhaps, by using that voice, he can come to terms with who he is, where he is, what has happened, and what the future holds. When David Malouf reconstructed Ovid's years in exile in *An Imaginary Life*, he tried to capture this experience of being voiceless. Malouf shows the poet actually finding his twin in a feral child, as unable to communicate with other humans as Ovid claims to be with the other inhabitants of Tomis. Poetry provides for Ovid the sole means of communicating with those who might be able to understand him, even though they live at a considerable distance from Tomis.[14]

Another reason for him to write exists, however—a reason which has not changed since he was a young man, yet one which acquires new importance in his old age. Ovid still claims that poetry has power to bestow immortality on its author. The difference now is that in the face of his own death, Ovid's claims for the power of song are much more compelling. This is the same poet who had challenged the claims of *livor edax*, or consuming Envy, that in the vigor of young manhood he should heed the call to the soldier's life or the lawyer's or the orator's (*Am.* 1.15). Refusing to follow the recommended *cursus honorum*, or the traditional ladder to success in public life, Ovid chose to write instead because he sought the immortal fame which only poetry could bestow.

At the end of his career and in spite of the hardships of exile, Ovid is as insistent on the power of poetry as he was in his early years. In fact, in his letter to his stepdaughter Perilla, Ovid as poet is at his most convincing when he announces that although he has suffered acutely for his art, he is returning to his Muse. It is nothing new for a writer to insist on the immortality of poetry or to advise younger poets about their art, but *Tr.* 3.7 goes beyond the poetic commonplace. Here Ovid writes not from the comfort of a mature poetic career enjoyed in Rome but from a painful old age spent in exile; and he writes not to some generic poet but to his literary and literal descendant, Perilla. His advice to her acquires even greater poignancy precisely because of their relationship and because of his age. Asking if Perilla is still writing, Ovid recalls how he nurtured her earliest efforts, reading her verse and acting as critic; she returned the favor. Always, he had urged her to keep writing. Now he is afraid, however, that the example of his banishment will frighten her away from poetry. He admonishes Perilla to stop making excuses and to keep at her poetry because she will not be a lovely young woman forever: there will come a day when reminders of her former loveliness will reduce her to tears. Things change—youth and beauty give way to the ravages of old age; the rich become poor. The products of the mind, however, do not succumb to change or decay: "In brief, we possess nothing that is not mortal except the blessings of heart and mind" (43–44).

Here Ovid describes himself, an old man, exiled, deprived of family and companions, yet he does not betray the depression we find in many of the other exile poems. Instead, as he writes to this talented young woman, he claims the immortality of his poetry[15] as vigorously as he had at the end of the *Metamorphoses,* where he wrote: "Wherever Rome's power extends over the conquered world, I shall have mention on men's lips, and, if the prophecies of bards have any truth, through all the ages shall I live in fame" (15.877–79). To Perilla, Ovid declares: "My mind is nevertheless my comrade and my joy; over this Caesar could have no right. Let any you will end this life with cruel sword, yet when I am dead my fame shall survive. As long as Martian Rome shall gaze forth victorious from her hills over the conquered world, I shall be read. Do thou too . . . ever shun what way thou canst the coming pyre!" (47–54).

If we can judge by Ovid's productivity in the last ten years of his life, the poet can write with this confidence for two reasons. In the first place, much in keeping with Cato's arguments for a vigorous old age in *De senectute,* Ovid had prepared for a lifetime of writing even as a young man, when he abandoned his father's plans for him and chose instead the life of a poet. It is inconceivable that the realities of growing old in Tomis would compromise Ovid's determination to keep writing. Moreover, at fifty Ovid engaged in the life review that Butler describes, and did so in isolation, without the support of family or friends. His reaction to the review was an extreme one: it included depression, bouts of anxiety, and persistent and repeated reflections upon the past. Despite the threat to his confidence and to his sense of identity, however, Ovid weathered more than the winters at Tomis and emerged from this review not only still writing but perhaps writing something new, if indeed the *Halieutica* is his work. He no longer reverted back to the poetry of his youth. Either he had given up trying to get help, or he had somehow made peace with his situation. In either case, writing poetry was as compelling an occupation in his old age as it had been in his youth, and Ovid was hard at work when death overtook him.

Notes

"Whatever I tried to write was a verse" (Tr. 4.10.26). Throughout the text, English translations follow the Latin. Where I have quoted an entire passage in English, I have included the translation in the reference list.

This chapter is reprinted, in revised form, from Thomas M. Falkner and Judith de Luce, eds., Old Age in Greek and Latin Literature by permission of the State University of New York Press, © 1989 State University of New York. It develops further my thesis in "Ovid as an Idiographic Study of Creativity and Old Age." Portions of this thesis were originally presented orally as "Representations of Old Age in Ovid" at the 1987 University of Maryland symposium "Aging and the Life Cycle in the Renaissance: The Interaction between Representation and Experience." I am grateful to the College of Arts and Science and the Department of Classics at Miami University for the leave which allowed me to begin studying Ovid's exile poetry.

I am indebted to my colleagues B. Lukens and M. Seltzer for their insights and unfailing patience as I worked through this material, K. Maitland Schilling and A. Winkler for their adroit cutting of a Gordian knot, and above all to L. Horvitz, amico doctissimo callidissimoque, for posing difficult questions about creativity and poetry which challenged me to reconsider my original reading of the exile poems.

1. While there remains some doubt as to the identity of this "Perilla," I subscribe to the tradition that she is in fact Ovid's stepdaughter. Our source for his own banishment, Ovid says that the reason for his exile was generally known in Rome (*Tr.* 4.10). Subsequent scholars, not entirely sure why the poet was banished, have usually assumed that the *Ars amatoria* provided the official excuse because the poem appeared to run directly counter to the emperor's avowed intentions to resuscitate Roman morality.

2. There now exist some useful models for studying literary aging: see, for example, Jon Hendricks and Cynthia Leedham, "Making Sense of Literary Aging"; the spring 1991 issue of *Generations* was devoted exclusively to creativity and aging.

3. John C. Thibault, *The Mystery of Ovid's Exile,* and P. Green, "Carmen et Error," provide useful and sober reviews of the evidence for Ovid's exile. I am not the first to question whether exile might operate as a metaphor for old age, but A. Fitton Brown, "The Unreality of Ovid's Tomitian Exile," has gone even further to propose

that Ovid did not go into exile at all. A. W. J. Holleman, "Ovid's Exile," disagreed strenuously.

4. Aulus Gellius (*Noctes Atticae* 10.28), however, cites Tubero who in turn refers to Servius Tullius's determination that after forty-six a man would be *senior*, that is, old.

5. For discussions of the Greek and Roman attitudes toward old age, see Thomas M. Falkner and Judith de Luce, "A View from Antiquity: Greece, Rome, and Elders"; M. I. Finley, "The Elderly in Classical Antiquity."

6. C. G. Harcum, "The Ages of Man: A Study Suggested by Horace, *Ars Poetica*," 118.

Because *De senectute* excludes entire classes of Romans, we cannot accept this as a universally applicable picture of old age. No woman, regardless of class, would have had the opportunities to enjoy the kind of influence and associations which Cato could claim. Furthermore, it is highly unlikely that anyone but a man of the middle or upper classes would have enjoyed such an old age. In fact, Laelius challenges Cato on that very point, suggesting that perhaps his old age is not so unhappy because of his "resources, means, and social position" (3.8). While Cato does not address this objection in any detail, he does grant that in abject poverty old age would be far from pleasant and goes on to conclude that old age even in the midst of great wealth would be unpleasant for the fool.

In a recent paper ("Heeding Our Native Informants: The Use of Latin Literary Texts in Recovering Elite Roman Attitudes towards Age, Gender, and Social Status") which she has kindly made available to me, Judith P. Hallett reconsiders *De senectute* from the added perspectives of gender and class.

7. For the range of scholarly opinion on the exile poetry, see Hermann Frankel, *Ovid,* and Betty Rose Nagle, *The Poetics of Exile.* Harry B. Evans, *Publica Carmina* includes useful comments on Ovid as an old man. Other recent scholarship which contributes to a new appreciation of these poems includes J. P. Bews, "The Metamorphosis of Virgil in the *Tristia* of Ovid"; E. Block, "Poetics in Exile: An Analysis of *Epistulae ex Pont.* 3.9."; Mary T. Davisson, "Duritia and Creativity in Exile *Epistulae ex Ponto* 4.10" and "*Tristia* 5.13 and Ovid's Use of Epistolary Form and Content"; S. Hinds, "Booking the Return Trip"; R. G. M. Nisbet, "Great and Lesser Bear (Ovid *Tristia* 3.4)."

8. Lawrence Lipking, *The Life of the Poet,* 78.

9. Robert N. Butler, "The Life Review."

10. Betty Rose Nagle, *The Poetics of Exile.*

11. Carol C. Esler, "Horace's Old Girls: Evolution of a Topos."

12. For a full discussion of Latin invective poetry, including Horace's position within that tradition, see Amy Richlin, *The Garden of Priapus.*

13. David Armstrong, *Horace,* 122. Although Armstrong goes so far as to suggest that Horace is possibly engaging in a "life review," he does not develop that claim, however, nor does he refer explicitly to Robert Butler's work.

14. David Malouf, *An Imaginary Life.* In a manuscript which she has made available to me, Elizabeth Forbis has provided a provocative and persuasive discussion of the relationship between voicelessness in the *Metamorphoses* and the exile poetry. Her work on voicelessness contributes significantly to our understanding of those poems written at the end of Ovid's life. Forbis considers the relationship between the poet's vigorous control over the narrative of the *Metamorphoses* and his subsequent silencing in the exile poetry, his transformation from "a thriving poet into mere poems."

Her conclusion bears directly on the current chapter, although she arrives at that conclusion on the basis of a very different kind of analysis. The difference between the transformation stories which Ovid tells in the *Metamorphoses* and his own "transformation" after exile is that "Ovid's metamorphosed form is verbal/articulate after all. . . . Ovid's poetry retains a *vox humana* which has preserved the poet's identity."

15. As it turned out, Ovid's confidence in his art was not misplaced; the exultant *vivam* (I shall live), the final word of the *Metamorphoses,* was prophetic.

BETHANY LADIMER

Colette: Rewriting the Script for the Aging Woman

IF aging is the most significant "missing category in current literary theory,"[1] it is also of particular importance to understanding the life and work of the French writer Sidonie-Gabriel Colette, or "Colette," as she came to be known. Critics usually have stressed the effects of her moving back in time, to her childhood and a newfound source of strength related to her mother Sido. But the effects of going forward into old age are also important and in fact generally have been undervalued. Colette changed not only her writing style as she aged but also her view of the writing process and the benefits it could yield.

While the origin of Colette's strength and continued productivity in old age certainly lies in her childhood, the trajectory of her life represents a continuous process of maturation, rather than a circular return. Her late style reached a culmination in her last novels, *The Evening Star* and *The Blue Lantern*. In particular, her maturation involved a movement away from the conventional romance plots of her early fiction and the discovery of an erotic satisfaction in the process of writing itself which offered her, as a writer and as a woman, an alternative to the eroticism of heterosexual love. The satisfaction in this transformation came from a sense of empowerment associated with authorship and subjecthood. Increasingly, she turned from the passivity associated with being looked at by men to the more active stance of one who gazes at the world in order to record what she sees, and the act of writing about this sensory pleasure became the source of a new sensual satisfaction.

This evolution began and gathered momentum in Colette's middle years, beginning with *The Vagabond*. This novel, published in 1910 when

Colette was close to thirty-eight, was the first that she wrote independently of her first husband, "Willy" (Henri Gauthier-Villars). Her early works had been written at his insistence and published under his name, then under their combined name, "Colette-Willy." These include the well-known "Claudine" novels, which despite their relatively independent heroine are essentially love stories with conventional plots ending in marriage. With *The Vagabond*, Colette presents the evolution of a woman artist in early middle age. Renée Néré, who works as a mime in the music hall like Colette, has also been a writer and married, most unhappily. She receives an attractive offer of love and marriage from Max, a devoted suitor, but she leaves Paris on a tour of France with her troupe. She finally decides in favor of a solitary, wandering existence in which she remains free to write, and in particular to observe and describe according to a perspective of her own.

Part three begins with Renée's first love letter to Max. Gradually, she comes to the decision to leave him; and as she does this, she turns back to writing, to and for herself. Fear of aging and of loss of beauty also play a role, as they will in *Chéri*, especially when Max sends her a snapshot of himself playing tennis with a young girl. But there is also her identification of the true, and very limited, role of love in a woman's life. Mature age is an essential factor in this beginning of self-discovery: "If giving myself were the only thing at stake! But there is more than pleasure. . . .In the boundless desert of love, the burning fire of passion occupies only a small place, but it glows so brightly that at first one can see nothing else: I am not an innocent young girl, to let myself be blinded by its blaze" (*V*, 1211).

Most of all, Renée fears the threat to her autonomous gaze; as Nancy K. Miller formulates it, "Against the familiar logics of possession in which a woman is fatally seen, and evaluated in her femininity, Renée opposes the need to see for herself."[2] To Max, Renée writes: "You offer a young, ardent, jealous companion, who is tenderly in love? I know: he is called a master, and I want no more of that. . . . I refuse to contemplate the most beautiful countries on earth, reduced in size, in the amorous mirror of your gaze" (*V*, 1126, 1132). To herself, she clearly posits the "erotic pleasure of writing" (*V*, 1084) as an alternative to the erotic pleasure in love: "For how long had I been forgetting Max, for the first time? Yes, forgetting him, as if I had never known his gaze nor the caress of his mouth, forgetting him, as if I had no more urgent task in my life than to seek the words, the words to say how yellow is the sun, how blue the sea" (*V*, 1120–21).

In her refusal of Max, in her choice of solitude in the interest of seeing for herself, Renée announces the importance of the gaze and its tropes in Colette's work, which will evolve over the rest of her life. Colette was one of the first women writers to describe the male character as the object of the feminine gaze.[3] In wanting to see for herself, she increasingly insists on autonomy in relation to men and love, although romantic love certainly remains her principal thematic material almost until the end of her life. An evolving shift in her identity, her sense of self, and those of her female protagonists, thus begins at midlife and continues until *The Evening Star* and *The Blue Lantern* in old age.

Inseparable from the discussion of seeing, and looking in order to record, is the recurring theme of the woman writer's sensuality. The above quotations from *The Vagabond* illustrate the way in which the development of Renée's independent self is inextricably linked to finding an alternative sensuality in writing. In other words, writing became for Renée as for the aging Colette, not only a means to independence but also, necessarily, a way of experiencing and expressing the world through the senses. By capturing and re-creating in words the pleasures of sight, touch, sound, and smell, Renée possesses the world, and this possession in turn is a sensual pleasure inseparable from a feeling of mastery. Renée's letters make clear that above all the vision she will transcribe will be her own. She will dedicate her life to exploring her own sensory reality and to deriving satisfaction from the writing of it. Her pleasure is not so much a substitute for sex as it is a kind of generalized, protean sensuality, which sometimes takes for its subject a pair of lovers but at other times focuses on phenomena of the natural world, people, or a landscape. Regardless of the subject of her discourse, however, Renée feels that the position of mastery implied in writing her own "take" on reality means that to be a writer is somehow deeply incompatible with a love relationship with a man.

The slow disengagement from heterosexual love and pleasure was not easy, as the last paragraphs of *The Vagabond* also predict: "I escape, but I am not yet free of you, I know. How many times shall I return to you, my dear refuge where I rest but also wound myself? For how long will I yearn for what you could give me, that long voluptuousness first suspended, then inflamed, and then renewed? You will be for a long time one of the strongest desires of my solitary path" (V, 1232). Only with advanced age does Colette herself manage to become fully detached.

In her discussion of Eleanor in Virginia Woolf's *The Years*, Kathleen Woodward notes a similar phenomenon. Expanding on theories of narcissism first presented by Kohut, Woodward hypothesizes a different transformation of narcissism from that proposed by Lacanian psychoanalysis. Instead of Lacan's basically regressive, repetitive model of narcissism as aggression, Woodward proposes a developmental account of a maturation of primary narcissism over the life course. The difference, which involves the transfer or displacement of narcissistic energies to other domains beyond the self in a gesture that is fundamentally benevolent rather than aggressive, may have to do with the aging process itself and its accompanying decrease in libido. This difference translates itself into the way we see others and the way we feel about being seen by them, and Woodward further speculates that the way we look at other people may vary significantly at distinct points along the life course. She notes that Kohut distinguishes between the look and the gaze in early childhood: the idealized parent is gazed at, whereas the narcissistic self wants to be looked at. The child is the subject when he or she actively gazes at the parent but is the passive object of someone else's look. In the course of psychic development, Woodward believes, the individual passes through several stages with respect to looking and being looked at, finally returning to the gaze as narcissism undergoes a basically constructive transformation in old age. She considers Eleanor in this light: "From this perspective too, then, the figure of the elderly Eleanor invites us to speculate that at a certain point in our lives we may give up a large measure of our narcissistic self. Accordingly, we may relinquish our desire to be looked at in admiration. In turn we become those who gaze at others."[4] Woodward also notes the intense pleasure afforded to the gazer by the gaze.

Like Eleanor, the aged Colette, self-assured, writing with ease in her own name at the end of her life, gazes at others and at "youth." The pleasure for Colette in her late writing, as predicted by Renée Néré, is the sensory pleasure of imagining and describing other people, as well as the natural world, the seasons, and personal memories. For this woman writing, the gradual abandonment of narcissistic self was primarily an alteration of her position as the object of the male gaze and desire. Like Eleanor, she no longer hopes to be the one looked at. But unlike Eleanor, she continues to derive some narcissistic satisfaction from the exercise of an authorial subjectivity, a form of control or possession of others and of the world, and this pleasure is intensified by the fact that it has been so difficult for her to acquire as a woman. Colette spent her early years acutely aware of her position as object of an evaluative male gaze, both as an object of sexual desire and as a writer who was kept subordinate to her husband. She only began to exercise her own critical, authorial gaze when she was almost forty. One might say that Eleanor's fully disinterested benevolence is not entirely available to Colette, whose experience was shaped by gender as well as by age. Perhaps it is harder for real women than for fictional ones to abandon or entirely transform their narcissism.

She left to the aging women characters in her mature works of fiction the difficult task of resolving the pain occasioned by the loss of their attractiveness to men—and, perhaps more difficult still, of how they would fulfill or express their own sensuality after this had occurred. Women inevitably lose their attractiveness, as Léa's story reveals in both *Chéri* and *The End of Chéri*, Marco's in "Le Képi," or the character "Colette's" in *Break of Day*. Léa is a forty-nine-year-old demimondaine who is the mistress of Chéri, a man of twenty-four. Their liaison ends with Chéri's marriage to a very young woman, but during their separation both come to the realization that the other had been the great love of both their lives. At the end of the novel, Chéri returns to Léa, but in the morning light he, and she, finally understand that she has aged and can no longer correspond to the Léa of his fantasies. It is her body that has aged and changed, that is the cause and emblem of her tragedy; her dignity and nobility enable her to preserve Chéri's esteem, by facing the truth on that last morning: "Sitting up very straight now, [Léa] showed him in the full light of day her face, noble and ruined, glazed by her bitter tears. . . . An invisible weight was pulling down her chin and her cheeks. . . . In this wreckage of her beauty, Chéri could retrieve, intact, her lovely strong nose, her eyes as blue as a flower." What follows reveals the irreversibly destructive effect of this change in her. He tells her: " 'So, Nounoune, I arrive here and . . .' He stopped, frightened by what he had almost said. 'You arrive here, and you find an old woman,' said Léa in a weak and tranquil voice" (C, 185). The loss of their physical attractiveness and desirability is an almost unbearable catastrophe to Colette's women characters and to the narrator.

In *The End of Chéri*, written several years later when Colette was fifty-three, Léa has removed herself as an object of the male gaze, and indeed from any apparent expression of sexuality. While Chéri, fundamentally weak like many of Colette's male characters, actually dies because he cannot reconcile himself to living without the Léa of the past, Léa herself has no regrets about losing him and finds much healthy enjoyment in the present. Like other Colettian women she has seen her reflection in the mirror and benefited from the lesson; at the end of *Chéri* Léa believes Chéri has decided to stay with her after all: " 'He's coming back, he's coming back!' she cried, raising her arms. An out-of-breath old woman repeated her gesture in the oblong mirror, and Léa wondered what she could possibly have in common with that madwoman" (C, 90). She has had a moment of insight into the foolishness of trying to appear as a young lover when she is in fact fifty years old, and the scene is perhaps the cruelest of Colette's mirror scenes. Yet even while we admire Léa's ability to face reality, it is clear that Colette can only regret her character's subsequent loss of gender identity as expressed by her sexuality. The repeated grotesque descriptions of her body in *The End of Chéri* betray a fundamental ambivalence toward the aging woman that arises from Colette's unshaken conviction that femininity and even female gender identity, in the only ways she conceived of them, must disappear with age: "She was not monstrous, but vast, and weighted down by a lush development of all of her body parts. Her arms, like round thighs, stood away from her hips. . . . The solid colored skirt, the long impersonal jacket . . . announced the normal abdication and disappearance of femininity, and a sort of sexless dignity" (*FC*, 87).

The same loss of "femininity" occurs in a much later work, written when Colette was seventy. In "The Képi" bodily changes in a forty-five-year-old woman named Marco are observed by the much younger character "Colette," whose judgment is as harsh as the narrator's in *The End of Chéri*. Marco gains weight while in love with a young army lieutenant, and the change is not appealing: " 'She's got a behind like a cobbler's,' I thought . . . 'and, in addition, breasts like jellyfish, very broad and decidedly flabby.' For even if she is fond of her, a woman always judges another woman harshly" ("K," 522). When the lieutenant has left her after a fateful moment in which he looks and "sees" her for the middle-aged woman that she is, Marco loses weight quickly and begins to resemble a priest: "When a woman, hitherto extremely feminine, begins to look like a priest, it's the sign that she no longer expects either kindness or ill-treatment from the opposite sex" ("K," 520).

Given the intensity of this ambivalence about aging, it is impossible for her characters to resolve it while remaining involved in the dynamic of a heterosexual love relationship. Thus Colette as writer, narrator, and character sought refuge and a way out of the impasse by means of a figurative return to her mother Sido, or to a certain idea of her mother she constructed. In *Break of Day*, published in 1928 when Colette was fifty-five, a semifictional character named Colette is spending a season in her house on the Mediterranean coast. While she meditates on her aging, she turns to a few of her mother's letters, written before "Sido's" death, in search of lessons on "the supreme elegance of knowing how to finish" (*BD*, 142). The title of the work refers to the beginning of a time when she will renounce the sensual power of love and will devote herself, as Nancy Miller has described it, to the "project . . . of (*renaming:*) to transform through time and memory the aleatory of life and fiction into a new text punctuated by another order." [5] Sido's letters connect her to a female line of literary descent, to "another order," from which she establishes a feminine literary identity. It is distinct from the masculine literary tradition and excludes amorous relationships with men. The latter are represented by the fictional character Vial, a younger man who figures in a sketchy love story that illustrates the necessity of "leaving off" heterosexual love. She muses: "Love, one of the great commonplaces of existence, is slowly leaving mine" (*BD*, 18). In the end, "Colette" refuses Vial's love, although at this same point in her own life the author Colette was to marry Maurice Goudeket, also a man younger than herself who became her third husband and to whom she remained married for the rest of her life. One might speculate that in writing *Break of Day* in these terms, Colette was in effect exorcising those aspects of a love relationship that she feared most, or more simply that her relationship to men at midlife, at a time when she was seeking an autonomous identity as a woman writer, was complex or ambivalent enough to admit of both refusal and acceptance. It may be that she attempted through her fiction to eliminate the possibility of a certain kind of heterosexual relationship, one that had caused her much pain, and which had interfered with her sense of herself as an autonomous writing subject.

While *Break of Day* is obviously concerned with renouncing a particular feminine role and the love of men, it also addresses the question of a more general sensuality which is developed from *The Vagabond* on. But here Colette is not yet able to construct another sensual relationship to the world, a new extension of the sensorial by the sensual. At this point "Colette" has understood the impasse of sexual pleasure and possession, the failure of love between man and woman, and this love is inseparable for Colette from the domain of the senses. Thus in *Break of Day* her character feels she must go on to renounce her sensuality itself, "[her] sensuality whose eyes, thank God, were always bigger than its belly" (*BD*, 28). To do this, she must learn "Sido's" essential lesson, which is one of renunciation and the paradoxical notion that true possession comes only with abstention.

In this respect, "Sido" will always be superior. She has spent her life in the garden, nurturing and observing the passing of the seasons, and she knows how to renounce. Indeed, the book opens with a letter in which "Sido" says that she cannot accept an invitation to come to see her daughter and son-in-law. If she did, she would miss the flowering of a pink cactus which might not bloom again. The half-fictional "Colette," on the other hand, has spent her life indulging her sensual appetites, as Nancy Miller states: "Colette would have the sensual match the natural, but the analogy is always a faulty construction, a harvest destined to inferiority."[6]

It is important to realize that the letters in *Break of Day* were all rewritten by Colette for inclusion in her text, and many were significantly altered, including the one that opens the book, for in fact Sido did not decline her son-in-law's invitation. In coauthoring the letters she had received from her mother, Colette engaged in a deeply satisfying altering or "mothering" of her own mother. The image that she presents of her mother's middle and old age is thus in large part a creation of her imagination. Her distortions may have been in part responsible for her difficulty in coming to terms with her own aging. One can speculate that her character's declared feelings of inferiority to her mother in *Break of Day* result in part from a failure to perceive that the mother, in her seventies and very near death from cancer, was led to "renounce" sensual pleasure in a very different spirit from her daughter, at the time in healthy middle age.[7]

In any case, it is obvious from her later work that Colette did not in fact renounce her sensuality. Indeed, she finally came to terms with it, a most significant psychological development of her old age. Colette was a hedonist in the original sense of the term, in that she continued to believe that sensuality and pleasure might provide a path to a deeper understanding of the world. Although she believed that the sexes found it difficult to understand each other, and sensual pleasure had offered her no real communication or understanding with men, her disappointment finally was with love, not with sensuality. Thus her interpretation of her mother's aging as a "leaving off" was finally a fiction she invented to enable herself to leave off the love of men and to cease to write about it.

It is clear even in *Break of Day* that "Colette" will not renounce writing any more than she will renounce her sensuality. On the contrary, she will derive inspiration from her mother's writing in order to transform the love objects of her sensuality into new objects, newly named: "I think I hear her, and pull myself together, Fly, my favourite! Don't reappear until you have become unrecognizable. Jump through the window, and, as you touch the ground, change, blossom, fly, resound. . . . When you return to me I must be able to give you, and my mother did, your name of 'pink cactus' or some other flame-shaped flower that uncloses painfully, the name you will acquire when you have been exorcised" (*BD,* 140). What needs to be renounced and "exorcised" is the "story" of the heterosexual love affair, the "plot" that had shaped most of her works. *Julie de Carheilhan,* Colette's last full-length fictional work, published when she was sixty-eight, finally closes the series of "sentimental retreats" begun in her early years, and *Gigi,* a short work published at age seventy-one, reminds us that she gave up the writing of fiction only very late. Finally, what may be the fairest statement of the "problem" of the fictional love plot in her work is that beginning with *The Vagabond,* she often resisted the strictly fictional account, with its conventions of plot and ending, often inserting a "self" into the text (as in "The Képi," *Break of Day,* etc.) that is more or less verifiable as an autobiographical figure and which places the text in an indeterminate area in which the boundaries of fiction are blurred. At times, Colette also sought to separate her fiction from the conventional fiction of love, as in *Break of Day* where she refuses the man for reasons that have no literary precedent, or in *Bella Vista,* written when she was sixty-four. In the latter collection of short stories, she wrote about encounters other than those of love: "It is folly to think that those periods in a woman's life that are devoid of love are 'blanks' in her existence. On the contrary . . . When love has gone, there comes a welcome calm that calls up friends, passers-by, normal feelings such as fear, gaiety, boredom, awareness of time in its flight" (*BV*, 7).

In *The Evening Star,* written and published when she was seventy-three, Colette finally has abandoned the fictional love plot. Although she still claims she will try to stop "writing," in fact it will only be to substitute for ordinary writing a form of tapestry writing, embroidery in the colors of Sido's garden, an alternative to the ordinary alphabet that she originally had glimpsed in *Break of Day:* "You wrote to me that same day, a year before you died, and the loops of your capital B's, T's and J's, which have a kind of proud cap on the backs of their heads, are radiant with gaiety" (*BD,* 33–34). Again, she plans to continue, but in her mother's footsteps rather than within masculine literary traditions.

In *The Evening Star* and *The Blue Lantern,* then, fictional plot has been abandoned altogether in favor of the meditation begun in *Break of Day.* These works make explicit that ordinary narrative structures and novelistic conventions do not work for Colette writing from and about a perspective of old age. In *The Blue Lantern,* she no longer apologizes for her sensuality, now that its focus and object are different; instead, sensory pleasure can be marshaled against the grinding pain of her arthritic leg. She notes: "It is a far hark back to my fiftieth birthday. What is left to me is my avidity. Of all my forces it alone has not humbled itself to time" (*BL,* 104). In *The Evening Star* and *The Blue Lantern* there is also a culmination of thematic material introduced in *The Vagabond.* For these stylistic and thematic reasons, these two works together represent Colette's late style, a new kind of prose to which age, immobility, and pain also contributed in their way. In the remainder of this chapter I would like to look more closely at these works, and to try to describe more fully the feelings and perceptions of their author and subject as she entered into full possession of the riches of her own active contemplation of the world, i.e., of the "gaze" that she sought to cultivate from her late thirties until the end of her life.

Colette wrote *The Evening Star* in the immediate postwar period, confined most of the time to her room, from which she looked out on the gardens of the Palais Royal. She suffered from an arthritic lesion which had complicated a broken leg and was increasingly immobilized and in chronic pain until her death in 1954 at age eighty-one. By this time Colette was a widely read author and journalist much appreciated in France by her readers, if not by the critical establishment. Her last years were filled with gratifying attention from her public and enhanced by memories of her long literary career with many collegial friendships. She devotes considerable space in *The Evening Star* to evocations of the male colleagues she knew in her early career as a journalist and to a number of women writers, clearly identifying herself as a member of a profession.

There is no nostalgia here for past lovers; she has burned her love letters, while carefully preserving other ones. Relationships with colleagues are now considered to comprise the real past. The portraits of women writers consist of a series of lessons, of exercises meant to prepare her for certain perils of extreme old age. In this respect, they remind us of the "lessons" of "Sido's" letters in *Break of Day*. They also provide a meditation on the role of love and art in a woman artist's life. She reminds us that she was an author before she was a mother, and she valued that role more, though only now has she reached a time in her life when it is possible to say this (*ES*, 131, 138). Colette's affirmation of the value of reminiscence in these texts recalls Robert Butler's well-known essay "The Life Review: An Interpretation of Reminiscence in the Aged." Like some of the elderly patients Butler observed, she achieves a sense of personal integration in the face of impending death by examining her past. She grows to understand herself and the way she has resolved conflicts throughout her life, as the example of her reflection on her maternity shows. She includes in this review the creation of her works and literary characters. She reveals to herself and to her readers the sources of her inspiration. She still compares herself at times to her mother, but she is serene because she has at last "renounced" the amorous relationships that had made the comparison to Sido so unfavorable.

In the present Colette is not alone: her third husband is not named but referred to lovingly as "my best friend." Goudeket, who was Jewish, was sent to a prison camp during the war, and although he was released unharmed, Colette remained haunted by the separation and by the pain and will to survive, almost "ferocious" at times, of the women who had to stay behind (*ES*, 52–53). The pain of her anxiety coincided with the deaths of a good many of her contemporaries. Therefore she associates the war with her own old age, proudly emphasizing her difference from postwar society and sometimes refusing to adapt. She makes clear the Platonic nature of her present relationship with Goudeket, now that she is old and no longer feels herself to be a desiring or desirable woman (*ES,* 116). Their rapport is interesting. While it is clear that he is very dear to her, she feels the constant need to deceive him in new ways: to reassure him that she is not suffering when she is. Above all she seeks not to admit that she is often lost in her memories, her reveries of the past, and that she considers this a valuable and fruitful activity for this time in her life. She is surrounded by loving friends, but she often chooses solitude, for only when she is alone can she discover an authentic self and devise a way of writing that will prepare her for the end (*ES,* 144). She compares herself to a rose: "I've just heard fall on a nearby table the petals of a rose which also only waited to be alone before shedding its blossom" (*ES,* 30). She is also the "evening star," the planet Venus, often mistakenly thought to be rising at sunset when it is in fact setting: "With her third name, Vesper, I associate, I link that of my own decline" (*ES,* 17). She is at once the planet of erotic love and of a certain idea of old age, one of a "leaving off," or decline, with respect to love.

The meditation is structured by the figure of a boat, a symbol which refers in fact to the bed on which Colette must spend most of her time. People come to her by appointment, and her talking to them is followed by contemplation and moments of self-discovery. She welcomes them: "Come in, it's the appointed time, you whom I call my idleness and my recreation. Come in, just a few. . . . Come in, you who travel from the steppes of Neuilly for me, just for me!" (*ES,* 100) By selecting her visitors in advance, she is deliberately constructing a world. She paradoxically regards her stasis as a voyage. Each visit sets off reflection and reminiscence, an alternation between past and present which also structures the meandering, free-associating style of the book. Thinking about the past was always important to Colette. She remembered her happy childhood, but she also always refused to reduce her existence or that of her characters to this dimension alone. Indeed, the protagonist Chéri in *The End of Chéri* dies when he is unable to live in the present. He cannot let go of his past, and in particular his memories of how lovely Léa used to be. His only accomplishment in life is a brief act of heroism on the battlefield in World War I, but once the war is over, he cannot manage to find any kind of meaningful activity or occupation. In the same text Léa finds happiness in the much-changed society of the 1920s without forgetting her past, a far wiser choice because her sensitivity coexists with a strong sense of reality about the present. This basic attitude remained in place throughout Colette's life, though the relative status or role of the past necessarily changed with advancing age. A balance and a harmony subsist, so that the past can now truly be a source of joy because the present is also an unending source of sensory pleasure and the particular satisfaction of writing about it.

The pleasure of writing for Colette was most evident in her primarily descriptive, nonfictional texts like *The Evening Star,* where her rich, sometimes playful descriptions reveal the passionate intensity of her gaze. She seeks to record the immediate sensation, the fleeting impression. Her attention to the sensory impression of the moment reveals the importance of the present in her work. "Everything alters the moment I take my eyes off of it," she writes in *The Evening Star,* for "the life of a virtually immobilized being is a vortex of hurry and variety" (*ES,* 141). In *The Blue Lantern:* "On my outings I drive along at the leisurely pace of a lady of the Second Empire. . . . There is always so much to look at when one travels slowly" (*BL,* 29). The project of capturing the moment, of giving duration to the instant, thus reveals the corollary project of mastering time, of creating a leisurely pace in both her and the reader's experience of her text. She expands the moment of observation, amusing herself by saturating her text with concrete details and metaphors which call attention to themselves and finally lend to her descriptions of ordinary things an air of discovery. Speaking to her "best friend," she denies being bored: "Why, the sky alone is distraction enough," she declares, and "the moon enters my room at will, advances at a cat's pace, extends a white paw to attack my bed: she is satisfied with waking me, she at once loses heart and climbs down again. At the time when she is at the full I rediscover her at dawn, all pale and bare, straying in a chill region of the sky. Returning to its slumbers, the last bat slashes her with a zig-zag stroke" (*ES,* 69).

In her last two works, the vast reserve of Colette's memories are called up by an association with a sensation in the present. To remember is to reexperience, and it has the immediacy of the present. Her memories pierce her: "The husk is beginning to split and through this cleavage can be seen the gleam of the three light mahogany fruits. By a trick of my peculiarly tenacious memory, all I have to do is to clamber up as far as the solid wall of leaves to reach the neighboring pines. . . . Just let me go there, I shall not lose myself. Shut the door of my bedroom. I need nobody to guide me on my walk. All that I needed were these three chestnuts. . . . Au revoir, au revoir, I may be a little late for dinner" (*BL,* 81).

Because it made possible—even necessary—her leisurely contemplation of the world, Colette can say that her enforced immobility actually served her insatiable need for active contemplation. Although she suffers and resents the pain, and on occasion complains, she can also say: "We do well to adapt misfortune to our requirements and even to our convenience. This is a mode of exploitation to which the young and robust are ill-suited, and I can well appreciate, for instance, that near-immobility is a gift" (*ES*, 11). Her work expresses a hunger to possess the world, inexhaustible in its richness, and this sensual desire to possess the aesthetic dimension of things is a fundamental attitude toward life: "We do not look, we shall never look enough, never carefully enough, never passionately enough" (*PF*, 109). She will possess the world through writing, experiencing the pleasure of possession in the act of transcribing the world as revealed by her gaze. Here, there is also an immediate physical connection. Throughout *The Evening Star*, writing is depicted as an intensely physical act that reveals, through graphological analysis, a writer's true sexuality, his photographic image, his portrait (*ES*, 57, 119).

At the end of her life, she not only accepts her sensuality but actually cultivates and exploits it to distract her from her pain. At the end of the day, a jeweler comes to her by arrangement so that she may delight in the display of his creations and treasures. There are pages of descriptions in *The Blue Lantern* of dazzling colors. The effect of this visual pleasure on her is complex and essential to her well-being: "My friend and neighbor, the jeweler, assures me that the contemplation of precious stones brings relief to arthritic pains, that the majority of the gems snatched from the bowels of the earth are of beneficent effect" (152). But the jeweler insists that few stones are truly beautiful. It is a mistake, he declares, to try to include the semiprecious. They aren't genuine and can only disappoint us (*BL*, 154). Similarly, when enumerating the cats, dogs, and birds who come to visit her in the evening, she acknowledges that there are few: "It is a short list, the list of my evening visitors. The Eden permitted us has nothing of a Noah's Ark about it" (*BL*, 158). The list is short, even in Eden, but it is enough. We have only the earthly splendors that we have been given, and Colette counsels herself not to make the mistake of wanting others or of wanting more. Accepting these limits, she seeks to possess the sensory world through writing.

Colette's consistent use of paradox creates a sense in the reader that even while she is describing the world in minute detail, she is playing with the possible and various meanings it possesses, illustrating duplicities or unsuspected and contradictory dimensions to her object, thereby destabilizing the relation between the meanings pointed to by her description and the referent. Thus while awaiting the arrival of spring in the early pages of *The Evening Star*, she catalogues and describes various kinds of paradoxical spring weather, including a spring hot like summer, a wet one that ruins the cider, and a snowy one that afforded her great pleasure on the day of her wedding to Goudeket. The pleasure of reading her texts may derive precisely from these breaks with our cultural and psychological assumptions, which are set against the background of otherwise familiar phenomena, in the manner described by Barthes in his discussion of the reader's *jouissance* in *The Pleasure of the Text*.[8]

But of course the most significant paradox in Colette's last works may be that she is a bedridden, aged woman, once a great traveler and physically active, but that she is not to be pitied. This type of paradoxical characterization is found throughout Colette's work, as in the happy relationship between the young Chéri and the aging Léa who fly in the face of the received notion that a couple must be well-matched in age.[9] The character of the *ingénue libertine*, who returns frequently in her novels, also confounds our expectations, even a cultural norm, and explains why Colette so often provoked scandal. She perceives herself in the same way. Just as she once revised the stereotype of women by insisting on their strength, now she insists that the immobilized old woman is a voyager, and the slower pace of her life is in fact an advantage.

Colette takes this spirit of contradiction even further, engaging in a sort of "constructive denial" of certain aspects of her existence. Rather than thinking about her friends' deaths, she remembers the way they were when they were with her (*BL*, 9). She refuses to contemplate her leg and its misery: "This leg . . . yes, we know. Enough about this leg. We'll do without that. I am a normal old person, that is, one who is easily amused. Miserable old people are abnormal, sick or wicked. Sometimes they have the excuse of being frightfully oppressed by the generation they have engendered. Which is certainly not my case" (*ES*, 127).[10]

Another defensive process of the same kind is her acceptance and even enjoyment of her "illusions," or failure to understand the rapidly changing modern world: "For anyone not able to dawdle along a pavement and indulge the fortuitous whims and luck of the stroller, there remain only superficial sights . . . buildings enhanced by alluring optical illusions. . . . Illusions crowd thick upon me. What I take to be a hedging implement, can it really be the latest invention for making coffee!" (*BL*, 15–16). Again, she turns her infirmity to advantage in a paradoxical reversal. Her willed evasion into her past, as in the "journey" described above, is another such mechanism, but Colette knows the limits and will not escape into madness, as the poetess Hélène Picard did at the end of her life (*ES*, 83). Her escape remains within the bounds of her art.

Colette claims in *The Evening Star* that her new kind of nonfictional writing is finally honest and unpretentious precisely because the "lies" of fiction are no longer possible for her: "But now the inability to get about, and the years, make it impossible for me to sin by fabrication any longer, and exclude me from any chance of romantic encounters. So it is to the glory of God that I accumulate these sheets, devoid of any dialogue between imaginary characters, of an arbitrary ending that kills, maims, separates" (*ES*, 119). The welcome passing of romantic love and its fictions has freed her writing and in a final paradox has freed the writer from her formerly exaggerated claims of independence, to acknowledge greater dependence on others, a state which her physical condition has of course also made necessary (*ES*, 128).

In *The Blue Lantern*, Colette asserts that she will go on writing until the end: "Now, if I am lying here motionless tonight, there is good reason for it, for I can feel stirring within me—apart from the twisting pain, as if under the heavy screw of a wine-press—a far less constant turnscrew than pain, an insurrection of the spirit which in the course of my long life I have often rejected, later outwitted, only to accept it in the end, for writing leads only to writing" (*BL*, 161). She ends her book "To be continued . . ." (*BL*, 161). She seems no longer to feel a need to impose an end to writing or to the sensual enjoyment of the world which it expresses. Her example recalls Erik Erikson's hypothesis in *The Life Cycle Completed* on sensuality in old age: "And what final psychosexual state can we suggest for (presenile) old age? I think it is *a generalization of sensual modes* that can foster an enriched bodily and mental experience even as part functions weaken and genital energy diminishes."[11] Colette seems to have known such a "generalization" at the end of her life. Her sensuality at the end of her life was much less ambivalent than her prior sexuality, in large part because her experience of traditional gender roles was an unhappy one. Romantic love was an unhappy preoccupation, even an obsession. Its passing was difficult for the woman as for the author, but as a writer she was able to accept and even welcome it. As an old woman she was at last able to possess the world of the senses to which she was so much attached, for as she says in eulogy to Hélène Picard in *The Evening Star*, "Poetry alone possesses, seizes, lets fall, distributes to its eternal champions that which human love scatters so parsimoniously among its creatures" (*ES*, 79).

Notes

1. See Introduction, this volume. Translations of passages from *Paris de ma fenêtre*, *La Vagabonde*, and *La fin de Chéri* are mine.

2. Nancy K. Miller, *Subject to Change*, 253.

3. This insight forms the basis of Marcelle Biolley-Godino's ground-breaking study, *L'Homme-objet dans l'oeuvre de Colette*.

4. Kathleen Woodward, *Aging and Its Discontents*, 81–87.

5. Nancy K. Miller, "The Anamnesis of a Female 'I,'" 169.

6. Ibid., 167.

7. Margaret Morganroth Gullette provided this insight into the distortions of our mothers' midlives and the difficulties this may pose to an aging daughter, for which I am grateful.

8. Roland Barthes, *Le Plaisir du texte*, 25–26.

9. The importance of the paradox in Colette, both in her descriptions and in the events of her narratives, is discussed in depth in Danielle Deltel's excellent article, "Le Scandale soufflé." I owe these insights on characterization to her.

10. This observation follows a reverie about where her daughter might be at this moment. Whatever difficulties her daughter might have experienced in having Colette for a mother, at least in the view of many Colette scholars, these were apparently not problems of the same magnitude for Colette.

11. Erik Erikson, *The Life Cycle Completed*, 64.

GLORIA G. FROMM

Being Old:
The Example of Dorothy Richardson

Breaking Down

AS AN ANOMALY, Dorothy Richardson is hard to beat. She fits into none of the paradigms familiar to us: of old age as a time of loss and mourning, and creativity as the province of youth. She was already forty when she began to write *Pilgrimage,* the multivolume autobiographical fiction that inaugurated the modernist novel in England and won for her a place in literary history. *Pilgrimage,* however, did not come into being as a fully developed entity. It was published in twelve separate parts between 1915 and 1938, with a thirteenth part composed over the next decade and a half and added to the collected edition of 1967, which appeared ten years after Richardson's death at the age of eighty-four.[1] Moreover, not only had Richardson's heroine begun her fictional life at the relatively advanced age (for a bildungsroman) of seventeen, but she had barely reached forty by the thirteenth part, still being written late in Richardson's life. In other words, Dorothy Richardson the author had grown old but her heroine had not, or—to put it still differently—Dorothy Richardson became middle-aged twice, reliving and reshaping in fiction the years from seventeen to forty that, in her eyes, best explained who she was when *Pilgrimage* began to take shape. But who was she becoming as *Pilgrimage* slowly developed over the second half of her life? The answer lies in the relationship between Dorothy Richardson the aging author and her fictional character, who never grew old. Though it would seem that Richardson was privileging her middle years as the most creative period of her life, this turns out to be not the case at all.

There is little doubt, of course, that her own primary aim was to tell, in the form of an impersonal narrative (i.e., third person), the subjective story of her developmental years. In essence, *Pilgrimage* is a cultural autobiography read initially as a new kind of fiction that would come to be called "stream of consciousness." The label would also come to seem more suited to the work of James Joyce, Virginia Woolf, and Marcel Proust, but it was the early volumes of *Pilgrimage* that were instrumental in changing the contours of the English novel. Yet what Richardson had in mind from the start was to document the education of a woman's sensibility in the late Victorian and Edwardian climate of her own youth. One of her long-term admirers, the historical novelist Bryher, said that when, in 1916, she first read *Backwater* (the second volume of *Pilgrimage*), she "dashed to the telephone and shouted to the only friend of [her] own age then in London, '*Somebody is writing about us.*'"[2] For as Bryher went on to point out, though she was two generations younger than Richardson, there had been little change in conditions for women between 1890 and 1914; and *Pilgrimage*, taking place in just this twenty-five-year time frame, spelled out the struggle for independence that women had been forced to wage at a time when "the world for [them] was a prison, not a universe." Bryher knew the struggle firsthand, in spite of being the daughter of one of the wealthiest men in Europe. But money did not bring with it the freedom from stifling conventions that as Winifred Ellerman she had had to fight for; and to remind herself of the social forces historically arrayed against young women who wanted to live unfettered lives, she reread the whole of *Pilgrimage* every few years.

Still another reader as well as writer, Storm Jameson (born eighteen years after Richardson), saw the author of *Pilgrimage* as "the chronicler and painter of a vanished age" and kept returning to the novels, too, but for a slightly different reason. Whenever she felt her brain "getting slack or flabby," a few pages of Richardson's demanding prose would act invariably "as a tonic, an object lesson and a whip."[3] Jameson's playful description of her experience reading *Pilgrimage* is meant, no doubt, to contrast with Richardson's persistent reputation as the ungainly pioneer in a genre that became much more sophisticated and complex in the hands of Joyce and Woolf. As a further anomaly, however, *Pilgrimage* presents its own brand of difficulty that literary critics have yet to fully recognize as well as overcome. For one thing, the language of *Pilgrimage* is literally being forged as the novels progress, and—like poetry—it is being taught by the novels themselves as one reads them and learns their system of signs and symbols. Furthermore, the rhythms of Richardson's prose, which is reflective, undramatic, shunning both highs and lows, are unfamiliar and sound almost atonal to the ear attuned to more traditional harmonies. Not least, the point of view throughout *Pilgrimage* is not only limited—in the technical sense—to one central character, Miriam Henderson, but it is also highly individualistic; it unfolds gradually in the novels, along with Miriam herself, whose developing consciousness is the prime matter of *Pilgrimage*. But because the central character was introduced as a naive, parochial, opinionated seventeen-year-old girl and progressed at what contemporary readers soon felt was a snail's pace, her little hard-won, cumulative victories over the restraining, gender-based conventions of English society seemed small potatoes indeed, if they registered at all. In sum, *Pilgrimage* has come across for years now as both *too* modern, even anticipating, for some, *le nouveau roman* and therefore ahead of its time, and not modern enough, superseded by the pyrotechnics of *Ulysses* and *Finnegans Wake* and overshadowed by the musicality of *To the Lighthouse* and *The Waves*.

It is no surprise, however, that for the most part *Pilgrimage* has been seen as lagging behind, fixed in a world long gone, for while Richardson neared her eighties in 1952, she had yet to finish *March Moonlight,* the thirteenth chapter, in which her fictional self was just entering middle age and the Great War was not even on the horizon. Richardson knew very well how *Pilgrimage* was regarded by a generation that had lived through a second great war. Indeed, she had been aware since the 1930s that *Pilgrimage* was proceeding much too slowly and incrementally for current tastes, but she also thought that an edition bringing together all the separately published novels in the series might gain new readers among those who did not know the earlier volumes. For this reason, she welcomed the proposal made to her in the early 1930s that J. M. Dent and the Cresset Press jointly publish an "omnibus" edition of *Pilgrimage*. Unfortunately, as often happens, negotiations dragged out, and the project was seriously hampered not only by misunderstandings on the publishers' side but also by illness on the author's.

Dent and Cresset had been led to believe from the start, probably by S. S. Koteliansky[4] (who worked for Cresset and had initiated the project), that they would be publishing a *Pilgrimage* complete at last in twelve parts and could advertise it as such, indeed as the work of a lifetime brought to a triumphant conclusion. Richardson had never promised anything of the sort, and when she learned of the false belief, quite late in the negotiations, it made her feel as though she herself were being brought to a premature end. But she was not up to engaging in controversy or calling a halt to the proceedings. She had fallen ill from overwork in 1934 and felt hard-pressed as it was to finish the eleventh novel, *Clear Horizon,* which was scheduled for publication by Dent in 1935. When *Pilgrimage* finally appeared in 1938, in the much-delayed "omnibus" edition of four hefty volumes, each containing two or three novels, it included a twelfth part that was clearly not the last, despite the publishers' advertisements, which had continued to suggest that it was. The misleading publicity, combined with the crisis in the world at large, resulted in reviews that were either puzzled or exasperated—and in precious few sales. Richardson decided, ruefully, that *Pilgrimage* might well be finished, that her publishers would scarcely agree to bring out the thirteenth part, which she had already begun to write. For years afterward, she claimed to be working on it anyway, determined to leave it to posterity, but all the evidence suggests that as an old woman she—along with the world—had finally lost interest in her middle-aged self, who was fighting cultural battles that many considered had been won. Richardson realized that both she and *Pilgrimage* were aging at a faster pace than Miriam Henderson, which meant that her heroine's "thought-life" was no longer as revolutionary and iconoclastic as it had been at first.

It is certainly reasonable to suppose as well that the failure of the collected edition had a great deal to do with Richardson's changed attitude toward *Pilgrimage*. But there are signs that a shift had begun to take place even earlier, suggesting a rearrangement of priorities as Richardson approached old age. One would expect the present to assume more and more importance as the future became less reliable, and Richardson's illness at sixty-one was surely a precipitating factor, but the nature of the illness complicates the case, for it is not at all clear what had happened to her in 1934.

The apparent cause of Richardson's physical and mental breakdown—as she herself assigned it—was the strain of translating five books from French and German, one after another. Desperately poor, married to an artist (Alan Odle) whose career was as unremunerative as hers,[5] Richardson hoped to carry them through a particularly bad period (resulting from the American stock market crash of 1929) by undertaking translation, which had to be done quickly but for which payment was made at once. In principle, this seemed both plausible and rational, but in practice Richardson found herself riding the proverbial tiger from which she could not dismount. Alternating between French and German was difficult enough, especially since she was virtually self-taught in both languages and needed constant recourse to the dictionary. With weak eyes long a problem for her, the threefold shift from original text to dictionary to translation gradually produced physical symptoms: dizziness and nausea. Yet as soon as one translation was finished, she undertook another—all this time trying also to finish *Clear Horizon*, begun in 1931. It is hard not to see self-destructive impulses at work here.

For in 1927 Richardson (at fifty-four) had published *Oberland*, the ninth novel in the *Pilgrimage* series, to some of the most favorable reviews she had ever received.[6] While sales and royalties were not correspondingly large, it would have seemed wise and prudent to follow up this succès d'estime as soon as possible with another book. But the next volume of *Pilgrimage* (*Dawn's Left Hand*) did not appear until 1931, by which time she also had embarked on the sequence of translations that kept her from finishing *Clear Horizon*, even though the prospect of a collected edition had already emerged. One suspects that Richardson was not ready yet to face her own mounting resistance to the continuation of *Pilgrimage*, whose heroine would have to become increasingly outmoded if the integrity of the series—its method and scale—was to be maintained.

Until this time, the public identity of Dorothy Richardson quite literally merged with *Pilgrimage*. She *was Pilgrimage*—or one should say Miriam Henderson—despite the fact that the autobiographical basis of her novel was not generally known. But precisely because very little was known about Dorothy Richardson herself—an intensely private person, who spent most of her time in remote north Cornwall—her novel and its distinctive heroine came to stand for the author. It came as quite a shock to her, then, that in the late 1920s an American writer of the same name began to be confused with her. Not only was she getting her namesake's press cuttings, but she was also having the American's books attributed to her. And when the *New York Times*, along with an "ecstatic" review of *Oberland*, printed a photograph of the wrong Dorothy Richardson, the right one felt as though she had been obliterated. Perhaps it was then that she began to think of constructing a brand-new self outside of *Pilgrimage*.

Significantly enough, she actually succeeded in building a reputation as a first-rate translator. Bertolt Brecht, just beginning his own career, knew her work and wrote to ask whether she would consider translating the novel he was writing. Though nothing was to come of this query (probably because of political conditions in Germany), it testified to the measure of renown she had achieved in a highly competitive arena. But just when she had reached the point of being able to name her own price as a translator, her breakdown forced her to withdraw completely from the field. It was a heavy price to pay for demonstrating that the author of *Pilgrimage* could be someone else as well.

The favorite diagnosis of an illness like hers, which made the slightest movement or sound excrutiatingly painful, was still neurasthenia. Richardson embraced the doctor's explanation with relief and took herself to bed. But her anxious friend Bryher wanted to know what she was going to *do* in order to get better and kept suggesting that she see a psychoanalyst.[7] Richardson's response was that at her advanced age (sixty-one) she ought not to need one, that life itself should provide the materials for psychoanalysis. And she did recover, though not without help from a most unorthodox source—a young American "healer" she had recently met, named William Macmillan. His remarkable "cures" had earned him the backing of two influential figures in London's religious circles: Dr. Maud Royden, the well-known preacher and women's suffragist; and Dick Sheppard, the popular vicar of St. Martin-in-the-Fields. They supported Macmillan's petition to the Home Office for a license to practice psychotherapy. It was granted in 1934, and after briefly treating patients in the vestry of Maud Royden's church in Eccleston Square, Macmillan rented a maisonette in St. John's Wood, where Dorothy Richardson and her husband had been spending every summer since their marriage in 1917.

Macmillan intrigued her at once, mainly because the results he achieved could not be explained, defying logic and science. She saw him, in other words, as someone like herself—an anomaly, whose lifework seemed to have come upon him almost by chance, through a series of fortuitous meetings and events, in the way that Richardson's invention of "stream of consciousness" had been the by-product of an entirely different goal: to render her own experience as representative of a generation and a class of women. Macmillan's effectiveness seemed to her to derive from some mysterious source that he alone—for equally mysterious reasons—could tap, just as *Pilgrimage* had emerged from a deep well of experience into which she unexpectedly found she could dip. Macmillan, then, was a kindred spirit, and she turned to him at a time when it seemed that both her past and present selves were reaching a crossroads. She saw Macmillan every day for six weeks in the summer of 1935 and claimed that it was he who enabled her to "keep going." By this she appeared to mean that *Pilgrimage* had become important once again as an embodiment of her past and a guarantee of her survival in the future. From then until 1938, the negotiations and the plans for the omnibus edition dominated her life, with Richard Church at Dent impressing upon her that this was a "final bid" to establish *Pilgrimage,* and Koteliansky at Cresset dealing with the firm's mounting fears of financial disaster. The Cresset Press was not ruined by the failure—practically speaking—of the collected edition, but Dorothy Richardson realized that she had come to a parting of the ways, and it was by no means insignificant that in the spring of 1938 she had also turned sixty-five.

Old Age as New Experience

Richardson marked her entry into this new phase of life with a piece called "Old Age," not published until several years after her death in 1957.[8] Curiously enough, it is a projection of what she imagined old age would be like rather than a record of her own experience, which one might say was just beginning. In fact, she added a note to the manuscript, when she happened upon it in 1951, expressing her surprise (and satisfaction) that she had been so accurate at the "early" age of sixty-five: convenient testimony that at seventy-eight she had not changed her mind.

The view of old age Richardson expressed in this short piece is remarkable, considering what was happening to her. With *Pilgrimage* failing in several senses at once and the immediate future holding the prospect of a terrible war, she drew up a kind of balance sheet listing the benefits and the liabilities of old age. Chief among the liabilities, of course, was the inevitable decline of physical and mental faculties, which "we take," she said, "according to our nature. Rebelliously, futilely. With dismay. With a rueful or half curious satisfaction to feel ourselves on the move, getting into the sere and yellow, attesting our common humanity, achieving a degree in life." Note the double-sided character gradually being given to decline, as though it had distinct advantages, amusingly pictured: getting to be old was not only an achievement that gained you respect, but it also made you fully human—surely Dorothy Richardson's wry acknowledgment of her lifelong "difference" from others, her separatist nature.

Even death does not seem to her an unmitigated negative. It may well be a "final cataclysm" but just as plausibly "a peaceful sliding away." And perhaps the "really old" are so near death that "they fight and keep it off but do not see or think" of it. Primarily, however, it was not one's own demise so much as "the death all about us of the world we knew" that constituted for Richardson the important "lesson" to be learned by all of us. With the dismantling—"piecemeal"—of our world, the disappearance "of those we loved or thought we loved," comes the realization that we relied on all those people for what lay "in store for *us*," and that what we chiefly loved in all of them was ourselves. "Illusion is gone," as Richardson put it; "people become . . . objects of indifference, and our acute nostalgia for youth is our nostalgia for things to count upon. We get the first glimpse of what is called dotage—and know why the old man remembers life years ago better than last week. [But] this so called failure of memory is really its beginning," and the beginning as well of Richardson's principal thesis about old age— that it is the final stage in the making of us as artists. She means that we learn "the artist's detachment and what appears to be his cynical indifference to all things but his art, . . . the free movement of his spirit." And in old age we "hold on nowhere," are free; "we can move everywhere. All our intolerance and exclusions and fixities are gone. In a world, more amazing, more beautiful, than . . . the trailing clouds of glory [ever were], we dance the lightest footed dance of all."

As the years to follow bear out, this was not wishful thinking on Dorothy Richardson's part. In the fiction and the letters she wrote during the war and after, as well as in the solitary life she led in a tiny Cornish village (especially after Alan Odle died in 1948), Richardson maintained the unusually positive view of old age adumbrated in the preliminary sketch she penned at sixty-five. But its roots lay in the attitude toward life expressed most fully in *Pilgrimage*—the joy in all phenomena, from the simplest things like doors and bars of soap to the complex effects of light and sound and the wonder at the sheer *fact* of existence. Put another way, what had always mattered most to Dorothy Richardson was consciousness—her own individual response to the world around her—and it seemed entirely possible that old age might enhance or enlarge consciousness rather than diminish it, precisely because the mind would have been freed or "detached" from its exclusionary circle of preoccupations. In contrast with the standard view that old age is characterized by physical stasis, Richardson saw it conversely as all movement—the unhampered motion of the mind.

The crucial element in Richardson's redefinition of the aging process is memory. When, at sixty-five, she described the so-called failure of an old person's memory ("dotage") as "really its beginning," she was herself just beginning to formulate an idea that would become the cornerstone of her conception of old age. A few years later, in 1941, Richardson's elder sister Kate died, setting off—as one would expect—a chain of experiences involving memory and the past. Since another sister had died much earlier (before the First World War) and her remaining (younger) sister lived abroad, it fell to her to correspond with all the childhood and girlhood friends who had kept in touch with Kate. Richardson was struck by the sharpness of their memories, even though some of them must have been—in her words— "amazing ages." They reminded Richardson of details, events, and people she found she had not forgotten, that sprang into being out of "an everlasting present" within her. It was "wrapped about [her]," she said, "the whole of [her] life, fold upon fold," as it had been years before when she first began to write *Pilgrimage,* that is, to perform the creative act of unfolding. Not for a long time had she felt so in touch with the world that had nurtured her art. And as the letters from her sister's friends continued to come, along with replies from relatives to whom she had written the news, Richardson felt they were opening new doors and windows in her mind. The phrase "so long ago," which occurred so often in the letters, grew more and more meaningless to her.

Still another death soon after her sister's—of a cousin-in-law who had been part of an important phase of Richardson's personal development— involved her again in correspondence with people she had not heard from for half a lifetime. It surprised her to find how easily she could talk to them and "how well, during the years of silence, [she had] grown to know them," as if to say that no experience ever really came to an end, that it continued to work within, whether one was aware of it or not.[9]

The letterwriting and the insights it generated had further consequences. In the bomb-ridden England of the early 1940s, extinction was on everybody's mind as an ever-present likelihood. Richardson believed that one had to fight against the possibility of "giving in," no matter how much destruction and annihilation went on. One way to do so was to recognize—and illustrate—the duration and the continuity of experience. Kate's death had sent her back to the period before *Pilgrimage,* to her own childhood, which had scarcely figured in the novels, designed as they were to begin with her seventeenth year. The child she had been, rather than the middle-aged heroine who had come to seem stale and obsolete, took hold of her imagination. The more distant past was closer, fresher, and fraught with new meanings, which she felt compelled to explore in three short stories that she wrote in the early 1940s instead of going on with *Pilgrimage.* Moreover, in one of them, the character representing the old woman she had become conjures up the child she had been, as if to show how life—and old age—can make artists of us all.

"Visitor" and "Visit," the two stories devoted exclusively to the experience of children, were published in *Life and Letters* in September 1945. The third story, "Excursion," appeared the same year in the annual volume *English Story,* sixth series. There is no doubt who are the models for the little girls in the first two stories: Richardson herself and her younger sister Jessie, given the names Berry and Pug, as she reported to Jessie. In "Excursion," though only Pug is named, the children are the same. In fact, all four Richardson girls come into the picture that the old woman, who is both central consciousness and narrator, draws from "memory."

Although one cannot tell exactly when—or in what order—the three stories were written, they are linked not only by the children appearing in all of them but also by the same impetus: Richardson's need to hold on to herself in a time of loss and disintegration. "Excursion," for example, is set in a wartime present, with one of the young people in the story a soldier about to return to active duty and Richardson's treatment of him resembling her account (in letters) of the young American army man stationed in the Cornish village with whom she and Alan Odle had developed a "parental" relationship. The old woman in "Excursion" is called Gran, but Richardson never makes clear any of the relationships in the story. She is much more interested in Gran's consciousness, as it attends to the present so acutely that the past is called into being.

Briefly summarized, "Excursion" takes place in a rented cottage at a seaside resort, where Gran and the three younger people (two women and the soldier) have been on holiday. The three women plan to remain after the young man's departure and therefore are concerned that the noisy family across the road have not gone home yet, as they had seemed to be getting ready to do in the morning. Gran realizes they are still there when she hears the bark of their dog, a sound that none of the others catches. It has the instantaneous effect of plunging her back sixty years into the past, to a morning in Weymouth when a dog had also barked and she and her three sisters had learned that their holiday had been extended for a week. The two sounds suddenly merge in the old woman's mind, and she becomes again the small, passionate child in pigtails, with one sister close to her in age and two older sisters: Richardson's own family on one of their seaside holidays.

What Richardson has Gran realize, as she herself had come to believe, is that this is not memory. The dog across the road had barked many times before; other dogs, on other occasions, had barked just as suddenly and abruptly and wildly, with no effect on her. But this time the conditions and her state of being are exactly right, producing, instead of an experience remembered, the experience itself, seen no longer chronologically but composed, "after the manner of a picture, with all the parts in true perspective and relationship." Age has made this possible. When one is old (and, as the saying goes, "wandering in mind"), Richardson's character concludes, the accumulated "wealth" of consciousness can finally be discovered—the "immortal, inexhaustible" moments that all of us possess, that we mourned when they passed, only to find them opening out in old age, "reveal[ing] fresh contents every time we go back into them, grouping and regrouping themselves as we advance." She even thinks it possible that "one of these days, perhaps before long, as I sit listening to the talk of others, a chance phrase, or some sudden evocative sound, will so deeply involve me in experience that I shall be unaware of speaking from the midst of it, irrelevantly, into a current occasion. Perhaps, even worse, I shall produce the sound known as a senile giggle" (*JP*, 102).

What Richardson has Gran describe in "Excursion" she had been working out for herself since the death of her sister and had been hinting at in letters to friends. In the story, however, she achieved the full expression she was trying for, and she complemented it with the new projection of herself as a very young child in "Visitor" and "Visit," enabling her to experience further the "opening out" of certain rich moments that her mind possessed. But one can also see how these stories fit into Richardson's larger project— the revaluation of old age. Both of them proceed as if from the child's consciousness, and the burden in each is the effort on the part of the child to find something beautiful in what strikes her (and most people) as ugly. In "Visitor," it is the deformed, pain-ridden body and homely face of crippled and Nonconformist Aunt Bertha that little Berry is determined to transform. She succeeds at this by deciding, after sustained and careful observation, that one of the most repulsive aspects of Aunt Bertha, her "chapel-ness," is precisely what brings her peace and renders her whole. Therefore one does not need to pity her. Having reached this comforting conclusion, the child is filled with rage at her "stupid, stupid Mother" whom she hears murmur, "Poor *Bertha!*" To Berry this means that her mother "only knows Aunt Bertha is a cripple"; she has seen nothing more, thus ruining the birthday gift that Berry gave her, the embroidered text, "I Know that my Redeemer liveth," done under the watchful eye of Aunt Bertha and, in the mind of the child, *containing* her. Her mother "is spoiling the text, because she can't *see*" Aunt Bertha there, within it, beyond either the compassion or pity that the crippled person mechanically inspires (*JP*, 9).

The independent-thinking child of "Visitor" is much the same in "Visit," determined not to see Aunt Bertha's country cottage—to which she and her younger sister have come for three days on a return visit— through conventional eyes. Even Berry, however, is stymied at first by the cramped and musty cottage that houses not only Aunt Bertha but also her two odd bachelor brothers and their old, blind, partially deaf mother—all of whom seem to Berry trapped in a dull, lifeless routine, the very anti-type of Dorothy Richardson's sense of the plenitude of old age. It takes the grimness of a chapel Sunday, when the children are deprived of the single pleasure the cottage offers, its garden, to tax Berry's transformative powers to the limit. She slips away with Pug to find "the country" they thought they were coming to see but so far has been nowhere in sight. And what she discovers has the effect at last of transmuting the experience of their visit:

> A green hill, going up into the sky. . . . Berry runs up the bright green grass. Into nowhere. Sees the wind moving the grass. Feels it in her hair. No one knows about this hill. No one knows it is there. Near the top she stands still, to remember how it looked from the door; long, long ago. It will always look like that. Always. Always. She lies down, to smell the grass, puts her cheek against it, feels grass blades in her ear.
> "Pug! This is the country. . . . We've found it." (*JP*, 20)

Tranquillity

On the surface, all three stories are curious productions indeed, coming as they did during the most intensely anxious years of the war. And they might well seem examples of what Anna Freud called *Altersgedanken,* old-age thinking. But in the context of Richardson's evolving view of old age as a time of renewed and recharged creativity, when she could still see experience so freshly through childish eyes, they tell us what we need to know—how it was that she did not shrink from either the prospect or the reality of advancing years. Unlike Proust, with whose *Remembrance of Things Past* and its demonstration of "involuntary memory" Richardson's work bears comparison, she was not repelled by old age, perhaps because she had not looked at herself in the mirror of society in the way that most of us are prone to do—and Proust certainly did. The "hideous vision" of his narrator—when he returns to Paris in *The Past Recaptured,* after years spent in a sanatorium, and meets his friends who have grown shockingly old in the meantime—is described by Kathleen Woodward in her book *Aging and Its Discontents.* She argues persuasively that what Marcel finds most loathsome in the old bodies and faces in the Guermantes' drawing room is his own reflection: he, too, is aging; and the old people around him "hold up the mirror to him." But "what he will never see," Woodward points out, is "that he has himself made the mirrors in which he sees himself reflected. Unable to identify himself sympathetically even in any small way with 'this old man' or 'that old woman', . . . he thus dooms himself to a similar future, perpetuating a cycle of ageism." [10]

There is no single—or simple—explanation for Dorothy Richardson's seeming escape from the pervasive cycle that Woodward and others have documented, but surely Richardson's attitude toward soma and psyche as well as toward life in general and her own in particular must be considered. It was the sensory system rather than the body as physical organism that Richardson valued most. Put more crudely, sex did not dominate—not even in her marriage, which took place when she was a middle-aged forty-four and Alan Odle an ailing, if not tubercular, twenty-nine, with a passion for art and literature above all else. In both their lives, then, the waning of sexual desire and capacity would have been a negligible factor. Equally important, however, in Richardson's case was the almost total absence of the familiar wish that her life had turned out differently or that she had been born in another time and place. One of the striking refrains in her letters is the satisfaction she claimed to get from simply *being* in the world then and there. It was—she thought—a period of transition, and she wanted to see the shape of things to come. There is no doubt, needless to say, that Richardson had also hoped for more success with *Pilgrimage,* but that is something else. Not regretting either the natural boundaries of her existence or the life choices she had made meant that Richardson's old age was tranquil and accepting, unusually free of inner conflict—as her letters amply testify. Yet they also show that she had good reason—in worldly terms—to feel bitter, resentful, aggrieved at the undervaluation of her life's work. But she—and not the world—was the final arbiter of her own life—a role relatively few of us are psychologically prepared to take on.[11]

Notes

1. *March Moonlight,* the thirteenth part of *Pilgrimage,* was discovered in type-script among Richardson's papers after she died. Three sections had appeared years before, as "Work in Progress," in *Life and Letters* (April, May, and November 1946), but whether the whole of *March Moonlight* can be regarded as "finished" remains in question.

2. Bryher, "D. R.," 22–23. Bryher (1894–1983) was born Winifred Annie Eller-man.

3. Storm Jameson, "More on D. R.," 24. Margaret Storm Jameson (1891–1986) is perhaps best known now for her own autobiography, *Journey from the North* (1960–70).

4. S. S. Koteliansky (1880–1955) is perhaps better known for his friendship with D. H. Lawrence and Katherine Mansfield.

5. Alan Odle (1888–1948), fifteen years younger than Dorothy Richardson, was himself an anomaly: a graphic artist of ferocious power, with a vision of humankind as unremittingly greedy and lustful, and a man of uncommon gentleness. A taste for Odle "grotesquerie" was specialized indeed, and his work did not sell, but he never stopped drawing. When he died quite suddenly at sixty, on his weekly walk to the local library, Richardson found consolation in the belief that he had reached his full growth as an artist. For a fuller account of the marriage, see Fromm, *Dorothy Richardson* (1977).

6. *Oberland* had even been nominated for the French Femina-Vie-Heureuse Prize, which was won, however, by H. M. Tomlinson's novel *Gallions Reach.*

7. Bryher herself had undergone analysis with the eminent Freudian Dr. Hanns Sachs.

8. Dorothy Richardson, "Old Age," 25–26.

9. I quote throughout from Richardson's unpublished letters in the Beinecke Rare Book and Manuscript Library at Yale University, some of which will be included (with the permission of Ms. Elizabeth Susan Howell, literary executrix of the Richardson Estate) in my forthcoming selection of her letters.

10. Kathleen Woodward, *Aging and Its Discontents,* 59. This is not to say that Richardson ignored society. On the contrary, she was as sharply aware as Proust of social class and gradations.

11. Richardson's letters cease quite suddenly at the end of 1952, when she fell ill with shingles, the painful nerve infection. Though she seemed to recover physically, her mind was affected to the point of not being able to distinguish at all between past and present. Moved against her will (by her sister-in-law and literary executrix) from Cornwall to a nursing home in Kent, she spent her last years in virtual silence, dying in June 1957 at the age of eighty-four.

14

CAROLYN H. SMITH

Old-Age Freedom in
Josephine Miles's Late Poems, 1974–79

IN HER LAST chapter of *Writing a Woman's Life,* Carolyn Heilbrun talks about five women writers writing about themselves when over fifty (Virginia Woolf, May Sarton, Doris Grumbach, Colette, Kathe Kollwitz). To Heilbrun, their late writings disclose refusals to narrate the traditional story in which a woman is dismissed once she is seen as "aged." Instead of the silence and timidity such dismissal elicits, Heilbrun finds in these writers an "old-age freedom." This freedom prompted them to speak more boldly about their daily events, art, and social and philosophical views, or, in Heilbrun's words, to use seniority "to take risks, to make noise, to be courageous, to become unpopular." [1]

Josephine Miles (1911–1985) is another writer who in her later years speaks with this extraordinarily powerful "old-age freedom" about her personal life. Miles's late poems, collected in *To All Appearances* (1974) and *Coming to Terms* (1979), are especially engaging because they are vivacious, humorous, and sympathetic toward the young as well as self-liberating even in the face of pain and death. Miles also spoke with verve in her early poems, but not about herself. The disclosures she makes about herself in the poems she wrote when she was in her middle and late sixties follow in a remarkable way years of virtual silence about her personal life. In her early poems (1930s to 1950s), her references to herself are diffident, even veiled. Her focus is on daily events in the lives of others or in nature. In her late poems, however, she reveals more about herself, and each disclosure is in itself astonishing and instructive.

If related to studies of aging by psychologists Robert Butler, K. Warner Schaie, Daniel J. Levinson, Robert Lifton, and a group called postformal cognitive psychologists, Miles's change from a reserved to a free-speaking poetic persona can be seen as a means of meeting three acute needs typical of those in their later stages: reconsideration and, if possible, reintegration of painful memories and emotional needs; accommodation to the changes involved when retiring from a core of activity to possible marginality; and preparation for death. At the same time, her late persona continues to express the earlier persona's enjoyment of the quotidian, a continuity that Erik Erikson finds essential for a satisfying late stage in life.

The change from diffidence to openness is most clearly evident in Miles's poems on teaching. In her early poems her persona is an ordinary, even inept teacher, as in "Denial" (*CP*, 65–66), in which the "I" stands helpless before a crying student. The one hint in the earlier poems that she had the knowledge and ability to teach on the college level is in the title "Preliminary to Classroom Lecture" (*CP*, 37). Quite surprising, then, is the revelation in one of her later poems, "How I Caught Up in My Reading" (*CP*, 187–88), that "I" had spent her summer joyfully reading not merely "many accumulated magazines," "A number of old novels like *Anna Karenina* / And a number of new science fictions" but also "Your thesis and Betty's thesis" as well as "Clinton's / Thesis," and had "advised alterations / In marginal notes of great thickness."

Although only a few details about Miles's life are available, they indicate that her career was far more remarkable and significant for those interested in gender and aging than her few poems on teaching would indicate. For one reason, she received advanced degrees in the 1930s, the years when, as Paul Lauter has documented, the number of women earning advanced degrees was declining to make room for male "breadwinners."[2] After graduating in 1928 from Los Angeles High School, where she studied Latin and Greek, she attended UCLA as a language major. She received her B.A. in 1932. She then attended the University of California at Berkeley, receiving her M.A. in 1934 and doctorate in 1938 for studies in literary style (her dissertation was on Wordsworth's style). Miles must have been considered worthy of the competition because she was awarded not only coveted degrees but also an instructorship in the University of California's English department in 1940, when, as Lauter shows, the proportion of women holding positions on college campuses was declining.

Also exceptional are the number of Miles's scholarly works and her rapid rise within a profession in which other women scholars were not progressing, mainly, according to Lauter, because of the reluctance by such professional groups as the MLA to recognize their work. Miles rose from instructor in the English department on the Berkeley campus in 1940 to full professor in 1952, a position she retained until her retirement in 1978. For many years she was the only woman in Berkeley's English department, where she was a popular teacher. Besides her departmental duties and teaching, she served on several important university committees, helped plan the Bay Area Writing Project and participated annually in its summer institute, wrote eight scholarly books, and had over a dozen articles published in such scholarly journals as *Studies in Philology, PMLA,* and *Style.* Also testifying to her extraordinary abilities as a scholar are the prestigious fellowships she received to pursue her work. In spite of the MLA's general disdain for women scholars, the association honored Miles in 1975 with the James Russell Lowell Prize. The University of California named her professor emerita at the time of her retirement in 1978. In the midst of this illustrious career, she continued to write poems, many receiving acclaim.[3]

Miles never married, and she reveals no desire for marriage in her early poems. If we knew only Miles's early poems and her professional life at Berkeley, we could easily conclude that the reason she did not marry was that she was too interested in her poetry, teaching, and scholarship. We could then ask, how did this single woman, so involved with and deeply committed to professional service and teaching, face the prospect of aging, with its possible diminution of energy and mental quickness, and retirement, with its losses in status, companionship, and sense of importance? Answers to this question alone would make a study of Miles significant for those interested in gender and aging. But Miles had another dimension to her life. She suffered from degenerative arthritis, a condition that became evident when she was only four. Even though her parents tried various cures, including a temporary move from Chicago to southern California in 1916 when she was five and a permanent move there when she was eight, her condition got so progressively worse that from the 1950s until her retirement, she had to have help getting to and from her home in Berkeley to classroom, meetings, and the few other events she could attend. Yet she did not openly disclose her situation in her poetry until *Coming to Terms.* Knowledge of how she dealt with her disease in her later years can expand questions about how she faced aging.

Her physical suffering and debilitation must have severely limited chances for romantic attachments. In her poems, Miles never openly disclosed any regrets over this limitation, but in an interview with Karla Hammond in October 1979, about a year after her retirement, suggests that moon imagery in her poetry has sorrowful overtones: "The moon is not a particularly positive image for me." She cited in particular the moon in "Lumber Yard" and "Moonrise over Dentist's Office." She added, "I feel sorrow in that moon. On the other hand, sun is almost always a positive image. The moon is part of my life that I have not lived, so it's an absence. . . . The actual moon may be a good center for someone else's poem. Also the sun is very important to me because my arthritis really needs the sun; it doesn't need coldness."[4]

If there were disappointments and griefs over being disabled, Miles apparently was able to find consolation in scholarship, teaching, and poetry, as well as in a wide circle of friends. Gregory Rochlin has argued that much attention in psychoanalysis has been given to the pain of losses and failure but too little to the restitution and creativity these generate in the ordinary person and also in those with special skills and talents.[5] In her interview with Hammond, Miles intimates that she found restitution for loss of romance not merely in writing but also in her professional identification with those women who took new roles at the end of World War I, especially in the world of scholarship at Berkeley. She more openly links herself with the scholarly world in one of her earliest poems, "Physiologus" (*CP, 7*). Although speaking about people in general rather than about herself (the poem is in the third person), Miles associates herself with all who feel the need for intellectual relief when "the mind is dark with the multiple shadows of facts." She adds that this search for intelligibility "can have no cure— / This weight of knowledge dark on the brain is never / To be burnt out like fever," whereas "sunset and summer" and "Sulphur's good medicine" can help "the rheumatic." She does not say that she is the "rheumatic," but she implies that whatever physical handicap she might have, it is not as debilitating as lack of discernment and sound judgment.

Miles wrote some four hundred poems, about three hundred of which appear in *Collected Poems,* with the others in manuscript or not reprinted from earlier collections. This number suggests that Miles found compensation not only in scholarship but also in writing poetry. She did not write about herself, however, until she was in her sixties. In her early poems Miles's main images involve the play of light on daily objects, the surprising ways in which routine events unravel, and an ordinary person's extraordinary gestures and words. In a few of her early poems, Miles appears to make observations of nature and people while she is walking freely and in control of her destiny, as in "Entry," in which "we" walk from the suburbs to see the city sights (*CP, 15*) and "Peak Activity in Boardwalk Ham Concession," in which "I" strolls along an oceanfront's boardwalk enjoying various sights and sounds as well as "hot ham" and a "strawberry sucker" (*CP, 32*). Miles's mid-life persona is also a mobile and affirming observer of daily oddities and wonders, as in "The Plastic Glass," in which "I" walks by Herndon's credit store on a sunny day and stops to enjoy reflections in the globe outside (*CP*, 102).

What these poems mask are the elaborate plans Miles had to make in order to get to such places as the credit store or the coast, plans that became even more complicated as she aged. For the most part, she had to observe rather than participate. She admits in her conclusion of "Now That April's Here" that she would enjoy getting ice cream and seeing "meadows of evening" from "races of pavement" "if I were there" (*CP*, 35). Instead of actually being "there," she had to participate imaginatively. Her lack of mobility, however, seemed to intensify rather than dampen her interest in daily events and details, her belief in life's goodness, and her skill in creating the impression of being present in a scene or situation. She also maintained an ironic humor, as in "Sale," with its contrasts between the speaker's timid request in a shoe store for an unusual "triple A" shoe and the salesman's more assertive reaction of "humming the blues" after sucking on a "peppermint lifesaver" and then, surprisingly, plucking "from the mezzanine the very shoe" (*CP*, 83). Similarly, in "Outside," the speaker finds the fantasy of the movie's world ironically undone when she leaves the movie because the sidewalk outside has too many gum papers and is too slippery to make walking and fantasizing easy: "What does it give sea legs after a sea picture? / Gum papers. / What does it give spurs after range riding? / A slippery basement tilt" (*CP*, 75).

The only early poems in which Miles seems to be talking directly about her struggle with painful arthritis are "Physiologus" and the very brief (two quatrains) poem she wrote on the day World War II began, "Dec. 7, 1941," a poem not published until her *Collected Poems* (48). In this poem the "I" contrasts "the little wars" of civilians—at least they seem freely chosen—with the lot of the soldiers who must go off to war. Among the "little wars" are the fight of "crutch with stair." In the 1955 poem "Education" (*CP*, 96), the "I" is Miles recalling how as a student at Los Angeles High School, she "would sit in the window's ledge" of the school to feel the sun on "coldest bone" while watching "pecking sparrows" and the "warm and lively life" of "bickering girls." At the end, however, she asks where has all of this gone, thus turning the poem into an *ubi sunt* poem rather than a confession about suffering with "coldest bone" because of arthritis.

In other early and midlife poems Miles talks even more indirectly about her personal awareness of pain, at times through characters who are suffering in some way, at other times through images connoting agony. Although the poems are more startling once we know about Miles's condition, they have their own moving effects. For example, the very early "Dialogue"

(*CP,* 4) poignantly suggests that love was lost when "he" told "her" that she should "move with the fierce motion of the sea" instead of hearing life "only as a bright and silver ripple." She felt compelled to say that she must remain with the "red" pebbles she loves (connoting intense pleasure in the domestic realm of womanhood, but also, if read biographically, an admission that she must remain behind to care for her burning bones because they are the only bones she has).

Poignant scenes about suffering are also created in other early poems, each enriched by effects of realism and ironic humor created through such contrasts as formal, traditionally poetic language and the informal language of conversations and phrases from songs and clichés; a character's intense pain and ordinary objects in the environment; high expectations and deflated results. These poems include "Appointment in Doctor's Office," in which a "pale" woman in the "intense parlor atmosphere" of her doctor's office tries to look at "the framed pictures," read *Harper's Bazaar,* and think about Hawaii, but she is too profoundly afraid that "her little broken bone" has brought her to the brink of being "sick unto death" (*CP,* 31). In "The Sympathizers" "we" are a mighty group, but we are helpless when facing a man upon whom "Came the descent of pain. / All kinds, / Cruel, blind, dear, horrid, hallowed," and this pain "Rained, again, again" (*CP,* 69).

In an interview with Stanley Pinsker in the winter of 1979, shortly after her retirement, Miles connected her reticence in many of her early poems with uncertainty about her status as a poet, lack of experience in the world at large, and training as a student and poet in the heyday of Eliot's poetry, with its reserve, ambiguity, and indirectness through associative (or, in Eliot's term, correlative) objects. She said, "I felt more distant in that I was less familiar with what I was doing and I felt more wary of the world. And also that was the code of the time, that was the literary tradition—to have distance." Yet her conscious desire to be part of a poetic tradition cannot alone explain the long period of time in which she wrote from a distanced position. During part of this period, in the 1950s and 1960s, she was defending poets like Allen Ginsberg who were writing confessional poetry.[6]

One cause of concealment was undoubtedly the anxiety of deprivation and the need for restitution that all people feel. According to Rochlin in his chapter "The Loss of Function," these feelings are especially intense among those who as children were deprived of some bodily function by accident or illness. Rochlin argues that disengaging from a lost part of the body and accepting the altered body image involves more than mourning. Denial and fantasies about restitution are also essential. In his chapter "Creativity,"

Rochlin argues further that even an ordinary person will creatively use such defenses as denial to manage or transcend deeper discontents. Thus, defense can result in the person's "greatest inventions that enrich his life and in his little contrivances that comfort him." [7]

According to Rochlin's view of the psychodynamics of loss and restitution, Miles's reticence about herself in her early poems can be seen as a means of managing anxiety about her image of her arthritic body. Her creation of a mobile, wryly humorous, affirming, although reserved, poetic persona was, thus, her means of transcending both the anxiety and the defense of reticence. Her unwillingness to speak about her pain until later in life can also be attributed to the very difficulty of speaking about suffering. In her study of pain, Elaine Scarry agrees with Virginia Woolf that language "runs dry" for the sufferer trying to describe pain. [8]

In the poems she wrote during the 1970s and after retirement, however, Miles speaks more openly about her physical pain. In one group of poems on her childhood, she speaks of the pain and constraints she had when about eight because of arthritis. In another group, she talks freely about the pains of aging, and in a third group, she recalls the shock she felt over the way student protesters were treated on the Berkeley campus during the 1960s and the unease she experienced in realizing how little she had done to prevent this treatment. As in her earlier poems, she creates complex effects of poignancy, realism, and ironic humor by associating pain and dismay with ordinary objects and by mingling formal with unexpected conversational language and rhythms. The details, however, are more clearly autobiographical and more intensely felt and confessional than those in earlier poems.

Why the change? Her interviews and her poems suggest that her aging prompted her to discuss her inner life, just as other aging people, according to such psychologists as Robert Butler, feel compelled to confront their changing status. In her interview with Hammond, Miles said that she wrote the poems in *Coming to Terms* after an awareness of aging "just really hit me." When Hammond asked whether the poems were an attempt to make peace with the past or disavow it, Miles gave a somewhat ambiguous answer, as though searching for a clear explanation of what was a complex intertwining of attempts. She answered that she wanted to find "words" for "scenes of my past, recollections" so that the travel backwards in time could be "a metaphor for *Coming to Terms*. You know, getting somewhere else. A consciousness of aging, questions about professions, the bureaucratic nature of society, industrial politics . . . well, it's a traveling toward these things." As though to emphasize her desire both to recover the past and to move beyond it through better understanding, she also told Hammond that she wanted her late poems to show that "being able to move ahead [is] at least a relief," a relief, she added, from "unending need." She confessed a need to write poems that would not only recover her childhood but also express what it had been like living as a professor at Berkeley with "the feeling of tremendous pressure, working in bad times, and having to work too hard and not finding solutions under those wartime circumstances [of the Vietnam War]." [9]

According to Robert Butler, a "life-review mechanism" is brought into play by the biological changes of aging. These changes arouse an intense sense of imminent death and cause a person to evoke reminiscences (in Miles's words, "scenes of my past"). Also, the process encourages one to reintegrate parts of the personality unattended to (Miles's longing to get "somewhere else"). Sometimes the way to this reintegration may be through experiences of guilt, regret, and anger over the way past events have turned out. Butler argues that if the elderly person is adaptable and self-aware, reintegration will occur. K. Warner Schaie and the group called postformal cognitive psychologists also view the late stage as a time when, barring severe illness or poverty, review and reintegration are possible. Schaie maintains, however, that the search for reintegration begins not from a fear of death but from memories and thoughts so complex that they demand attention to ensure physical, emotional, and intellectual well-being. For postformal psychologists, late-stage thinking is complex, but this complexity elicits thinking that is reflexive and exploratory rather than demanding, simplified, or fearful. [10]

For Butler, the first disturbing awareness of aging is typically caused by an unexpected reflection in a mirror. Among the examples he cites is a woman who caught sight of herself in a mirror and was so shocked by the reflection of her aged face that she feared death was imminent and felt compelled to recall and rectify any unfinished business. [11] None of Miles's late poems describes a mirror experience, but three recount a sudden and disturbing awareness of aging; of these, one is like an unexpected encounter with a mirror. The first is "Retrospective" (*CP*, 190–91), in which Miles recalls how "a quarter-century" of teaching Chaucer "went very fast," and suddenly she was aware that she had "lived to the time" when she had to review her past and wonder "what I have been doing." The second is "Sleeve" (*CP*, 213), which begins with her admission that just as 1973 had been a "dark year for Spiro Agnew" (he had to resign as vice-president because of income tax evasion), it had been "a dark year for me too." She explains that she had become aware (as if for the first time) that when her sleeve (a metonymy for bone) is touched, it "rends / In the dark, in the hidden dust / To moth and rust" as if unusually old and worn-out.

A more startling but more positive experience is dramatized in "Concert."[12] Miles recalls sitting behind a woman neatly dressed except that her hat is "Tilted at a curious angle left to right"; Miles is startled to see that when the woman impatiently "pulled the hat" off, she revealed "wild white hair." This sudden awareness of an old person is like the one Freud had when an elderly person suddenly intruded into his train compartment as the train made a violent jerk. Freud quickly realized that he was looking at his own reflection in the compartment mirror behind the door flung open by the train's jerking motion. He also realized that he was dismayed and repulsed by his reflection.

Miles's white-haired person is not in a mirror, but she catches Miles unawares like an unexpected double. Miles, however, seems fascinated, even liberated, rather than dismayed by her double. Her description of the woman's white hair as "wild" carries connotations that are positive (strong passions and freedom) as well as negative (crazy, desolate). Miles also implies acceptance of her double in the title (with its double meanings of music concert and in harmony with another). And in giving the detail of the woman's impatient removal of her hat, Miles signifies her own desire to liberate herself from the codes she had been obeying in her profession.[13]

These three poems reflect the occasion that "hit" Miles into an awareness of her aging, prompting her to evoke scenes of her past, as evident in the first seven poems of *Coming to Terms*, most especially "Trip," "Doll," and "Parent," as well as in several in the middle of *Coming to Terms*, particularly "Study" and "Why We Are Late." What is especially striking about the first seven poems is that they evoke those moments in Miles's past when she was suffering from arthritis. According to Butler, life review among the elderly typically calls up unresolved conflicts that must be dealt with before life draws to a close. Butler does not give a taxonomy of such unresolved conflicts, but Rochlin suggests one in his study of the psychodynamics of loss of functions. According to Rochlin, the disabled are trapped in the conflict between acceptance of the disablement and despair, a conflict normally managed, he says, through various levels of denial, recognition, and sublimation. Miles's life review seems to have led her back to the earliest remembered experiences of dismay over loss of mobility, the very memory from which her scholarship and early poetic persona had been defending her.

As a result, Miles moved away from a reserved persona to a persona speaking more freely about her own childhood and pain, as in "Before" (about her first "flame of arthritis" and deathlike fatigue), "Blocks" (about the "many chloroformed walls" and "white sheets" of hospitals she experienced because of arthritis), and "Motive" (about how "Heat in bones under blankets burned / With aspirin" during some of her worst days). Miles also may have been more willing to speak out about pain because after years as a poet, she had at least found ways to express pain she could not find earlier.[14]

At the same time such poems and their travel metaphors suggest a means of "getting somewhere else" that can help a person facing retirement and aging. Miles recalls that her journeys back and forth between hospitals involved pain but also renewed strength (in "Blocks," she leaves the hospital with a fantasy about going "with Mme. Montessori home again"; in "Motive," once home, she still feels pain, but she finds that "Oho! There is something to life!" when her stepgrandmother brings her some small bottles of colored perfumes; in "Parent," her father stops on the way back from the hospital to buy her "the sherbet / Of your eight-year-old dreams"). And in the midst of the pain and stoic endurance come moments of play, even though they are brief and end in more pain: in "Before," running in meadows; in "Doll," playing with the doll Lillian under willow trees; in "Parent," eating sherbet.

According to Butler, constructive effects can result from seeing past conflicts in the light of positive understandings. When telling Hammond that the poems in *Coming to Terms* involved the sense of "getting somewhere else," Miles suggests that her recollections of childhood pain and survival helped her recover from the shock of aging. In this respect, Miles recounting her childhood experiences with arthritis can be compared with the invalid and elderly Malone in Beckett's *Malone Dies*. Kathleen Woodward describes him as a person trying to deal with pain and imminent death by telling stories about his past, including, ironically, even painful bodily changes. Like Malone, Miles deflates movements toward self-pity by making fun of her condition: she associates her fatigued self with Aunt Rhodie's dead goose ("Before"); when in the hospital, she says she is "scotched," either dried out like a radiator or scored like a piece of meat ("Blocks"); when coming home with a cast, she intimates that she feels like the tires that blew out "on our trusty Mitchell" ("Doll").

Also like Malone, Miles represents parts of her body in focused and intense images—her leg in a cast ("Blocks," "Parent," "Doll," "Album") and aching bones ("Motive"). Woodward cogently argues that the image of a part of the body is psychologically like one of D. W. Winnicott's transitional objects. Thus, she concludes, just as a child finally abandons the transitional object without mourning, so Malone (or, by extension, any elderly person such as Miles) can abandon a bodily part or function without mourning if it has been represented in an image, an image Woodward calls "the transitional or reparative phantasy." [15] In "Doll," Miles most poignantly signifies abandonment of her body in the fragments of her broken doll. Miles finds consolation in the fantasy that she and her doll can strengthen one part still intact, the eyes, so that they can "see in the dark"; by implication, they can face the unknown with hope, courage, and insight even if they are physically impaired.

The paper on which Miles wrote her poems also can be interpreted as Woodward perceptively interprets the exercise book in which Malone writes his thoughts, as a reverse form of the transitional object. Woodward explains that whereas a transitional object helps a child move away from a mothering figure to the objective world, Malone's accounts of his past in the exercise book help him face departure from the world with all of its attachments (including detachment from the body, however painful that loss might be). Miles's choice of title for her collection of late poems, *Coming to Terms,* suggests that she too wanted the contents of her poems to help her come to terms with aging and its detachments. Her image of "getting somewhere else" also signifies departure.

Unlike Malone, who is in his eighties and isolated in a house when writing in his exercise book, Miles was in her late sixties and still part of the academic community when writing the poems for *To All Appearances* and *Coming to Terms.* She was thus not yet ready to stop looking for "somewhere else" in society. However, she was facing retirement from her academic position. Thus, her search for "somewhere else" can be understood in the light of not only Butler's life-review concept, and its connection with Rochlin's ideas about loss and restitution, but also the theories of aging which view the late stage as a process of adaptation to the new social patterns involved in retiring from accustomed roles. One proponent of this view is Daniel J. Levinson, who concluded from his studies of aging men that if life is to be satisfying, it should be viewed as a series of developmental periods, or seasons, each eventually coming to termination and each, therefore, entailing the tasks of acceptance of termination, review of the past to find what to keep and what to reject, and the search for new possibilities. Earlier than Levinson, Erik Erikson similarly viewed the late stage as a time when one struggles between despair over terminations and the hope that what one has done in the past has coherence and significance. For Erikson, this conflict will continue until the person has formed an acceptance "of one's one and only life cycle and of the people who have become significant to it." [16]

Although Levinson and Erikson studied men, their conclusions about aging help explain what Miles has to say in many of her late poems. The playtime incidents in poems recalling her childhood as well as the reference in the Hammond interview to "getting somewhere else" suggest that as Miles neared retirement, she was reviewing the past for reminders of more playful experiences than those possible in the world of scholarship and university teaching. Other statements to Hammond—those about "working in bad times, and having to work too hard and not finding solutions under those wartime circumstances"—indicate that she felt not only fatigue because of work but also despair over the meaningfulness of the work done during the period of the Vietnam War, when student protestors on Berkeley's campus were harassed and even beaten. By adding that she wanted to "move ahead" and transcend "unending need," Miles intimates that she did not want to succumb to despair or reject the past as much as she wanted to find new ways of looking at old problems and a vantage point from which to look back and find coherence in what seemed chaotic and discordant.

In several of her poems of the 1970s, she reflects this willingness to admit her troubled memories over her political life while working as an academic. Unlike her statement to Hammond, these poems range from events of the 1940s to ones of the 1970s. Their value is in Miles's honesty and in the care she paid to the means of confessing her own shortcomings, a care indicative of her desire not only to speak freely about her academic life in a time of political unrest but also to understand her actions, make amends, and move forward. Her means include dramatic turns in a poem's structure, startling diction, and an interweaving of dreamlike and realistic images.

"Retrospective," while about the sudden awareness of aging, is also one of the first of the poems in which Miles admits that she had been blind to ramifications of political events. She sets her confessional mode and time frame in the beginning line when she says, "Once I didn't think that much about making the bomb." She then indirectly but powerfully confesses that her academic pursuits had made her thinking politically superficial and even callous: "I said sorry / To Japanese friends, especially one from Hiroshima / I agreed with in liking Isaac Walton." Looking back, she is horrified by her earlier behavior: "Now in one way, by a foreshortened view and exaggerated, / I have lived to the time in this free city where I say, / Look what I have been doing." Like many involved in life review who, according to Butler, feel guilt over past actions, Miles blames herself for allowing political problems to come about because of her academic preoccupations: "I have been making the bomb, creating, / Letting be created, the following real people: / John Mitchell, General Westmoreland, / Sheriff Madigan, John Mitchell, /

The list keeps sticking so it doesn't get to the bit names." She ends with the perception of possibilities for amends and a new sense of direction by becoming a poet writing about her political experiences: "How to keep from making / John Mitchell, General Westmoreland. / Composition: to think again / To work again the slow used-over clay" (*CP*, 190–91).

In "Witness," the poem that follows "Retrospective," Miles speaks more critically, this time, however, not about herself but about the police who used tear gas to stop student protests against Vietnam. She implies that even though she could be judged adversely for not doing more to stop the police, thinking rationally and productively under the warlike conditions at Berkeley was difficult. Nevertheless, she laments her inability to communicate her horror even afterwards: "Gassed going between classes / Students said little" and "My throat alive still cries, / But how to tell without dying / Is not told by the dying trees."

As in "Retrospective," so in her two "Luncheon" poems (*CP*, 214–15), Miles reviews her career from its start, and she honestly concedes that when concentrating on her academic work and life, she failed to work actively against political decisions she considered deplorable, not just during the Berkeley riots but earlier during World War II. The scene she recalls in "Luncheon" is a luncheon at her home, when friends assembled to talk about poetry. Because writing about a past event, she begins in the past tense. The scene was apparently so real and important in her memory, however, that toward the end of the poem, she shifts to the present tense to picture what happened as the luncheon drew to a close. The afternoon was "great with peace," but then it is interrupted by the cry of a bird ("cries / Far off, and once, a bird") as if warning that this peacefulness is a mirage. This warning is reinforced in the last line by the word "mirage" in the title of George Sterling's *Sails and Mirage and Other Poems,* a title alluded to either in the conversation or in Miles's mind after the bird's cry.

The cry of the bird in "Luncheon" can be interpreted as similar to the cry of Keats's nightingale, a reminder of life's transiency and death. But in the context of its companion poem, "Luncheon 2," the cry is more immediately a reminder that citizens are vulnerable to political abuses and war unless they are politically vigilant. In "Luncheon 2," Miles's admission of her political failures earlier in her career is presented as openly as in "Retrospective" but in a more dramatic manner. She recalls the luncheon when she was one among several American and Soviet writers who, in spite of language difficulties, managed to speak amicably about various other writers (Gogol, Pasternak) by nods or shaking heads. Then an interpreter arrived, and as if speaking on behalf of the group, he discharged a jolting and confrontational question: "Why did you drop the bomb on Hiroshima?"

Because the interpreter's question about Hiroshima concludes "Luncheon 2," it implies that Americans, including Miles, have no defensible answer. This implication of complicity in the atomic bomb is like that in "Retrospective." Just as Miles balances "Retrospective" with "Witness," so she balances "Luncheon 2" with "Officers" and "Memorial Day" (*CP*, 216–18), thus counterbalancing her failure to act politically with the ruthless actions of university officials and the police. The first two of the four stanzas of "Officers" have images recalling the everyday courteous and constructive conversations Miles had with two campus police officers for many years until the Berkeley riots. The third and fourth stanzas, however, have images of bullying and collision.

In the third stanza Miles remembers the officer who stopped her and her driver "When we were going to a senate meeting, strikebound by pickets." Before noticing that Miles was in the car, the officer smashed "his billy club" on her driver's arm resting innocently on the car window. When he realized his error, the officer ran away, but he had already become a terrible "giant" in Miles's eyes. In the fourth stanza Miles describes police running through the basement where she was teaching to spread "tear-gas in the corridor / To rise and choke in offices and classrooms." The officers' gas masks "distorted their appearance," although like the other officers, Miles had known two of them long enough to call them by name.

Miles reinforces her meaning in "Officers" by line arrangements. The first two stanzas have seven lines each, but the last two stanzas have eight lines each. The difference emphasizes the difference between the genial, simple way of life of the first two stanzas and the new way of life in the last two, when unrealistic fears over war protests complicated relationships between police, administrators, faculty, and students. In addition, in the fourth stanza lines seven and eight are set apart: "Since then, I have not met an officer / That I can call by name." By letting these lines stand out, Miles discloses more openly the depth of her horror over the way in which political forces can turn otherwise personable officers into dehumanizing and dehumanized brutes.

In "Memorial Day" she also memorializes the callous treatment she and her students received during the days of the Vietnam protests. Miles speaks in the present tense, as if still living the experience. The setting is the afternoon when a "rifle waves in the window" and tear gas "gusts" during Miles's Milton class. She adjourns the class to her front yard, where, after working through "the patristic part" of *Paradise Lost*'s part 7, she urges her students to tell their parents about the "sorts of pressures, absences of aid, / Losses of understanding you are working under." Ironically, as the students are telling her that their parents refuse to believe they are in danger, an army helicopter "In its regular rounds of surveillance drops down low," as though the mere "twenty figures in a courtyard" could really "mean trouble."

Miles ends "Memorial Day" with a desperate cry for some kind of sign to the police in the helicopter that she and her students protest the war because they want peace, although the only immediate action she can envision is throwing camellias into the air: "Couldn't we pick these flowers to throw at them / All these camellias overgrown and wasting?" Like repressing the names of officers, this action of throwing flowers is politically ineffective. But both actions signify not merely Miles's protest against police state tactics but her wish as she neared retirement to speak more openly about political issues than she had in the past.

Miles's desire to develop a more political persona and the willingness to admit that the persona may fail are poignantly expressed in the two stanzas of "Institutions" (*CP*, 218). In the first stanza, in eight lines, Miles admits that as each term has ended over her long career, she has at times fallen "into a reverie of dismay" over not only how poorly she has done in the academy but also how even more "terrible" she might do if she were working in a hospital or prison, where she might fail "to aid survival" or fail "to foster." In the second stanza she admits that at the end of each term, she can also believe that she did achieve some of what "I hoped, much that I tried," enough to give her hope, "like a rift of cloud," that she should not give up, but "Begin a new demand." The sense of new beginning in the last line is reinforced by its position as the seventh line when eight are expected, as in the previous stanza; the drop of the eighth line adumbrates possibilities that cannot yet be recorded because in the future.

In addition to serving as the means of working out new positions to take during retirement, poems like "Institutions" and "Retrospective" can be seen in Rochlin's terms as Miles's creative means of regaining mastery over, or coming to terms with, the losses in self-image that occurred during life review. As her political poems in *To All Appearances* and *Coming to Terms* disclose, she discovered in reviewing her past that while known in the academic world as someone with knowledge, status, power, and a willingness to work in search of solutions, she had made no contributions of any significance in the political arena. In "Concert 2" Miles presents an uncanny signifier of her desire to reshape her poetic persona from a political nonentity into a political critic.[17] As in her companion poem, "Concert," Miles describes an old woman at a concert who seems to be her double.

This woman is odd because she carries a purse with a hook from which hang her cane, a shoe, and a ladle. At intermission she "Fights her way to the refreshments," where presumably she startles the thoughtless, self-centered, and formal concertgoers clustered around the refreshment stand by waving her cane and ladling punch into her shoe. Whatever her actions, they cause agitation like that aroused when "a macho / Cyclist" harasses a small town "To bully the scattering citizens / And to set fires to doorways."

Miles presumably dropped "Concert 2" from *Collected Poems* not because she dropped her desire to be like the old woman but because she wanted to sever connection with the "macho / Cyclist," who is a bully intimidating all citizens without thought of differences. Miles makes clear her sympathy for students in her early poems on teaching and her later poems on the Berkeley protests. In expressing this sympathy of the old for the young, Miles reveals the empathy that according to postformal psychologists is possible as one ages because of the complex reflexiveness of late-stage cognition. In this empathy Miles resembles Virginia Woolf's elderly Eleanor in *The Years*. At the end of the novel, Eleanor looks with pleasure on a young couple she sees from the window of her home. Woodward cogently interprets Eleanor's look as motivated not by the Lacanian lure of desire nor by the Freudian longing for self-sufficiency but by benevolence (a reaction Woodward connects with Kohut's concept of benevolent narcissism accompanying maturity). For Woodward, Woolf did not intend to portray Eleanor's benevolence toward the young as springing from an unrealistic desire to return to youthfulness but, rather, as coming from a belief in the possibilities of the future. This belief is evident, as Woodward points out, in Woolf's comment on Eleanor's perceptions during her dream before the end ("Nothing was fixed; nothing was known; life was open and full before them") and in Eleanor's comment when she awakens that she expects old age to have the same openness as previous periods in her life ("So when I was a child; so when I was a girl; it's been a perpetual discovery, my life, a miracle").[18]

Similarly, in "Witness" and "Memorial Day," Miles looks at the young not to recapture their youthfulness or supplant them but to express sympathy for their plight during the Vietnam War and to encourage them to believe in their abilities to reshape the future in better ways than the adults before them. In one of her longest poems, "Views from Gettysburg" (*CP*, 192–97), Miles also portrays students as more peaceful than well-placed adults. She begins the poem with a series of dreamlike fantasies prompted by a visit to Gettysburg with some students. In these fantasies she imagines male soldiers at Gettysburg and in other wars killing each other, a male lecturer in a math class using his power to undercut a student, male real estate developers marring the environment and mistreating the poor to benefit themselves and rich home buyers, and male astronauts manipulating nature in order to soar in space. Presumably because she saw these men as embodiments of the kind of aggressive masculinity that was being denounced by NOW and other women's groups in the late 1960s and early 1970s, Miles linked the poem with the women's movement.[19] By connecting the soldiers and the other men with deadly machines, bloody wounds, and gunsmoke and the astronauts with an electric map (a sign, she told Pinsker, of "the conventions of power" and ordering), Miles powerfully criticizes well-established militarists, scientists, and businessmen who believe that power and victory at all costs will lead to peace and order.

Although linking "Views from Gettysburg" with the women's movement, Miles does not criticize all men, only those who misuse whatever power they have. In the final scene she pictures herself with her students, male and female, "students all," riding around Gettysburg in a car as ideal lawmakers, not seeking the hilltop but "the plain ground / To parley." She does not give the parley, but she says that from it emerges a better understanding of how to achieve peace through negotiation than has emerged from the soldiers, developers, and scientists pictured earlier in the poem. In affirming a dialogic relationship between male and female students at the end of "Views from Gettysburg" and in implying throughout the poem the need for mercy rather than justice, Miles reveals thinking that, according to Nancy Chodorow, Jean Baker Miller, and Carol Gilligan, is typical of women.[20] Miles, however, makes clear that a relationship based on accommodation and mercy is not easy to obtain or maintain. By contrasting the brevity of the final scene with a long series of scenes in which men have committed violence in order to achieve power, Miles reveals the extent to which those seeking an accommodating dialogue are vulnerable to the aggression of others. Significantly also, Miles and her students drive around in an old car, one that might break down, suggesting that the riders will have difficulty reaching their goals, even the limited goal of getting home.

Nevertheless, Miles, like Woolf's Eleanor, puts her hope in the ongoing processes of life and in the young in spite of the cultural limitations facing them, a hope also expressed in other poems about students in *Coming to Terms* ("Teacher," "Reading," "Supper," "Makers"). She also affirms other adults besides herself who look with benevolence on the young: the businessmen and holiday seekers who move to protect children on an airplane when the news comes of a possible crash landing in "Delay"; the two businessmen who help a little girl who seems troubled traveling alone with only her doll in "Travelers"; the parents and parishioners who, in spite of a poor desert setting, richly nurture three young girls in a "flat adobe mission" in "Easter."

Miles's hope in new life is also expressed in several of her life-review poems that are also paradoxically about death. The basic cause of life review according to Butler is a perception of death. Robert Lifton defines life's main crisis at any age as awareness of coming death. Although most of his studies have analyzed the experience of survivors of such devastating events as the Holocaust, the atomic explosion at Hiroshima, and the Vietnam War, Lifton sees the elderly as similar to these survivors in several ways. Like Butler and also like Erikson, Lifton argues that anyone facing death searches the past for explanations. Lifton, however, adds that such a person looks also for connections with others and for some sense that freedom of movement is still possible. The result is what Lifton calls a "Protean style" of thinking, that is, a complex of images connoting what is imminent (death, figured in images of the inexplicable, alienation, stasis) and what is wanted (life, characterized by words connoting clarity, affiliation, action). Lifton concludes that those who overcome suicidal and murderous reactions to death do so because they maintain this "Protean style" rather than letting death images overwhelm them.[21] Miles's "Fanatic" (*CP*, 213) can be defined as "Protean" since it begins with images of dissolution and death but ends with images of new life, even if painfully gained. The images in "Fanatic" are cryptic, but they are associated with aging and death by the poem's placement right after "Sleeve," a poem obviously about aging. In "Fanatic," Miles recalls one of the many conferences she attended as a scholar and teacher; as the conference "rolls on," she begins to see uncanny "Multitudes of white-robed figures" coming from behind the auditorium's curtains "As out of vaults," their "arms lifted." They flow "smoothly" but relentlessly across the room. Miles does not move; instead, "I sit tight and here / *Phagocytes.*" The pun on "here / hear" indicates that she is so preoccupied sitting "here" thinking about her own condition and imminent death that she "hears" the bacteria (phagocytes) moving to repair her diseased tissues at the same time that the white figures make her think of death. As someone steeped in Latin and Greek, Miles undoubtedly selected the word "Fanatic" to bring out the poem's double or, as Lifton might say, Protean connotations, that is, she feels "fanatic" (frantic, unbalanced) because of fear of death but "fanatic" (visionary, enthusiastic) because of life's promises. In this respect the white-robed figures coming "out of vaults" signify both death and the phagocytes repairing the body for ongoing life. The auditorium, then, is a *fane,* or temple, where both death and life are recognized.

Although Lifton does not connect "Protean" with humor, images of action can include playful movement, including the kind of play on words Miles uses in "Fanatic." Miles uses wordplay more humorously in "Intensives," in which she adds snatches of the popular song "Hello Dolly" as well as a play on the word *intensive* to encourage a friend, Margaret, who is in intensive care because of a grave illness. Miles affirms the connections and motions possible in life by intensively urging Margaret "to live intensely / At the moment of your medication" so that "the intensive moment" will come all the sooner when "you flip, turn over, look around," and your friends can sing, "Well hello, Dolly." At that moment, Miles assures her, she will be "back where / Hello Dolly. / Where you belong" (*CP*, 226–27).

That Miles herself wanted to "live intensely" as long as possible is evident in "Stroke," a poem recalling one of her periods of illness.[22] In the state of feeling "so far" from the world, "eyes, ears blurred, / Memory forsaken," with voices ringing out as if from "a round bell far away," she wanted "to hurry to get back into the world." To emphasize this wish for motion and connectedness in the midst of alienation, she ends with a double play on the word *stroke*. This time the word means not a physical impairment but the strike of the "round bell" in the land of the living she wants to hear and also the strike that would swing her back to the world of motion: "Strike me back into the world."

"Trip" is more obviously both a life review and a "Protean" poem. It is not only the first of the life-review poems in *Coming to Terms* but the poem Miles cited in her interview with Hammond as one whose ending she considered important because it conveys what she called "a sense of beyondness." In her Hammond interview, Miles also identifies the narrator as herself, presumably when her parents made their first trip from Chicago to southern California when she was five to ease her arthritic condition.[23] Like many journeys in literature, this one begins inexplicably from some unnamed place (here, an anonymous train station) and moves toward an unnamed destination (an oasis out West). From the beginning of the trip, the train offers a phantasmagoria of ominous, surreal sounds and visual images connoting death. The train leaves the "hothouse roses" of the station on a "rough night, wind blowing rain slantwise / On the train windows." It travels through "a tunnel of dark" and "into Halloween," with "some good scares" in the vestibules "Between cars, roaring and clashing at the heavy doors." In a misguided effort to cheer her, Miles's father tries to get her to sing "Hail, hail, the gang's all here," but she sings to herself "those going-away blues." She feels similarly betrayed by her mother. As they near El Paso, her mother seems to promise a pleasurable view by calling El Paso "The Pass," but it turns out to be a "burning deck" with only a few men, who are frightening because their faces are hidden by their sombreros as they sit "against the sun."

To counter the disappointing view of El Paso, someone on the train assures her that she will soon see a grove of fragrant orange trees. However, when Miles and her family arrive at their station, she finds it deserted and surrounded by "Sandy ranges of an infinite distance / Under a hot-white sky." Such breadth is at first "hurtful" to her "small heart, / A scope which beached our debris on its shore / Abandoned, lost from a tide of life." Miles's dismay fades, however, when she joins her parents in looking at the distant sky and sensing some kind of mystical nurturing in that free space: "Thirsty we drank its infinite sources, / Eyes brimmed with tears." This connection between free space and an infinite source of water leads to the perception of going "farther away" from the immediate death-life setting and the other figure in the setting, a hotelkeeper in "pith hat and jodhpurs." In the final lines the hotelkeeper meets the family, drives "our baggage into the Springs," and seems in an uncanny way to represent both life and death (he is affiliated with both the desert and the oasis, and he is silent, as if the keeper of special knowledge).

If connected with Lifton's concept of Protean thinking, the move at the end of "Trip" from a deathlike desert scene and an uncanny hotelkeeper to a family vision of nurturing, free-flowing water embodies Miles's willingness to admit inevitable death but to replace fears of dying with a more stabilizing view that until death comes, there should be an affirmation of the free-flowing nature of life and its possibilities for connections with others. In view of Butler's and Schaie's reintegration concepts, the poem also provided Miles a means of reviewing those moments of conflict she felt with her parents, a review leading to the reintegration dramatized in the family unity at the end. Then too, if the journey has the larger implication of a journey through life, the oasis represents the place of retirement—a green space where one can be free to carry on new pursuits and exploratory reflections away from "hothouse" institutions like the station at the beginning of the poem.

As in "Views from Gettysburg," Miles recognizes the reality that visions and freedom are hard to maintain because of life's pain and brevity. Of the poem's sixty-seven lines, only the last six are formed by oasis and fountain imagery. Even so, the thrust of the poem is toward liberation from fear, manifestly the fears Miles remembered as a child on a trip but underneath, the fears she had as an aging and arthritic writer nearing retirement. The final vision of a nurturing fountain and an oasis implies liberation not only from fear but also from the station at the beginning, with its "hothouse roses," signs of the belief that a woman, like a rose, is worthy only when young, beautiful, and passively waiting for a male to take charge. At the end of "Trip," Miles is still young, but as the writer she is in her late sixties, and she is actively and freely writing. And in writing in the first person, as she does in "Trip" and in most of her other late poems, she intimates her sense that she is in charge of herself. "Trip" also initiates a collection of poems in which Miles speaks out in her own voice about her life with the "old-age freedom" that Heilbrun finds admirable in other women writers over fifty.

The poems in *To All Appearances* and *Coming to Terms* make abundantly clear that Miles in her late sixties wrote with honesty and also with intense feeling, deep thoughtfulness, and careful attention to poetic structure so that readers would visualize and feel her late-stage condition. In her late poems she lives up to the role prefigured by the old woman in "Concert," whose "wild" hair links her with the impassioned and visionary young poet with "floating hair" and "flashing eyes" at the end of "Kubla Khan." The hair of Miles's late-stage persona, however, is not only "wild" but "white," signifying the desire to speak freely and passionately not as a male or young poet but as an aging woman about the concerns such a woman has regarding bodily pain, disintegration, role loss, and dying. Unlike the poems of the young poet with floating hair, which arouse "holy dread," Miles's late poems arouse joy because they show how one aging woman resists despair and marginality by speaking freely about pain, with empathy for the young and with longing for connectedness and mobility when facing death. Life drawing to a close arouses urgent needs, such as an understanding of what lies behind outer appearance and of how to come to terms with pain, role loss, and final stasis. Miles meets such needs with humor, compassion, and a profound sense of self-liberation in *To All Appearances* and *Coming to Terms*.

Notes

1. Carolyn G. Heilbrun, *Writing a Woman's Life*, 127, 131.

2. Paul Lauter, "Race and Gender in the Shaping of the American Literary Canon," 25–28. Lauter notes that by the 1950s women received only 19 percent of the doctorates in the modern languages, and by the 1960s they held only 22 percent of university positions. Lauter also observes that as early as the 1920s, the MLA had virtually foreclosed women scholars from presenting papers except in sections considered to be marginal, those on folk material and writings by women. To show that this decline was caused in great part by a widespread belief that women's endeavors

are not as mentally vigorous and significant as men's, Lauter quotes Professor Robert Archibald Jelliffe of Oberlin College (from 1907 to 1949), who, when appealing for a new teacher of composition in 1920, argued: "In my opinion the new instructor, when appointed, should be a man. . . .despite the excellent teaching being done by the women of the English faculty, the students are quick to infer that the work is considered by the faculty itself of less importance than that to which the men devote their time" (27).

Sources of information about Miles's life are scanty. Other than obituaries, the main source is Vernon H. Liang's sketch of Miles in *The Dictionary of Literary Biography*. Miles recalls some details and indicates beliefs about certain issues in two interviews: with Sanford Pinsker in Riverside early in 1979 ("Interview with Josephine Miles," 181–87) and with Karla Hammond at Columbia University in October 1979 ("An Interview with Josephine Miles," which first appeared in the *Southern Review* 19 [July 1983]: 606–31). I have been kindly given permission by Karla Hammond to quote from her interview and by the University of Illinois Press to quote from Pinsker's interview. I have also looked at some of the letters to Miles in the Miles Collection, Bancroft Library, University of California, Berkeley. The Bancroft has also prepared a brief "Biographical Chronology."

3. Her earliest poems, published in an anthology of new poets in 1935, won the Shelley Memorial Award in 1936 and the Phelan Memorial Award in 1937. Her first three collections (1939, 1941, 1955) earned a National Institute of Arts and Letters Award for Poetry in 1956 and the Oscar Blumenthal Prize from *Poetry* in 1959. Because of their regard for these and her subsequent collections (1960, 1962, 1966, 1968, 1974), members of the Academy of American Poets in 1978 named her as the thirty-seventh poet to receive a fellowship.

I have received information about connections between Miles's poetic career and her academic standing from personal conversations with Motley Deakin, professor emeritus, University of Florida. Professor Deakin, one of Miles's graduate students, attributes Miles's high status at Berkeley to her own scholarly brilliance (she was "just exceptionally good," he said), her unusual ability to work with students majoring in literature and those pursuing creative writing interests, and (because of her poetic talents) her sensitivity to matters of style, a sensitivity not often found in scholars (with the exception, Professor Deakin added, of Mark Schorer, one of Miles's colleagues at Berkeley).

According to Margaret Cortes, a friend of Miles in Berkeley from 1960 who was in the poetry group that met with Miles from 1970 until her last illness in 1985, Miles was "greatly loved by her students, crowds of students, for whom she made room even when classes were overfilled. She was sharp, witty and generous, and definitely not saccharine." Margaret Cortes has kindly given permission to quote from her letter.

Miles's fellowships and administrative service included (according to the Bancroft Library's "Biographical Chronology"): an American Association of University Women Research Fellowship in Literature, 1939–40; a Guggenheim, 1948–49; Fellowship, American Council of Learned Societies, 1965; Chair, Campus Committee on Prose Improvement, 1958–60; member, Committee on Research, Academic Senate, 1963–64; member, Chancellor's Committee on the Arts, 1968–71; member, President's Committee on Search for Chancellor, 1970–71. Miles's essays on her methods and rationale for teaching composition classes at Berkeley and in the Bay Area Writing Project are collected in *Working Out Ideas*. Her contributions to the Bay Area Writing Project are summarized by James Gray in his "Preface" to *Working Out Ideas,* iii, and in his essay with Miles Myers, "The Bay Area Writing Project," 410–13.

4. Hammond, "Interview," 620–21. The two poems she cites are not in *CP;* they are in her 1974 *To All Appearances*, somewhat differently titled: "Moonrise over Dentist's Office" is "Moonrise in City Park," 61, and "Lumber Yard" is "Moonrise in a Lumber Yard," 71. In her midlife collections Miles expresses the disappointments that can come with romance in the following poems, but she may have been imagining how someone else might feel rather than expressing what she was personally feeling: "Matter of Fact,"; the fourth song of "Four Songs,"; "Location," and "Dream" (*CP*, 106, 128–29).

Miles may have had early romantic longings like those felt by Rosemary Sutcliff (1920—), the British writer of historical novels and Member, Royal Society of Miniature Painters. Sutcliff was also crippled by Still's disease, the type of rheumatoid arthritis that affects children and that usually causes crippling deformities (unlike osteoarthritis, which only rarely cripples and which affects adults). Sutcliff recalls her struggles and her two romantic disappointments in her autobiographical *Blue Remembered Hills*. She seems to have found compensation in her writing and art.

5. Gregory Rochlin, *Griefs and Discontents*, 121–64. Rochlin argues that the search for compensation is prompted by the psychodynamics of self-esteem, which begin in early childhood and make "the need to fulfill wishes" as "formidable as the events and conditions which thwart them" (135). From his clinical studies and from his readings in myth, art, and literature, Rochlin concludes that primary means of restitution are substitute gratifications found in dreams, fantasy, mythmaking, identification with what has been lost, and sublimation, especially in occupations.

6. For Miles's support of poets in the Bay Area Beat movement, see Michael Davidson, *The San Francisco Renaissance*, 174–75. Miles's statement to Pinsker is in Pinsker, "Interview," 187.

7. Rochlin, *Griefs*, 222. Rochlin begins his chapter "The Loss of Function" by declaring: "Disabilities, impairments, or the loss of a function are such distressing experiences that no matter when in life they occur, they rarely fail to produce lasting emotionally disturbing results and influence behavior more than has been generally recognized" (321). Rochlin links this distress with the distress all children feel during childhood over various losses and deprivations, but he finds the distress intensified when the ego feels threatened by an alteration in its image of the body, to which it is narcissistically attached. The disabled may have felt even more emotional disturbance in the 1960s when Rochlin was writing because, as Sutcliff indicates in *Blue Remembered Hills*, they were then seen more negatively by the able-bodied than now.

8. Elaine Scarry, *The Body in Pain*, 4. Scarry adds, "Physical pain does not simply resist language but actively destroys it, bringing about an immediate reversion to a state anterior to language, to the sounds and cries a human being makes before language is learned"; she concludes that the expression of physical pain eventually relies on metaphors and "as if" depictions (22). Like Rochlin and Scarry, Gilbert Rose, "The Creativity of Everyday Life," 349, argues that expression of personal pain through metaphoric language, art, or other forms of socially and culturally accepted activity is not "escape through wishful distortion of the world, but orientation in it . . . all in the service of the reality principle."

9. Hammond, "Interview," 618–19.

10. Robert N. Butler, "The Life Review," 66; K. Warner Schaie, "Toward a Stage Theory of Adult Development," 261–70; Francis A. Richards, Cheryl Armon, and Michael L. Commons, "Perspectives on the Development of Thought in Late Adolescence and Adulthood," and Gisela Labouvie-Vief, "Logic and Self-Regulation from Youth to Maturity," 3–27, 158–79. Schaie argues that the cause of life review is the

moment when "the complexity of the adult cognitive structure has reached an over-load stage" (268). The "postformal" pychologists argue that late-stage thinking is too complex and reflexive to be measured adequately by recall alone or by Piaget's concept of "formal operational," or propositional thought, which Piaget called the highest form of thinking.

11. Butler, "Life Review," 68.

12. "Concert" is in *Coming to Terms;* it was not reprinted in *CP* but in *The Norton Anthology of Literature by Women,* ed. Sandra M. Gilbert and Susan Gubar, 1762.

13. Freud's double story appears in his essay "The Uncanny"; it is quoted and explicated by Kathleen Woodward, *Aging and Its Discontents,* 63–65. Woodward links Freud's dismay over his double with his masculine fear that old age is a late form of castration. Miles may have held a more positive view of an aging double because women in Western culture are more likely to want a friendship with, rather than separation from, the other, according to Carol Gilligan, "Adolescent Development Reconsidered," xviii–xix. Miles also had lived with her mother during most of her career; Miles's father died early in her life, in 1930. "Conception" (*CP,* 199), Miles's elegy for her mother, reveals the respect she had for her mother's activities, which over the years went beyond the home to include participation in play-reading groups, the League of Women Voters, and local politics.

14. Sutcliff did not talk about her pain until her sixties, when she wrote *Blue Remembered Hills,* as if she too had to learn how to articulate her experience. Miles's poems about pain are short; Sutcliff's passages on pain in *Blue Remembered* are also short. Scarry claims that even though words from a sufferer "may be meager," "to be present when a person . . . projects the facts of [painful] sentience into speech is almost to have been permitted to be present at the birth of language itself" (*Body,* 6).

15. Woodward, *Aging,* 184. For Woodward's rich and provocative insights on the fragmenting body and Malone, cf. *Aging,* 132–42, 167–90.

16. Erik Erikson, *Insight and Responsibility,* 115. Levinson's studies appear in *The Seasons of a Man's Life.*

17. "Concert 2" appears in *Coming to Terms* but not in *CP.*

18. Woodward, *Aging,* 78–87. For a postformal explanation of old-age empathy, see Cheryl Armon, "Ideals of the Good Life and Moral Judgment," and Suzanne Benack, "Postformal Epistemologies and the Growth of Empathy," 340–56, 357–80.

19. Pinsker, "Interview," 187. Miles told Pinsker that until "Views from Gettysburg," she felt "outside the women's lib problem in that I haven't had any power exercised upon me nor have I exercised power," a comment that seems disingenuous in light of the power she had over dissertations and departmental decisions on Berkeley's campus. In the light of poems like "Retrospective" and "Witness," however, she must have meant that she had little power in the political arena, nor had she wanted political power until realizing too late that she might have done more to prevent the holocaust at Hiroshima and to alleviate the political turmoil at Berkeley during the Vietnam War. By the 1970s she must have realized that she had affinities with the women's movement, which had turned from demands for equal access to the workplace (which Miles already had) to demands for new definitions of masculinity and a cessation of war (which Miles wanted, as evident from poems like "Views on Gettysburg" and "Officers").

20. Nancy Chodorow, *The Reproduction of Mothering;* Jean Baker Miller, *Toward a New Psychology of Women;* Carol Gilligan, "Remapping the Moral Domain." Chodorow, Miller, and Gilligan argue that in a culture where the mother is

the main nurturer of children—but where the father is more socially affirmed because of his autonomy—a daughter feels torn between two desires: to remain attached to her mother, a desire prompted by the wish for the mother's continued love and by culture's expectation that a daughter will become a nurturer like her mother; yet to possess her father's autonomy and all that it signifies—power, freedom, self-sufficiency. In Chodorow's terminology, a daughter typically reaches some accommodation with issues of primary identification and separateness (*Mothering,* 129). However, unlike a son's accommodation to familial ties, a daughter's is more ambiguous and tenuous because it involves relationships with both the mother and father, or at least with the polarizations they culturally represent—nurturing and attachment as opposed to autonomy and separation. Because of this ambiguity, Miller argues that women should replace the word *autonomy* with a word meaning the kind of relationships they understand, those involving both freedom and attachment (*New Psychology,* 95). At the same time, according to Gilligan, this ambiguity can be an advantage since it leads to a deeper and more flexible understanding of relationships and mercy than men traditionally have had.

21. Robert Lifton, *The Life of the Self,* 63, defines the Protean style of thinking as a struggle to keep the self moving away from an obsession with death alone "toward the nurturing that will keep it intact, connected, and active (in movement)."

22. "Stroke" was first published in *CP,* 245. Miles was presumably recalling her very severe illness in 1978, although this was caused by gall bladder complications. She did not then or subsequently suffer from a stroke; apparently in "Stroke," she was imagining what a stroke might be like as well as playing on the connotations of the word *stroke* as a means of expressing her feelings during her illness.

23. Hammond, "Interview," 618.

15

BERTRAM WYATT-BROWN

Aging, Gender, and the Deterioration of Southern Family Values in the Stories of Peter Taylor

PETER TAYLOR'S short stories chiefly concern the transition of the South from rural to city values. They also describe the vast changes in family ties, codes of manners, and conduct that such a transformation has entailed. What has seldom received critical attention, however, is the southern writer's understanding of aging as it relates to these matters as well as to the age-old struggles between men and women and the rivalry among different generations for dominance.[1] By taking account of the aging factor we perceive that the ambiguities with which all of Taylor's stories are concerned are not just reflections of cultural shifts. Nor are they simply engaging issues of male versus female. Rather, they also include the difficulties arising from the way individuals handle the problems associated with a particular time in their lives. These characters find themselves in the unaccustomed position of being marginal—no longer at the crux of events. As a result their assertions of individuality seem at once pathetic and invigorating, a bittersweetness that signifies the author's rejection of sentimentality.

Unlike modern society, in which young peer groups dominate, families of a traditional kind, as Taylor once explained, used to involve a mix of ages. Custom and convention supported an unequivocal sense of good and evil. Consequently in this system tensions, anxieties, and repressions were manageable. A sense of "authority" could exist in contemporary society only "by force of will, assertion" and no longer by an older "tradition" that inculcated inherent respect between the generations.[2] A number of his stories deal with personal disorientation or confused mourning resulting from such cultural changes and shifts of values. "Their Losses" (1950), "What You Hear from 'Em?" (1951), and "Miss Leonora When Last Seen" (1960) all involve the fate of women who are old and facing the ultimate solitariness of death. When they are confronted with a new order in which their familial codes of conduct are unappreciated, these figures find themselves temperamentally unable to enter the new situation with confidence. The rigidity of old habits inhibits their ability to adjust, but always Taylor asks, what are the costs in terms of personal integrity and autonomy in meeting the altered circumstances? The figures he portrays largely remain on the fringes of their world, occupying an intermediate social space which, he emphasizes, is neither completely isolated nor fully blended. Age and gender—that is, the relative unimportance of womanhood in the male scheme of things—both conspire against them. They are lonely but are not left completely alone. They would like to belong but also stubbornly insist on being their cranky selves. Idiosyncratic though Taylor's old women may be, they fulfill roles of dependency that society has already assigned them, but their status sets them apart (*CS*, 199–215, 232–51, 502–35).

With regard to the marginality of aging, Taylor illustrates matters that Margaret Kuhn of the Gray Panthers and Jeanne Bader discussed recently in the *Gerontologist*. In the context of contemporary American society, they, like Taylor in fiction, draw attention to the marginality of those who are just entering and those who are soon to leave life. These observers point out that "one rarely truly listens to the Young or to the Old the way one listens to middle aged adults."[3] As if to illuminate their point, "Three Heroines," a prose-poem, and "In the Miro District," two of Taylor's most penetrating narratives, represent the conflicts of the generations to which these advocates for the aging allude. The tales provide a striking opportunity for analyzing the difference that gender makes in understanding the relative positions of aging men and women in family life and the ruptures in connectedness that arise. What Taylor achieves is a special rendering of southern culture that illuminates areas seldom recognized even by the region's closest literary observers. He shows that growing old in a South that is undergoing rapid social change poses special dilemmas. The predicament is not the soulless impersonality of the nursing home, an issue that might have greater pertinence in a northern setting, but rather the misunderstandings of family members—the southern caregivers for the young and the old. Taylor does not seek to illustrate an abstraction but to explore the subtle interplay of highly individualistic temperaments, cultural factors, and physical and emotional problems in growing old.

"Three Heroines" offers a study of ways in which the modern world is destroying the venerable ties that once linked the generations. The story's chief figures are all women whose viewpoint, says critic Jane Casey, Taylor had previously employed as an observation post looking down upon masculine "disorder." In this story, though, he expresses a new theme: the significance and moral vigor of the domestic function in a world in which men sometimes find their ambitions and pretensions set at naught.[4] Each of the women fulfills her proper role even though it is largely confined to domestic and decorative functions. In the eyes of southern men, as Taylor recognizes, women's activities too often are seen as irrelevant to the main concerns of life—at least according to male definitions. Sensitive to the effects of that bias upon its victims, Taylor in "Three Heroines" deals with aging and its particular effect upon women, whose lives have been subordinated to the dictates of a male world. Yet while Taylor respects women, although they are outsiders, he has no political agenda that a feminist would celebrate. The use of the term "Heroines" suggests that he deliberately intends an old-fashioned connotation. The women in question are by no means presented as "heroines" in a Hollywood–Scarlett O'Hara way. Nor are they really portrayed as "heroes" in drag, as it were, taking on attributes associated with men at a loss to their femininity.

Taylor's narrator in this story is traditional in his attitudes. Seen through this unnamed character, the story reveals that the three women involved—his dead grandmother, dying mother, and Willie Mae, her aging black maid and caregiver—are heroic in their sense of dignity and clear understanding of themselves—as women loyal to tradition itself. Thus, to a degree, the reader comes to share the narrator's unvoiced assumption that such women are marginalized, but we do not accept the narrator's further presumption that such liminality is appropriate. According to hard southern custom, as the author makes clear, they are expected primarily to dedicate themselves to making life comfortable for their husbands or employers, as the case may be. They are supposed to raise their children to be loyal to community values. As a result, even the three women at the center of the story—particularly his fatally ill mother—generally have played supporting roles. One senses that the author himself finds the ancient function of womanhood a richer, more dignified role than we, in modern times, can imagine.

The marginality of the first "heroine," the narrator's mother, becomes clearer only as the story progresses. At first we see her as a grand southern lady of eighty-six. With death looming only weeks away, she is being readied for a ball at the country club. Ambivalent, somewhat conflicted in his responses, her middle-aged son observes the elaborate preparations that the old servant Willie Mae performs for her mistress with her "powerful brown" and "handsome hands" ("TH," 143, 144.) Distinctly masculine in his interests, he is both touched and bored with the cosmetic process. Because of his mother's great age and illness, the procedure cannot be other than slow and laborious. So time-consuming is the caregivers' toil of dressing and beautifying the old that "institutional plain," as Jaber Gubrium reports, is the general rule in the modern nursing home.[5]

The narrator chafes at the significance of his mother's attempt to rise to the occasion. His ambivalence stems from his love for his mother on the one hand and the traditional reaction of men who insist upon freedom from apron strings—a differentiation from the other sex that helps to establish their separateness. She yearns to retrieve some sense of identity and belonging through the rituals of beautification and partygoing. Yet, for him, who remembers her as a younger woman, the process dramatizes her impending dissolution and the end of his ties to her. On the one hand, love and gratitude stir him as he contrasts the thinness of her silver strands with the abundance of dark hair that once bent over him as a child who "needed attention" when ill with "the mumps or measles" ("TH," 144).[6] On the other hand, there is a curious detachment in his reminiscence. Perhaps he has not reconciled himself either with her forthcoming death or with her past. The attempt to distance himself may indicate his fear of future pain from her loss.

At the ball Taylor has the character play the role of the "faithful son," in a rather self-mocking way. He serves as "everybody's hero," but the tone throughout is self-deprecating and insecure. He remembers his own derelictions when much younger—his academic difficulties and the failed first marriage that had embarrassed his father. Apparently both the narrator and Taylor as author do not see that the mother may have been disappointed, too ("TH," 148). Even before their arrival at the affair, he feels a touch of boyish mortification. The son anticipates how others in attendance may react to the sight of his dying mother: "Who does the woman think she is? Where does she think she is going in that outfit?" ("TH," 143). In such manner men in the South had always denigrated the secondary roles that women took, even though they would have them play no others. They placed them in a double bind, insisting that they be objects to admire, a role that is rendered increasingly difficult as age inevitably saps beauty and vigor. In reaction, the women, with little self-examination, might grow irritable, selfish, hard—traits not at all to be admired. As Taylor once pointed out, when tales like this one were told in the days of his youth, he had listened uncritically but only later realized that "in all these fine old Southern stories blacks were getting the short end from women, who were getting the short end from men." In the story the son's sense of humiliation stems from the close identification of family members in the South; he fears that her temerity in attending the party will affect how others will react toward him—feeling, as he does, somewhat marginal himself.[7]

Yet in "Three Heroines" Taylor makes clear that in the old regime female bravery—when appropriate within the requisite limits of its gender—held an honored place. The old woman's struggle to defy age and death, to make a final presentation of herself as she once used to be, upholds the principles by which she was raised and to which she will subscribe until her dying hour. Both factors are represented in her recollections of her Grandmother Haynes, the second "heroine" of the story. In honor of her own grandmother, the old mother wears to the ball the diamonds that her grandmother had saved from looters during the Civil War. Confederates had suspected her of Unionist sentiments in wartime Tennessee. For the partygoing old woman, the Civil War progenitor serves as a model of stoic determination, a characteristic usually associated with men but which also was an ideal of southern ladyhood. By wearing a gold lamé gown and her grandmother's heirlooms, she recapitulates that sense of familial daring, soon to be lost in the rush of modernity.

Gone is the code of behavior that had enabled Grandmother Haynes to be "frivolous"—as she had been in the pre–Civil War era—and then "capable" and intrepid in running the farm when the men had become soldiers at the front. In the late Victorian era the exigencies of war no longer existed. The men had returned, and women once more were ornaments rather than surrogate breadwinners and plantation managers, wrestling with the problems of the workaday world ("TH," 152). Limited, however, though her role might be, the dying mother seeks in her struggle against death to emulate the bravery of her mother. One senses, too, that the writer wishes the reader to detect that the aged partygoer's interest in the past somehow excludes her son. She had an existence apart from him, but that distinctiveness is not one to which he is totally reconciled. She seeks to please herself, not her son. This kind of personal statement represents a traditional mode of escape from the toils of male disparagement that he, although modern enough, finds a little unsettling.

The raw clash of culture and gender is evident in the reaction of the old woman's youthful physician to her appearance at the party. He is unable to comprehend this terminal act of defiance and pride. Although Taylor's character has summoned up her last reserves to be as witty and gracious as she once had been, the doctor looks at his patient as if seeing a ghost.

Gradually learning something about himself from watching the physician's expressions, Taylor's narrator observes, "there can be no *proper* greeting for death." Master of a "primitive profession," the doctor knows nothing of death's meaning but only about the biological "cessation of life." The narrator-son sees that his mother's doctor has yet to reach the stage when maturity and experience can teach him wisdom and compassion about such matters. The scientific culture in which the physician lives provides no deeper perspective on death ("TH," 150). But still more important, the young doctor, like her son, finds her self-assertiveness at the party disconcerting. She departs from the accustomed role of dependency upon him as physician and adviser. She rejects the role of marginality and insists upon being in the midst of life and social pleasure.

In the final section of the brief prose-poem, the focus abruptly shifts to provide another signal of familial decline and gender separateness by focusing on the one who made the occasion possible by dressing the old lady for the ball. As the narrator observes, the old woman is "something [that] Willie Mae, the house servant, has put together"—her own artistic creation with rouge and lipstick "as real as a doll's coloring," indeed, "more real than life" itself ("TH," 147). The son turns to Willie Mae, the third "heroine" of the brief tale, standing near the entrance upon their return home. He exclaims to Willie Mae how glad he is that "you waited up for her." "And Willie with a look of even deeper wonder, / Asks with her eyes: What else did you expect of *me?*" ("TH," 156). Willie Mae is herself nearing death; she knows that with the old woman's passing will come an end to her career, her significance, her slender hold on life. She loves her mistress and loyally serves her. She is not motivated, however, by sentimental feelings ascribed to the traditional black mammy. Her retort to the son suggests as much. Like her mistress, she is herself by no means resigned to dependency. Taylor wants the reader to consider her as fully alive as the others. Not for nothing does he include her as one of the heroines. Willie Mae discerns that her own life has been intimately connected with the dying woman, but by no means are we to think less of her for being a lowly black servant. Rather, the common link of gender and age transcend the division of race.

Unlike the doctor and the son, Willie Mae is no less determined than her mistress is to defy the men and their commonsensical rules which would deny a woman the chance to prove her mettle even if it seems ridiculous for a dying woman to attend a party. Thus, she, too, represents the dying order. Taylor does not, however, seek to evoke some dubious nostalgia. He has conceded that the relationship of employer and servant was "an inherently patronizing situation, and there was no future in it" for blacks. As literary

critic Jan Pinkerton has noted, "he often records the discontinuities of contemporary family life, but he does not imply that families of the past were
superior or preferable; there were always conflicts and neuroses, he makes
clear, and even a seemingly stable family façade has always been blighted
by the basic and constant flaws in human nature."[8] Failure to change to
meet new conditions is no less a blemish, in Taylor's view, than an inability
to recognize the need of others to cleave to old ways.

Nonetheless, the writer wishes to emphasize the disappearance of those
values of an earlier day, which have not been replaced by a more humane
system. Unlike her contemporaries, Willie Mae is dependent on the mistress
just as the mistress has had to rely on her. It is an antique but more intimate
relationship, it must be said, than that to be found in the modern nursing
home. In such a setting, impersonal, institutional duties would have made
family-based ties seem brittle or unauthentic. Generational compatibility
and the corresponding link between mistress and maid, Taylor implies, can
sometimes overcome the differences of class as well as race. The notion may
seem comically old-fashioned. Yet the contrast with the present-day world
of aged dependents placed in nursing warehouses suggests that it might be
preferable, despite the peripheral role that aged and dying women were left
to play.

In his story "In the Miro District," Taylor deals with the world of men
and their potential problems of liminality. In this case, rivalries separate
fathers and sons—a common oedipal theme. Still more significantly, however, Taylor explores the rivalry of grandfathers and grandsons, a topic
seldom treated in fiction despite the inherently explosive conflicts that could
arise from that too often romanticized relationship. As Kuhn and Bader
have observed, the old and young "are isolated from each other." They
live in separate worlds, yet both groups are curiously similar. They are expected to stay out of the full-time job market, to be sexually inactive, and
to remain outside the main discourse of life. As if to amplify upon Kuhn's
perception, Taylor believes that if the pressure of peers is ever to be diminished, children need more than simply parental authority. They require a
variety of role models. As if to illustrate this point in his story, Taylor has
said, "When I was a child, you could turn to other aunts and uncles and
old colored people. It wasn't just all mother and father. It was the whole
family," a contrast with the modern, more vulnerable nuclear form.[9]

"In the Miro District" richly illuminates the conventions and ideals
of southern male culture and the role of the life cycle in establishing the
norms—and building the tensions—of masculine behavior. Set in suburban
Nashville, in a part of the Old Southwest known in eighteenth-century

Spanish days as the "Miro District," the story chronicles the dramatic episodes by which a son—who serves as the narrator recalling his youth—forges ahead in juvenile indiscretion to build his own special place and sense of himself. It deals with the issues of sexual inequality, the anachronistic pull of old concepts of dignity, the meaning of generational roles within a changing family structure, and the conflicts of young and old against the middle-aged, or that which Kuhn and Bader call the "sandwich generation."

In Taylor's view the relation of men to each other in a family are more complex than are their individual ties with their mothers. Probably personal grounds inform this perspective: "I had great grievances with my father," he has admitted. Moreover, as in the reminiscences of the dauntless Grandmother Haynes in "The Three Heroines," Taylor represents in a portrayal of an indomitable grandfather how a primitive southern family ethic continued to exist into the twentieth century. The ethic was suited to the rural world in which he lived. By his lights virtue still resided in the Mosaic doctrine of justice, the ideal of absolute self-reliance, and the concept of virtually unanimous community agreement about who stood where in the ranks of local society. The ethic had long since been abandoned in the southern urban setting of Nashville, where his middle-aged daughter and son-in-law and his still more secularized grandson lived by less stringent, more sophisticated understandings. According to the new citified code, the old and young were to supply each others' emotional needs—if only to ease the burden of the middle generation, busy with issues of moneymaking and power. "The Young are assumed to need mothering; the Old, it is assumed, turn to God," as Kuhn and Bader remark.[10] But the clash of the two sets of ideals—the agrarian values of the grandfather and the modern and rebellious notions of the grandson—make a meeting of minds between youth and age very unlikely.

The narrator of the story recalls his troubled relationship with his grandfather. Entering upon middle age, he at last has the maturity and perspective to reflect on the hidden motives of the other members of his family and, most especially, his own desires and passions. Through the narrator, the writer makes abundantly clear that the conflict over power and family identity is not something to be happily resolved because the chief figures in the story remain on the fringe of the family dynamics just as they had at the beginning.

The story centers on the alienation of a grandson, the story's narrator when a youth, and his maternal grandfather, Major Basil Manley. Both feel powerless in the larger family's life. They are thrown together because they are both shoved out of the way for the convenience of the middle-aged, active generation of Manley's daughter and son-in-law. Having no brothers and sisters, the narrator is left to his own devices in growing up.

Grandfather Manley visits his daughter and son-in-law but refuses to move in with them. Worried about his safety and health as he grows older, the middle-aged couple implore him to give up the drafty place in the country and live under their roof. He is a widower who by no means has adjusted to the absence of his wife. Profoundly depressed, though unaware of his state of mind, he embraces solitude. He cannot imagine how to change old habits. Manley's wife no longer is there to set him straight, nag him about his appearance, insist that he keep the place up properly. As a result, he grows increasingly infirm but stays vigorously alive largely out of fear to change, for change might mean death. Despite the many entreaties of the Nashville couple, he insists on driving his own car and living by himself in the old home. When he arrives at his daughter's house in fashionable Acklen Park, he comes in tieless. Would the late Mrs. Manley have permitted such negligence? Never. She would know that both parents and grandson were used to stylish dressing even in leisure hours. The reader might guess that the grandson attends Montgomery Bell, a Nashville boys' academy that required coat and tie for classes in the 1920s. In the country club atmosphere of the suburbs, a tieless old man would seem quite out of place. The Major would have it so; he does not wish to belong to their fancy world. He will not surrender even on minor matters.

In contrast, the narrator as a youth eagerly awaits his entry into adulthood and the greater social order, free of the restraints imposed by his parents. Grandfather and grandson both seek independence—the former as a means of defense, the latter as a form of aggression and hope. Each resents the other's borderline standing in the family matrix, because it seems to be a reflection of his own. Yet, Grandfather Manley—who scarcely questions the necessity of constraining the young—thinks that his grandson understands and loves him. He does not base his conviction upon any sign of genuine rapport but only upon assumptions derived from the old southern ethic: the grandson should make at least an outward appearance of affection—in a properly reserved way, of course. Conversely, the grandson sees the grandfather as a gratingly authoritarian figure without any sympathy for or understanding of his needs.

Their frustration grows worse because neither party can enter the larger, secular environment in which the parents dwell. As Kuhn and Bader note, the young are supposed to be too inexperienced and the elderly too mentally worn down to participate in the major deliberations and activities of the middle generation. The rest of the family tacitly believe that the grandson is too young and uninitiated to join in decisions about important family business. The grandfather is an outsider, too. Yet, in contrast to the son, he can at least react openly to his marginalization—if only by retreating to his home in Hunt County. Unlike his Rebel cohorts, he would not turn himself "into an old woman," his grandson remarks ("MD," 166).[11] Unreconstructed, Major Manley pursues his timeworn routines in his isolated, unheated house in the backward part of the state, forty miles away from Nashville. He cherishes his autonomy and his memories of his dead wife too much to move.

At the heart of the story is the struggle over the role that women should be permitted in the lives of men. The generation to which Basil Manley belongs reflected the old customs that Thomas Jefferson, Andrew Jackson, and Sam Houston each had preserved in a way quite baffling to the grandson. These gentlemen seldom mentioned women in their public utterances—except as icons for abstract veneration. Like that older generation of heroes, the grandfather divided his private and public worlds. So complete was that division that in the presence of others he had never even called his own wife by her first name. To speak too familiarly about women—the respectable ones—in public would have been judged unseemly, a violation of decorum deemed as inappropriate as disrobing in front of strangers. The narrator and grandson asks, "Did they have too much respect for women? Were they perhaps, for all their courage in other domains, afraid of women or afraid of their own compelling feelings toward women?" ("MD," 197). The answer is yes, there was dread.

In a traditional society, as the South of Basil Manley's day had been, women exercise considerable power as moral arbiters. When men in the rural South violated conventional standards in some openly blundering way, southern matrons could muster opinion that assured the offenders' disgrace and even ostracism from polite company.[12] As a result, southern men told each other tales of sexual exploits, but delicacy, dignity, reticence—and indeed fear—forbade them from broaching such matters in mixed company. When the grandfather's son-in-law has to have a prostate gland removed, for instance, Major Manley is horrified that the operation should be reported to him by his own daughter.

The code of honor required strict separation of a man's world from that of a woman's. According to its rubrics, by which Basil Manley lived, a woman ought never to intrude upon the preserves of male indulgence, habit, or circumstance—a prohibition always explained in terms of protecting feminine modesty. Yet it also provided a greater latitude for men about whose activities women were not to learn too much. Such views are alien to the grandson's more egalitarian understanding of the world. Taylor implies that as the South became more industrialized and urban in character, its people became more attuned to the secular styles of the rest of the nation. The ethic that ruled the world of slaves and plantations, Confederate glory, and noble defeat was quickly vanishing, undermining the moral certainties upon which Major Manley took his stand. The narrator admits that he had not thought of such matters at the time. Yet the grandson recalls having felt that "his generation and my own were a thousand years apart" ("MD," 197).

Contrasting the pair in this fashion, however, reveals only part of their relationship. Strangely, both grandson and grandfather need each other as foils to carry on their separate wars for identity. Their incomprehension of the other's sensibilities is a wall that they erect against each other, but also, briefly, it is also a bond of sorts as well. Just as the son refuses to be the "good little boy" his parents expected him to be, so the grandfather rejects the accustomed roles of a quavery, doddering martinet, ignored or laughed at, or of a spinsterlike dependent, "washing up little stacks of dishes" in a relative's house ("MD," 166). Instead, he is himself. Coming to town in his dusty touring car, Basil Manley, age seventy-nine, used to arrive like a Prussian general on inspection, unannounced. He would wear a broad-brimmed hat and worn gabardine topcoat. Usually he would ask such abrupt and unanswerable questions of his citified, immature grandson as: "Young man, what have you to say for yourself?" The question was a blunt assault, a gruff means of distancing himself as if fearing that even this boy might draw him into a demeaning sense of dependence. Major Manley has too much on his mind—his declining powers, his grief for his dead wife, his confusion over the changing world around him. The narrator, as the son reflecting upon his early years, does not give us this perspective. Yet the clues are there in his description of the grandfather's behavior.

Each of three disastrous encounters during the summer of the boy's eighteenth year drive home the differences between them. The first occurs when Grandfather Manley suddenly appears when the son and two friends are helping themselves to the contents of the absent parents' liquor closet. After the scurrying departure of his companions and angry confrontations over the liquor, the grandson enters the room set aside for Major Manley's use and questions him rudely about a famous incident in Manley's past— the time when night riders, involved in a land dispute, kidnapped him and his law partner, killing the latter. While the rednecks were preoccupied with their grisly task, Manley managed to break free and hide in the swamp. Eventually, he returns to civilization, but as a changed and rather resentful figure. (The Reelfoot Lake tragedy was a famous incident in which one of Peter Taylor's grandfathers [Robert Taylor] experienced the same ordeal as Manley does in the story.) [13] We are given no explanations for why Manley, a Civil War veteran who had seen much blood in action, was so painfully affected by the trauma. But the incident clearly had triggered deep feelings of guilt and anxiety for him as the survivor, in contrast to the fate of his partner. As a hostage to fate, as a victim of mindless cruelty, he had learned a rueful lesson of human vulnerability. He had often told his grandson about the incident, clearly as a way to instruct him in the dangers of chaos and the depravities to which all men can sink. But it was also a way to avoid discussion of his youthful Civil War experiences under Nathan Bedford Forrest. The Major had grown wary of talking about those earlier heroics because to do so would mean a capitulation to the conventional conversational mode of other Rebel veterans, who had been compelled to abdicate their liberty and live meekly with their younger kinfolks.

On this occasion, though, the Major refuses to talk about the Reelfoot Lake adventure. The boy begins the account himself. His grandson was half-mocking him, drunkenly seeking his own independence, a freedom from the old man's domination. As the boy rattles on rather incoherently, Manley begins to see in the child something of his own self-possession. The struggle to gain parity with the old man by repeating the old man's story has come too soon. At the end of the contest of wills, smiling wickedly, Major Manley turns aside his grandson's queries and brusquely sends him off to bed.

The struggle over storytelling bears much meaning for an understanding of the South of these separated generations. As historian Darden Pyron recently has pointed out, oral narration empowers the teller. He or she has possession of knowledge that is conveyed by word of mouth. As Pyron notes, the dramatic and disastrous events of Civil War lent the storytelling custom greater urgency than ever before. "Like the Trojan Wars, the 'War for Southern Independence' provided an epic source and object that focused and concentrated the narrative and oral impulse of the South," Pyron writes. Margaret Mitchell, who belonged to the same generation as the author of "In the Miro District," pointed out that her male relatives "didn't talk of these happenings as history nor as remarkable events but just part of their lives and not especially epic parts." [14] Yet, it must be added, the effect upon hearing of narrow escapes from battle death or of a miraculous surmounting of wartime deprivations was to instill a sensation of awe in the listener. That feeling of reverence was not one which the teller wished to dispel. In tradition-bound societies, tales of past deeds or sketches of personalities long since departed help to define an individual, a family, a people. Through narration lessons are provided in how to behave, win fame or favor, and not fall into trouble. This ancient ritual, long since departed from the general American experience, was not to be surrendered lightly at the time Taylor's representation, Basil Manley, lives. The Major, as the writer has it, would tell his stories—ones he chooses—at his own leisure and sense of appropriateness. He would not do so when somebody, even a grandson, makes demands. Yet, in contrast to Pyron's notion of narrative empowerment, mythmakers like the aging Major Manley are mostly themselves on the fringes of power. They enjoy a degree of prestige perhaps, but to whom do they usually retell the old legends and anecdotes? Generally to the very young or to their elderly peers. Active household members have other duties to meet: in the case of the Major and his grandson, the absence of busy parents throws them together.

Like the boy's rude mockery, the offense of youthful overdrinking was meant to demonstrate his coming of age but only proved his continuing state of immaturity. Major Manley had no objection to alcohol as such— far from it. Like other licit male vices, it was supposed to be an indulgence undertaken solely with other men. The old gentleman believes that getting drunk should always be a surreptitious amusement that preferably takes place on hunts in the woods with close friends and never in the presence of women. Such precaution, he feels, "signified respect for the public" sanctions against an undoubted evil. His logic of honor describes the new fashion of drinking in mixed company as a 1920s hypocrisy. The pretense gives the illusion that nothing is morally amiss when in fact order has fallen to ruin. In his view the old code by which he lives calls a spade a spade. At the same time the rubric permits men considerable license. They can do as they wish so long as they do not drag their dependent women into seamy affairs that might become matters of public notoriety.

At the second confrontation, six weeks later, the grandson, once again freed of parents, brings in friends and some low-class girls. The next morning, predictably enough, Manley drives up, discovers the situation, and flails his walking cane on the sleeping couple's bottoms. In like manner, he rouses the other miscreants. Being the old-fashioned patriarch he is, Major Manley feels a sense of noblesse oblige and treats the girls with uncommon courtesy—what Taylor once called a sense of "genuine responsibility" toward young women of "the demi-monde."[15] They respond to the Major's gallantry, gratefully, politely. So, once again the grandson feels that he is outsmarted. He cannot muster the nerve to take on the Major in a heated confrontation that might reveal their mutual antipathy.

In fact, they spend the day cleaning up. Thus, Major Manley conspires, in effect, to hide the incident from parental discovery. The effort, however, does not bring them together. The boy is too insecure, and so, too, in a way, is the old man. In its way, Manley's participation is yet another expression of the ethic by which he so long had lived, and the youth senses it. The Major is simply following the rules of his own class and day in expecting that young men should do such things as part of their growing up. He is not trying to save the boy from humiliation but rather to guard the narrator's mother from revelations of strictly male business. According to the honor code of the Old South, female innocence was a greater value than naked truth. As a result, both grandfather and grandson are engaged in a rather boyish effort to conceal indiscretion, as if the new moral authority were vested in the middle generation and the old man and young one were guilty of infraction. In a sense Major Manley is implicated, too, because throughout the story his course is to stave off—rebelliously—the inevitable dependency of old age.

But the third incident finally snaps the tension and permits outright confrontation—as well as a degree of resolution in their relationship. It takes place when parents and grandfather are all supposed to be at Beersheba, a well-known Tennessee resort. This time the grandson seduces a girl of his own social class. Moreover, at the house on Division Street in Nashville, the young couple, very much in love, spend the day in Grandfather Manley's room, which was always set aside for him, amidst the ugly, cranky furniture. They make love in his bed, no doubt the one in which the old man will come eventually to die. The site symbolizes the transfer of power and life from the very old to the very young. It dramatically represents the death of the Old South's traditions which the previous contests over drinking and wenching prefigured. Recognizing that he does not belong to the new country club generation, the Major is unable to stand the "swells" or their city manners at Beersheba Springs and abruptly departs. He turns up at his daughter's house on Division Street. The Major hopes to find at last some grounds for a rapprochement with his grandson.

Nonetheless, the secret is soon exposed. This time, Manley reacts with silent indignation upon discovering the naked Ward Belmont schoolgirl in the wardrobe and departs. Taylor emphasizes the naturalness of the young couple's making love, casting it as an authentic experience. It serves as hard commentary challenging the repressiveness of the chivalric code, false and empty, that the grandfather still espouses.[16] The boy's violation of his grandfather's bed in an act of unabashed passion represents the decisive overthrow of southern honor, a rebellion that sweeps away its tattered remains. That violation may be understandable—eighteen-year-olds will experiment. The narrator recalls the lovemaking with pleasure. Yet, the reader can see how it would be a most disagreeable and even humiliating episode for the grandfather. The moral perspective of the Major has been challenged. He still believes that women are either all good or all evil, and that good ones never give themselves in love outside of marriage. Thus, he could even smile to himself at the earlier episode. To make love with a respectable, marriageable girl, however, is almost beyond imagining. Still more important, Manley realized that the boy has deliberately profaned his territory in order to stake out his claim as a new source of power in the family circle. It is almost a primitive act of replacement—the old patriarch must make way for the new authority. Major Manley had hoped that the grandson would understand his values and appreciate his life, but instead, he had met with boyish defiance and then overthrow.

Thus the crisis brings on the final defeat of Manley's long-maintained autonomy and the shattering of his outmoded faith in gentlemanly reticence, family honor, and the proper separation of the sexes. Never again does he wear the gabardine coat. He puts on a string tie; he attends Confederate jamborees. For years he had refused to join his cohorts at these annual affairs for fear that he would receive promotion to colonel as all the other veterans had, regardless of their wartime rank. Moreover, with "his cheeks wet with tears," he, "like an old general," accepts the terms of surrender with soldierly fortitude ("MD," 200). He agrees to live in Nashville, moves his handsome farmhouse four-poster bed and other furniture into his room, and renounces his old life in the decrepit farmhouse. He gives up driving the touring car. These details reveal that when Major Manley left behind his old rural life, he signified his recognition that his generational authority had to be relinquished and acknowledged resignation to death itself.

Formerly Manley told stories only in the bosom of the family about the fearsome Reelfoot Lake kidnapping and the hallucinations about the legendary New Madrid Earthquake of 1811 which haunted him during his escape through the swamps. These tales are emblematic of his link with a primitive world stretching back from the Old South to prehistory, but their telling was strictly to enlighten his kindred. It was a part of family, not of public culture. In his changed role, he tells Confederate war anecdotes to the admiration of the young fraternity boys whom he meets at the house or club. No longer does he decide what stories to recount and when. Instead, he ritualistically regales an audience upon demand. At one time, master of the situation, he becomes the servant of his listeners. Thus, Taylor provides us with a curious resolution. At last Grandfather Manley has come to recognize that he is living in another world so different from his youth that he might as well enter into the role expected of him. The patriarchal order has disappeared. He is simply an impotent old man. "In those days in Nashville," Taylor recalls in his story, "having a Confederate veteran around the place was comparable to having a peacock on the lawn, or, if not that at least comparable to having one's children in the right schools. It was something anybody liked to have" ("MD," 201).

Nowadays the old are compelled to play a submerged and generally irrelevant role in the American tribal system, Taylor seems to say. If "lawn ornament" is the customary designation for the aged, then so be it. Lacking the means to insist upon respect for his autonomy, Basil Manley turns in the end toward those of his own age—the Confederate veterans. He joins their reunions, marches in their parades, and accepts the colonelcy so long resisted as a debasement of the war's meaning. Yet such a submersion into the mass of his cohorts only reinforces the anonymity and powerlessness that old age entails. The victory of the middle-aged—the parental generation— is complete. But, of course, their triumph must eventually give way to their own defeat years later. The middle generation still holds to the outward forms of the old principles but no longer practices them.

Should we see the grandfather's domestication as a healthy reconciliation with the passage of time? Is it a new maturity in which the limitations of aging are at last accepted? Or does it signify a death of the spirit, a capitulation imposed for tawdry reasons of convenience and gentle amusement for the middle generation, confidently in command? The answer that the writer, through the voice of the narrator, leaves for us is deliberately and artfully left unclear. On the one hand, the grandson and narrator has learned something of identity, the beauty of love, and has come to see that his own generation had been liberated from a repressed and repressive code of honor. The vitality that Major Manley had once enjoyed has suddenly dissolved. The grandson's part in destroying it acts as a means of empowerment—or does it? The answer is revealed in the narrative itself. In his evident decline the Major cannot fully distinguish between his grandson and the other admiring college boys who listen to his stories of General Forrest and conjectures on the strategies of the war. He answers his grandson's questions as politely as he does those of the others. The Major does not merely suffer from a natural forgetfulness and vagueness that may come with old age. The young man has himself become incorporated into his age cohort: he now belongs, a goal long sought. He has melted into the crowd. In this respect both grandson and grandfather have adopted the roles which society has designed for them, and in the process they have both gained in social acceptability. The one does so, however, in promise of bright future, the other in anticipation of death. Yet they both, too, have lost in the breaking of their connection as male rivals for that yearned-for incorporation, so to speak. And both are somewhat morally diminished in submitting to the pressures of convention.

One senses that the author laments the loss of individuality and old family links that the generational battle revealed—even as the writer recognizes their primitive character and imperfection. Yet, true to his craft, he allows the narrator to draw a rather idyllic picture of the old man as keeper of the region's memory of an honorable past. In an interview Taylor admitted that the old man "faced things more realistically toward the end of the story, after he saw a different set of mores in the city." [17]

Nonetheless, the reader must question the reliability of Taylor's narrators in these stories, as in many others. The author himself has hinted as much. He notes that by reverting to the role of Civil War veteran, Major Manley "is defeated by a changing world." [18] This kind of irresolution in which both the contradictions and the benefits of intergenerational conflict are so simply rendered is the essence of Taylor's art. As a writer aware of the aging process—in himself and in others—he has learned that for some questions there are no answers and no solutions, no right and wrong. In his view this truth offers cause to be neither cynical nor despairing. Even though younger critics and readers sometimes become impatient with such signs of incompleteness, writers in their maturity like Taylor make us aware of life's complications. They apprehend the ambiguities which we all must face in a world of shifting values. Thus, the author furnishes no easy reconciliations. Instead, he sees the marginality of the old—but also the young— as part of everyone's experience in life. The lesson is perhaps simple, but in its simplicity Taylor discovers the tensions and pain of ordinary living that he so skillfully lays bare.

Notes

1. J. William Broadway, "A Conversation with Peter Taylor" (1985), 80; Jane Barnes Casey, "A View of Peter Taylor's Stories, 215; Herschel Gower, "The Nashville Stories," 37–47. An exception is a paper by Anne Wyatt-Brown, "Approaches to Gender Issues in Molly Keane and Peter Taylor," which concerns Taylor's Pulitzer Prize–winning novel, *Summons to Memphis.*

2. Broadway, "Conversation," 95. Apart from short popular newspaper reviews and the articles mentioned herein, the chief studies of Taylor's writings are relatively

slim; they include Andrew Lytle, "The Displaced Family," 115–20; Albert J. Griffith, *The Achievement of Peter Taylor;* Alan Williamson, "Identity and the Wider Eros," 71–84; James Curry Robison, *Peter Taylor.*

3. Margaret E. Kuhn and Jeanne E. Bader, "Old and Young Are Alike in Many Ways," 274; see also Richard A. Easterlin, Christine MacDonald, and Diane J. Macunovich, "Retirement Prospects of the Baby Boom Generation," 776–83; and Nancy J. Chapman and Margaret B. Neal, "The Effects of Intergenerational Experiences on Adolescents and Older Adults," 825–32.

4. Casey, "Peter Taylor's Stories," 215, 219.

5. See Jaber F. Gubrium, *Life and Death at Murray Manor,* 140.

6. On one occasion Peter Taylor declared: "My father used to say, 'There are no old gentlemen in the South. The old ladies seem to go on reproducing old ladies without the old gentlemen.' And it was true" (Broadway, "Conversation," 80).

7. Wendy Smith, "*PW* Interviews: Peter Taylor," 63.

8. W. Hampton Sides, "Interview with Peter Taylor," 134; Jan Pinkerton, "The Non-Regionalism of Peter Taylor," 434.

9. Broadway, "Conversation," 96.

10. Kuhn and Bader, "Old and Young," 274; Broadway, "Conversation," 96; see Bertram Wyatt-Brown, *Southern Honor.*

11. Broadway, "Conversations," 90.

12. Wyatt-Brown, *Southern Honor,* 35–40, 52–54.

13. Louise Davis, "Just Who Was That Ward-Belmont Girl Nude in the Closet?" 23.

14. Mitchell and Pyron quoted in Pyron, *Southern Daughter,* 35.

15. Don Keck Dupree, "An Interview with Peter Taylor," 57.

16. Casey, "Peter Taylor's Stories," 223.

17. Davis, "Just Who Was?" 27.

18. Ibid.; Robert Brickhouse, "Peter Taylor," 53.

DIANA HUME GEORGE

"Keeping Our Working Distance": Maxine Kumin's Poetry of Loss and Survival

To be a poet in a destitute time means: to attend, singing, to the trace of the fugitive gods. This is why the poet in the time of the world's night utters the holy."
—Martin Heidegger

A DECADE AGO I began a sustained reading of modern and contemporary women poets on the subjects of memory, mortality, and aging in the literature of the life cycle. Exploring Denise Levertov, May Sarton, Marie Ponsat, May Swenson, and Muriel Rukeyser, I found that the writing of women poets on aging is confrontational, angry, tender, and unashamed. Their works indicate that they wish to do the work of aging, and of facing their own deaths, with fearlessness. But their poetry records the process of confronting their fear rather than the accomplishment of having defeated it. Theirs are poems of death and loss, and they would permit me no wishful projection that mature poets of demonstrated achievement, and presumably personal wisdom, had come entirely to terms with mortality or aging.[1] What I did find was that such poets use their fears, deliberately and creatively. Their works embody the fact that we all, as we age, tally our losses, remember what has passed, think of our personal histories, our families, our unfinished business.

Memory and loss have always been among Maxine Kumin's primary subjects, and in that respect her poetry has consistently shared the preoccupation that becomes more concentrated in older poets. When Kumin was in her fifties, she wrote a series of elegies to deal with the loss of Anne Sexton, whose biography by Diane Wood Middlebrook was a controversial best-seller of 1991. Anne Sexton and Maxine Kumin had been dear friends from the time they met in a Boston poetry workshop in the late fifties until Sexton's death by suicide in 1974. Their friendship surprised many people in the poetry community because they seemed to be opposites in almost every respect, both personally and poetically. Sexton, though she became a fine crafter of poetry, was unschooled and unintellectual, whereas Kumin was steeped in the great traditions of English formalism. Sexton's apprenticeship began in the mental asylum, Kumin's in universities and libraries. Sexton wrote uninhibitedly about her own madness and suicide attempts, but Kumin's early work was restrained, formal, decorous. In person Sexton was outgoing, often flamboyant, while Kumin's style was understated. Yet for seventeen years, they were inseparable, raising their children together, enduring deaths and losses, and always keeping the work at the heart of their lives. They workshopped their poems together over kitchen tables and telephones year after year, serving as each other's editors as well as soulmates and sisters.

The ultimate contrast between them became survival: Sexton chose to die, and Kumin chose to live. Cast by Sexton's death into the personal and poetic role of "survivor," Kumin spoke of endurance in direct connection to life-cycle issues. Now in her sixties, Kumin continues to represent and embody the survivor. In the late 1980s and early 1990s she makes it a matter of stubborn celebration as well as of constant, subtle, necessary mourning. The mourning of loss, particularly of loss generated by mortality, remains fundamental to her poetic vision. Her recent poetry, especially *Nurture* (1989) and *Looking for Luck* (1992), develops and sustains the terms of survival and endurance first fully articulated in the period following Sexton's death.

Here I discuss Kumin's elegies to Anne Sexton, especially as they apply to the issues of aging, loss, and survival for the living poet. I also look at the ways in which the representational aspects of poetic language make her poetry not only elegiac but in some respects epitaphic. The mourning of loss generated by mortality and the representation of absence remain fundamental to her recent poetry and to what I would call her poetics.

Kumin's poems to Sexton demonstrated the double haunting of lyric elegy—the poet haunted the dead as she herself was haunted.[2] Through the dream site of elegy, Kumin attempted in the late 1970s and early 1980s to come to terms with her own middle age and her mortality. She "gathered up our words," both to fend off aging and to ready herself for it. While Sexton remained in the perpetual youth purchased by the flight from life, Kumin grew into the middle age that transformed her from the dead poet's "sister" into her "mother." Kumin's haunting by Sexton is overlaid by the living poet's words, carved as a monument to her (and our) mortality.

The five poems to Anne Sexton in *Our Ground Time Here Will Be Brief* (some reprinted from *The Retrieval System*) participate in an old poetic tradition: an address by a living poet to a dead poet much loved or admired. Sexton's death left Kumin, as she says in "Apostrophe to a Dead Friend," with a tremendous burden to carry, "like a large infant, on one hip": "I who am remaindered in the conspiracy, / doom, doom on my lips" (*GT*, 24). The large infant is carried on the hip of a poet past her childbearing years, a woman experiencing the aging her friend escaped and preparing for the death Sexton embraced in an untimely hurry. Kumin knows she will never fully recover from this loss. How could it be otherwise, for the poet-sister left alive, who wears the dead poet's clothes, her shoes, who must "put my hands in your death / as into the carcass of a stripped turkey?" Yet this infant, this stripped carcass, instructs the survivor on how to endure into the night of life.

"Where Presence—is denied them, they fling their speech," wrote Emily Dickinson. Poetry has always taken as one of its domains the representation of loss, has always attempted to give body to memory, flesh to ghostly form. Karen Mills-Courts calls the spectral power of the written word essential rather than incidental to poetry; she suggests that poetic language is both epitaphic and elegiac, that every linguistic gesture can be seen as a kind of speaking monument. During the act of writing, every poet becomes, momentarily, a carver of gravestones. Even as one constitutes a self through writing, that self slips away at the moment of inscription, so that the haunting is always double, the gravestone carved always that of the poet as well as whom she intends to memorialize. Wordsworth called the human urge to memorialize in epitaphs our "tender fiction"—we bring the dead to life through the process of inscription.[3]

Especially since Sexton's death, Kumin has engaged in the tradition of the "tender fiction," continuously developing and playing upon the extent to which her poems about the dead become a part of her attempt to ready herself for death. The voice in her poems is her own, however highly mediated it is by representational considerations. She observes death and loss in the barn, the pasture, the woods, as well as in the rooms of her life, with clear-eyed, clean-sighted toughness. Life is irrepressibly stubborn and delightful, and throughout her work she knows that it will renew itself, will go on without her. In "A Mortal Day of No Surprises" (*GT*, 86), the speaker watches the abundance of life—a frog in the pasture bathtub, weeds in the zucchini patch, sparrows making their "departmental claims," the dog bringing in "one half a rank / woodchuck no angel spoke up for"—and fits her own into the recurring cycle this way:

When I'm scooped out of here
all things animal
and unsurprised will carry on . . .
me gone to crumbs in the ground
and someone else's mare to call
to the stallion.

Kumin is thus elaborately aware of how she uses her observations in the natural world and their connection to the fact of her own death. Loss and death are Kumin's dominant themes in the poetry of the 1970s and 1980s, in poems to and about her uncles, her brother, her animals, her Anne. And although many of these poems were written before Anne Sexton's death, that death seems to have allowed her to do sustained instead of intermittent mourning. When her poetry grows from solidity to stunning power, it does so in the elegiac tradition, as dirge; nor is this strength divorced from celebration, for it is the infinitely renewed mystery of life, as well as its brutality, that Kumin sings of and mourns. As the survivor who nevertheless knows that anyone's survival is only temporary, she uses her poetry to come to terms with as many permanent losses as she can before that final loss of self. Kumin's own statement on the purposes of poetry reflects her understanding: "I believe very strongly that poetry is essentially elegiac in its nature, and that all poems are in one sense or another elegies. Love poems, particularly, are elegies because if we were not informed with a sense of dying we wouldn't be moved to write love poems. The best love poems have that element of longing in them, that either they'll lose that love or that time will take it away. Behind the love poem there's always that sense of regret, that sense of doom." In this respect love poems are essentially elegiac, for they cast before them what Kumin calls "the premonitory shadow of your own mortality." [4]

In Kumin's poems to Sexton in the early 1980s, the conversation between the live and the dead poet has gone on for nearly a decade; we overhear on occasion. Sexton joins Kumin in every activity of daily life: while she is walking in the woods, cutting and splitting logs, flying over Paris, listening to the pope in St. Peter's Square. Kumin picks up each conversation in medias res, lending a sense of immediacy and intimacy. In all of these poems Kumin entangles her complicated passions toward this dearest friend: she is loving, compassionate, bereaved, betrayed, sometimes ironic to the point of bitterness.

The first line of "How It Is" (*GT*, 86) becomes an underlying theme for the series: "Shall I say how it is in your clothes?" The intimate paradoxes of their sisterhood are continually symbolized by this neat, biographical, entirely feminine detail: Kumin's and Sexton's shoe sizes were the same, their clothing sizes close enough that they could share everything from a blue jacket to "public-occasion costumes." Who shares clothes this way? Sisters and friends who call themselves sisters. When Kumin wears Sexton's clothing after her death—"A month after your death I wear your blue jacket"—she is in a sense trying on that other self who died by her own hand to escape old age and despair, to check the fit. "My skin presses your old outline." The question of identity between the living poet and the dead friend becomes and remains central. This otherwise self-possessed speaker, who knows perfectly well who she is, must keep calling into question that knowledge when she thinks of her friend. Repeatedly the poems declare: I know who I am; and then they ask: but since who I am has so much to do with you, then who am I without you?

Still in Sexton's jacket, Kumin runs the home movie backward, from "the death car idling in the garage," through the rituals Sexton used to prepare for her death that day, to "a space / we could be easy in, a kitchen place" where they sit and speak together, "our words like living meat." The unspoken allusion is perhaps to the dead meat of the body that no longer speaks, for both Sexton and Kumin had used the metaphor of the body as meat. "Our words" is the object of the poet's wish, and also the richly troubled legacy of Sexton's death, as Kumin says in the end of "How It Is": "I will be years gathering up our words, / fishing out letters, snapshots, stains, / leaning my ribs against this durable cloth / to put on the dumb blue blazer of your death."

To "gather up our words" is to claim them, to put them back together, to hoard them as the only constants left, to use them both to mourn what has passed and to celebrate what still lives; it is also to claim them from and give them back to both poets' readers: writing this poem is part of the "gathering." In this first poem Kumin has conflated Sexton's dead absence and her living presence in the doubly haunted metaphors of clothing and words. Now that Sexton has gone, the living poet-friend must wear her clothing and speak their collective words from within the dumb blue blazer of Sexton's death. She must grow slowly, painfully, from within that death, to an acceptance of it; and she must also learn to lean into her aging body and its eventual death.

In "Progress Report," Kumin keeps Anne Sexton informed about how life is without her, two years after her death, and it is here that she is first specific about the aging process. "The middle age you wouldn't wait / for now falls on me" as the speaker walks through the woods, fighting her way through gnats and blackflies. There is less time now, and perhaps less need, for comforting the absent friend or reassuring her that the one left behind understands. Kumin had expected, after all, to share this time of life with Anne Sexton, and since she is alone in the flesh, it is her own dilemma, and not Sexton's, that concerns her. Her eye watches what is permanent: time goes on, marked by regular rhythms and returns, and the only constant is this loss. Last year's scarlet tanager, "a red / rag flagging from tree to tree," lends a "rakish permanence to / the idea of going on without you." The smile in that line is grim; for her "empty times"

> still rust like unwashed dogfood cans
> and my nights fill up with porcupine
> dung he drops on purpose at
> the gangway to the aluminum-
> flashed willow, saying that
> he's been here, saying he'll come
> back with his tough waddle, his pig eyes,
> saying he'll get me yet. ("Progress Report," *GT*, 51)

The haplessly vicious porcupine is more than incidentally connected with Sexton's death: "He is / the stand-in killer I use / to notarize your suicide." No sun-yellow souls here—only the open-eyed, frankly acknowledged desperation of just how bad the bad times are, just how stupidly horrible the natural world becomes when seen through the refracting lens of this senseless death that would not await the natural process of aging.

From this grotesque image of the world gone unaccountably awry, Kumin turns to a vision of possible peace to be wrested from this moment of madness. She notes that Thomas Mann's permit to take refuge in Switzerland said, "For literary activities and the passage of life's evening." She wonders if his loved and dear dead came to him in reverie there, "he taking both parts, working it out." She sees that she has been doing much the same thing with Anne Sexton, "Me taking both parts in what / I suppose is my life's afternoon." She seems to find this both faintly ridiculous and comforting, this dialogue with the dead friend with whom she had always supposed she would have time to work it out. She is compelled to keep talking to this dead love, compelled to both ask the questions and answer them in words she imagines Sexton might say. As in "Splitting Wood," the medium of their communication is dreaming:

> Dear friend, last night I dreamed
> you held a sensitive position,

you were Life's Counselor,
coming to the phone in Vaud or Bern,
some terse one-syllable place,
to tell me how to carry on. ("Progress Report," *GT,* 52)

For both Maxine Kumin and Anne Sexton, the dream is at the root of
poetry. Kumin speaks of "the nightmare of one's choice," as described by
Conrad in *Heart of Darkness:* "One must descend into the abyss and dream
the nightmare of one's choice and dream it through to the very end." She
will endure the decay of the organism, unpleasant though it be. For the
period of her life beginning in 1974, Anne Sexton's death seems to be the
nightmare of her choice. Waking from this dream, Kumin swears to Sexton
that she

will break
your absence into crumbs
like the stump of a punky tree
working its way down
in the world's evening
down to the forest floor. ("Progress Report," *GT,* 52)

The movement of the metaphor is double and even contradictory, for Kumin
will break Sexton's absence into crumbs that will finally, like the punky
tree, disintegrate down into the forest floor. She seems to be saying both
that she will finish with this loss once and for all by breaking down what's
left of Sexton, forgetting her, learning to be done with the dead, and at
the same time that it is only Sexton's absence that will break into crumbs,
leaving the distillation of her presence, her very essence.

Another several years pass before "Apostrophe to a Dead Friend." As a
continued progress report, "Apostrophe" has many confidences to impart.
Everything is still the same; yet everything is different as Kumin ages, as
Sexton's death and life recede:

It fades, the glint of those afternoons
we lay in the sun by the pond.
Paler, the intimate confidences.
Even the distances we leapt in poems
have shrunk. No more parapets. ("Apostrophe," *GT,* 24)

With flat frankness, Kumin details what happens when you stay alive and
embrace the aging process. The men have "grown smaller, drier, / easier to
refuse;" their mutual children, grown up into "exacting adults," are "no

kinder or wiser than we." Kumin won't pretend otherwise. Yet the poem has begun with the same event that began "How It Is" years before; an interview with Sexton's biographer has stripped her back down to "the bones of this person / whose shoe size was your size / who traded dresses in our pool / of public-occasion costumes."

If the years have made her somewhat less sentimentally attached to "the glint of those afternoons," it still takes very little to bring her back to "How It Is." "Apostrophe" ends on the note of doubleness that began it, calling over the chasm of the distance that separates them, yet whispering into the ear right next to her mouth:

> Soon I will be sixty.
> How it was with you now
> hardly more vivid than how
> it is without you. ("Apostrophe," *GT*, 24)

It has been nearly a decade, at the time of this poem, and Kumin has had to develop some distance from that death. As always, Kumin tells her dead friend the truth: that Sexton has faded, that life grows more constricted as we age. The time between Sexton's death and this poem is almost half the number of years of their friendship, and Kumin has been busy living in the intervening years—and changing. For these two women poets who came together over creative acts that included both poems and babies, the "large infant, on one hip" is an especially powerful image. Kumin, old enough to be a grandparent now, carries the weight of the "telling" of this old love like a baby who never grew up. Locked in the past, the "infant" of their relationship has not grown up, or older, with Kumin. Just as Sexton would not wait for her own middle age, Kumin will not be able to stop her own old age from arriving. Perhaps that is the "doom, doom on my lips": she, like Sexton, will someday die, and with her, their old conspiracy.

In "Itinerary of an Obsession," Kumin speaks to Sexton in a voice as newly raw as it is familiar.[5] The isolated notes of bitter irony in the other poems here gather into a chiding chorus of resentment, both good-humored and earnest. The "Obsession" of the title is the speaker's concern with Sexton's death—and with her own as she ages. She is telling Sexton the story of her trip to the Holy Land with a "planeload of pilgrims, / none under seventy."

All through the trip to the Holy Land that this poem describes, we might infer that Kumin, in however secular a fashion, is searching out some spiritual truth. Yet even here she is haunted by visions of Anne Sexton dead, Anne Sexton alive, Anne Sexton resurrected and restored to her. Sexton's own search was for transcendent sacredness, for a patriarchal God of unquestionable authority and comfort. Kumin's search seems to be for connection of the human sort, transcendent over aging and time. While Sexton searched for God, Kumin searched for whatever it was she had, and lost, with Anne Sexton: a friendship stronger than death, a solidarity of souls that must continue. "Words are the only 'holy' for me. The only sanctity really, for me, is the sanctity of language."[6] That language is the words between friends who are poets—"our words like living meat"—words turned by Sexton's death into a "carcass," which the living poet must try to reconstruct. She can do so, in these poems, only by bringing Sexton back from the grave. And she does so one final time in the last section of "Itinerary," where she finds that even if she "dreams of you less," she is still obsessed:

> Still, when the phone rings in my sleep
> and I answer, a dream-cigarette in my hand,
> it is always the same. We are back at our posts,
> hanging around like boxers in
> our old flannel bathrobes. You haven't changed.
> I, on the other hand, am forced to grow older.
> How I am almost your mother's age.
> Imagine it! Did you think you could escape?
> Eventually I'll arrive in her
> abhorrent marabou negligee
> trailing her scarves like broken promises
> crying yoo-hoo! Anybody home? ("Itinerary," *GT,* 23)

Recalling their old friendship, one of sisters and equals, the poet asks her dead friend to imagine the impossibility that she has been left to become the age of the monumental parental presence of Sexton's mother, Mary Gray. In these final lines of "Itinerary," Kumin transforms herself into Mary Gray and follows Sexton to the grave, arriving as a gaudy, inappropriately dressed ghost who promises to continue disturbing Sexton's sleep. Because she is now Mary Gray's age, she can take on her identity by the same act through which she has taken on Sexton's identity throughout the series: she is wearing the dead woman's clothes.

As Kumin wanders up the mountain with her body, which she called "Old Paint, Old Partner," in this "sedate roundup" in the "meander of our middle age," looking for the "same old cracked tablets," her "airmail half-ounce soul" touches tongues with "Old Paint"; but "somehow it seems less sure; / somehow it seems we've come / too far to get us there" ("Body and Soul," *GT,* 66).

It was in part by working through Anne Sexton's death, and through the relationship between Sexton's body, so like Kumin's, and Sexton's soul, that small round entity like a "sun-yellow daisy heart," that Kumin tried in this middle period of her life and her poetry to unite her own body and soul, always uneasy partners. Sexton gave up the search. Kumin was left to puzzle her way through, aware that "our ground time here will be brief."

Since the mature period signaled by the publication of *The Retrieval System* and building through *Our Ground Time Here Will Be Brief, The Long Approach, Nurture,* and *Looking for Luck,* Maxine Kumin's poetry is fundamentally informed by the mourning of loss, such as we have seen in the Sexton elegies. While her earlier work included occasional poems of mourning for particular deaths or losses, *The Retrieval System* (1978) announced her clear intention to get down to the necessary business of confronting and then mourning loss, in the lived and in the written life. But this conscious embrace of mourning is not by any means a rejection of celebration. Quite the contrary: to live in the presence of a cultivated (self)-consciousness is to understand the necessity of loss, and to mourn it so that one may continue to live, so that one may experience delight.

The titles of three consecutive Kumin volumes clarify her position. "Fact: it is people who fade, / it is animals that retrieve them." The title poem of *The Retrieval System* indicates the nature of that system, i.e., the explicit, transmuted recovery of the dead. *Our Ground Time Here Will Be Brief* has its source in the pun on airport announcements between flights; the analogy, of course, is to the shortness of the human life span. And *The Long Approach* is the approach to death as well as from air to ground. The Sexton elegies appear in *Ground Time* and *Retrieval,* where fistfuls of other poems sustain the mood of mourning. "In Memoriam P.W., Jr., 1921–1980," for instance, is a series of five poems for her dead brother.

The P.W. poems are different from the Sexton elegies in that the latter were composed over a period of years, thus most comprehensively signaling continuity in the mourning process; but in her two most recent collections, *Nurture* (1989) and *Looking for Luck* (1992), the beloved brother rises again, among the Kumin pantheon of dead aunts, cousins, parents, and living daughters, husband, son, and grandson, all the faces native to Kumin who form the core of the lifelong series she calls her "tribal poems." Even the mother-daughter poems, sustained over a period of decades, take mourning as their primary subject, beginning or ending in the leave-takings of physical or psychic separation.

Kathleen Woodward proposes the recognition of a state in between mourning and melancholia. As distinct from mourning, melancholia is a pathological state of mind, not a normal psychic process with a clear ending. Freud defined it as failed or unsuccessful mourning. Woodward finds that Freud "leaves us here with no room for another place, one between a crippling melancholia and the end of mourning." For some people, she argues, come to terms with their grief by learning to live with their pain. Moreover, she insists "that the distinction between mourning and melancholia has been cut too sharply, that we may point to something *in between* mourning and melancholia, that we may refer to a grief which is interminable but not melancholic in the psychoanalytic sense." Woodward contends that we all find mourning more difficult yet more familiar as we grow older and losses accumulate—and as we approach our own deaths.[7] In the women poets whose work I explored ten years ago, Woodward's theory certainly holds true: the quality of a continuous, even a cultivated mourning suffuses many of their finest poems, but it is in no sense pathological, dysfunctional, or debilitating, not the symptom of a disorder or a diseased mind.

I propose an essential in-betweenness as central to Kumin's vision, even to what might properly be termed her poetics. Perhaps, indeed, a state of continuous and sustained mourning is the necessary province of the poet— in which case Kumin is among its most deliberate practitioners, believing, as we have seen, that poetry is essentially elegiac, that it casts before it that haunting "premonitory shadow of your own mortality." The best lyric poets have always known this. Wordsworth called his poetry a "speaking monument" in *The Prelude*. And Hopkins expressed it eloquently in "Spring and Fall: To a Young Child," where he asks, "Margaret, are you grieving / Over Goldengrove unleaving?" Kumin's speaker knows Hopkins's answer: "It is the blight man was born for, / It is Margaret you mourn for." I choose the examples of Wordsworth and Hopkins carefully in their connection to Kumin, for it is through the observation of nature, fundamental to the Romantic and post-Romantic vision, that she attempts to come to terms with the blight.

While Kumin herself eschews the practice of theory about poetry, she has commented in her poetry on one of the great theorists, Heidegger.

> It is true, Martin Heidegger, as you have written,
> *I fear to cease,* even knowing that at the hour
> of my death my daughters will absorb me, even
> knowing they will carry me about forever
> inside them, an arrested fetus, even as I carry
> the ghost of my mother under my navel, a nervy
> little androgynous person, a miracle
> folded in lotus position. ("The Envelope," *GT,* 65)

Heideggerean hermeneutics seeks meaning, while deconstruction insists that meaning is only an illusory effect of an illusory system. Karen Mills-Courts uses Heidegger and Jacques Derrida to discuss theories of language that are incarnative on the one hand and representational on the other. Heidegger's central figure is of "gathering" (which we have seen literalized in Kumin's "gathering up our words"), Derrida's of "dissemination." While Heidegger thinks of language as presentational and incarnative, Derrida and deconstruction treat it as ungrounded representation. And while Heidegger insists on the unconcealment of "meaning," Derrida dismantles the very concept. Caught between the fundamental conflicts about the nature of consciousness articulated in our time by these theories, many poets create poetry that is overtly intended to work as "unconcealment," as the incarnation of a presence, the embodiment of a voice in words. Yet, says Mills-Courts, he or she displays that voice as an inscription carved on a tombstone. Poetry must function between the presentational and representational workings of language. It attempts to incarnate meaning and intelligibility, even perhaps Truth; but "no choice between representational and incarnative language is genuinely possible." The speaking monument of poetry presents this contradiction: "The maintenance of presence and its undermining occur in the same gesture." [8]

Poets, aware that their attempts to incarnate meaning are met with the limits of representation, grant poetry the same "privileges" one grants a gravestone. Having written extensively on burial stones, epitaphs, and iconography, I count the privileges of the monument, and our suspension of a certain kind of disbelief in its honor and presence, as considerable. [9] If lyric poems share the province of the monument, their work is monumental in every respect. They assert, as does the memorial, that inscription makes a difference, points to or even creates significance, expresses or incarnates loss, gives body to the memory of spirit, stands meaningfully at the intersection between the living and dead, between consciousness and its end.

Poetry, for Heidegger, reveals to the self its relationship to its own death. "It is true," declares Kumin, "*I fear to cease.*" Heidegger suggests that any evasion of this relationship creates a dearth of meaning. Poets must believe that their work offers, in one way or another, the lighting projection of truth: "This possibility motivates writing. Yet, most good poets have always understood that, as representation, poetry is always threatened by the possibility that words betray truth. As a result, poetry exists in an 'in-between' state, located on a fine-honed edge between the desire to present the 'thing-itself' and the knowledge that language can only stand in place of that thing." [10]

Maxine Kumin enacts the poetic form of this knowledge in any number of her mature works. She is explicit about the self-deceiving "tender fiction" Wordsworth associated with the epitaph form and with all poetic endeavor—and of its necessary attempt to embody presence in the process of composition:

> Poetry
> makes nothing happen.
> It survives
> in the valley of its saying.
> Auden taught us that.
> Next year another
> Consultant will sit
> under the hand with the arrow
> that props the door ajar
> for metaphor.
> New poets will lie on their backs
> listening in the valley
> making nothing happen
> overhearing history
> history time
> personal identity
> inching toward Armageddon.
>> ("Lines Written in the Library of Congress after
>> the Cleanth Brooks Lecture," *GT*, 36–42)

Brooks had spoken of history, time, and personal identity as three touchstones of poetry. Kumin was then the Library of Congress consultant in poetry, thus occupying a ritual place in the history of poetry she sometimes found faintly amusing, perhaps even self-parodic. In "Revisiting the MacDowell Colony," she echoes Hopkins while acknowledging that poets behave as if poetry mattered and as if poetry were connected to Wordsworth's intimations of immortality instead of its opposite. Visiting poets have signed the plaque above the hearth, "as evidence of tenancy and worth," but there are "too many pale ones gone to smudges:" "Use a penknife, I advise my friend, / then ink each letter for relief / —as if a name might matter / against the falling leaf" ("Revisiting," *GT*, 33).

It is such grim but light-hearted parody of poetic vocation that she deploys to make sure she does not take herself, or her vocation, too seriously. But of course she does take it seriously, because she believes in the sacredness of poetic language. What she cultivates is the in-betweenness expressed in poems such as "The Envelope." Here she confronts fear simply and cleanly, but then, once again with combined seriousness and self-parody (another kind of in-betweenness), she indulges in the fantasy of endurance through inheritance, embodying yet another "tender fiction" that is also, in Stevens's famous phrasing, supreme. The second section ends the poem with a half-tongue-in-cheek hope, intoned through a grammatical construction that both expresses a wish and confers a blessing: "May we, borne onward by our daughters, ride / in the Envelope of Almost-Infinity" (*GT*, 65). This though she knows that it is through reproduction that death announces itself, as she wrote much earlier: "But let there be / no mistaking how the dark scheme runs." The huntsman brings the mother a heart, which she eats, thinking it is the daughter's. "And as we both know, at the appropriate moment / I will be consumed by an inexorable fire / as you look on" ("The Fairest One of All," *GT*, 176). But she will have it both ways, alternating between a vision of death that seals a curse and another that confers a blessing. Her own mother's death was good. In her barn she hauls a hay bale, "and with my free hand pull / your easy death along" ("February," *GT*, 21).

In the work she has completed in her sixties, Kumin contemplates mutability, aging, and mortality by intensifying her alternating gaze: inward toward family and heritage in variations of the tribal poems and outward toward the natural environment. This shifting gaze extends her essential in-betweenness; she looks outward, then inward, outward, then inward, as if to say that the two perspectives need each other in order to avoid sentimentality or self-absorption on the one hand or rigid detachment and objectification on the other. The result is what she herself calls her "working distance," one that allows for, even insists on, legitimate forms of intimacy within the constraints of individual consciousness and inevitable difference. The self mediates and interpenetrates the world of the other, the human the world of the nonhuman; body becomes, as nearly as she can envision, the domain of soul.

In the recent *Nurture,* a volume replete with the doubleness of her acknowledged fictions, Kumin conflates these issues with the other enduring subject of her poetry: the relationship of humanity to nature. The clear and present delights of the natural world and our connections with it as creatures who know we are part of it infuse her sense of responsibility toward more fragile forms of life on the planet we share. She continues to express the necessity of endurance in the face of odds we cannot finally beat.

Kumin's stature as a nature poet, far from distancing her work from the poet of "consciousness," unites the two endeavors in an emblematically modernist Romanticism. While she is largely without the sentimentality we associate with the Romantics in their efforts at union with, and idealization of, nature, they were perhaps less dedicated to that sentimental vision than we have thought. Wordsworth says that the end of the journey in *The Prelude* is not reunion with nature but a courageous self-consciousness. Much of his writing on nature is explicitly cast as the emblem of a mind, which he is careful not to create as a symbol of unification with nature. Returning to the notion of the "tender fiction," Wordsworth explicitly identifies the notion of simple presence within inscription as such a fiction and relates it to the "intervention of the imagination." [11]

Kumin's consciousness of the interconnections among her visions of nature, mortality, and poetry is usually implicit, functioning as the subtle, never intrusive poetics underlying the poems. When she is explicit, as in "Surprises" (*N*, 47–48), it is almost a surprise; but never to be caught treating such sacred terms with reverence—she must remain "in-between"— she couches her hope in the wry intonations of self-parody. For the first time in fifteen years, her red peppers grow and "hang / in clustered pairs like newly hatched sex organs / . . . . Doubtless this means I am approaching / the victory of poetry over death." A string of associations leads her through her mother's roses, her mother's memories of horses' names in old age, her own coming old age, her mother's baked peppers "full of the leftovers she called"—what else?—"surprises."

Kumin's recent poetry also delineates that we are part of nature as well as its observer, formulator, victim, and victimizer. We must nurture it as it has us, and as it also refuses to do; comfort its creatures even though they can offer us little comfort in return—unless we relinquish our separation from them and lie down with horses, acknowledging that the mortal body (theirs at the mercy of ours) is also the soul. I would say that Kumin— or her poetry, at any rate—does not believe this for a minute, and also believes it utterly. The stakes are high, and consciousness (of mortality, in fact of anything) is the beloved enemy who must be embraced as well as extinguished.

She means us to ponder lovingly the webs of relationship that bind us to fates we both control and, ultimately, share. Stubborn celebration is the dominant tone: she bids us "rejoice to be circumpolar, all of us / on all fours obeying the laws of migration" ("With the Caribou," *N*, 4). She invites our gaze upon the parallels between us and her dog when he carries frogs from place to place in his mouth, "doing what he knows how to do / and we too, taking and letting go, that same story" ("Custodian," *N*, 14). We are better at taking than at letting go. But consciousness combines with nature to teach us that we must.

The animals she returns to most often are her own, who "run like a perfectly detached / statement by Mozart through all the other lines / of my life,

a handsome family of serene / horses glistening in their thoughtlessness."
She translates their conversation with her, "conveyed in a wordless yet perfect / language of touch and tremor" ("Sleeping with Animals," *N*, 22).
Yet she eschews both moralism and sentimentality through an insistence
on facing cruelty, predation, stupidity, whether committed by our fellow
animal travelers or by us: "Nature a catchment of sorrows. / We hug each
other. No lesson drawn" ("Catchment," *N*, 24).

The poet finds the tendency to anthropomorphize dangerous because
sentimental and falsifying; but its opposite, complete detachment, is equally
untenable because it begets the insensitivity that leads to imperialism and
destruction. A "being with" and "being in" that approaches but does
not reach identification with nature—crucially distinct from anthropomorphism—presents the opportunity to explore continuity in a world of mutability. It is significant that in the purest moments of this "being-with," the
poet must relinquish words, which are always, after all, representations
of separation brought into "being" by human consciousness. Relinquish
words, yes, but not "language," which is more like Mozart's music. The
"being-with" is expressed in that "wordless yet perfect / language." It is a
language both beyond and before human speech, the only one that escapes
consciousness, and therefore knowledge of death. Heidegger said: "Mor-
tals are they who can experience death as death. Animals cannot do so, but
animals cannot speak." [12] Kumin would correct Heidegger: animals cannot
speak, but they do have language. Ironically and appropriately, this indefin-
able concept, "language," that both includes and transcends poetry, that is
shared by the beast and the bard, is one Kumin and Anne Sexton developed
together decades ago.

Three poems, one near the end of *Nurture*, the other two the Prelude
and Epilogue to Kumin's new collection, *Looking for Luck*, bring together
Kumin's complex uses of nature in her confrontation with loss and mortality. "Distance" directly expresses the terms of her negotiation with aging.
"What does it mean," she asks herself while mowing the lawn, "how / do I,
who buried both my parents long ago, / attach my name and number to
another birthday?" In part by detaching herself from exclusively gendered
sexuality, the reproductive cycle that is also, ironically, the seal of death;
she says the old are androgynous, which does not preclude a vision of eros
but places it beyond the limitations of genital sex. And in part by acknowledging that life from now on will be that catchment of losses demonstrated
to her by the natural cycles around her:

> Around me old friends (and enemies) are beleaguered
> with cancer or clogged arteries. I ought to be

> melancholy inching upward through my sixties
> surrounded by the ragged edges of so many acres,
> parlaying the future with this aerobic mowing,
> but I take courage from a big wind staving off the deerflies,
>
> ruffling and parting the grasses like a cougar if there
> were still cougars. I am thankful for what's left that's wild:
> the coydogs who howl in unison when a distant fire siren
> or the hoot owl starts them up, the moose that muddled
> through the winter in the swampland behind us, the bears
> that drop their spoor studded with cherry pits in our swales.
>
> If I could free a hand behind this Tuff-Cut
> I'd tug my forelock at the sow and her two cubs I met
> at high noon last week on the trail to Bible Hill.
> Androgyny. Another birthday. And all the while
> the muted roar of satisfactory machinery.
> May we flourish and keep our working distance. ("Distance," N, 60–
>   61)

Once again she shifts between intimacy and separation, claiming her essential in-betweenness. Yet in *Luck,* where almost half of the poems are concerned with death and loss and with the necessity of continuous mourning, her "Credo" announces that "I believe in magic." The nature of that magic? The "rights of animals to leap out of our skins." In an Indian legend "that instant a bear appeared where a boy had been." Rejoicing in the magic of the wild, she also draws near to the domesticated wildness inherent in "the gift of the horse," who reminds her of her custodianship.

> I believe in myself as their sanctuary
> and in the earth with its summer plumes of carrots,
>
> its clamber of peas, beans, masses of tendrils
> as mine. I believe in the acrobatics of boy
> into bear, the grace of animals
> in my keeping, the thrust to go on. ("Credo," LL, 15)

In the Epilogue poem, "The Rendezvous," that "thrust" will be expressed in a transmutation of the eros the poet, now in her sixties, seemed to reject in "Distance." This renewed and reclothed, or newly naked, eros transcends the human by wishing for sexual/spiritual union with animals. Employing a legend that says a male bear is able to feel shame—a piece of anthropomorphism she would eschew outside of the poem—she says that a woman encountering a bear is advised to remove her clothes, causing him to run away. But in her rendezvous she slips off her skirt and blouse while he takes out his teeth. Then he works his way out of his pelt, casting it to the ground as a love-rug.

> He smells of honey
> and garlic. I am wet
> with human fear. How
> can he run away, unfurred?
> How can I, without my clothes?
>
> How we prepare a new legend. ("Rendezvous," *LL,* 89)

The fiction is tender, incarnative as well as representational. If the epitaph genre records hope as well as fear, celebration as well as mourning, this one could be an epitaph of renewal for the ravaged world at the close of the century, attended to and recorded in the valley of vision where the poet lies down in a destitute time, at the edge of the world's night, uttering her only holy. She is singing the traces of the vanished gods in whom she does not believe, and in whom she believes.

In May 1991 I interviewed Maxine Kumin in Princeton, where she was giving a reading. The following excerpts from her comments offer the poet's own views of issues related to aging and creativity.[13]

On the literary and personal perspective offered by aging:

DHG: You said that in your sixties, you have developed "a longer perspective than I ever would have believed possible." How so?

MK: It's very funny. You get to be a certain age and you look back and you see that you have arrived at that sort of long, informed, relativistic point of view that you never expected to be dispassionate enough to present.

DHG: And do you feel that you have arrived at that?

MK: Right. Maybe I'm deluding myself, but I feel that. I trust my judgment.

DHG: Do you know when you started to trust your judgment? . . . Can you give a sense in the cycle of your life of when you started to?

MK: I would say about ten years ago. The last ten years I've become increasingly churlish about my own opinions and now I almost feel I'm entitled to them. I'm not very easily dislodged from them.

DHG: And do you come to them more easily than you used to?

MK: Probably. I think it's a normal concomitant of age that you get more cantankerously opinionated. This is what I always said when I was a relative youngster about my parents and their generation. That was the thing that was so despicable about them. They were so cocksure about their opinions, and here I am getting terribly cocksure, too, and I'm not really proud of it.

DHG: Do you do much backing up to check yourself on that?

MK: I do. I think it's a trap. You can get overly opinionated. But it's very hard over a long period of years to have worked with so many students in a lot of different settings and not see some sort of a plan, and not be able to pretty readily sort out what you think is promising and what you think has been played awry.

On poetry and mortality:

DHG: Looking over what you have written from your life's work thus far, what are the things that you think will endure?

MK: It's probably wishful thinking. I suppose I think some of what I call the tribal poems are durable, poems about family relationships, mother and daughter. Probably it looks as if some of the Hermit poems, those persona poems, probably some of the animal poems. From there on up it's hard to say. I would hope that some of the animal poems hang around to remind people that there are other species out there, and we do have a connection to them.

DHG: Looking at the survival of natural things, do you find any analogy with poetry?

MK: Well, we were talking about cycles—it's very comforting to me year after year to watch things start up again in spring. Now I think I'm more tuned in to it, more sensitive to the change year by year as I go, and it's very reassuring to me in the fall.

DHG: Years ago, you said something I'd like you to talk about again, to see if you still stand by it. You said that all poetry is elegiac. Would you still say so?

MK: Probably I still do, yes. One does write poems in celebration, and I think I'm writing a little less about death than I was ten years ago. But I do think that the essential informing passion behind the writing of poetry is this knowledge of our mortal nature. If we were going to be here forever, we would not have the impulse to record our lives and our passions and our feelings. We wouldn't need to eulogize people that we love, to have respite. I'm pretty much convinced that that is the wellspring for poetry in general. Maybe you can't hold every poem to that, but I think that's where it comes from.

DHG: You really think that if there were no death, if we were not mortal, we would not feel the need to record ourselves?

MK: I think there wouldn't be any art . . . whatsoever if we were immortal.

On her own relationship to death and poetry:

DHG: I was thinking that although you're still struggling with it, your poetry has come more and more to real terms with death.

MK: Oh yes. I think maybe I am more clear-sighted about the fact that I obviously don't have another sixty-six years on this planet.

DHG: But it's still not all right with you?

MK: But it's still not all right with me. My husband and I have a joke about it. I have a nine-year-old gelding whom I birthed and if I loved him any better, he'd be in the living room with us. When he does something wonderful, I say, "Oh, God, this is my horse forever." I could never part with him. My husband said, "You'll still be driving him in your nineties." And I stopped and I said, "You know something, I don't think I'll be driving in my nineties." But then I said to myself, it's quite possible that I will in my eighties. And that was very reassuring. So you keep extending the background. As you move from the foreground to the middle ground, you want the horizon to recede and recede, and you keep hoping that you have a lot more time. There's still a lot that I want to do, like go to Yellowstone.

DHG: Is it important to have it be more all right with you that we are mortal? In other words, is this something that you're still working on, or not particularly any more? Have you given up on ever thinking you're going to come to terms with it?

MK: I don't think you ever come to terms with it. I don't think anybody ever comes to terms with it.

DHG: "You" meaning generic humans, period?

MK: Yes, generic humans. I think the life force is such that it is very difficult to override the desire to go on. But I think that if I had a terminal illness that was going to drag on and on, was going to be very painful for me, and was going to be very painful for my survivors and heirs, then I think I want the right to choose my exit.

DHG: Then you believe in that for all people?

MK: I do. I think one of the terrible things about medical science is we have the technology to keep people alive well beyond their appointed span or their desire to go on. We keep doing this with dreadful consequences. I think we should be able to choose.

DHG: You've got documentation to make sure that that happens for you?

MK: Well, you can't ever really be sure that happens to you because so much depends upon the individual caregiver. They can make most of those decisions. You can write "do not resuscitate" on the chart but maybe you don't want to let it go that far.

DHG: When I talk to people who are old, they're always saying things such as, I want to die in my sleep.

MK: That's the pious wish.

DHG: I don't feel that way. Do you want to die in your sleep?

MK: Well, I listened to my mother say that for many, many years, and her wish was granted. She had the most peaceful exit. It was quite wonderful to see. On the other hand, our kids are always after me about this dangerous avocation I have that involves the horses, the younger horses especially. I just got kicked on Mother's Day. My Mother's Day present was quite a kick. If it had been a couple of inches lower, it probably would have shattered my kneecap. Luckily he got me in the fleshy part of the leg, and I'm really fine. My rejoinder to my kids is, say to yourselves, well, Mother died untimely young, but at least she died doing something she loved. So if I have a fatal accident on a horse, kismet. I'm not seeking that, but I'm aware that it's a possibility.

On aging and creativity and the relationship of creativity to physical labor:

DHG: We were talking at lunch about the ways in which you have to realize that you can't any longer ride horses a certain way for a certain length of time and so forth. So Old Paint [Kumin's nickname for her body], your Old Partner, is hanging in there, but you are having some problems that make you confront those issues. What about the mind, the writer in you? What do you think about creativity and aging, about imaginative powers and aging as you have experienced it?

MK: I don't see any diminishment in creative energy. I really don't. In fact the only positive thing to say for being mashed in the [horse] stall or being kicked and having to lie low for a few days is it gives you the physical leisure to let your mind enter into a freer flow. My life is so crowded in the spring and summer that there's hardly time for common play or rambles. It's almost a liberation. . . . Winter is a luxury. The sun rises later which means I sleep later. I've got the whole morning to myself at my desk because anything I want to do outdoors isn't going to get done until the sun is at its peak, around midday. And then it gets dark early. At about four o'clock everybody's fed and done with. There's a whole lovely evening to do, to write, think, whatever. So I'm very much a creature of the seasons.

DHG: You need the quiet, the break from the physical routine in order to have the meditative time to do the creating, but I suppose that if you weren't cyclically busy in a physical way, it would also affect your imaginative time?

MK: Absolutely, I know this is so. I think I'm extremely lucky that I have the two, that I can balance it. If I lived in a Manhattan apartment and I couldn't open the door and put my feet on the soil, I would probably be in a loony bin. I have got to be able to go out and do things with my body, almost as a soporific for my brain.

On what matters when you're a young writer and when you're older:

DHG: Are there any things that were important to you when you were a young writer that aren't important to you now?

MK: Yes.

DHG: What kinds of concerns or issues have endured for you from the time that you were young until now? And what things that you used to think were important don't matter any more?

MK: Form matters less. Although I still love it, I'm a lot less rigid about it. I think I can accept my dry periods much more casually. I don't panic when I can't write. I don't immediately think, Oh, it's gone, it'll never come back. . . . I do to some extent. I get a little queasy about it, but you know, it's always come back. Right now I'm in a total sterile time, dry as a bone. . . . But I know that it'll work through. And I don't worry about reputation any more. I really don't give a damn. I said this last night: About the only good thing I can say for getting older is there's not so much riding on it. You say what you think, and screw it. If people don't like it, then they don't like it. If they take you to task, then they take you to task. But you don't have to lie awake at night worrying what Helen Vendler said about you. She's entitled to her opinion, and so it goes.

I don't feel competitive in the least any more, and I certainly did in my thirties. There were times when I felt jealous of other poems, desirous of fame at least. I don't find myself lusting for awards, or prizes, or positions, or any of that. That's a kind of, I guess a kind of compromise, or security maybe. I feel very strongly that I've got to do what I'm doing, that I can't do it any other way. Much as I've loved my time here in Princeton, which is so fertile for me, unbelievably wonderful, and I've been invited back to teach—but I won't come for a whole semester because I don't know how much time Victor and I have left together and I just know that we don't want to spend the whole semester apart. I do still believe in magic.

DHG: Yes, talk about the things that still do compel you.

MK: The life close to nature is very compelling, life among the animals, the harvest of the crops, all these things. If I were a believer, I guess I would have to say every year that I encounter the glut of the cucumbers and start making bread-and-butter pickles, I would thank God for all those cucumbers. But I really know I have only myself to thank, and whoever developed this wonderful new cultivar that makes it so prolific. The botanists—I have a lot of faith in the botanists. . . . I'm fascinated by the growing of things. I find I spend more time now starting my seedlings indoors and leaving them out (we have a glassed-in porch so it's almost like a greenhouse) and tending them and getting ready to put them in the garden and mixing up my own fertilizers, becoming more scientific about it, and just loving it. So that I figure if the arthritis worsens and I have to give up a lot of the horse stuff, I'll still have this other thing to do that means a lot to me. So I'm sort of planning for my old age. I know I'm certainly not there yet.

On "tribal seniority" in family versus in poetry (after discussion of "A Game of Monopoly in Chavannes," from *Nurture*, in which the grandson's "ultimate task is to stay to usher us out"):

DHG: How do you find yourself connecting your roles now as a grandmother in your tribe with your tribal seniority role in poetry?

MK: Oh, dear. See, I'm not ready to acknowledge that I've got a tribal seniority role in poetry. That's very hard for me to live up to. It really is. I know that I am now sort of a part of the history of contemporary American women's poetry. That's really scary for me.

DHG: Scary?

MK: That's really scary because that's a position of responsibility that I find difficult to live up to. I don't really know what to do with it.

DHG: Really?

MK: Really. Does that surprise you?

DHG: Yes. I would have thought that you'd feel real easy and comfortable in that role, that it almost wouldn't be an issue for you.

MK: No, I really don't. I feel a little bit timorous about it. I don't like to play myself up. Women come up to me and say, "You've been a role model to me." I'm just taken aback partly because I think there weren't any role models in my life. . . . No women poet models. Who was there, Marianne Moore?

DHG: Right, and you did everything that could be done with that connection in "Marianne, My Mother, and Me," which really works. But you had to make the stretch because she wasn't yours. . . . You had to make her belong to you.

MK: Neither she nor Bishop gave me permission to write in the way that, say, Sexton and Rich and Levertov and Plath and Van Duyn and Kumin gave "permission" to young women poets today. It's a whole new world.

DHG: Alicia Ostriker is starting to function that way for younger writers.

MK: Absolutely. I think Alicia and I share a fairly strong sense of responsibility, more highly developed in her than in me, toward young writers. I have never felt as I feel so many male poets have felt—each one shoot one. I've never felt that way. . . . Among women I think that should not pertain. I hope it never will. I'm sure there are jealousies and rivalries and so on. But I feel that if we could—I give blurbs to young women writers whose work I admire. . . . And older women, too. Jean Berwin, she's terrific. She's seventy-five or six, and she's bringing out the first book she's brought out since the late fifties. It's a really culled manuscript. It has been very carefully edited, and there's some wonderful poems. I think, what can I say that hasn't been said yet, because they're so rich and so witty and so to the point, and they reflect her generation. Damn it, we need those books.

DHG: I guess one of the reasons I would have thought you'd be comfortable in your—what could we call your role—it's motherly. It's nurturing . . .

MK: Queen mother? [laughs]

DHG: I don't know what to call it because the language of mentoring is so inflected with gender and hierarchy issues. And I also don't want to reduce you to a maternal function here, that's not what you do, not quite what you represent. But you do have some sort of role model or nurturing function for younger women writers, and one of the reasons I assumed you were comfortable in it is that you look comfortable in it, self-assured. You move comfortably, and since you write about nurture in the animal world and in your family world, I guess I thought . . . I didn't know you weren't at home in that leader role.

MK: No, I'm not. I'm uneasy about it.

DHG: I'm not disappointed about your discomfort. That means you're not assuming the mantle of authority. The very fact that you're not comfortable with it, that you question and wonder about it, suggests that you'll be careful with how you use your power.

Notes

1. Diana Hume George, "Who Is the Double Ghost Whose Head Is Smoke?" 134–53.

2. Diana Hume George, "Itinerary of an Obsession, 243–66.

3. Karen Mills-Courts, *Poetry as Epitaph*, 21, 34–35.

4. Maxine Kumin, "Interview with Karla Hammond," 53.

5. In my earlier essay on the Sexton elegies, I discussed only "Itinerary of an Obsession" in detail. I take some of my comments here from that essay.

6. Maxine Kumin, "Interview with Martha Meek," 25.

7. Kathleen Woodward, "Late Theory, Late Style," this volume; see also Kathleen *Aging and Its Discontents,* chap. 6.

8. Mills-Courts, *Poetry,* 1–4, 7.

9. With Malcolm A. Nelson I wrote *Epitaph and Icon,* a study of eighteenth-century burying grounds and gravestones in New England. My discussion of epitaphic function here is informed by our research.

10. Mills-Courts, *Poetry,* 13–15, 18.

11. Ibid., 166–68.

12. Martin Heidegger, "What Are Poets For?" *Poetry,* 97.

13. The full text of this interview will be published in 1993 in the *Associated Writing Programs Chronicle.*

Abbreviations
Bibliography
Contributors
Index

Abbreviations

Atherton, Gertrude, *Adventures of a Novelist*	AN
Barthes, Roland, *Camera Lucida*	CL
Bogan, Louise, *Journey around My Room*	Journey
Bogan, Louise, *What the Woman Lived*	Letters
Bowen, Elizabeth, *Bowen's Court*	BC
Bowen, Elizabeth, *Eva Trout*	ET
Bowen, Elizabeth, *The Little Girls*	LG
Bowen, Elizabeth, *Pictures and Conversations*	P&C
Bowen, Elizabeth, *Seven Winters*	SW
Cather, Willa, *A Lost Lady*	LL
Cather, Willa, *The Professor's House*	PH
Cather, Willa, *The Song of the Lark*	SL
Cheever, John, *Oh What a Paradise It Seems*	Paradise
Cixous, Hélène, "Extreme Fidelity"	"EF"
Colette, *Bella Vista*	BV
Colette, *The Blue Lantern*	BL
Colette, *Break of Day*	BD
Colette, *Chéri*	C
Colette, *La Fin de Chérie*	FC
Colette, *The Evening Star*	ES
Colette, *Julie de Carneilhan*	JC
Colette, "The Képi"	"K"
Colette, *Paris de ma fenêtre*	PF
Colette, *La Vagabonde*	V
Freud, Sigmund, *Standard Edition*	SE
Glendinning, Victoria, *Elizabeth Bowen*	EB
Horace, *Epistulae*	Ep.
Horace, *Odes*	O.
Kumin, Maxine, *Ground Time*	GT
Kumin, Maxine, *Looking for Luck*	LL
Kumin, Maxine, *Nurture*	N
Lawrence, D. H., *The Complete Plays*	CPL
Lawrence, D. H., *The Complete Poems*	CP
Lawrence, D. H., *Letters* (Cambridge edition)	L
Lawrence, D. H., *The Plumed Serpent*	PS
Lawrence, D. H., *Sons and Lovers*	S&L

Lawrence, D. H., *The Virgin and the Gipsy*   *V&G*

Miles, Josephine, *Collected Poems, 1930–83*   *CP*

Montherlant, Henry de, *La Mort qui fait le trottoir*   *MFT*

Montherlant, Henry de, *La Reine morte,* in *Théâtre*   *RM*

Montherlant, Henry de, *La Rose de sable,* in *Romans II*   *RS*

Montherlant, Henry de, *Va jouer avec cette poussière*   *VJP*

Ovid, *Amores*   *Am.*

Ovid, *Epistulae ex Ponto*   *Pont.*

Ovid, *Tristia*   *Tr.*

Richardson, Dorothy, *Journey to Paradise*   *JP*

Sarton, May, *The Education of Harriet Hatfield*   *HH*

Swift, Jonathan, *The Prose Works of Jonathan Swift*   *PW*

Taylor, Peter, *Collected Stories*   *CS*

Taylor, Peter, "In the Miro District"   "MD"

Taylor, Peter, "Three Heroines"   "TH"

Woodward, Kathleen, *At Last*   *AL*

Bibliography

Abraham, Karl. "A Short Study of the Development of the Libido, Viewed in the Light of Mental Disorders" (1924). In *Selected Papers of Karl Abraham*, trans. Douglas Bryan and Alix Strachey, 418–501. London: Hogarth Press and Institute of Psycho-Analysis, 1973.

Abraham, Nicolas, and Maria Torok. *Cryptonymie: Le Verbier de l'homme aux loups*. Paris: Aubier-Flammarion, 1976.

——. "The Topography of Reality: Sketching a Metapsychology of Secrets." Trans. Nicholas Rand. *Oxford Literary Review. Psychoanalysis and Literature: New Work* 12 (1990): 63–68.

Albert, Marilyn S., and Mark B. Moss, eds. *Geriatric Neuropsychology*. New York: Guilford, 1988.

Alvarez, A. *The Savage God: A Study of Suicide*. New York: Bantam, 1973.

Anderson, Philip. "Transformations of 'Swift' and the Development of Swift's Satiric Vision in *Verses on the Death of Dr. Swift*." *Publication of the Arkansas Philological Association* 6 (1973): 19–31.

Andreasen, Nancy C. "Creativity and Mental Illness: Prevalence Rates in Writers and Their First-Degree Relatives." *American Journal of Psychiatry* 144 (1987): 1288–92.

Armon, Cheryl. "Ideals of the Good Life and Moral Judgment: Ethical Reasoning across the Lifespan." In *Beyond Formal Operations: Late Adolescent and Adult Cognitive Development*, eds. Francis A. Richards, Cheryl Armon, and Michael L. Commons, 357–80. New York: Praeger, 1984.

Armstrong, David. *Horace*. New Haven: Yale Univ. Press, 1989.

Ashworth, Ann. " 'But Why Was She Called Portia?': Judgment and Feeling in Bowen's *The Death of the Heart*." *Critique: Studies in Modern Fiction* 28 (Spring 1987): 159–66.

Atherton, Gertrude. *Adventures of a Novelist*. New York: Liveright, 1932.

Austin, Mary. *Everyman's Genius*. Indianapolis: Bobbs-Merrill, 1925.

Bakhtin, M. M. "Epic and Novel: Toward a Methodology for the Study of the Novel." In *The Dialogic Imagination: Four Essays*, ed. Michael Holquist, trans. Caryl Emerson and Michael Holquist, 3–40. Austin: Univ. of Texas Press, 1981.

——. "Forms of Time and of the Chronotope in the Novel: Notes toward a Historical Poetics." In *The Dialogic Imagination: Four Essays*, ed. Michael Holquist, trans. Caryl Emerson and Michael Holquist, 84–258. Austin: Univ. of Texas Press, 1981.

Bagnell, Prisca von Dorotka, and Patricia Spencer Soper, eds. *Perceptions of Aging in Literature: A Cross-Cultural Study*. Contributions to the Study of Aging, no. 11. New York: Greenwood Press, 1989.

Banner, Lois. *American Beauty*. New York: Alfred A. Knopf, 1983.

——. "The Meaning of Menopause: Aging and Its Historical Contexts in the Twentieth Century." Center for Twentieth Century Studies, Univ. of Wisconsin-Milwaukee. Working Paper no. 3 (Fall/Winter 1989–90): 1–38.

Barnett, Louise. *Swift's Poetic Worlds*. Newark: Univ. of Delaware Press, 1981.

Barr, Barbara Weekley. "Memoir of D. H. Lawrence." In *D. H. Lawrence: Novelist, Poet, Prophet,* ed. Stephen Spender, 8–36. New York: Harper & Row, 1973.

Barraclough, B. M., and D. J. Pallis. "Depression Followed by Suicide: A Comparison of Depressed Suicides with Living Depressives." *Psychological Medicine* 5 (1975): 55–61.

Barthes, Roland. *Le Plaisir du texte*. Paris: Seuil, 1973.

——. *Camera Lucida: Reflections on Photography* (1980). Trans. Richard Howard. New York: Hill and Wang, 1981.

Bateson, Mary Catherine. *Composing a Life*. 1989. Rept. New York: Plume, 1990.

Beauvoir, Simone de. *A Very Easy Death*. Trans. Patrick O'Brian. 1964. Rept. New York: Warner Books, 1973.

Becker, Ernest. *The Denial of Death*. 1973. Rept. New York: Free Press, 1975.

Bell, Blair W. *The Sex Complex: A Study of the Relationships of the Internal Secretions to the Female Characteristics and Functions in Health and Disease*. London: Balliere, Tindall and Cox, 1916.

Bell, Quentin. *Virginia Woolf: A Biography*. 2 vols. New York: Harcourt, Brace, Jovanovich, 1972.

Benack, Suzanne. "Postformal Epistemologies and the Growth of Empathy." In *Beyond Formal Operations: Late Adolescent and Adult Cognitive Development,* eds. Francis A. Richards, Cheryl Armon, and Michael L. Commons, 340–56. New York: Praeger, 1984.

Benjamin, Jessica. *The Bonds of Love: Psychoanalysis, Feminism, and the Problem of Domination*. New York: Pantheon, 1988.

Bennett, Andrew, and Nicholas Royle. *Still Lives: Elizabeth Bowen and the Dissolution of the Novel*. (Manuscript under consideration.)

Benstock, Shari, ed. *The Private Self: Theory and Practice of Women's Autobiographical Writing*. Chapel Hill: Univ. of North Carolina Press, 1988.

Bews, J. P. "The Metamorphosis of Virgil in the *Tristia* of Ovid." *Bulletin of the Institute of Classical Studies* 31 (1984): 51–60.

Biolley-Godino, Marcelle. *L'Homme-objet dans l'oeuvre de Colette*. Paris: Klincksieck, 1972.

Birren, James E., and Vern L. Bengtson, eds. Preface to *Emergent Theories of Aging*. New York: Springer, 1988.

Blaney, P. "Affect and Memory: A Review." *Psychological Bulletin* 99 (1986): 229–46.

Block, E. "Poetics in Exile: An Analysis of *Epistulae ex Pont*. 3.9." *Classical Antiquity* 1 (1982): 18–27.

Bloom, Floyd E., and Arlyne Lazerson. *Brain, Mind, and Behavior*. 2d ed. New York: W. H. Freeman, 1988.

Blumenthal, Susan J., and David J. Kupfer, eds. *Suicide over the Life Cycle: Risk Factors, Assessment, and Treatment of Suicidal Patients*. Washington, D.C.: American Psychiatric Press, 1990.

Bogan, Louise. *Body of This Death*. New York: McBride, 1923.

——. *The Sleeping Fury*. New York: Charles Scribner's Sons, 1937.

——. "The Catalpa Tree." *Voices: A Quarterly Review of Poetry,* Sept.–Dec. 1941, 8.

——. *Poems and New Poems.* New York: Charles Scribner's Sons, 1941.

——. *Achievement in American Poetry, 1900–1950.* Chicago: Henry Regnery, 1951.

——. *Collected Poems, 1923–1953.* New York: Noonday Press, 1954.

——. *A Poet's Alphabet: Reflections on the Literary Art and Vocation.* Ed. Robert Phelps and Ruth Limmer. New York: McGraw Hill, 1970.

——. *The Blue Estuaries: Poems, 1923–1968.* New York: Ecco Press, 1977.

——. *Journey around My Room: The Autobiography of Louise Bogan.* Ed. Ruth Limmer. New York: Viking, 1980.

——. *What the Woman Lived: Selected Letters of Louise Bogan, 1920–1970.* Ed. Ruth Limmer. New York: Harcourt Brace Jovanovich, 1983.

Bond, Alma Halbert. *Who Killed Virginia Woolf? A Psychobiography.* New York: Human Sciences, 1989.

Bourne, Randolph S. *Youth and Life.* 1913. Rept. Freeport, N.Y.: Books for Libraries Press, 1967.

Bowen, Elizabeth. *Bowen's Court.* In *Bowen's Court and Seven Winters: Memoirs of a Dublin Childhood.* 1942. Rept. London: Virago Press, 1984.

——. *Seven Winters.* In *Bowen's Court and Seven Winters: Memoirs of A Dublin Childhood.* 1942. Rept. London: Virago Press, 1984.

——. *The Little Girls.* 1963. Rept. Harmondsworth, Middlesex, Eng.: Penguin Books, 1982.

——. *Eva Trout or Changing Scenes.* 1968. Rept. Harmondsworth, Middlesex, Eng.: Penguin Books, 1982.

——. *Pictures and Conversations.* New York: Alfred A. Knopf, 1975.

——. "The Move-In." In *Pictures and Conversations,* 67–76. New York: Alfred A. Knopf, 1975.

Bowlby, John. *Separation: Anxiety and Anger.* Vol. 2 of *Attachment and Loss.* 1973. Rept. Middlesex, Eng.: Penguin Books, 1975.

——. *Loss: Sadness and Depression.* Vol. 3 of *Attachment and Loss.* New York: Basic Books, 1980.

Bowles, Gloria. *Louise Bogan's Aesthetic of Limitation.* Bloomington: Indiana Univ. Press, 1987.

Braithwaite, William Stanley. "The Novels of Jessie Fauset." *Opportunity* 12, no. 1 (Jan. 1934): 24–28.

Brawley, Benjamin G. *The Negro Genius.* 1937. Rept. New York: Biblo and Tannen, 1972.

Breslau, Lawrence D., and Marie R. Haug, eds. *Depression and Aging: Causes, Care, and Consequences.* New York: Springer, 1983.

Breslau, Naomi. "Migraine, Suicidal Ideation, and Suicide Attempts." *Neurology* 42 (1992): 392–95.

Brewster, Earl, and Achsah Brewster. *D. H. Lawrence: Reminiscences and Correspondence.* London: Secker, 1934.

Brickhouse, Robert. "Peter Taylor: Writing, Teaching, Making Discoveries" (1983). In *Conversations with Peter Taylor,* ed. Hubert H. McAlexander, 48–53. Jackson: Univ. Press of Mississippi, 1987.

Broadway, J. William. "A Conversation with Peter Taylor" (1985). In *Conversations with Peter Taylor,* ed. Hubert H. McAlexander, 67–114. Jackson: Univ. Press of Mississippi, 1987.

Brown, A. Fitton. "The Unreality of Ovid's Tomitian Exile." *Liverpool Classical Monthly* 10 (1985): 19–22.

Brown, Felix. "Bereavement and Lack of a Parent in Childhood." In *Foundations of Child Psychiatry*, ed. Emanuel Brown, pp. 435–55. London: Pergamon, 1968.

Bryher. "D[orthy] R[ichardson]." *Adam International Review*, nos. 310–12 (1966): 22–23.

Buckley, Jerome H. *Season of Youth: The Bildungsroman from Dickens to Golding*. Cambridge: Harvard Univ. Press, 1974.

Bureau of Vocational Information. *Training for the Professions and Allied Occupations*. . . . New York: Bureau of Vocational Information, 1924.

Butler, Robert N. "The Life Review: An Interpretation of Reminiscence in the Aged." *Psychiatry: Journal for the Study of Interpersonal Processes* 26 (Feb. 1963): 65–76.

Cameron, Sharon. "Representing Grief: Emerson's 'Experience.'" *Representations* 15 (Summer 1986): 15–41.

Caramagno, Thomas C. "Manic-Depressive Psychosis and Critical Approaches to Virginia Woolf's Life and Work." *PMLA* 103 (1988): 10–23.

——. *The Flight of the Mind: Virginia Woolf's Art and Manic-Depressive Illness*. Berkeley: Univ. of California Press, 1992.

Casey, Jane Barnes. "A View of Peter Taylor's Stories." *Virginia Quarterly Review* 54 (Spring 1978): 213–30.

Cather, Willa. *The Song of the Lark*. 1915. Rept. Boston: Houghton Mifflin, 1988.

——. *A Lost Lady*. 1923. Rept. New York: Knopf, 1951.

——. *The Professor's House*. 1925. Rept. New York: Knopf, 1953.

Chapman, Nancy J., and Margaret B. Neal. "The Effects of Intergenerational Experiences on Adolescents and Older Adults." *Gerontologist* 30 (Dec. 1990): 825–32.

Cheever, John. *Oh What a Paradise It Seems*. New York: Random House (Ballantine paperback), 1982.

Chinen, Allan B. *In the Ever After: Fairy Tales and the Second Half of Life*. Wilmette, Ill.: Chiron, 1989.

——. *Once Upon a Midlife: Classic Stories and Mythic Tales to Illuminate the Middle Years*. Los Angeles: Jeremy P. Tarcher, 1992.

Chodorow, Nancy. *The Reproduction of Mothering: Psychoanalysis and the Sociology of Gender*. Berkeley: Univ. of California Press, 1978.

Cicero. *De senectute, De amicita, De divinatione*. Trans. W. A. Falconer. London: Heinemann, 1923.

Cixous, Hélène. "Castration or Decapitation." Trans. Annette Kuhn. *Signs* 7, no. 1 (Autumn 1981): 41–55.

——. "Extreme Fidelity." In *Writing Differences: Readings from the Seminar of Hélène Cixous*, ed. Susan Sellers. Milton Keynes: Open Univ. Press, 1988.

Claridge, Gordon, Ruth Pryor, and Gwen Watkins, eds. *Sounds from the Bell Jar: Ten Psychotic Writers*. New York: St. Martin's Press, 1990.

Cohen-Shalev, Amir. "Old Age Style: Developmental Changes in Creative Production from a Life-Span Perspective." *Journal of Aging Studies* 3 (Spring 1989): 21–37.

Cole, Thomas R. *The Journey of Life: A Cultural History of Aging in America.* Cambridge: Cambridge Univ. Press, 1992.

——, and Sally A. Gadow, eds. *What Does It Mean to Grow Old? Reflections from the Humanities.* Durham: Duke Univ. Press, 1986.

——, David D. Van Tassel, and Robert Kastenbaum, eds. *Handbook of the Humanities and Aging.* New York: Springer Publishing, 1992.

Colette. *Chéri.* Paris: Fayard, 1920.

——. *Bella Vista.* Paris: Ferenczi, 1937.

——. *Julie de Carneilhan.* Paris: Fayard, 1941.

——. *Paris de ma fenêtre.* Paris: Editions du Milieu du monde, 1944.

——. *Break of Day.* Trans. Enid McLeod. New York: Farrar, Straus Cudahy, 1961.

——. *The Blue Lantern.* Trans. Roger Senhouse. New York: Farrar, Straus and Co., 1963.

——. *The Evening Star.* Trans. David Le Vay. New York: Bobbs-Merrill, 1973.

——. *La fin de Chéri.* Paris: Flammarion, 1983.

——. "The Képi." In *The Collected Stories of Colette,* ed. Robert Phelps, trans. Antonia White. New York: Farrar, Straus, Giroux, 1983.

——. *La Vagabonde.* In *Oeuvres,* 1:1067–1232. Paris: Gallimard, Bibliothèque de la Pléiade, 1984.

Collier, Virginia MacMakin. *Marriage and Careers: A Study of 100 Women Who Are Wives, Mothers, Homemakers, and Professional Workers, for the Bureau of Vocational Information.* New York: Channel, 1926.

Colt, George Howe. *The Enigma of Suicide.* New York: Summit, 1991.

Cornell, Dewey G., Ronald Suarez, and Stanley Berent. "Psychomotor Retardation in Melancholic and Nonmelancholic Depression: Cognitive and Motor Components." *Journal of Abnormal Psychology* 93 (1984): 150–57.

Cowley, Malcolm. "Three Poets." In *Critical Essays on Louise Bogan,* ed. Martha Collins, 58. Boston: G. K. Hall, 1984.

Craig, Patricia. *Elizabeth Bowen.* Lives of Modern Women, gen. ed., Emma Tennant. Harmondsworth, Middlesex, Eng.: Penguin Books, 1986.

Crimp, Douglas. "Mourning and Militancy." *October* 51 (Winter 1989): 1–18.

Csikszentmihályi, Mihály. "Society, Culture, and Person: A Systems View of Creativity." In *The Nature of Creativity: Contemporary Psychological Perspectives,* ed. Robert J. Sternberg, 325–39. Cambridge: Cambridge Univ. Press, 1988.

——. "The Domain of Creativity." In *Theories of Creativity,* ed. Mark A. Runco and Robert S. Albert, 190–212. Newbury Park, Calif.: Sage, 1990.

Curtis Brown, Spencer. Foreword to *Pictures and Conversations,* by Elizabeth Bowen, vii–xlii. New York: Alfred A. Knopf, 1975.

Dante Alighieri. *Inferno.* Trans. Charles S. Singleton. Princeton, N.J.: Princeton Univ. Press, 1977.

Davidson, Michael. *The San Francisco Renaissance: Poetics and Community at Mid-century.* Cambridge and New York: Cambridge Univ. Press, 1989.

Davis, Louise, "Just Who Was That Ward-Belmont Girl Nude in the Closet?" In *Conversations with Peter Taylor,* ed. Hubert H. McAlexander, 22–27. Jackson: Univ. Press of Mississippi, 1987.

Davisson, Mary T. "Duritia and Creativity in Exile: *Epistulae ex Ponto* 4.10." *Classical Antiquity* 1 (1982): 28–42.

———. "*Tristia* 5.13 and Ovid's Use of Epistolary Form and Content." *Classical Journal* 80 (1985): 238–46.

de Leo, Diego, and Rene F. W. Diekstra. *Depression and Suicide in Late Life.* Lewiston, N.Y.: Hogrefe and Huber, 1990.

Deltel, Danielle. "Le Scandale soufflé: Le Paradoxe dans l'écriture de Colette." In *Colette, Nouvelles Approches Critiques,* ed. Bernard Bray, 151–65. Paris: Nizet, 1986.

de Luce, Judith. "Ovid as an Idiographic Study of Creativity and Old Age." In *Old Age in Greek and Latin Literature,* ed. Thomas M. Falkner and Judith de Luce, 195–215. Albany: SUNY Press, 1989.

Derby, Irving M. "Manic-Depressive 'Exhaustion' Deaths." *Psychiatric Quarterly* 7 (1933): 436–49.

Derrida, Jacques. "Fors." *Georgia Review* 31, no. 1 (Spring 1977): 64–116.

Donaldson, Scott. *John Cheever: A Biography.* New York: Random House, 1988.

Dorr, Rheta Childe. *A Woman of Fifty.* New York: Funk and Wagnalls, 1924.

Drake, William. *Sara Teasdale: Woman and Poet.* San Francisco: Harper and Row, 1979.

DuPree, Don Keck. "An Interview with Peter Taylor" (1984). In *Conversations with Peter Taylor,* ed. Hubert H. McAlexander, 54–59. Jackson: Univ. Press of Mississippi, 1987.

Eachus, Shirley. "Elinor Glyn." In *British Women Writers: A Critical Reference Guide* ed. Janet Todd, 277–79. New York: Continuum, 1989.

Easterlin, Richard A., Christine MacDonald, and Diane J. Macunovich. "Retirement Prospects of the Baby Boom Generation: A Different Perspective." *Gerontologist.* 30 (Dec. 1990): 776–83.

Eastman, Crystal. "Birth Control in the Feminist Program" (1918). In *Crystal Eastman on Women and Revolution,* ed. Blanche Wiesen Cook, 46–49. New York: Oxford, 1978.

Echols, Alice. "The Demise of Female Intimacy in the Twentieth Century." *Michigan Occasional Papers* 6 (Fall 1978): 1–29.

Ehrenpreis, Irvin. *Swift: The Man, His Works, and the Age.* 3 vols. Cambridge: Harvard Univ. Press, 1962–83.

Elbow, Peter. "The Doubting Game and the Believing Game—An Analysis of the Intellectual Enterprise" (1973). In *Writing without Teachers,* 147–91. London: Oxford, 1973.

Ellis, Havelock. *Man and Woman: A Study of Human Secondary Sexual Characteristics.* 3d ed. London: Walter Scott; New York: Scribner's, 1902.

———. *Psychology of Sex: A Manual for Students.* New York: R. Long and R. R. Smith, 1933.

———. *Studies in the Psychology of Sex.* Vol. 3. New York: Random House, 1936.

Ellmann, Richard. *Yeats: The Man and the Masks.* Oxford: Oxford Univ. Press, 1979.

Erikson, Erik. *Childhood and Society.* New York: Norton, 1950. 2d ed. New York: Norton, 1963.

———. *Insight and Responsibility.* New York: Norton, 1964.

———. "Reflections on Dr. Borg's Life Cycle." In *Aging, Death, and the Comple-*

tion of Being, ed. David Van Tassel, 29–67. Philadelphia: Univ. of Pennsylvania Press, 1979.

——. *The Life Cycle Completed: A Review.* 1982. Rept. New York: Norton, 1985.

——, Joan M. Erikson, and Helen Q. Kivnick. *Vital Involvement in Old Age: The Experience of Old Age in Our Time.* New York: W. W. Norton, 1986.

Erkkila, Betsy. "Greta Garbo: Sailing beyond the Frame." *Critical Inquiry* 7 (1985): 595–619.

Esler, Carol C. "Horace's Old Girls: Evolution of a Topos." In *Old Age in Greek and Latin Literature,* ed. Thomas M. Falkner and Judith de Luce, 172–82. Albany: SUNY Press, 1989.

Evans, Harry B. *Publica Carmina: Ovid's Tomitian Exile.* Lincoln: Univ. of Nebraska Press, 1983.

Falkner, Thomas M., and Judith de Luce. "A View from Antiquity: Greece, Rome, and Elders." In *Handbook of Humanities and Aging,* ed. Thomas R. Cole, David D. Van Tassel, and Robert Kastenbaum, 3–39. New York: Springer Publishing, 1992.

——, eds. *Old Age in Greek and Latin Literature.* Albany: SUNY Press, 1989.

Ferber, Edna. *A Peculiar Treasure.* New York: Doubleday Doran, 1939.

Fernandez, Dominique. *Le Rapt de Ganymède.* Paris: Bernard Grasset, 1989.

Finley, M. I. "The Elderly in Classical Antiquity." *Greece and Rome* 28 (1981) 156–71. Rept. in *Old Age in Greek and Latin Literature,* ed. Thomas M. Falkner and Judith de Luce, 1–20. Albany: SUNY Press, 1989.

Fischer, John Irwin. *On Swift's Poetry.* Gainesville: Univ. Presses of Florida, 1978.

Forbis, Elizabeth. "Voice and Voicelessness in Ovid's *Metamorphoses* and Exile Poetry." Paper presented at the 1991 annual meeting of the Classical Association of the Middle West and South.

Forster, E. M. *Commonplace Book.* Ed. Philip Gardner. Stanford, Calif.: Stanford Univ. Press, 1985.

Fowlie, Wallace. "On Writing Autobiography." In *Studies in Autobiography,* ed. James Olney, 163–70. New York: Oxford Univ. Press, 1988.

Frank, Elizabeth. *Louise Bogan: A Portrait.* New York: Alfred A. Knopf, 1985.

Frankel, Hermann. *Ovid: A Poet between Two Worlds.* 1945. Rept. Berkeley: Univ. of California Press, 1969.

Freud, Anna. *The Ego and the Mechanisms of Defence.* 1936. Rev. ed. London: Hogarth Press and Institute of Psycho-Analysis, 1986.

——. "About Losing and Being Lost." *Psychoanalytic Study of the Child* 22 (1967): 9–19.

Freud, Ernst L., ed. *Letters of Sigmund Freud.* Trans. Tania and James Stern. New York: Basic Books, 1969.

Freud, Sigmund. *The Interpretation of Dreams* (1900). In *The Standard Edition of the Complete Psychological Works of Sigmund Freud.* Trans. and ed. James Strachey. 24 vols. London: Hogarth Press and Institute of Psycho-Analysis, 1953–74. SE 4–5:xi–338, 339–627.

——. "The Transformations of Puberty" (1905). In *Three Essays on the Theory of Sexuality,* trans. and ed. James Strachey, 73–96. New York: Basic Books, 1975.

——. "On Transience." 1916. SE 14:304–7.

——. "Mourning and Melancholia." 1917. *SE* 14:239–58.

——. *Beyond the Pleasure Principle*. 1920. *SE* 18:7–64.

——. *Inhibitions, Symptoms and Anxiety*. 1926. *SE* 20:77–175.

Fried, Debra. "Andromeda Unbound: Gender and Genre in Millay's Sonnets." *Twentieth-Century Literature* 32 (1986): 1–22.

Fromm, Gloria G. *Dorothy Richardson: A Biography*. Urbana: University of Illinois Press, 1977.

Fry, P. S. *Depression, Stress, and Adaptations in the Elderly: Psychological Assessment and Intervention*. Rockville, Md.: Aspen, 1986.

Furness, Clifton Joseph. Introduction to *The Genteel Female: An Anthology*. New York: Knopf, 1931.

Furst, Lilian R. "Realism and Its 'Code of Accreditation.'" *Comparative Literature Studies* 25 (1988): 101–26.

Garnett, David. *The Golden Echo*. New York: Harcourt, 1954.

George, Diana Hume. "Who Is the Double Ghost Whose Head Is Smoke? Double Haunting and Double Discourse in Women's Poetry on Aging." In *Memory and Desire: Aging—Literature—Psychology*, ed. Kathleen Woodward and Murray M. Schwartz, 134–53. Bloomington: Indiana Univ. Press, 1986.

——. "Itinerary of an Obsession: Maxine Kumin on Anne Sexton." In *Original Essays on the Poetry of Anne Sexton*, ed. Frances Bixler, 243–66. Conway: Univ. of Central Arkansas Press, 1988.

——, and Malcolm A. Nelson. *Epitaph and Icon*. Orleans, Mass.: Parnassus Imprints, 1983.

Georgotas, Anastasios, and Robert Cancro. *Depression and Mania*. New York: Elsevier, 1988.

Gilligan, Carol. *In a Different Voice: Psychological Theory and Women's Development*. Cambridge: Harvard Univ. Press, 1982.

——. "Adolescent Development Reconsidered." In *Mapping the Moral Domain: A Contribution of Women's Thinking to Psychological Theory and Education*, ed. Carol Gilligan, Janie Victoria Ward, Jill McLean Taylor, with Betty Bardige, vii–xxxviii. Cambridge: Center for the Study of Gender, Education and Human Development, Harvard Univ. Graduate School of Education, 1988.

——. "Remapping the Moral Domain: New Images of Self in Relationship." In *Mapping the Moral Domain: A Contribution of Women's Thinking to Psychological Theory and Education*, ed. Carol Gilligan, Janie Victoria Ward, Jill McLean Taylor, with Betty Bardige, 3–19. Cambridge: Center for the Study of Gender, Education and Human Development, Harvard Univ. Graduate School of Education, 1988.

——, Janie Victoria Ward, Jill McLean Taylor, with Betty Bardige, eds. *Mapping the Moral Domain: A Contribution of Women's Thinking to Psychological Theory and Education*. Cambridge: Center for the Study of Gender, Education and Human Development, Harvard University Graduate School of Education, 1988.

Gilmore, Thomas B. "The Comedy of Swift's Scatological Poems." *PMLA* 91 (1976): 33–43.

Glaser, Barney G., and Anselm L. Strauss. *The Discovery of Grounded Theory:*

Strategies for Qualitative Research. New York: Aldine de Gruyter, 1967.

Glasgow, Ellen. *The Woman Within.* New York: Harcourt, Brace, 1954.

Glendinning, Victoria. *Elizabeth Bowen: Portrait of a Writer.* 1977. Rept. Harmondsworth, Middlesex, Eng.: Penguin, 1985.

Glück, Louise. *The House on Marshland.* New York: Ecco Press, 1975. 14.

Goleman, Daniel. "Erikson, in His Own Old Age, Expands His View of Life." *New York Times,* June 14, 1988 (National ed.), 13, 16.

——. "New Studies Find Many Myths about Mourning." *New York Times: Science Times,* Aug. 8, 1989 (National ed.), 17, 20.

Goodwin, Frederick K., and Kay Redfield Jamison. *Manic-Depressive Illness.* New York: Oxford Univ. Press, 1990.

Gower, Herschel. "The Nashville Stories." *Shenandoah* 28 (Winter 1977): 37–47.

Gray, James. Preface to *Working Out Ideas: Predication and Other Uses of Language,* by Josephine Miles, iii. Univ. of California, Bay Area Writing Project, Curriculum Publication no. 5. Berkeley, 1979.

——, and Miles Myers. "The Bay Area Writing Project." *Phi Delta Kappan,* Feb. 1978, 410–13.

Green, Georgia M. *Pragmatics and Natural Language Understanding.* Hillsdale, N.J.: Lawrence Erlbaum Associates, 1989.

Green, Peter. "Carmen et Error. πρόφασι ς and αἰΤί α in the Matter of Ovid's Exile." *Classical Antiquity* 1 (1982): 202–20.

Greenwell, Bill. "Goose Corn." Review of *Oh What a Paradise It Seems,* by John Cheever. *New Statesman,* Nov. 23, 1982, 22–23.

Griffith, Albert J. *The Achievement of Peter Taylor.* Boston: Twayne, 1970.

Grunes, Jerome, and Wendy Wasson. "The Significance of Loss and Mourning in the Older Adult: Clinical and Research Findings." In *The Problem of Loss and Mourning: Psychoanalytic Perspectives,* ed. David R. Dietrich and Peter C. Shabad, 175–84. Madison, Conn.: International Universities Press, 1989.

Gubrium, Jaber F. *Life and Death at Murray Manor.* New York: St. Martin's Press, 1975.

——. "New Thoughts on Identity in the Upward Years." Paper presented at symposium, Writing in the Upward Years, Santa Fe Community College, Gainesville, Fla., March 17, 1990.

Gullette, Margaret Morganroth. "The Exile of Adulthood: Pedophilia in the Decline Novel." *Novel* 17, no. 3 (Spring 1984): 215–32.

——. *Safe at Last in the Middle Years: The Invention of the Midlife Progress Novel: Saul Bellow, Margaret Drabble, Anne Tyler, and John Updike.* Berkeley: Univ. of California Press, 1988.

——. "The Deaths of Children and the Fear of Aging in Contemporary American Fiction." *Michigan Quarterly Review* (Winter 1992): 56–72.

——. "The Cultural Invention of the 'Postmaternal' Woman (1897–1926): Idle, Useless, and Out of a Job." (Manuscript under consideration.)

——. "The Invention of Male Midlife Sexual Decline." *Midlife Fictions: The Construction of the Middle Years of Life, 1880–1935.* In progress.

Gussow, Adam. "Cheever's Failed Paradise: The Short-Story Writer as Novelist." *Literary Review* 27, no. 1 (Fall 1983): 103–16.

Gutmann, David L. "Psychoanalysis and Aging: A Developmental View." In *The Course of Life: Psychoanalytic Contributions toward Understanding Personality Development.* Vol. 3. *Adulthood and the Aging Process,* ed. Stanley I. Greenspan and George H. Pollock, 489–517. Washington, D.C.: National Institute of Mental Health, Department of Health and Human Services, 1981.

——. *Reclaimed Powers: Toward a New Psychology of Men and Women in Later Life.* New York: Basic Books, 1987.

Hall, G. Stanley. *Senescence: The Last Half of Life.* New York: D. Appleton, 1922.

Hallett, Judith P. "Heeding Our Native Informants: The Use of Latin Literary Texts in Recovering Elite Roman Attitudes towards Age, Gender, and Social Status." Paper delivered at the Univ. of Cincinnati, 1991.

Hamilton, Cicely. *Life Errant.* London: J. M. Dent, 1935.

Hammond, Karla M. "An Interview with Josephine Miles." *Southern Review* 19 (1983): 606–31.

Hanscombe, Gillian, and Virginia L. Smyers. *Writing for Their Lives: The Modernist Women, 1910–1940.* Boston: Northeastern Univ. Press, 1987.

Harcum, C. G. "The Ages of Man: A Study Suggested by Horace, *Ars Poetica.*" *Classical World* 7 (1914): 114–18.

Hareven, Tamara. "The Last Stage: Historical Adulthood and Old Age." *Daedalus* 105, no. 4 (Fall 1976): 13–27.

Harrington, David M. "The Ecology of Human Creativity: A Psychological Perspective." In *Theories of Creativity,* ed. Mark A. Runco and Robert S. Albert, 143–69. Newbury Park, Calif.: Sage, 1990.

Harris, Elaine. *L'Approfondissement de la sensualité dans l'oeuvre romanesque de Colette.* Paris: Nizet, 1973.

Harrison, Michael. *Clarence: The Life of H.R.H. the Duke of Clarence and Avondale (1864–1892).* London: W. H. Allen, 1972.

Heath, Stephen. *The Sexual Fix.* New York: Schocken, 1984.

Heidegger, Martin. *Poetry, Language, and Thought.* Trans. Albert Hofstadter. New York: Harper & Row, 1957.

——. *Basic Writings.* Ed. David Farrell Krell. New York: Harper and Row, 1977.

Heilbrun, Carolyn. "Edna Ferber." In *Notable American Women: The Modern Period,* ed. Barbara Sicherman and Carol Hurd Green. Cambridge: Harvard Univ. Press, 1971.

——. *Writing a Woman's Life.* New York: Norton, 1988.

Hendricks, Jon, and Cynthia A. Leedham. "Making Sense of Literary Aging: Relevance of Recent Gerontological Theory." *Journal of Aging Studies* 1 (1987): 187–208.

Hildebidle, John. *Five Irish Writers: The Errand of Keeping Alive.* Cambridge: Harvard Univ. Press, 1989.

Hinds, Stephen. "Booking the Return Trip: Ovid and *Tristia* 1." *Proceedings of the Cambridge Philosophical Society* 31 (1985): 13–32.

Hofstadter, Beatrice K. "Gene Stratton Porter." In *Notable American Women, 1607–1950,* vol. 3, ed. Edward T. James, Janet Wilson James, Paul S. Boyer. Cambridge: Harvard Univ. Press, 1971.

Holland, Norman N. "Unity Identity Text Self." *PMLA* 90 (1975): 813–822.

——. "Not So Little Hans: Identity and Aging." In *Memory and Desire: Aging*

—*Literature—Psychoanalysis*, ed. Kathleen Woodward and Murray M. Schwartz, 51–75. Bloomington: Indiana Univ. Press, 1986.

——. *The Brain of Robert Frost: A Cognitive Approach to Literature*. New York: Routledge, 1988.

——. *The Critical I*. New York: Columbia Univ. Press, 1992.

Holleman, A. W. J. "Ovid's Exile." *Liverpool Classical Monthly* 10 (1985): 48.

Hollingworth, Leta S. "The New Woman in the Making." *Current History* 27 (Oct. 1927): 15–20.

Holtby, Winifred. *Women and a Changing Civilization*. New York: Longmans, Green, 1935.

Homans, Margaret. *Women Writers and Poetic Identity*. Princeton, N.J.: Princeton Univ. Press, 1980.

——. *Bearing the Word: Language and Female Experience in Nineteenth-Century Women's Writing*. Chicago: Univ. of Chicago Press, 1986.

Homans, Peter. *The Ability to Mourn: Disillusionment and the Social Origins of Psychoanalysis*. Chicago: Univ. of Chicago Press, 1989.

Honan, Park. "The Theory of Biography." *Novel: A Forum on Fiction* 13 (Fall 1979): 109–20.

Horace. *Satires, Epistles, and Ars Poetica*. Trans. W. H. Fairclough. London: William Heinemann, 1926.

——. *The Odes of Horace*. Trans. J. Michie. New York: Orion Press, 1963.

Hough, Graham. *The Dark Sun: A Study of D. H. Lawrence*. New York: Octagon Books, 1973.

Hull, Gloria T. *Color, Sex, and Poetry: Three Women Writers of the Harlem Renaissance*. Bloomington: Indiana Univ. Press, 1987.

Jameson, Storm. "Delicate Monster." *Women against Men*. New York: Knopf, 1933.

——. "More on D[orothy] R[ichardson]." *Adam International Review*, nos. 310–12 (1966): 24.

Jamison, Kay Redfield. "Psychotherapeutic Issues and Suicide Prevention in the Treatment of Bipolar Disorders." *Psychiatry Update: American Psychiatric Association Annual Review* 6 (1987): 108–24.

——. "Mood Disorders and Patterns of Creativity in British Writers and Artists." *Psychiatry* 52, no. 2 (1989): 125–34.

Jaques, Elliot. "Death and the Mid-Life Crisis." *International Journal of Psychoanalysis* 46 (1965): 502–14.

Jeffares, A. Norman. *William Butler Yeats: A New Biography*. London: Hutchinson, 1988.

Jelinek, Estelle. *The Tradition of Women's Autobiography from Antiquity to the Present*. Boston: Twayne, 1986.

Jones, Ernest L., ed. *Letters of Sigmund Freud*. Trans. Tania and James Stern. New York: Basic Books, 1969.

Kaminsky, Marc. "Story of the Shoe Box: On the Meaning and Practice of Transmitting Stories." In *Handbook of the Humanities and Aging*, ed. Thomas R. Cole, David D. Van Tassel, and Robert Kastenbaum, 307–27. New York: Springer Publishing, 1992.

Kaplan, Robin, and Shelley Neiderbach. "I Live Alone in a Very Beautiful Place: An Interview with May Sarton" (1977). In *Conversations with May Sarton*, ed. Earl G. Ingersoll, 52–63. Jackson: University Press of Mississippi, 1991.

Kastenbaum, Robert. "The Creative Process: A Life-span Approach." In *Handbook of the Humanities and Aging*, ed. Thomas R. Cole, David D. Van Tassel, and Robert Kastenbaum, 285–306. New York: Springer Publishing, 1992.

Kaufman, Sharon R. *The Ageless Self: Sources of Meaning in Late Life.* 1986. Rept. New York: New American Library, 1987.

——. "Illness, Biography, and the Interpretation of Self Following a Stroke. *Journal of Aging Studies* 2 (1988): 217–27.

Kennedy, J. Gerald. "Roland Barthes, Autobiography, and the End of Writing." *Georgia Review* 35, no. 2 (Summer 1981): 381–98.

Kenyon, Gary M. "Basic Assumptions in Theories of Human Aging." In *Emergent Theories of Aging*, ed. James E. Birren and Vern L. Bengtson, 3–18. New York: Springer Publishing, 1988.

Kershner, R. B., Jr. "Bowen's Oneiric *House in Paris*." *Texas Studies in Literature and Language* 28 (Winter 1986): 407–23.

Kirby, Kathleen. "Indifferent Boundaries: Studies in the Subject, Language and Power." Manuscript, 1989.

Klein, Melanie. "Mourning and Its Relation to Manic-Depressive States." *International Journal of Psycho-Analysis* 21 (1940): 125–53.

Kopald, Sylvia. "Where Are the Female Geniuses?" In *Our Changing Morality*, ed. Freda Kirchwey, 107–26. New York: Albert and Charles Boni, 1924.

Kuhn, Margaret E., and Bader, Jeanne E. "Old and Young Are Alike in Many Ways." *Gerontologist* 31 (April 1991): 273–74.

Kumin, Maxine. Interview with Karla Hammond. In *To Make a Prairie: Essays on Poets, Poetry, and Country Living*, by Maxine Kumin, 47–65. Ann Arbor: Univ. of Michigan Press, 1979.

——. Interview with Martha Meek. In *To Make a Prairie: Essays on Poets, Poetry, and Country Living*, by Maxine Kumin, 19–34. Ann Arbor: Univ. of Michigan Press, 1979.

——. *To Make a Prairie: Essays on Poets, Poetry, and Country Living.* Ann Arbor: Univ. of Michigan Press, 1979.

——. *Our Ground Time Here Will Be Brief: New and Selected Poems.* New York: Penguin Books, 1982.

——. Interview with Diana Hume George. *Poesis: A Journal of Criticism* 6, no. 2 (1984): 1–18.

——. *Nurture.* New York: Viking Penguin, 1989.

——. *Looking for Luck.* New York: Norton, 1992.

——. Interview with Diana Hume George. *Associated Writing Programs Chronicle*, forthcoming, Spring 1993.

Kunitz, Stanley J., and Howard Haycraft, "Temple Bailey." In *Twentieth Century Authors: A Biographical Dictionary of Modern Literature.* New York: H. W. Wilson, 1942.

Labouvie-Vief, Gisela. "Logic and Self-Regulation from Youth to Maturity: A Model." In *Beyond Formal Operations: Late Adolescent and Adult Cognitive Development*, eds. Francis A. Richards, Cheryl Armon, and Michael L. Commons, 158–79. New York: Praeger, 1984.

Lacan, Jacques. "The Function and Field of Speech and Language" (1953). In

Ecrits: A Selection, trans. Alan Sheridan, 30–113. New York: Norton, 1977.

———. "Desire and the Interpretation of Desire in *Hamlet*" (1959). Trans. James Hulbert. *Yale French Studies* 55/56 (1977): 11–52.

Lang, Elsie M. *British Women in the Twentieth Century.* London: T. Werner Laurie, 1929.

Laslett, Peter. *The World We Have Lost.* New York: Scribners, 1965.

Lassner, Phyllis. *Elizabeth Bowen.* Women Writers, gen. ed., Eva Figes and Adele King. Houndmills, Basingstoke, Eng.: Macmillan Education, 1990.

Lauter, Paul. "Race and Gender in the Shaping of the American Literary Canon: A Case Study from the Twenties." In *Feminist Criticism and Social Change: Sex, Class, and Race in Literature and Culture,* ed. Judith Newton and Deborah Rosenfelt, 19–44. New York and London: Methuen, 1985.

Lawrence, D. H. *The Plumed Serpent.* 1926. Rept. New York: Vintage-Knopf, 1959.

———. *The Collected Letters of D. H. Lawrence.* Ed. Harry T. Moore. 2 vols. New York: Viking, 1962.

———. *The Complete Poems of D. H. Lawrence.* Ed. Vivian de Sola Pinto and Warren Roberts. New York: Viking Press, 1964.

———. *The Complete Plays of D. H. Lawrence.* New York: Viking, 1966.

———. *Sons and Lovers, St. Mawr, The Fox, The White Peacock, Love among the Haystacks, The Virgin and the Gipsy, Lady Chatterly's Lover.* London: Heinemann, 1976.

———. *The Letters of D. H. Lawrence.* Ed. James T. Boulton. Vol. 1. Cambridge: Cambridge Univ. Press, 1979.

Leavis, F. R. *D. H. Lawrence: Novelist.* Chicago: Univ. of Chicago Press, 1955.

Lee, Hermione. *Elizabeth Bowen: An Estimation.* London: Vision Press and Totowa, N.J.: Barnes & Noble, 1981.

———. *Willa Cather: Double Lives.* New York: Pantheon, 1989.

Lee, Jae Num. *Swift and Scatological Satire.* Albuquerque: Univ. of New Mexico Press, 1971.

Levinson, Daniel J., with Charlotte N. Darrow, Edward B. Klein, Maria H. Levinson, and Braxton McKee. *The Seasons of a Man's Life.* 1978. Rept. New York: Ballantine, 1979.

Liang, Vernon H. "Josephine Miles." *Dictionary of Literary Biography: American Poets, 1880–1945,* 2d ser., 48 (1986): 298–304.

Lifton, Robert Jay. *The Life of the Self: Toward A New Psychology.* New York: Simon and Schuster, 1976.

Lipking, Lawrence. *The Life of the Poet: Beginning and Ending Poetic Careers.* Chicago: Univ. of Chicago Press, 1981.

Loewald, Hans W. "Internalization, Separation, Mourning, and the Superego." *Psychoanalytic Quarterly* 31 (1962): 483–504.

Lombroso, C. *The Man of Genius.* London: Walter Scott, 1891.

"Louise Bogan, Noted Poet Who Wrote about Love, Dead." *New York Times,* Feb. 5, 1970, 39.

Lowry, Edith. *The Woman of Forty.* Chicago: Forbes, 1919.

Luhan, Mabel Dodge. *Lorenzo in Taos.* New York: Knopf, 1932.

Lytle, Andrew. "The Displaced Family." *Sewanee Review* 66 (1958): 115–20.

McDowell, Margaret B. "Mary Webb." *Dictionary of Literary Biography: British Novelists, 1890–1929: Traditionalists* 34 (1985): 281–91.

Malouf, David. *An Imaginary Life.* New York: Braziller, 1978.

Marcus, Jane. Introduction to *The Judge,* by Rebecca West. London: Virago, 1980.

——. "Invincible Mediocrity: The Private Selves of Public Women." In *The Private Self,* ed. Shari Benstock., 114–46. Chapel Hill: Univ. of North Carolina Press, 1988.

——. "Virginia Woolf and Her Violin: Mothering, Madness, and Music." In *Virginia Woolf: Centennial Essays,* ed. Elaine K. Ginsberg and Laura Moss Gottlieb, 27–49. Troy, N.Y.: Whitson, 1983.

Maris, Ronald, ed. *Biology of Suicide.* New York: Guilford, 1986.

Martin, Emily. *The Woman in the Body: A Cultural Analysis of Reproduction.* Boston: Beacon Press, 1987.

Meisel-Hess, Grete. *The Sexual Crisis: A Critique of Our Sexual Life.* Trans. Eden and Cedar Paul. New York: Critic and Guide, 1917.

Mencken, H. L. "Fiction Good and Bad." *American Mercury* 6, no. 23 (Nov. 1925): 379–81.

Mercer, Ramona T., Elizabeth G. Nichols, and Glen Caspers Doyle. *Transitions in a Woman's Life: Major Life Events in Developmental Context.* Springer Series: Focus on Women, vol. 12. New York: Springer, 1989.

Merrild, Knud. *A Poet and Two Painters.* 1938. Rept. *With D. H. Lawrence in New Mexico.* New York: Barnes and Noble, 1965.

Metchnikoff, Ilia Ilich. *The Prolongation of Life: Optimistic Studies.* Trans. P. Chalmers Mitchell. New York: Putnam, 1908.

Meyers, Jeffrey. *D. H. Lawrence: A Biography.* New York: Knopf, 1990.

Middlebrook, Diane Wood. *Anne Sexton: A Biography.* Boston: Houghton Mifflin, 1991.

Miles, Josephine. *To All Appearances: Poems, New and Selected.* Urbana: Univ. of Illinois Press, 1974.

——. *Coming to Terms.* Urbana: Univ. of Illinois Press, 1979.

——. *Working Out Ideas: Predication and Other Uses of Language.* Univ. of California, Bay Area Writing Project, Curriculum Publication no. 5. Berkeley, 1979.

——. *Collected Poems, 1930–83.* Urbana: Univ. of Illinois Press, 1983.

——. "Concert." In *The Norton Anthology of Literature by Women: The Tradition in English,* ed. Sandra M. Gilbert and Susan Gubar. New York: Norton, 1985.

Miller, Jean Baker. *Toward a New Psychology of Women.* 1976. 2d ed. Boston: Beacon Press, 1986.

Miller, Nancy K. "The Anamnesis of a Female 'I': In the Margins of Self-Portrayal." In *Colette: The Woman, The Writer,* ed. Erica Eisinger and Mari McCarty, 164–75. Univ. Park: Pennsylvania State Univ. Press, 1981.

——. *Subject to Change: Reading Feminist Writing.* New York: Columbia Univ. Press, 1988.

Milner, Marion. *The Suppressed Madness of Sane Men: Forty-four Years of Exploring Psychoanalysis.* New Library of Psychoanalysis, 3, gen. ed., David Tuckett. London: Tavistock Publications, 1987.

Mills-Courts, Karen. *Poetry as Epitaph: Representation and Poetic Language.* Baton Rouge: Louisiana State Univ. Press, 1990.

Money, John. *Lovemaps: Clinical Concepts of Sexual/Erotic Health and Pathology, Paraphilia, and Gender Transposition in Childhood, Adolescence, and Maturity.* New York: Irving Publishers, 1986.

——. *Gay, Straight, and In-Between: The Sexology of Erotic Orientation.* New York: Oxford Univ. Press, 1988.

Monks House Papers. Leonard Woolf's diary housed in the Univ. of Sussex Library.

Monroe, Harriet. *A Poet's Life: Seventy Years in a Changing World.* New York: Macmillan, 1938.

Montherlant, Henry de. *Romans I.* Bibliothèque de la Pléiade. Paris: Gallimard, 1959.

——. *Va jouer avec cette poussière.* Paris: Gallimard, 1966.

——. *La Mort qui fait le trottoir (Don Juan).* Paris: Gallimard, 1972.

——. *Théâtre.* Bibliothèque de la Pléiade. Paris: Gallimard, 1972.

——. *Romans II.* Bibliothèque de la Pléiade. Paris: Gallimard, 1982.

——, and Roger Peyrefitte. *Correspondance.* Paris: Laffont, 1983.

Moody, Harry R. *Abundance of Life: Human Development Policies for an Aging Society.* Columbia Studies of Social Gerontology and Aging, ed. Abraham Monk. New York: Columbia Univ. Press, 1988.

Moss, Howard. "Elizabeth Bowen: Interior Children." In *Minor Monuments: Selected Essays by Howard Moss,* 224–36. New York: Ecco Press, 1986; orig. in the *New Yorker,* 1979.

Murry, John Middleton. *Between Two Worlds: An Autobiography.* New York: Julian Messner, 1936.

Nadel, Ira Bruce. *Biography: Fiction, Fact and Form.* New York: St. Martin's Press, 1984.

Nagle, Betty Rose. *The Poetics of Exile: Program and Polemic in the* Tristia and Epistulae ex Ponto *of Ovid.* Bruxelles: Latomus, 1980.

Nisbet, R. G. M. "Great and Lesser Bear (Ovid *Tristia* 3.4)." *Journal of Roman Studies* 82 (1982): 49–56.

Norris, Kathleen. *Noon: An Autobiographical Sketch.* Garden City, N.Y.: Doubleday, Page, 1925.

O'Brien, Sharon. *Willa Cather: The Emerging Voice.* New York: Oxford Univ. Press, 1987.

Olney, James. *Metaphors of Self: The Meaning of Autobiography.* Princeton, N.J.: Princeton Univ. Press, 1972.

——, ed. *Autobiography: Essays Theoretical and Critical.* Princeton, N.J.: Princeton Univ. Press, 1980.

——, ed. *Studies in Autobiography.* New York: Oxford Univ. Press, 1988.

Opfell, Olga S. *The Lady Laureates.* 2d ed. Metuchen, N.J.: Scarecrow Press, 1986.

Ostriker, Alicia Suskin. *Stealing the Language: The Emergence of Women's Poetry in America.* Boston: Beacon Press, 1986.

Ottaway, Robert. "Terrible Beauty." Review of *Oh What a Paradise It Seems,* by John Cheever. *Listener,* Aug. 12, 1982, 24.

Ovid. *Metamorphoses.* Trans. F. J. Miller. Cambridge: Harvard Univ. Press, 1968.

——. *Tristia and Epistulae ex Ponto.* Trans. A. L. Wheeler. Loeb Classical Library. Cambridge: Harvard Univ. Press, 1975.

——. *Heroides and Amores.* Trans. G. Showerman. Loeb Classical Library. Cambridge: Harvard Univ. Press, 1977.

Parsons, Alice Beal. *Woman's Dilemma.* 1926. Rept. New York: Arno, 1974.

Percy, Walker. *The Last Gentleman.* 1966. Rept. New York: New American Library, 1968.

——. *The Thanatos Syndrome.* New York: Farrar Straus Giroux, 1987.

Peyrefitte, Roger. *Propos secrets.* Paris: Albin Michel, 1977.

Pinkerton, Jan. "The Non-Regionalism of Peter Taylor." *Georgia Review* 24 (Winter 1970): 432–40.

Pinsker, Sanford. "Interview with Josephine Miles." In *American Poetry Observed: Poets on Their Work,* ed. Joe David Bellamy, 181–87. Urbana: Univ. of Illinois Press, 1984.

Pollock, George H. "Mourning and Adaptation." *International Journal of Psycho-Analysis* 43 (1962): 341–61.

——. "Mourning and Memorialization through Music." *Annual of Psychoanalysis* 3 (1975): 423–36. New York: International Universities Press, 1975.

——. "On Mourning, Immortality, and Utopia." *Journal of American Psychoanalytic Association* 23, no. 2 (1975): 334–62.

——. "Aging or Aged: Development or Pathology." In *The Course of Life: Psychoanalytic Contributions toward Understanding Personality Development.* Vol. 3. *Adulthood and the Aging Process,* ed. Stanley I. Greenspan and George H. Pollock, 549–85. Washington, D.C.: National Institute of Mental Health, 1981.

——. "The Mourning Process, the Creative Process, and the Creation." *The Problem of Loss and Mourning: Psychoanalytic Perspectives,* ed. David R. Dietrich and Peter C. Shabad, 27–59. Madison, Conn.: International Universities Press, 1989.

Pontalis, J.-B. *Frontiers in Psychoanalysis: Between the Dream and Psychic Pain* (1977). Trans. Catherine Cullen and Philip Cullen. New York: International Universities Press, 1981.

——. "On Death-Work in Freud, in the Self, in Culture" (1978). Trans. Susan D. Cohen. In *Psychoanalysis, Creativity, and Literature: A Franco-American Inquiry,* ed. Alan Roland, 85–95. New York: Columbia Univ. Press, 1978.

Porter, Laurel, and Laurence M. Porter, eds. *Aging in Literature.* Troy, Mich.: International Book Publishers, 1984.

Project on the Status and Education of Women, Association of American Colleges. *Minority Women and Higher Education,* no. 1. Washington, D.C., 1984.

Pym, Barbara. *Quartet in Autumn.* 1977. New York: Dutton, 1978.

——. MSS, Bodleian Library, Oxford, England.

Pyron, Darden. *Southern Daughter: The Life of Margaret Mitchell.* New York: Oxford Univ. Press, 1991.

Rand, Nicholas. "Psychoanalysis with Literature: An Abstract of Nicolas Abraham and Maria Torok's *The Shell and the Kernel.*" *Oxford Literary Review. Psychoanalysis and Literature: New Work* 12 (1990): 57–62.

Rankin, Sally H. "The Emergence of Creativity in Later Life." In *Transitions in a Woman's Life: Major Life Events in Developmental Context,* ed. Ramona T.

Mercer, Elizabeth G. Nichols, and Glen Caspers Doyle, 167–78. Springer Series: Focus on Women, vol. 12. New York: Springer, 1989.

Resch, Yannick. "Colette ou le Plaisir-Texte." In *Colette, Nouvelles Approches Critiques*, ed. Bernard Bray, 167–73. Paris: Nizet, 1986.

Revere, Virginia, and Sheldon S. Tobin. "Myth and Reality: The Older Person's Relationship to His Past." *International Journal of Aging and Human Development* 12 (1980): 15–24.

Richards, Francis A., Cheryl Armon, and Michael L. Commons. "Perspectives on the Development of Thought in Late Adolescence and Adulthood: An Introduction." In *Beyond Formal Operations: Late Adolescent and Adult Cognitive Development*, ed. Francis A. Richards, Cheryl Armon, and Michael L. Commons, 3–27. New York: Praeger, 1984.

Richardson, Dorothy. "Women in the Arts: Some Notes on the Eternally Conflicting Demands of Humanity and Art," *Vanity Fair* May 24, 1925, 47, 100.

——. "Excursion," *English Story*, 6th ser., 1945:107–12.

——. "Visitor," *Life and Letters* 46 (Sept. 1945): 167–72.

——. "Visit," *Life and Letters* 46 (Sept. 1945): 173–81.

——. "Old Age." *Adam International Review*, nos. 310–12 (1966): 25–26.

——. *Pilgrimage*. London: J. M. Dent and the Cresset Press, 1967.

——. *Journey to Paradise*. Ed. Trudi Tate. London: Virago, 1989.

Richlin, Amy. *The Garden of Priapus: Sexuality and Aggression in Roman Humor*. New Haven: Yale Univ. Press, 1983.

Robinson, William J. *Sexual Problems of Today*. New York: Truth, 1921.

Robison, James Curry. *Peter Taylor: A Study of the Short Fiction*. Boston: Twayne, 1988.

Rochlin, Gregory. *Griefs and Discontents: The Forces of Change*. Boston: Little, Brown, 1965.

Roethke, Theodore. "The Poetry of Louise Bogan." In *Critical Essays on Louise Bogan*, ed. Martha Collins, 87–96. Boston: G. K. Hall, 1984.

Rooke, Constance. "Hagar's Old Age: *The Stone Angel* as *Vollendungsroman*." In *Crossing the River: Essays in Honour of Margaret Laurence*, ed. Kristjana Gunnars, 25–42. Winnipeg, Manitoba: Turnstone Press, 1988.

——. "Old Age in Contemporary Fiction: A New Paradigm of Hope." In *Handbook of the Humanities and Aging*, ed. Thomas R. Cole, David D. Van Tassel, and Robert Kastenbaum, 241–57. New York: Springer Publishing, 1992.

Rosaldo, Renato. "Grief and a Headhunter's Rage." In *Culture and Truth: The Remaking of Social Analysis*, 1–21. Boston: Beacon, 1989.

Rose, Gilbert. "The Creativity of Everyday Life." In *Between Reality and Fantasy: Transitional Objects and Phenomena*, ed. Simon A. Grolnick, Leonard Barkin, and Werner Muensterberger, 345–62. New York: Jason Aronson, 1978.

Roy-Byrne, Peter P., et al. "Suicide and Course of Illness in Major Affective Disorder." *Journal of Affective Disorders* 15 (1988): 1–8.

Royle, Nicholas. "Crypts in London: The Novels of Elizabeth Bowen." In *Proceedings of the Eighth International Conference in Literature and Psychoanalysis, London, July, 1991*, ed. Frederico Pereira, 143–44. Lisbon: Instituto Superior de Psicologia Aplicada, 1992.

Sacks, Oliver. "A Matter of Identity." In *The Man Who Mistook His Wife for a*

Hat, and Other Clinical Tales, 103–10. New York: Summit Books, 1985.

Sagar, Keith. *D. H. Lawrence: A Calendar of His Works (with a Checklist of the Manuscripts of D. H. Lawrence by Lindeth Vasey).* Austin: Univ. of Texas Press, 1979.

Salomon, Roger B. *Desperate Storytelling: Post-Romantic Elaborations of the Mock-Heroic Mode.* Athens: Univ. of Georgia Press, 1987.

Salvaggio, Ruth. *Enlightened Absence: Neoclassical Configurations of the Feminine.* Urbana: Univ. of Illinois Press, 1988.

Salvatori, Mariolina. "Thomas Hardy and Eugenio Montale: In Mourning and in Celebration." *Journal of Aging Studies* 1 (Summer 1987): 161–85.

Sarde, Michèle. *Colette, Free and Fettered.* Trans. Richard Miller. New York: William Morrow, 1980.

Sarton, May. *The Single Hound.* 1938. Rept. New York: Norton, 1991.

——. *The Bridge of Years.* 1946. Rept. New York: Norton, 1985.

——. *Faithful Are the Wounds.* 1955. Rept. New York: Norton, 1985.

——. *I Knew a Phoenix: Sketches for an Autobiography.* 1959. Rept. New York: Norton, 1969.

——. *The Small Room.* 1961. Rept. New York: Norton, 1976.

——. "The Design of a Novel" (1963). In *Writings on Writing,* 25–37. Orono, Maine: Puckerbrush Press, 1980.

——. *Mrs. Stevens Hears the Mermaids Singing.* 1965. Rept. New York: Norton, 1975.

——. *As We Are Now.* 1973. Rept. New York: Norton, 1982.

——. *A World of Light: Portraits and Celebrations.* 1976. Rept. New York: Norton, 1988.

——. *The Education of Harriet Hatfield.* New York: Norton, 1989.

——. Poetry reading at symposium, Writing in the Upward Years, Santa Fe Community College, Gainesville, Fla., March 16, 1990.

Scarry, Elaine. *The Body in Pain: The Making and Unmaking of the World.* New York: Oxford Univ. Press, 1985.

Schaie, K. Warner, "Toward A Stage Theory of Adult Cognitive Development." 1977. Rept. *Philosophical Foundations of Gerontology,* ed. Patrick L. McKee, 261–70. New York: Human Sciences Press, 1982.

Schakel, Peter. *The Poetry of Jonathan Swift: Allusion and the Development of Poetic Style.* Madison: Univ. of Wisconsin Press, 1978.

Schiesari, Juliana. "Appropriating the Work of Women's Mourning: The Legacy of Renaissance Melancholia." Center for Twentieth Century Studies. University of Wisconsin/Milwaukee. Working Paper no. 2 (1990–91).

Schroeder, Fred E. H. "Eleanor Hodgman Porter." In *Notable American Women, 1607–1950,* ed. Edward T. James, Janet Wilson James, Paul S. Boyer. Cambridge: Harvard Univ. Press, 1971.

Showalter, Elaine, ed., *These Modern Women: Autobiographical Essays from the Twenties.* New York: Feminist Press, 1973.

Sides, W. Hampton. "Interview with Peter Taylor" (1987). In *Conversations with Peter Taylor,* ed. Hubert H. McAlexander, 129–36. Jackson: Univ. Press of Mississippi, 1987.

Siggens, Lorraine D. "Mourning: A Critical Survey of the Literature." *International Journal of Psycho-Analysis* 47 (1966): 14–25.

Simonton, Dean Keith. "Creativity, Leadership, and Chance." In *The Nature of Creativity: Contemporary Psychological Perspectives,* ed. Robert J. Sternberg, 386–426. Cambridge: Cambridge Univ. Press, 1988.

——. "Does Creativity Decline in the Later Years? Definition, Data, and Theory." *Late Life Potential: The 1987 Presidential Symposium,* ed. Marion Perlmutter, 83–112. Washington, D.C.: Gerontological Society, 1990.

——. "History, Chemistry, Psychology and Genius: An Intellectual Autobiography of Historiometry." In *Theories of Creativity,* ed. Mark A. Runco and Robert S. Albert, 92–115. Newbury Park, Calif.: Sage, 1990.

Smith, Carolyn H. "Richard Eberhart's Poems on Aging." *Journal of Aging Studies* 3 (1989): 75–80.

——. "Images of Aging in American Poetry, 1925–1985." In *Handbook of the Humanities and Aging,* ed. Thomas R. Cole, David D. Van Tassel, and Robert Kastenbaum, 217–40. New York: Springer Publishing, 1992.

Smith, Joseph. "Identificatory Styles in Depression and Grief." *International Journal of Psycho-Analysis* 55 (1971): 259–66.

Smith, Wendy. "*P[ublishers] W[eekly]* Interviews: Peter Taylor" (1985). In *Conversations with Peter Taylor,* ed. Hubert H. McAlexander, 60–65. Jackson: Univ. Press of Mississippi, 1987.

Spencer, Anna Garlin. *Women's Share in Social Culture.* New York: Mitchell Kennerly, 1913.

Spicker, Stuart F., Kathleen M. Woodward, and David D. Van Tassel, eds. *Aging and the Elderly: Humanistic Perspectives in Gerontology.* Atlantic Highlands, N.J.: Humanities Press, 1978.

Stern, Karl, Gwendolyn M. Williams, and Miguel Prados. "Grief Reactions in Later Life." *American Journal of Psychiatry* 108 (Oct. 1951): 289–94.

Stewart, Susan. *On Longing: Narratives of the Miniature, the Gigantic, the Souvenir, the Collection.* Baltimore: Johns Hopkins Univ. Press, 1984.

Stokes, Geoffrey. Review of *Oh What a Paradise It Seems,* by John Cheever. *Village Voice,* March 16, 1982, 93.

Storr, Anthony. *Churchill's Black Dog, Kafka's Mice, and Other Phenomena of the Human Mind.* New York: Grove, 1988.

Strachey, James, ed. Introduction to *Inhibitions, Symptoms, and Anxiety,* by Sigmund Freud. *SE* 20:77–86.

Sutcliff, Rosemary. *Blue Remembered Hills.* New York: William Morrow, 1984.

Swift, Jonathan. *The Prose Works of Jonathan Swift.* Ed. Herbert Davis. 13 vols. Oxford: Basil Blackwell, 1939–59.

——. *The Correspondence of Jonathan Swift.* Ed. Harold Williams. 5 vols. Oxford: Clarendon Press, 1963–65.

——. *Jonathan Swift: The Complete Poems.* Ed. Pat Rogers. English Poets Series. New Haven and London: Yale Univ. Press, 1983.

Tannen, Deborah. "What's in a Frame: Surface Evidence for Underlying Expectations." In *New Directions in Discourse Processing.* Advances in Discourse Processes, ed. Roy O. Freedle, 2:137–81. Norwood, N.J.: Ablex Publishing, 1979.

Taylor, Peter. "Three Heroines" (1975). In *In the Miro District and Other Stories,* 143–56. New York: Alfred A. Knopf, 1977.

——. "In the Miro District" (1977). In *In the Miro District and Other Stories,* 159–204. New York: Alfred A. Knopf, 1977.

——. *The Collected Stories.* New York: Farrar, Straus and Giroux, 1979.

Thibault, John C. *The Mystery of Ovid's Exile.* Berkeley: Univ. of California Press, 1964.

Tiverton, Father William [Martin Jarrett-Kerr]. *D. H. Lawrence and Human Existence.* London: Rockcliff, 1951.

Tolchin, Neal L. *Mourning, Gender, and Creativity in the Art of Herman Melville.* New Haven: Yale Univ. Press, 1988.

Trombley, Stephen. *All That Summer She Was Mad: Virginia Woolf, Female Victim of Male Medicine.* New York: Continuum, 1982.

Tsuang, Ming T., Robert F. Woolson, and Jerome A. Fleming. "Causes of Death in Schizophrenia and Manic-Depression." *British Journal of Psychiatry* 136 (1980): 239–42.

Tynan, Kenneth. *Show People: Profiles in Entertainment.* New York: Simon and Schuster, 1979.

Updike, John. *Rabbit at Rest.* New York: Knopf, 1990.

——. "His Mother inside Him." *New Yorker,* April 20, 1992, 34–36.

Uphaus, Robert. "Swift's 'Whole Character': The Delany Poems and 'Verses on the Death of Dr. Swift.'" *MLQ* 34 (1973): 406–16.

Vaillant, George E. *Adaptation to Life.* Boston: Little, Brown, 1977.

Vanity Fair, editorial. March 1914, 15.

Van Tassel, David D., ed. *Aging, Death, and the Completion of Being.* Philadelphia: Univ. of Pennsylvania Press, 1979.

Vieth, David. "The Mystery of Personal Identity: Swift's Verses on His Own Death." In *The Author in His Work: Essays on a Problem in Criticism,* ed. Louis L. Martz and Aubrey Williams. New Haven: Yale Univ. Press, 1978.

Vivas, Eliseo. *D. H. Lawrence: The Failure and the Triumph of Art.* Evanston, Ill.: Northwestern Univ. Press, 1960.

Waxman, Barbara Frey. *From the Hearth to the Open Road: A Feminist Study of Aging in Contemporary Literature.* Contributions in Women's Studies, 113. New York: Greenwood Press, 1990.

Weiland, Steven. "Aging according to Biography," *Gerontologist* 29 (April 1989): 191–94.

Welter, Barbara. "Mary Roberts Rinehart." In *Notable American Women: The Modern Period,* ed. Barbara Sicherman and Carol Hurd Green. Cambridge: Harvard Univ. Press, 1980.

West, Rebecca. "Woman as Artist and Thinker." In *Woman's Coming of Age,* ed. Samuel D. Schmalhausen and V. F. Calverton, 369–82. New York: Horace Liveright, 1931.

Wharton, Edith. *A Backward Glance.* New York and London: D. Appleton-Century, 1934.

Whybrow, Peter C., Hagop S. Akiskal, and William T. McKinney, Jr. *Mood Disorders: Toward a New Psychobiology.* New York: Plenum, 1984.

Wilberforce, Octavia. *Octavia Wilberforce: The Autobiography of a Pioneer Woman Doctor.* Ed. Pat Jalland. London: Cassell, 1989.

Williams, Leonard. *Middle Age and Old Age.* London: Oxford Univ. Press, 1925.

Williamson, Alan. "Identity and the Wider Eros: A Reading of Peter Taylor's Stories." *Shenandoah* 30 (Fall 1978): 71–84.

Windholz, Martha, et al., eds. *The Merck Index: An Encyclopedia of Chemicals, Drugs, and Biologicals*. Rahway, N.J.: Merck, 1983.

Winkler, Mary G. "Walking to the Stars." In *Handbook of the Humanities and Aging*, ed. Thomas R. Cole, David D. Van Tassel, and Robert Kastenbaum, 258–84. New York: Springer Publishing, 1992.

Winnicott, D. W. "Child Department Consultations" (1942). In *Through Paediatrics to Psycho-Analysis*, 70–84. New York: Basic Books, 1975.

——. "Transitional Objects and Transitional Phenomena" (1951). In *Through Paediatrics to Psycho-Analysis*, 229–42. New York: Basic Books, 1975.

——. "Ego Distortion in Terms of True and False Self" (1960). In *The Maturational Processes and the Facilitating Environment: Studies in the Theory of Emotional Development*, 140–52. Madison, Conn.: International Universities Press, 1965.

Winters, Yvor. "The Poetry of Louise Bogan." In *Critical Essays on Louise Bogan*, ed. Martha Collins, 31–34. Boston: G. K. Hall, 1984.

Women of 1924 International. New York: Women's News Service, 1924.

Woodress, James. *Willa Cather: A Literary Life*. Lincoln: Univ. of Nebraska Press, 1987.

Woodward, Kathleen. *At Last, the Real Distinguished Thing: The Late Poems of Eliot, Pound, Stevens, and Williams*. N.p.: Ohio State Univ. Press, 1980.

——. "May Sarton and Fictions of Old Age." In *Gender and Literary Voice*, ed. Janet Todd, pp. 108–27. Women and Literature, n.s., 1. New York: Holmes and Meier, 1980.

——. "Reminiscence and the Life Review: Prospects and Retrospects." *What Does It Mean to Grow Old: Reflections from the Humanities*, ed. Thomas R. Cole and Sally A. Gadow, 135–61. Durham: Duke Univ. Press, 1986.

——. "Simone de Beauvoir: Aging and Its Discontents." In *The Private Self: Theory and Practice of Women's Autobiographical Writing*, ed. Shari Benstock, pp. 90–113. Chapel Hill: Univ. of North Carolina Press, 1988.

——. *Aging and Its Discontents: Freud and Other Fictions*. Bloomington: Indiana Univ. Press, 1991.

——, and Murray M. Schwartz, eds. *Memory and Desire: Aging—Literature—Psychoanalysis*. Bloomington: Indiana Univ. Press, 1986.

Woolf, Leonard. *The Journey Not the Arrival Matters: An Autobiography of the Years 1939 to 1969*. New York: Harcourt, Brace & World, 1969.

Woolf, Virginia. *A Room of One's Own*. New York: Harcourt, Brace, 1929.

——. *The Letters of Virginia Woolf*. Ed. Nigel Nicolson and Joanne Trautmann. 6 vols. New York: Harcourt, 1975–80.

——. *The Diary of Virginia Woolf*. Ed. Anne Olivier Bell and Andrew McNeillie. 5 vols. New York: Harcourt, 1976–84.

——. *Moments of Being: Unpublished Autobiographical Writings*. Ed. Jeanne Schulkind. New York: Harcourt Brace, 1976.

Wright, Celeste Turner. "Elinor Wylie: The Glass Chimaera and the Minotaur." *Women's Studies* 7 (1980): 159–70.

Wyatt-Brown, Anne M. "A Buried Life: E. M. Forster's Struggle with Creativity."

Journal of Modern Literature 10 (March 1983): 109–24.

——. "Late Style in the Novels of Barbara Pym and Penelope Mortimer." *Gerontologist* 6 (Dec. 1988): 835–39.

——. "*Eva Trout* and the Return of the Repressed: Elizabeth Bowen's Swan Song." Paper presented at seminar, Psychological Approaches to Fiction, IPSA Conference in Literature and Psychology, the Univ. of Florida, Gainesville, March 10, 1989.

——. "Approaches to Gender Issues in Molly Keane and Peter Taylor." Paper presented at IPSA Conference on Literature and Psychology, the Univ. of Florida, Gainesville, March 11, 1989.

——. "Creativity in Midlife: The Novels of Anita Brookner." *Journal of Aging Studies* 3 (Summer 1989): 175–81.

——. "A Message in the Bottle: *The Education of Harriet Hatfield*." Paper presented at symposium, Writing in the Upward Years, Santa Fe Community College, Gainesville, Fla., March 16, 1990.

——. "Life Review in the Novels of Molly Keane, Elizabeth Bowen, and Peter Taylor." ERIC Document Reproduction Service no. ED 308 540, 1990.

——. "The Coming of Age of Literary Gerontology." *Journal of Aging Studies* 4 (Fall 1990): 299–315.

——. "The Politics of Old Age: Another Model of the Aging Writer." Paper presented at symposium, Late Life Artists and Writers: Maturing of the Psychology of Creativity, annual meeting of the Gerontological Society of America, Boston, Nov. 19, 1990.

——. *Barbara Pym: A Critical Biography*. Columbia: Univ. of Missouri Press, 1992.

——. "Literary Gerontology Comes of Age." In *Handbook of the Humanities and Aging*, ed. Thomas R. Cole, David D. Van Tassel, and Robert Kastenbaum, 331–51. New York: Springer Publishing, 1992.

Wyatt-Brown, Bertram. *Southern Honor: Ethics and Behavior in the Old South*. New York: Oxford Univ. Press, 1982.

——. "Walker Percy: Autobiographical Fiction and the Aging Process." *Journal of Aging Studies* 3 (1989): 81–89.

Yeats, W. B. "Per Amica Silentia Lunae." In *Mythologies*. London: Macmillan, 1962.

Young-Bruehl, Elisabeth. *Anna Freud: A Biography*. New York: Summit Books, 1988.

Contributors

MARCIA ALDRICH is an Assistant Professor of English at Michigan State University in East Lansing, Michigan. She is at work on a critical book, *Lethal Brevity: Louise Bogan, Modernism and the Feminine Lyric.*

JOSEPHINE V. ARNOLD is an independent scholar living in Staunton, Virginia. She has published articles on George Sand and Emily Brontë and Henry de Montherlant. She has coedited, with A. James Arnold, an issue of *Callaloo* devoted to Caribbean literature. At present she is working on a book-length study of Montherlant. In addition, she is part of an international team of editors, headed by A. James Arnold, who are putting together for the first time a three-volume history of Caribbean literature under the sponsorship of the International Comparative Literature Association.

THOMAS C. CARAMAGNO is an Associate Professor in the Department of English at the University of Nebraska. A specialist in Virginia Woolf and psychobiological criticism, he is the author of *The Flight of the Mind: Virginia Woolf's Art and Manic-Depressive Illness* and has published essays on Woolf, Wordsworth, Dickens, Twain, and E. S. Dallas. He won the William Riley Parker Prize for the outstanding article in *PMLA* with his January 1988 essay on Woolf, "Manic-Depressive Psychosis and Critical Approaches to Virginia Woolf's Life and Work." He has held an Andrew W. Mellon Faculty Fellowship in the Humanities at Harvard University.

BRIAN A. CONNERY teaches eighteenth-century literature in the English department of Oakland University. He has published essays on both Swift and satire and is currently completing a book on Swift and editing a collection of essays on satire.

JUDITH DE LUCE is Professor of Classics and an affiliate in Women's Studies at Miami University where she has been on the faculty since 1974. Her primary research interests are in the areas of Latin literature of the late Republic and early empire, humanistic gerontology, and women's studies. She is coeditor, with Thomas Falkner, of *Old Age in Greek and Latin Literature.* She has been a visiting scholar at the Scripps Gerontological Program in Miami and currently teaches a course on old age in classical antiquity.

GLORIA G. FROMM (d. 1992) was Professor of English at the University of Illinois at Chicago, the author of *Dorothy Richardson: A Biography,* and the editor of a forthcoming selection of Dorothy Richardson's letters. She had also edited *Essaying Biography: A Celebration for Leon Edel* and had published numerous essays on both Edwardian and modern literary figures.

DIANA HUME GEORGE teaches English and women's studies at the Behrend College of Penn State University. She is a poet, essayist, and literary critic who has written or edited six books, including *Blake and Freud* and *Oedipus Anne: The Poetry of Anne Sexton*. With Sexton's biographer, Diane Wood Middlebrook, she is the editor of Sexton's *Selected Poetry*. George has written feminist psychoanalytic criticism for a number of publications. Right now she is writing a book on Maxine Kumin and Anne Sexton's friendship and working on a collection of personal essays titled *The Lonely Other: A Woman Watching America*.

MARGARET MORGANROTH GULLETTE is the author of *Safe at Last in the Middle Years* and has received an NEH fellowship for a companion volume, *Midlife Fictions: The Constructions of the Middle Years of Life, 1900–1935*. She is also the editor of the Feminist Press edition of Mona Caird's 1894 novel, *The Daughters of Danaus*. Her writings on age theory have appeared in *Representations, Novel, North American Review, Harvard Magazine,* the "Hers" column of the *New York Times Magazine,* and *Lear's*. One of her essays has been cited as notable in *Best American Essays 1991*. She has been a Bunting and an ACLS fellow and a Visiting Scholar at Radcliffe's Schlesinger Library, Wellesley's Center for Research on Women, and Northeastern's Women's Studies Program. She has taught at Harvard, the University of California at Berkeley, and the Radcliffe Seminars. In 1992–93 she is a Visiting Scholar in the Department of English at Harvard University.

BETHANY LADIMER is Associate Professor and Chair of French at Middlebury College, where she teaches courses in twentieth-century French prose and women's studies. She is the author of a number of articles on modern French writers, including Colette, Duras, Tournier, Breton, Camus, and Proust. She is currently working on a book-length study of "novels of discovery" by French, English, and American women writers.

M. M. LALLY, an Associate Professor of English at The Citadel in Charleston, South Carolina, teaches creative writing and English literature and is currently working on a study of D. H. Lawrence. A member of the Poets' Prize Committee, Lally has published in, among other places, *Ohio Review, Literary Review,* and *Kenyon Review; Juliana's Room* (1988) was nominated for the *Los Angeles Times* Book Prize in Poetry.

CONSTANCE ROOKE is Professor and Chair of English at the University of Guelph in Ontario. She is author of *Reynolds Price, Night Light: Stories of Aging,* and *Fear of the Open Heart: Essays on Contemporary Canadian Writing*. She is also a widely published short-story writer and the editor of Canada's most distinguished literary magazine, the *Malahat Review*. She is the author of several articles in the field of literary gerontology and is currently writing a book on old age and contemporary fiction.

JANICE ROSSEN has published *The World of Barbara Pym, Philip Larkin: His Life's Work,* and *The University in Modern Fiction: When Power is Academic*. She has edited *Independent Women: The Function of Gender in the Novels of Barbara Pym* and (with Rosemary M. Colt) *Writers of the Old School: British Novelists of the 1930s.*

CAROLYN H. SMITH is Director of Freshman English at the University of Florida, Gainesville. She has recently published "Images of Aging in American Poetry, 1925–1985" in the *Handbook of the Humanities and Aging* and articles on aging and gender in poetry in the *Journal of Aging Studies* and the *International Journal of Aging and Human Development.* In addition to giving papers on gender, aging, and mourning at the Gerontological Society of America, MLA, and drama conferences, she is working on a biography of Josephine Miles. She is also a published poet.

KATHLEEN WOODWARD, Director of the Center for Twentieth-Century Studies and Professor of English at the University of Wisconsin-Milwaukee, is the author of *At Last, the Real Distinguished Thing: The Late Poems of Eliot, Pound, Stevens, and Williams* and of *Aging and Its Discontents: Freud and Other Fictions.* She has edited two collections of essays on aging, *Aging and the Elderly: Humanistic Perspectives in Gerontology* (with Stuart Spicker and David D. Van Tassel) and *Memory and Desire: Aging—Literature—Psychoanalysis* (with Murray M. Schwartz).

ANNE M. WYATT-BROWN is an Assistant Professor of Linguistics and Coordinator of Scholarly Writing at the University of Florida. She is the author of *Barbara Pym: A Critical Biography.* Wyatt-Brown has recently published "Literary Gerontology Comes of Age" in the *Handbook of the Humanities and Aging,* as well as articles and review essays in the *Journal of Aging Studies,* the *Gerontologist,* and the *Journal of Modern Literature.* She has also presented papers on literature, aging, psychoanalysis, and writing at the Gerontological Society of America, MLA, and writing conferences.

BERTRAM WYATT-BROWN, Richard J. Milbauer Professor of History at the University of Florida, is the author of *Southern Honor: Ethics and Behavior in the Old South* (1982) and other books in history. Besides his numerous articles and review essays in historical journals, he has made three presentations at meetings of the Gerontological Society of America and has published an article on Walker Percy in the *Journal of Aging Studies.* He is currently completing *The House of Percy: Honor, Art, and Melancholy in a Southern Family.*

Index